'Cobham and Kanafani, aided by the rich contributions of an impressive array of international experts, have produced what is clearly the most learned and comprehensive work on the economy of the future state of Palestine. This volume combines the indispensable objectivity of economic analysis, a clear understanding of the policy experience and practices of successful countries, as well as a thorough appreciation of the political context, to derive highly relevant conclusions and policy implications. We owe Messrs. Cobham and Kanafani a debt of gratitude for so ably informing us about economic conditions and prospects in Palestine and, more significantly, for their considered and timely contribution to the cause of a Middle-East peace that is anchored in an economically viable and sovereign Palestinian state.'

Dr George Abed, Director, Middle East and Central Asia Department, IMF, 2002–2003

'A peaceful solution between Israel and a Palestinian State will be sustainable and stable only when the Palestinians will enjoy the economic dividends of peace. This book captures the main economic issues and presents the required economic policies that will secure economic prosperity for a newly born Palestinian State.'

Haim Ben-Shahar, Emeritus Professor, Tel Aviv University

'This book is a solid contribution to our understanding of the economic policy issues that will face decision makers in a sovereign and independent Palestinian state in the context of separation from Israel. It presents interesting recommendations regarding key issues that are more than likely to evoke intense debate amongst economists and politicians alike.'

Nabeel Kassis, PNA Minister of Planning

'Any well-functioning sovereign market economy requires sound institutions that guarantee Property Rights in the market place, restrict the Power of the Executive in setting intrusive policies, provide social safety nets, and craft forward-looking economic policy strategy through the political process. The book is the first of its kind to put forth an agenda for economic policies and institutional reforms, necessary for a viable Palestinian economy that could be integrated into the world economy, and serve as a host for foreign direct investment. A well-functioning Palestinian economy will definitely be a boon for the entire Middle East region.'

Assaf Razin, Professor of Public Finance, Tel Aviv University

'To be viable, any Palestinian state will need to make a series of important economic policy and institutional decisions. This volume edited by David Cobham and Nu'man Kanafani presents a series of carefully reasoned analyses of, and recommendations for, some of the most important policy and institutional reforms. Coming from an impressive list of international scholars including both Arabs and Israelis, the book is 'must reading' for economists and policy makers interested in identifying the policy and institutional requirements of any Palestinian state and indeed of any small state.'

Jeffrey B. Nugent, Professor of Economics, USC and President, Middle East Economic Association

The Economics of Palestine

This book aims to set the intense political debates on one side in order to do some serious economic analysis. It assumes that a sovereign independent Palestinian state comes into existence in the West Bank and Gaza Strip, and proceeds to examine the economic policies and institutional reforms which would be appropriate for it. Key recommendations are that such a state should:

- adopt a non-discriminatory trade regime;
- introduce a new currency with a currency board and later a hard peg to the euro;
- establish a new type of pension scheme combining universal and work-based elements;
- adopt an economic strategy geared to the modern knowledge-based global economy and based on the identification of clusters; and,
- take a forward-looking approach to the compensation of refugees which relates compensation to the cost of absorbing returning refugees in a viable and growing economy.

Budgetary policy, corporate governance, financial sector reform and foreign aid strategy are also discussed, and an incomplete contracts model of integration is presented.

The contributors are internationally respected economists from a variety of countries and perspectives. Their analysis should be accessible and relevant to readers of many kinds, from students and academics involved with development economics, politics and international relations through to policy makers and those with a general interest in the Middle East.

David Cobham is Reader in Economics at the University of St Andrews, Scotland. **Nu'man Kanafani** is Associate Professor at the Royal Veterinary and Agricultural University in Copenhagen, Denmark.

Routledge studies in development economics

1 **Economic Development in the Middle East**
Rodney Wilson

2 **Monetary and Financial Policies in Developing Countries**
Growth and stabilization
Akhtar Hossain and Anis Chowdhury

3 **New Directions in Development Economics**
Growth, environmental concerns and government in the 1990s
Edited by Mats Lundahl and Benno J. Ndulu

4 **Financial Liberalization and Investment**
Kanhaya L. Gupta and Robert Lensink

5 **Liberalization in the Developing World**
Institutional and economic changes in Latin America, Africa and Asia
Edited by Alex E. Fernández Jilberto and André Mommen

6 **Financial Development and Economic Growth**
Theory and experiences from developing countries
Edited by Niels Hermes and Robert Lensink

7 **The South African Economy**
Macroeconomic prospects for the medium term
Finn Tarp and Peter Brixen

8 **Public Sector Pay and Adjustment**
Lessons from five countries
Edited by Christopher Colclough

9 **Europe and Economic Reform in Africa**
Structural adjustment and economic diplomacy
Obed O. Mailafia

10 **Post-apartheid Southern Africa**
Economic challenges and policies for the future
Edited by Lennart Petersson

11 **Financial Integration and Development**
Liberalization and reform in Sub-Saharan Africa
Ernest Aryeetey and Machiko Nissanke

12 **Regionalization and Globalization in the Modern World Economy**
Perspectives on the Third World and transitional economies
Edited by Alex F. Fernández Jilberto and André Mommen

13 **The African Economy**
Policy, institutions and the future
Steve Kayizzi-Mugerwa

14 **Recovery from Armed Conflict in Developing Countries**
Edited by Geoff Harris

15 **Small Enterprises and Economic Development**
The dynamics of micro and small enterprises
Carl Liedholm and Donald C. Mead

16 **The World Bank**
New agendas in a changing world
Michelle Miller-Adams

17 **Development Policy in the Twenty-First Century**
Beyond the post-Washington consensus
Edited by Ben Fine, Costas Lapavitsas and Jonathan Pincus

18 **State-Owned Enterprises in the Middle East and North Africa**
Privatization, performance and reform
Edited by Merih Celasun

19 **Finance and Competitiveness in Developing Countries**
Edited by José María Fanelli and Rohinton Medhora

20 **Contemporary Issues in Development Economics**
Edited by B.N. Ghosh

21 **Mexico Beyond NAFTA**
Edited by Martín Puchet Anyul and Lionello F. Punzo

22 **Economies in Transition**
A guide to China, Cuba, Mongolia, North Korea and Vietnam at the turn of the twenty-first century
Ian Jeffries

23 **Population, Economic Growth and Agriculture in Less Developed Countries**
Nadia Cuffaro

24 **From Crisis to Growth in Africa?**
Edited by Mats Lundal

25 **The Macroeconomics of Monetary Union**
An analysis of the CFA franc zone
David Fielding

26 **Endogenous Development**
Networking, innovation, institutions and cities
Antonio Vasquez-Barquero

27 **Labour Relations in Development**
Edited by Alex E. Fernández Jilberto and Marieke Riethof

28 Globalization, Marginalization and Development
Edited by S. Mansoob Murshed

29 Programme Aid and Development
Beyond conditionality
Howard White and Geske Dijkstra

30 Competitiveness Strategy in Developing Countries
A manual for policy analysis
Edited by Ganeshan Wignaraja

31 The African Manufacturing Firm
An analysis based on firm surveys in Sub-Saharan Africa
Dipak Mazumdar and Ata Mazaheri

32 Trade Policy, Growth and Poverty in Asian Developing Countries
Edited by Kishor Sharma

33 International Competitiveness, Investment and Finance
A case study of India
Edited by A. Ganesh Kumar, Kunal Sen and Rajendra R. Vaidya

34 The Pattern of Aid Giving
The impact of good governance on development assistance
Eric Neumayer

35 New International Poverty Reduction Strategies
Edited by Jean-Pierre Cling, Mireille Razafindrakoto and François Roubaud

36 Targeting Development
Critical perspectives on the millennium development goals
Edited by Richard Black and Howard White

37 Essays on Balance of Payments Constrained Growth
Theory and evidence
Edited by J.S.L. McCombie and A.P. Thirlwall

38 The Private Sector After Communism
New entrepreneurial firms in transition economies
Jan Winiecki, Vladimir Benacek and Mihaly Laki

39 Information Technology and Development
A new paradigm for delivering the internet to rural areas in developing countries
Jeffrey James

40 The Economics of Palestine
Economic policy and institutional reform for a viable Palestinian state
Edited by David Cobham and Nu'man Kanafani

The Economics of Palestine

Economic policy and institutional reform for a viable Palestinian state

Edited by David Cobham and Nu'man Kanafani

Routledge
Taylor & Francis Group
LONDON AND NEW YORK

First published 2004
by Routledge
2 Park Square, Milton Park, Abingdon, Oxfordshire OX14 4RN

Simultaneously published in the USA and Canada
by Routledge
29 West 35th Street, New York, NY 10001

Routledge is an imprint of the Taylor & Francis Group

Typeset in Times by Wearset Ltd, Boldon, Tyne and Wear
Printed and bound in Great Britain by MPG Books Ltd, Bodmin

British Library Cataloguing in Publication Data
A catalogue record for this book is available from the British Library

Library of Congress Cataloging in Publication Data
A catalog record for this book has been requested

ISBN 0-415-32761-X

Contents

Figures

Tables

Contributors

Christopher Adam is a University Lecturer in Quantitative Development Economics at the University of Oxford, UK. His research is mainly concerned with macroeconomic policy design in low-income countries, particularly those of sub-Saharan Africa.

Christopher Allsopp is Reader in Economic Policy at the University of Oxford and the Editor of the *Oxford Review of Economic Policy*. He was a member of the Monetary Policy Committee at the Bank of England from 2000 to 2003. He has also worked at the UK Treasury, the OECD and the Bank of England. He has published extensively on monetary, fiscal and exchange rate issues as well as on the problems of economic reform and transition

Arie Arnon is professor in the Department of Economics, Ben Gurion University. His areas of research include the history of economic thought, macroeconomics and monetary theory. A major focus in recent years has been the political economy of the Israeli–Palestinian conflict. He was a co-author of *The Palestinian Economy: Between Imposed Integration and Voluntary Separation* (Brill 1997), and is now working with colleagues from Palestine, Israel and elsewhere on economic aspects of a permanent peace agreement.

Christian Friis Bach is Associate Professor at the Royal Veterinary and Agricultural University in Copenhagen. His research has been primarily on issues of international trade and development.

David Cobham is Reader in Economics at the University of St Andrews. His main research interest is UK monetary policy, but he has also worked and published on European (and African) monetary integration, central bank independence, Islamic banking and financial systems.

Eduardo Anselmo de Castro is Associate Professor in the Department of Environment and Planning, University of Aveiro. His research interests are in the fields of regional economics, the economics of Information and Communication Technology and the economics of planning.

Sébastien Dessus is Senior Economist at the World Bank, where he has primary responsibility for monitoring the Palestinian and Lebanese economies. He holds a Ph.D. in economics from the University of Paris-Sorbonne. Before joining the World Bank in 1999, he worked at the OECD for eight years. He has published extensively on trade and growth, including several books.

Leila Farsakh is currently a post-doctoral research fellow at the Center for Middle Eastern Studies at Harvard University. She holds a Ph.D. from the University of London, and an MPhil from the University of Cambridge. She has worked with the OECD in Paris and the Palestine Economic Policy Research Institute in Ramallah, and has published research on the Palestinian economy and the Oslo Process, international migration and regional integration. Her book *Palestinian Labour Flows and the Palestinian State* is forthcoming from RoutledgeCurzon in 2004.

Felix FitzRoy is Professor in the Department of Economics at the University of St Andrews. He has also been a visiting professor at the European University Institute, Florence, and a research fellow at the Science Centre (WZB), Berlin. He has published extensively in the fields of labour economics and comparative economics.

Osama Hamed is author of a number of studies on the Palestinian economy, including the chapters on shocks and stabilisation, private investment, and financial intermediation in Ishac Diwan and Radwan Shaban (eds), *Development Under Adversity*, World Bank and MAS, 1999. He currently teaches economics at Rutgers University, Camden, New Jersey. He holds a Ph.D. in Economics from the University of California, Los Angeles.

Athar Hussain is the Deputy Director of the Asia Research Centre at the London School of Economics. He has worked extensively on the developing economies of Asia, in particular China, Vietnam and Pakistan. In 1993 he travelled to Iraq as a member of a team to study the effect of the sanctions on the civilian population, and the field study report, jointly authored with Haris Gazdar, was later published in K. Mahdi (ed.) *Iraq's Economic Predicament*, Ithaca Press, 2002.

Khaled Islaih has been working as an Economic Researcher at the Office of the United Nations Special Coordinator in the Occupied Territories (UNSCO) for the last six years. Prior to this, he served as an Economic Statistician at the Palestinian Central Bureau of Statistics and as the Economic Desk-Officer at Orient House in Jerusalem. He holds an MA in Economics from Eastern Michigan University, USA.

Chris Jensen-Butler is professor in the Department of Economics, University of St Andrews, Scotland. His research interests are in the fields of regional economics, regional economic modelling and urban economics.

Nu'man Kanafani is Associate Professor at the Department of Economics and Natural Resources, the Royal Veterinary and Agricultural University in Copenhagen. His research interests are in the fields of development economics, preferential trade agreements and stabilisation policies. He has authored a number of studies on the Palestinian economy.

Tony Killick is Senior Research Associate of the Overseas Development Institute, London. His principal work has been in the areas of economic policies in developing countries, and in the ways in which the policies of international agencies impinge upon developing countries. He has a special interest in the economies of Africa, and in the study of poverty. Much of his most recent work has been on aspects of relationships between aid donors and recipient governments.

Anne Le More is writing a doctoral thesis in International Relations at Nuffield College, Oxford University on international assistance to the Palestinian people during the decade following the signing of the Oslo Agreement. She has also worked for the Office of the United Nations Special Coordinator for the Middle East Peace Process (UNSCO) based in Gaza and Jerusalem.

Andy Mullineux is Professor of Global Finance in the Department of Accounting and Finance in the Birmingham Business School at the University of Birmingham. He has published extensively on financial sector restructuring and regulatory and supervisory reform in various countries and regions, including Central and Eastern Europe and East and South-East Asia.

Jennifer C. Olmsted is a Middle East economist who focuses on gender and labour issues, particularly in the context of the Palestinian economy. Her work has been published in a number of journals, including *Feminist Economics* and *World Development*. She is currently an Associate Professor of Economics at Sonoma State University.

Elizabeth Ruppert Bulmer is a senior economist at the World Bank, where she has spent the last 10 years researching a variety of issues affecting the countries of the Middle East and North Africa. Her areas of interest include the Palestinian economy, labour market programmes and unemployment insurance in particular, and labour issues more broadly. She holds a Ph.D. in Economics from the University of Maryland.

Edward A. Sayre is an Assistant Professor of Economics at Agnes Scott College in Decatur, Georgia. He previously taught at Kenyon College in Ohio, and from 1996 to 1997 he was a visiting research associate at the Palestine Economic Policy Research Institute (MAS) in Ramallah.

Radwan Shaban is an economist at the World Bank. He was the Director of Research at the Palestine Economic Policy Research Institute in its founding period, 1994–1995. He has written extensively on Palestinian economic development, including editing *Development under Adversity, the Palestinian Economy in Transition* (World Bank and MAS, 1999, with Ishac Diwan). Prior to joining the Bank, he was a professor of Economics at Georgia Institute of Technology and University of Pennsylvania. His main areas of expertise are poverty, labour markets, rural institutions, and economic development. He has a Ph.D. in Economics from Stanford University.

Avia Spivak is the Deputy Governor of the Bank of Israel, and Professor of Economics at Ben Gurion University of the Negev. He has been a visiting professor in the US universities of UCLA, Pennsylvania, Brown and Boston, and a visiting fellow at Harvard and MIT. He has published in the areas of economics of uncertainty, macroeconomics and pensions, and has co-authored a book on the Palestinian economy.

Oren Sussman was previously at Ben Gurion University of the Negev. He is now at the Said Business School, University of Oxford. His research interests are in macroeconomics and finance, bankruptcy law and general corporate finance.

Jonathan Thomas is Professor of Economics at the University of Edinburgh. His research areas have included long-term contracts, particularly in the absence of commitment and/or full information, repeated games of incomplete information, labour economics and international debt.

Clare Woodcraft is Director-Strategy at ASDA'A Public Relations, the exclusive Middle East affiliate of Burson-Marsteller, in the UAE. Before that, she was Banking and Finance Editor for Middle East Economic Survey (MEES). Clare has undertaken several research projects on Palestine, commissioned by the World Bank, the EU and the Center on International Cooperation at New York University. She holds an MSc in Development Studies from the London School of Economics.

Dr Adel Zagha is assistant Professor of Economics and Dean of the Faculty of Commerce and Economics at Birzeit University. He has a Ph.D. from the Free University of Berlin and an MA from Vanderbilt University. His areas of research include taxation, fiscal decentralisation and intergovernmental relations, trade relations between Israel and Palestine, and poverty reduction policies.

Abbreviations

AHLC	Ad Hoc Liaison Committee
BOI	Bank of Israel
CBJ	Central Bank of Jordan
CU	Customs Union
DoP	Declaration of Principles (signed in Washington on 13 September 1993)
EP	Economic Protocol (Paris Protocol)
EC	European Commission
EU	European Union
FTA	Free Trade Area
HEPG	Humanitarian and Emergency Policy Group
ICRC	International Committee of the Red Cross
INGO	International Non-Governmental Organisation
JD	Jordanian dinar
JEB	Joint Economic Board
JLC	Joint Liaison Committee
LACC	Local Aid Coordination Committee
MFN	Most Favoured Nation
MoF	Ministry of Finance
MoP	Ministry of Planning (created 2003)
MoPIC	Ministry of Planning and International Cooperation (until 2003)
NDTR	Non-Discriminatory Trade Regime
NGO	Non-Governmental Organisation
NIS	New Israeli sheqel
OCHA	UN Office for the Coordination of Humanitarian Affairs
PA	Palestinian Authority
PCSC	Palestinian Commercial Services Company
PECDAR	Palestinian Economic Council for Development and Reconstruction
PLC	Palestinian Legislative Council
PLO	Palestinian Liberation Organisation
PMA	Palestinian Monetary Authority

PNA	Palestinian National Authority
PP	Paris Protocol (Economic Protocol)
PPP	Purchasing Power Parity
PSE	Palestinian Stock Exchange
RSG	Reform Support Group
SACU	Southern African Customs Union
SWG	Sector Working Group
TAP	Tripartite Action Plan
TFP	Total Factor Productivity
TFPI	Task Force on Project Implementation
TFPR	Task Force on Palestinian Reform
UNCCP	United Nations Conciliation Commission for Palestine
UNCTAD	UN Conference on Trade and Development
UNRWA	United Nations Relief and Works Agency for Palestine Refugees in the Near-East
UNSCO	Office of the United Nations Special Coordinator in the Occupied Territories
USD	US dollar
WBGS	West Bank and Gaza Strip
WFP	World Food Programme
WTO	World Trade Organisation

1 Introduction

David Cobham and Nu'man Kanafani

This book sets out to offer an economic analysis based upon a clear political vision. It assumes a political settlement to the Palestinian–Israeli conflict which will lead to the establishment of an independent and sovereign Palestinian state. The book proceeds from this starting point to ask how resources can best be utilised, policies designed and institutions organised in this state to bring about substantial and sustainable improvements in the living standards of its inhabitants.

Economic visions with respect to the resolution of the Palestinian–Israeli conflict have gone through three phases.[1] The first, and probably the least known, came in the context of the UN General Assembly Resolution no. 181 of 1947, the so-called Partition Resolution, which recommended a two state solution with an economic union. The main economic concerns of the Resolution were with the issues of trade and currencies, two of the issues which figured so prominently later in the years after the Oslo Accords (the so-called Oslo period, *c.*1994–2000). The UN Resolution envisaged the creation of separate Arab and Jewish states with defined borders, with the city of Jerusalem under a special international regime. The two states would establish an Economic Union which would involve a full customs union, a system of currencies with a common foreign exchange rate and joint economic development initiatives in areas such as irrigation, energy and transport. Subject to the joint currencies system, each state could operate its own central bank, control its own fiscal and credit policy, grant import licences and conduct international financial operations. At the head of the Economic Union would be a Joint Economic Board (JEB) consisting of three members from each state and three foreign members appointed by the Economic and Social Council of the UN. The JEB would be in charge of collecting revenues from customs and other services and would allocate between 5 and 10 per cent to the city of Jerusalem. The rest would be allocated equitably between the two states with 'the objective of maintaining a sufficient and suitable level of government and social services in each state'. However, the share of either state would not exceed its contribution to the revenues by more than a specified amount in any year. The principle by which the revenue was distributed could be revised by the JEB after five years on the basis of equity. Furthermore, the Resolution stressed that the two states would bind themselves to implement the decisions of the JEB and that, in the event of refusal, the JEB might decide to withhold an appropriate share of the customs revenues due to the reluctant state.

The Partition Resolution was, of course, never applied: the state of Israel was established in 1948 on a much larger land area than that envisaged in the resolution, the West Bank was incorporated with Transjordan into the new state of Jordan and the Gaza Strip came to be administered by Egypt. In the following two decades hardly any serious Palestine-specific economic work was done except for some sporadic studies of a historical nature (e.g. Sayigh 1967). After 1967, when the West Bank and Gaza Strip (WBGS) came under Israeli occupation, a few economic studies and surveys of living conditions in the 'Areas' were made, mainly in order to facilitate their administration by the occupying power. However, some Palestinian and Israeli scholars made notable contributions, e.g. Ben-Shahar *et al.* (1971) and Hilal (1975).

Economic discussion revived in the late 1970s in conjunction with the political debate within the Palestine Liberation Organisation (PLO) which called for the acceptance of a two state solution to the conflict rather than a single state covering historic Palestine. The economic debate concentrated specifically on whether a Palestinian state in the WBGS would have enough resources to support political independence, that is, would be economically viable. An early contribution to the debate came from Vivian Bull (1975), who defined economic viability in terms of the availability of economic resources which would allow sustainable economic growth and increase in social welfare, sufficient to secure a minimum degree of social and political stability. She considered federation of the West Bank with Israel or federation with Jordan and concluded that federation with Israel was economically viable but politically unviable, while federation with Jordan was the opposite. The best solution for the West Bank, according to Bull, was for it to become a semi-independent 'region'; and if free trade and free labour movement were secured between this zone and Israel then it would be viable with an annual growth rate of 8 per cent. To achieve this growth, investment should be concentrated on irrigation and improvement of labour skills.

Ward (1977) took the view that viability would require at least the restoration of the pre-1967 GNP growth rate of 6–8 per cent in the West Bank and suggested that this would be possible if there was a peaceful settlement and a restoration of the pre-1967 productive sectors (including the 3,700 industrial firms in the West Bank). He argued that the required increase in the investment rate (from the pre-1967 rate of 15 per cent of GDP to 20 per cent) would be feasible in the context of a peaceful settlement. He identified the obstacles to viability in three other factors: access to markets, the budget deficit and the balance of payments deficit. However, he claimed that if the political settlement secured access to the Israeli markets and to the earnings from tourism in Jerusalem then a Palestinian entity on the West Bank would be economically viable.

However, the most comprehensive and perceptive contribution came from Tuma and Darin-Drabkin (1978). Unlike earlier works, this study covered the Gaza Strip as well as the West Bank and took into account the return of the refugees to the WBGS (1.3 million returnees over five years). The authors distinguish between two sets of conditions for viability: subjective conditions, connected with people's feelings of national identity and their readiness to defend and improve it, and objective conditions related to the characteristics of the economy and its factors of production. They assumed the presence of the former and proceeded to suggest that the objective conditions for economic viability could be assessed in terms of three criteria: the availability of a minimum ratio of land to labour; the availability of a certain amount of water for industry and agriculture; and the presence of a minimum level of human skills (technology). After reviewing the potential resources that would be available to the new state they formulated the central question as: what are the necessary conditions that would allow the population of the future Palestinian state to achieve a certain level of income ($800 per capita income), and are these conditions likely to be fulfilled? In quantitative terms they attempted to estimate the necessary increases in labour productivity and in investment that would be needed to achieve the target, taking into account the housing of the returnees, the sectoral allocation of the labour force and the availability of land and water. They concluded that with a labour productivity increase of 10 per cent per annum and investment of some $8.5bn over five years, the target per capita income could be achieved. Palestine was, therefore, viable because it would have the capacity to achieve productivity and income levels which were comparable to those of other countries in the region. They stressed, however, that the support of the international community would be decisive and that the human factor[2] of the Palestinian people would play the most important role in achieving this viability.[3]

The third phase started in the very early 1990s just before the signing of the first document of the Oslo Accords, the Declaration of Principles, in 1993. The Madrid Conference triggered a new and positive political mood which suggested that a political settlement might be attainable. The PLO, which at that time had its headquarters in Tunis, rushed to design a National Development Programme 1994–2000[4] and the World Bank was asked to prepare a comprehensive survey of the WBGS economy and its development needs. The result was six volumes of pioneering work (World Bank 1993) on the basis of which an Emergency Assistance Programme for the WBGS was designed.[5] The World Bank study concluded that:

> assuming a 'good policy', a growth rate in excess of 3 percent in per capita incomes is sustainable [in the WBGS], with a total rise in incomes on the order of 40 percent in a decade, provided the phaseout from the Israeli labour market is managed in a 'smooth' fashion and provided there are adequate external public and private capital inflows (about $2,500 million during the five-year transition period).
>
> (volume 1: 15)

A number of other studies were also carried out in this early period, notably those which came to be published in Fischer *et al.* (1993).

The breakthrough came in 1994 with the Economic Protocol (Paris Protocol, PP) which formed part of the Oslo Accords and defined the temporary economic arrangements between the emerging Palestinian Authority (PA) and Israel. The literature in the following few years concentrated on analysing and criticising the PP on the one hand, and discussing how these arrangements could be developed in the final settlement which was supposed to be in place by the end of the decade, on the other. More specifically, economic analysis in this phase concentrated on three broad issues: whether the WBGS would be better off with a trade arrangement with Israel other than the modified customs union specified in the PP; whether the WBGS should have its own currency and central bank in place of the Palestinian Monetary Authority set-up under the PP, whose responsibilities were limited mainly to banking supervision; and finally the advantages and disadvantages of different levels of labour flow from the Palestinian areas into Israel. As an extension of the first issue, questions of regional cooperation, both with respect to trade and large infrastructural projects, also received considerable attention. Generally speaking, the bulk of the economic literature produced during this short, but almost euphoric, period advocated more integration between the WBGS and Israeli economies, or at least called for their future relationship to be based on some modified version of the PP. One of the few exceptions to this general trend was the volume produced by Arie Arnon and his colleagues on the Palestinian economy (Arnon *et al.* 1997), which looked backward to the effects of occupation and forward to the possibility and importance of establishing an independent state.

By the mid 1990s it was already becoming clear that economic progress in the WBGS was being hampered by the lack of implementation of the letter and spirit of the PP at least as much as by its design. And with the increasing tension and political turmoil the Israeli government intensified its use of the policy of 'closure', i.e. physical siege of the Occupied Areas which effectively prevented the movement of labour and goods not only to and from the West Bank and Gaza but also within each of them. It was therefore natural for economic research to focus on the economic and social crisis which resulted from the closure policies. A landmark work in this field was the volume published by the Palestine Economic Policy

Research Institute (MAS) and the World Bank in 1999, entitled *Development Under Adversity* (Diwan and Shaban 1999). The interlinkages between security issues, the political setting and political will in general, and economic performance became even more obvious, and efforts to design 'closure-free' (i.e. politics-free) arrangements which would secure a smooth flow of goods and labour were unsuccessful. As the policy of physical siege intensified and became the norm rather than the exception during the second intifada (which started in September 2000) efforts were concentrated on how to implement emergency aid programmes to mitigate the effects of drastic increases in unemployment and poverty.[6]

This short exposition makes clear that economic work in this phase was closely associated with, and restricted by, the concurrent state of the political process. More particularly, the constraints embedded in the Oslo Accords and the uncertainties about the final status agreement have led most of the literature to concentrate on short-term crisis management.[7] The implicit, if not explicit, assumption that the new Palestinian entity would have a 'special' but as yet undefined relationship with Israel has discouraged work on more detailed economic analyses of policies for the future state. We think that the events of the last three years have gone a long way towards undermining the idea of, or perhaps even the possibility for, a 'special' relationship between Israel and Palestine of the kind assumed in previous research. It seems imperative now that borders and sovereignty must be clearly and unambiguously delineated and much less porous than previously assumed. This will have significant implications for the type of economic arrangements, institutions and policies appropriate to the new state. This book therefore starts from the position that a new economic analysis based on a revised framework of clear separation between the Israeli and Palestinian economies is needed. From that starting point, research should address the question of what institutions, policies and trade and other relationships, both with Israel and with other countries, would be optimal for Palestine. The new state may decide that close economic cooperation with Israel is desirable, but this must be a free choice made on the basis of its own interests and aspirations.

More specifically, we take as our starting point a hypothetical scenario for the political settlement defined by the following three principles:

1 an independent Palestinian state will be established in the WBGS, with borders essentially the same as those which existed between 1948 and 1967;
2 the Palestinian state will be a fully sovereign state with control of its own borders, natural resources, economic policy and international relations;
3 the core of the Palestinian refugee problem will find a solution within the geographic borders of the new state.

It might be argued that constructing a book on the basis of an assumed political settlement is merely an 'academic' exercise. On the contrary, we believe that there is a long-standing and widespread consensus, in Israel, Palestine and internationally, that the three principles identified above constitute the only solution to the Palestinian–Israeli conflict that offers the prospect of a lasting peace. The events of the last decade have only underlined the impossibility of any solution which does not incorporate all of these elements. So, although our starting point is a political scenario which is hypothetical in the current circumstances, it is arguably the only route for a lasting and dignified solution to the conflict. This book should also be looked upon as a modest contribution towards the realisation of that solution.

While much of the literature of the preceding period dwelt on the distortions to the WBGS economy created by the 'forced integration' to which it was subjected, or on the adverse economic effects of 'closures', this book is forward-looking and focused more clearly on economic policy and institutional reform. It assumes a political framework which we think is appropriate to the circumstances in which an eventual Palestinian state is likely to come into existence. It abstracts from the political uncertainties which overshadowed much of the earlier work in order to prioritise economic issues. Finally, in order to broaden the perspective of the book and to strengthen its focus on economics rather than politics, we deliberately invited economists who were experts, not on Palestine but on the relevant areas of economics, to contribute papers or to act as discussants.

Outline of the book

The political framework specified above provides the point of departure for the economic analysis. The first three chapters in the book examine the core areas of economic policy: trade, money and fiscal policy. Sébastien Dessus and Elizabeth Ruppert Bulmer present a dynamic computable general equilibrium model on which they simulate the effects on the WBGS economy of different trade regimes, under different assumptions about the magnitude of transactions costs, on the one hand, and labour flows to Israel, on the other. While the ranking of the various regimes varies with the other assumptions, notably on labour flow, they find that, while the transaction costs and labour flows assumptions make a difference to the ranking, the non-discriminatory trade regime performs best in most cases. Christopher Adam and Christian Friis Bach in their comment interrogate both the model and the results; they also provide a useful comparative perspective on the Southern African Customs Union.

David Cobham identifies the exchange rate regimes operated in comparable economies, reviews estimates of the possible seigniorage benefits from a new Palestinian currency and the results of gravity models on the prospects for Palestinian trade, and assesses the suitability of various possible anchor currencies. He then argues for the introduction of a new currency, initially under a currency board with a peg to the Israeli shekel but later moving to a peg to the euro, with at least some scope for discretionary monetary policy. Chris Allsopp in his comment is more sceptical about the near term establishment of both currency and currency board, and emphasises the importance of institutional development.

Christopher Adam, David Cobham and Nu'man Kanafani investigate the budgetary experience of the PA so far, discuss the constraints on the use of fiscal policy in the new state and examine the range of structural challenges which fiscal policy will have to confront, from reconstruction and development to demographic changes and immigration. They argue that the constraints arising from the fiscal structure (e.g. high dependence on indirect taxes and customs duties) and from the likely monetary arrangements mean that fiscal policy will have to be relatively conservative. The fiscal challenges are not insuperable but the reforms, which the PA has already initiated, will need to be taken further. Adel Zagha in his comment asks some pertinent questions about the allocation of public expenditure, argues for a comprehensive policy to control population growth and for improvements in the administrative capacity of the tax authorities. He stresses the need for democratic tax reform and for public expenditure to be diverted towards basic social services and development needs.

The next three chapters discuss the financial sector, corporate governance and pensions. Osama Hamed examines the development of the banks and other financial institutions since the opening up of this sector in 1994, including the Palestinian Stock Exchange and informal financial mechanisms. He identifies the key developments that are needed to underpin the growth of a financial sector which will be able to make a strong contribution to economic growth and stability, notably land registration to improve the availability of collateral, improved banking supervision (with appropriate arrangements for branches of Jordanian banks), the possible contribution of venture capital and the need to facilitate operation of the informal financial sector. Andy Mullineux brings the experience of other developing and, particularly, transition countries to bear on these issues in his comment, arguing that banks will continue to be the main source of finance, questioning the role for venture capital and emphasising the need for good banking supervision and regulation.

Khaled Islaih and Clare Woodcraft discuss the need for improvements in company law and corporate governance. They examine the existing legal framework and current draft legislation in the WBGS, on the one hand, and the operational reality that Palestinian firms face, on the other, and they offer a brief case study of the Palestinian IT sector. They then present concrete proposals for company law designed to introduce into Palestine the best modern practices for both foreign companies investing there and domestic companies. Oren Sussman articulates the important qualification that the separation of ownership and control, which is fundamental to modern company law in the Anglo-Saxon world, applies to only a small percentage of Palestinian firms, so that the introduction of the Anglo-Saxon framework in the new Palestinian state might not be optimal.

Edward Sayre and Jennifer Olmsted consider the distribution of poverty and the need for improvements in the social safety net in Palestine, with particular reference to gender, employment conditions, labour legislation and the importance of the informal sector. Arguing that the most important reform needed is the introduction of a pension scheme, they review previous proposals for pension schemes in the WBGS and put forward – with detailed quantitative projections of the likely pension benefits – a novel scheme for pension provision which combines universal and work-based elements. Felix FitzRoy argues for a system of unemployment benefits as well as pensions, while Radwan Shaban in his comment focuses on the poverty alleviation aspects of the pension scheme proposed.

The next four chapters address a more varied range of topics. Chris Jensen-Butler and Eduardo Anselmo de Castro contribute a chapter on the overall strategy for economic development which emphasises the importance of spatial structures and economies of localisation and agglomeration and pays particular attention to the existing refugee camps in the WBGS. They go on to argue that economic strategy should be based on the identification of potential clusters and that policy should be designed to develop them. They suggest that the new Palestinian state has good possibilities of developing comparative advantage in the modern knowledge-based global economy and they emphasise certain characteristics of the refugee camps and (unconventionally) of Gaza. Leila Farsakh in her comment expresses some doubts about the resettlement of refugees in Gaza, argues that there is a great potential for development of dynamic clusters in West Bank cities and emphasises the importance of the territorial issues in any future settlement. She also notes that there are intricate connections between Israeli settlements in the WBGS and the local economy.

Anne Le More considers foreign aid strategy. She discusses the rationale, scope and composition of aid to the Palestinian people in the Oslo period when the aid process was essentially donor-driven, while the PA had no clear development strategy, poor monitoring capacity and weak coordination between ministries. She then sets out the actions which the government of a new state would need to take in order to ensure 'independence and ownership in a context of high foreign aid dependency'. Tony Killick in his comment brings a wider experience of foreign aid to bear on the issues raised by Le More, arguing that 'dependence does not have to mean donor domination' and discussing in detail how a Palestinian government could and should manage both aid and donors.

Arie Arnon and Nu'man Kanafani address the linked issues of compensation to the Palestinian refugees living in Jordan, Lebanon, Syria and elsewhere, and their possible resettlement in the new Palestinian state.

They survey the various approaches taken in the past to the magnitude and form of compensation and argue strongly for a forward-looking approach which relates compensation to the cost of absorbing the returnees in a viable and growing economy. They discuss how many refugees would be likely to settle in the new state. They provide macro-economic estimates of the costs (measured in terms of the required capital inflow) of the return to the West Bank of different numbers of refugees over different time periods and under alternative assumptions about the labour flows to Israel. They also provide estimates of the costs of economic development in the Gaza Strip sufficient to ensure that living standards there converge with those in the West Bank and discuss alternative policies for absorbing refugees, partly on the basis of Israel's experience with immigrants. Osama Hamed in his comment emphasises the importance of personal compensation, particularly to those refugees who do not choose to settle in the new state, and the financial, but also political and symbolic, contribution which could be made by the handing over of Israeli settlements in the WBGS to the returning Palestinian refugees. Athar Hussain argues that the chapter's approach to compensation 'makes a lot of economic sense and is not encumbered by the divisive baggage of history', and goes on to discuss questions of who will receive and who will finance compensation, and who should be defined as a refugee.

Finally, Arie Arnon, Avia Spivak and Oren Sussman present a model of the case for constructing a port in Gaza with strategic assets and incomplete contracts, as a way of raising broader issues about economic integration between Israel and Palestine. Previous discussion had emphasised the lower costs of the Israeli port of Ashdod, with its excess capacity. However, they are able to show that if Israel is free to set (and reset) the price of its port services the first best solution will not be attainable. It is therefore better for both parties that a port should be built in Gaza, even if its costs are higher than those of Ashdod and it later turns out to be underutilised. They interpret their finding as showing 'that modern economic theory does not support a priori the view that the optimal level of integration is full integration'. In his comment Jonathan Thomas looks closely at the assumptions of the model, arguing the importance of unverifiability rather than the unenforceability of contracts on sovereign states.

The chapters in this book were originally presented at a workshop at the University of St Andrews in August 2003, and then revised in the light of comments by discussants and others. The editors wish to record their gratitude to the UK government's Department for International Development for funding the workshop; to Alex Cobham for acting as rapporteur at the workshop; and to John Beath and David Corner at St Andrews, Astrid Woollen at the Royal Agricultural University in Copenhagen and Birgitte Rahbek for their support.

Notes

1 What follows is not intended to be a comprehensive survey of work on the Palestinian economy. Rather, we highlight some key papers and books to illustrate how research in this area has developed, as a background to identifying the distinguishing characteristics of this book.
2 Tuma and Darin-Drabkin (1978: 115) refer to the human or subjective factor as 'the confidence of identity for the nation', and as including 'the ability to identify reasonable expectations, to recruit resources, to assess and respond to the demand, and to pursue economic goals with enterprise and efficiency'.
3 Another important contribution in this phase, which was not particularly concerned with the issue of viability, is the volume edited by Abed (1988).
4 A summary of the PLO's two volume economic plan can be found in Sayigh (1993).
5 The World Bank study can be seen as a continuation of earlier international efforts through the UN to monitor economic conditions in the Occupied Territories, notably via UNCTAD, whose Special Unit on Palestine had been established as early as 1985 and which had produced regular surveys and studies about the economies of the Occupied Territories since then.
6 Among the important contributions in the 'closure literature' see the monitoring reports of UNSCO (e.g. 2002) and World Bank (e.g. 2002a, 2003).
7 There are some notable exceptions to this, including UNCTAD (1996), Valdivieso *et al.* (2001) and World Bank (2002b).

References

Abed, G. (ed.) (1988) *The Palestinian Economy: Studies in Development Under Prolonged Occupation*, New York: Routledge.

Arnon, A., Luski, I., Spivak, A. and Weinblatt, J. (1997) *The Palestinian Economy: Between Imposed Integration and Voluntary Separation*, Leiden: Brill.

Ben-Shahar, H., Berglas, E., Mundlak, Y. and Sadane, M. (1971) *Economic Structure and Development Prospects of the West Bank and Gaza Strip*, Santa Monica: Rand.

Bull, V. (1975) *The West Bank – Is It Viable?* Lexington: D.C. Heath & Co.

Diwan, I. and Shaban, R. (1999) (eds) *Development Under Adversity*, Washington, DC and Ramallah: World Bank and MAS.

Fischer, S., Rodrik, D. and Tuma, E. (1993) (eds) *The Economics of Middle East Peace*, Cambridge: MIT Press.

Hilal, J. (1975) *The West Bank: Economic and Social Structures 1948–1974*, Beirut: PLO Research Centre (in Arabic).

Paris Protocol (PP) (1994) *Protocol on Economic Relations between the Government of Israel and the P.L.O., Representing the Palestinian People*, available at http://www.pna.gov.ps/key_decuments/Protocol_on_Economic_Relations.pdf (accessed 14 January 2004), also reproduced in Arnon *et al.* (1997).

Sayigh, Y. (1967) *The Israeli Economy*, Beirut: PLO Research Centre (in Arabic).

Sayigh, Y. (1993) *Assistance to the Palestinian People – Priorities and Needs – The Palestinian Position*, Paris: The PLO's Department of Economic Affairs and Planning, UNESCO.

Tuma, E. and Darin-Drabkin, H. (1978) *The Economic Case for Palestine*, London: Croom Helm.

UN (1947) 'Resolution Adopted on the Report of the Ad Hoc Committee on the

Palestinian Question', no. 181 (Partition Resolution), available at http://www.un.org/documents/ga/res/2/ares2.htm (accessed 21 December 2003).

UNCTAD (1996) *Prospects for Sustained Development of the Palestinian Economy: Strategies and Policies for Reconstruction and Development*, Geneva.

UNSCO (Office of the United Nations Special Coordinator in the Occupied Territories) (2002) *The Impact of Closure and Other Mobility Restrictions on Palestinian Productive Activities, 1 January 2002–30 June 2002*, New York: United Nations.

Valdivieso, R., Erickson von Allmen, U., Bannister, G., Davoodi, H., Fischer, F., Jenkner, E. and Said, M. (2001) *West Bank and Gaza: Economic Performance, Prospects and Policies*, Washington, DC: IMF.

Ward, R. (1977) 'The economics of a Palestine entity', in R. Ward, D. Peretz and E. Wilson, *The Palestine State: A Rational Approach*, Port Washington,: Kennikat Press.

World Bank (1993) *Developing the Occupied Territories: An Investment in Peace*, 6 volumes, Washington, DC: World Bank.

World Bank (2002a) *Fifteen Months – Intifada, Closures and Palestinian Economic Crisis: An Assessment*, Washington, DC: World Bank.

World Bank (2002b) *Long-Term Policy Options for the Palestinian Economy*, Washington, DC: World Bank.

World Bank (2003) *Twenty Seven Months – Intifada, Closures and Economic Crisis: An Assessment*, Washington, DC: World Bank.

2 The choice of trade regime depends on multiple other factors

Sébastien Dessus and Elizabeth Ruppert Bulmer[1]

Overview

As policy makers look beyond the ongoing hostilities to consider a post-conflict period of Palestinian sovereignty, the future shape and functioning of the Palestinian economy will depend on the economic policy framework in place, particularly vis-à-vis its major trading partner, Israel. Predicting the shape of things to come is a risky undertaking, even more so given the large number of evolving variables that interact to generate wide-ranging outcomes. As a theoretical exercise we can examine the trade policy options available to Palestinian policy makers in the future, but the resulting trade performance and economic outcomes will depend more broadly on factors largely beyond the control of Palestinian decision makers. These include, notably:

1 the degree of restrictions on the movement of goods;
2 Israeli demand for Palestinian labour.

In this context, we identify potential trade regimes and explore their impact under a range of scenarios that could possibly arise. Whereas this approach enables us to be comprehensive, it does not point to a single optimal trade policy but instead generates a list of second-best choices dependent on a given economic and institutional environment.

This analysis takes as its point of departure the assumption of sovereign decision-making by Palestinian policy makers. With respect to trade relations with dominant trading partner Israel, future policy designs will be considered against the backdrop of historical preferential trade arrangements between the West Bank and Gaza Strip (WBGS) and Israel, namely the modified customs union (CU) that effectively provides for the free exchange of goods between the two neighbouring entities.[2] Other regimes that might be considered include a non-discriminatory trade regime (NDTR), which would give the WBGS the opportunity to reform its trade relations with both Israel and third parties under a uniform approach, and a free trade area (FTA) with Israel, which would enable the WBGS to amend its trade policy only vis-à-vis third parties. We examine three options for reform: an 'open' NDTR, whereby trade barriers are set at low levels for all partners; a 'closed' NDTR, whereby the WBGS introduces barriers against Israeli imports; and an FTA with Israel, whereby the WBGS reduces trade barriers vis-à-vis third parties.

For each of these trade options, policy simulations are conducted for the period up to 2010 using a dynamic computable general equilibrium model. While this type of analytical tool cannot be used to forecast the evolution of the Palestinian economy, it nevertheless provides relevant findings on the comparative characteristics of the different options. Various conclusions arise from this exercise, the most important being that the relative merits of the different options tested in this analysis fundamentally depend on exogenously-determined conditions that could be imposed on a future sovereign Palestinian state. In particular, an 'open' NDTR would provide maximum benefits to the Palestinian economy in an environment characterised by low transaction costs and low Israeli demand for Palestinian workers; by contrast, a continuation of the existing CU would probably be more beneficial in an environment of high transaction costs and large Palestinian labour flows to Israel. An important conclusion that emerges irrespective of these exogenous conditions is that raising external trade barriers under a NDTR would be extremely detrimental to Palestinian households' standards of living and thus would constitute an inferior option. While somewhat more conditional on the economic environment, the analysis also suggests that a FTA is inferior to either a CU or an 'open' NDTR.

This chapter is organised as follows. The following section describes the nature of economic relations between Israel and the WBGS since 1967, which serves as a background for our analysis. The third section presents the methodology and assumptions employed to assess the impact of various trade options. The fourth section presents and discusses the results of the modelling exercise, and the last section draws conclusions.

Historical background

Incomes and growth

Analysing trade policies and economic performance both pre-Oslo and under the Paris Protocol points to a distorted incentive framework and dependence on the Israeli economy, with Palestinian production focused on low value-added activities. Since 1967, Palestinian economic development has followed a model of integration with Israel aimed at convergence or catching up with the Israeli economy. But rapid growth did not materialise in the WBGS. There was some convergence in incomes, especially during the 1970s and early 1980s, driven by short-run gains from market access, worker remittances and higher incomes. But these were offset by long-run losses due to low productivity, vulnerability to external shocks and weak competitiveness, which eventually led to diverging economic performance, as the WBGS fell further behind (see Figure 2.1).[3]

The Paris Protocol, signed in 1994, aimed to correct some of the observed development disparities – especially vis-à-vis trade and income – by improving the environment for private investment and growth in the WBGS through eliminating Israeli trade barriers on Palestinian agricultural products, removing restrictions on economic activities, reducing political and economic uncertainty by phasing out military occupation, developing financial institutions and creating a legal and regulatory framework. The Paris Protocol also led to the revenue sharing, or clearance, mechanism under which Israel transferred the taxes it collected from trade, purchase and value-added taxes on behalf of the PA, less a 3 per cent administrative fee. These measures were accompanied by substantial donor support in terms of infrastructure investment and technical assistance. Nevertheless, the economic integration model failed as incomes diverged between Palestinians and Israelis during the Interim Period.

Palestinian economic output was erratic post-Oslo, with distinct episodes mirroring the volatile evolution of political relationships with Israel, particularly with respect to the degree of internal and external closures. In the initial post-Oslo years the economy experienced a return of nationals and large inflows of public and private capital as the result of

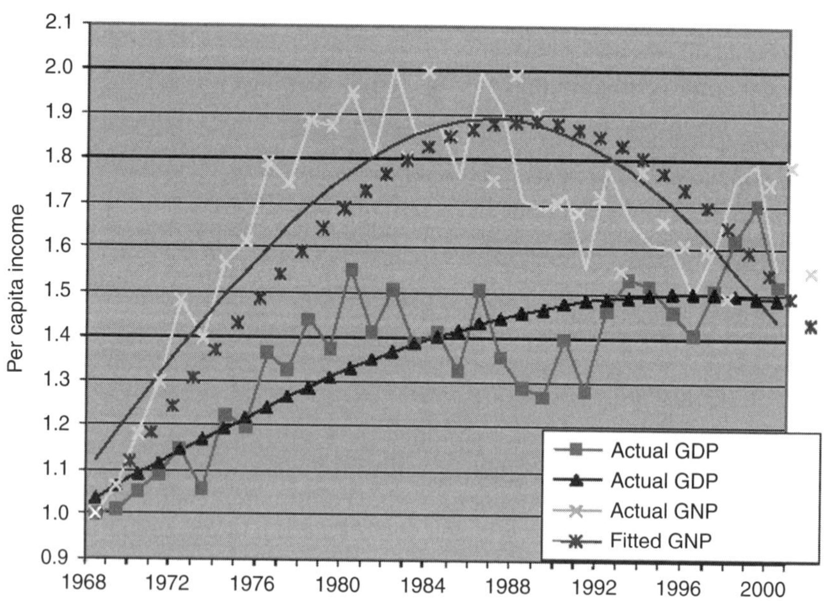

Figure 2.1 Convergence in GNI and GDP per capita between WBGS and Israel (authors' calculations based on ICBS for the period 1968–1993 and PCBS for the period 1994–2000).

positive expectations regarding the peace process. But two years of intermittent external closures in 1995–1996 and a sharp drop in Palestinian labour flows to Israel precipitated economic decline. From 1997 to September 2000, closures were less frequent, labour flows to Israel grew dramatically and transaction costs fell while private investment increased. The Palestinian economy also benefited from an economic boom in Israel, through enhanced opportunities for exports of Palestinian goods and labour. But the outbreak of the second intifada in late September 2000 halted this economic recovery.[4] Since 2000, real GDP is estimated by the World Bank to have declined by a third. Although this decline is the result of extraordinary events – and as such is not explicitly considered in the discussion on economic patterns – it nevertheless demonstrates the huge negative impact of closures and resulting high transaction costs on economic growth.

The Palestinian economy continues to depend on Israeli goods and labour demand. We construct a dependency index – defined as the sum of Palestinian goods and labour exports to Israel divided by Palestinian GNP – to capture the evolution of the Palestinian economy's reliance on Israel in conjunction with changes in the policy environment.[5] As illustrated in Figure 2.2 below, dependency on Israel peaked in the early 1980s and subsequently declined, driven initially by lower exports to Israel and then by more restricted access to the Israeli labour market in the mid 1990s.

Figure 2.2 also illustrates that the implementation of the Paris Protocol had little impact on reducing Palestinian dependence on Israel; in fact, Palestinian economic dependence actually increased between 1996 and 2000. The continued dependency observed post-Oslo did not enable the

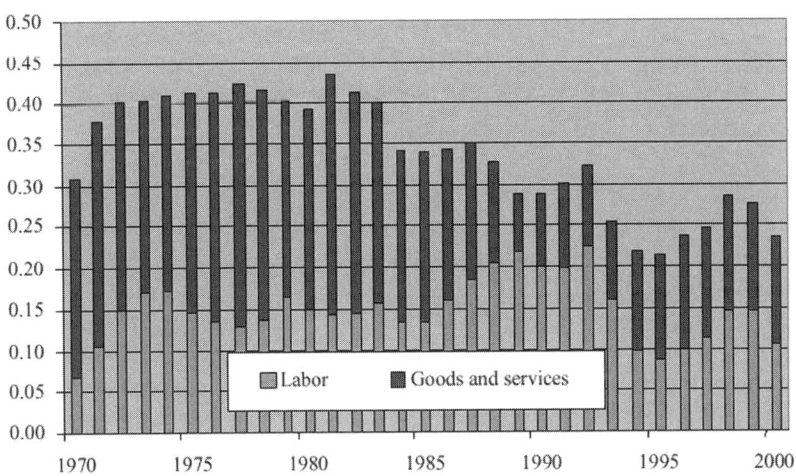

Figure 2.2 Dependency index (authors' calculations based on ICBS for the period 1968–1993 and PCBS for the period 1994–2000).

Palestinian private sector to diversify its risk and at the same time entailed significant trade diversion and high domestic wages. On the other hand, whereas dependence on Israel may not be desirable from the Palestinian political perspective, it did at least contribute toward higher household incomes, as discussed below.

Distorted trade outcomes

Israel is by far the West Bank and Gaza Strip's most important trade partner, dominating both imports and exports. In 1998, the WBGS imported US$2,849 million in goods and services (72 per cent of GDP excluding East Jerusalem), three-quarters of which was imported from Israel including indirect imports. WBGS exports amounted to US$697 million, 96 per cent of which was destined to Israel. The modified customs union currently in place is one-sided, favouring Israel in several ways. The external tariff on third party countries is set by Israel without regard to Palestinian comparative advantage. Although Israeli tariffs plus purchase tax averaged 11 per cent in 1998, the effective rate was a much higher 16.6 per cent on Palestinian imports due to the different types of goods imported by the WBGS.[6] Furthermore, the Paris Protocol allows only limited Palestinian access to Egyptian and Jordanian markets. Because Israel controls all borders in the Palestinian Territories, Palestinian trade must be conducted through Israel rather than directly with third party countries.

Requiring all goods to pass through Israel or Israeli-controlled borders creates at least two problems:

1 Palestinian traders incur higher transport costs than if trading directly;
2 the Palestinian Authority (PA) loses out on trade tax and VAT revenue from goods nominally imported into Israel but subsequently re-exported to the West Bank and Gaza Strip without being properly accounted for – and taxed – as a trade transaction.

Additional losses are incurred by the WBGS in welfare terms, because the US$900 million trade deficit with Israel constitutes a negative net transfer equivalent to US$99–140 million compared to a non-discriminatory trade regime (World Bank 2002). This means that Israel gains more than the WBGS from preferential access to Palestinian markets under the customs union.

On the other hand, the WBGS gains certain advantages from being in a customs union with Israel, such as preferential access to the large Israeli market, albeit still one-sided during closures. In addition, Israel's recent trade liberalisation has allowed liberalisation for Palestinian imports as well. And finally, starting in 1994, the Israeli tax authority collected taxes on behalf of the PA and remitted the proceeds to the PA (temporarily suspended under the intifada), greatly simplifying the PA's role and reducing its administrative costs by an estimated US$48 million annually.[7]

These factors together imply that the modified CU costs an estimated US$225–266 million each year compared to an alternative trade regime that is non-discriminatory (based on a comparative static analysis of 1998 trade data).[8] A NDTR is also superior to an FTA, based on a tax revenue/welfare calculation (World Bank 2002). Under an FTA, trade between the WBGS and Israel would remain free, implying the same welfare loss from the trade deficit as under a CU, plus additional costs for complying with rules of origin necessary to avoid trade deflection under an FTA. These costs would be borne by the PA in terms of border administration, as well as by exporters and consumers through higher import prices. Moreover, there are no border savings to offset these losses, such that in net terms an FTA would cost at least US$184 million more than the NDTR on an annual basis. In reality, an FTA would bring even higher costs associated with potential trade diversion, welfare losses due to the WBGS's higher propensity to import and enforcement complications resulting from multiple and overlapping FTAs.

Within this same static partial equilibrium framework, the CU is superior to an FTA from the perspective of tax revenues and administrative costs. An FTA would require setting up and administering customs border stations, but this added cost would not be accompanied by tax revenues from Israeli imports, which would continue to be free. Moreover, the introduction of rules of origin would reduce Palestinian access to Israeli markets. And finally, efficiency and welfare losses would arise under an FTA from trade diversion under which Palestinian producers use more expensive Israeli imports rather than less costly alternatives from third party sources in order to meet rules of origin criteria for exporting final goods to Israel duty-free.

Analysing trade policy choices in a partial equilibrium framework – that is, from a tax revenue and welfare perspective independent of other sectors of the economy – suggests that an NDTR is superior to both an FTA and the existing customs union, assuming an open and transparent trade policy enforced by credible lock-in mechanisms.[9] It is important to note, however, that the costs to a CU are offset to a large degree by Palestinian access to the Israeli labour market (addressed below).

Integrated labour markets and wage distortions

The historical integration of the Palestinian and Israeli labour markets and the resulting Palestinian access to Israeli jobs led to higher aggregate employment and incomes. On the other hand, this access distorts wages within the Palestinian economy, hindering competitiveness. Palestinian labour supply far exceeds demand on the domestic Palestinian market, despite low participation rates particularly among women, leading many workers to seek employment elsewhere, primarily in Israel.

Prior to the ongoing crisis, nearly a quarter of Palestinian employment was in Israeli jobs, where wages are significantly higher than in the WBGS. Israel began to restrict Palestinian labour inflows in the early 1990s by introducing work permit requirements. But the Oslo accords marked a fundamental shift in Israeli labour policy as mobility restrictions were enforced, including periodic border closures and at times extreme restrictions (i.e. internal closures) during which Palestinians could not leave their villages. During closures, very few workers from the Gaza Strip could reach their jobs in Israel or the settlements, but West Bankers had slightly more flexibility, due to the porous border with Israel. For both groups of workers, however, unemployment spiked in response to restrictive Israeli border policies. Figure 2.3 illustrates the strong negative correlation between Palestinian employment in Israel and unemployment. Closures were particularly severe in 1995 and 1996, leading to unemployment rates of 25 per cent in 1996, up from modest levels in the early 1990s. This represents a dramatic change from the 1980s when unemployment was negligible and movement restrictions did not exist.

The PA responded to skyrocketing unemployment by creating jobs in the civil service. Although this strategy coincided with the PA's expanded responsibilities post-Oslo and the need to set up the main institutions of governance and public service delivery, public employment grew faster than necessary, engendering an unsustainably large wage bill. As the security climate improved, labour flows to Israel regained much of their earlier importance in providing Palestinian jobs and unemployment declined in 1998 and 1999, falling below 10 per cent in mid 2000. The September 2000 outbreak of the intifada led to sharply higher unemployment as closures precluded workers from reaching their jobs and prolonged civil strife disrupted domestic economic activity.

Mincer-type wage regressions indicate that the returns to working in Israel are extremely high: 85 per cent for a worker from the Gaza Strip

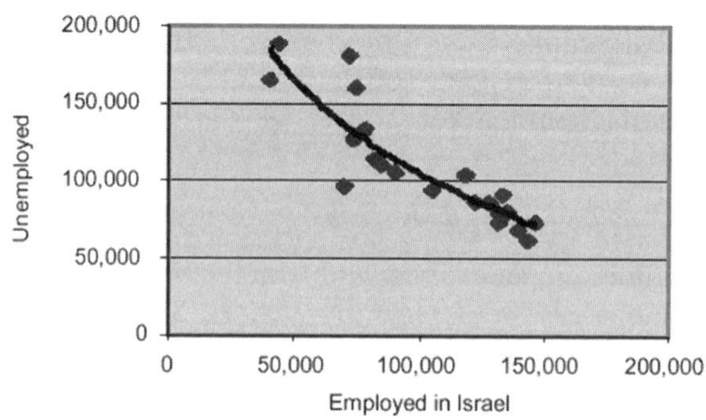

Figure 2.3 Correlation of Palestinian unemployment and employment in Israel (authors' calculations).

and 61 per cent for a West Banker, controlling for individual characteristics (World Bank 2002). In this environment, the domestic economy struggles to create adequate jobs for the fast-growing but fairly well-educated labour force, putting pressure on the PA to step in by creating more civil service jobs. Although the returns to education are positive and increasing, these are fully offset by the returns to working in Israel. This very real distortion from limited access to Israeli jobs and the resulting segmentation of the labour market gives rise to structural and therefore persistent unemployment (Ruppert Bulmer 2003). The Palestinian labour market also suffers segmentation within its domestic market: workers cannot commute freely between the West Bank and the Gaza Strip and, during closures and particularly the intifada, workers cannot leave their home villages to reach their jobs in nearby cities or even neighbouring districts. These rigidities manifest themselves in the mismatch between labour demand and supply (the supply exists but is unable to respond to demand) and the inability of wages to adjust sufficiently to clear the market. Since the outbreak of the intifada in 2000, for example, real wages have declined by 5 per cent while employment fell by 19 per cent, implying that employment rather than wages absorb most of the impact of closures.

Furthermore, the higher Israeli wage actually draws up domestic wages in the WBGS, making them less competitive and dampening domestic labour demand and thus hurting Palestinian economic development by underutilising available human capital resources and creating a labour market that specialises in low value-added activities. This in turn does not facilitate skills acquisition through knowledge-sharing or learning-by-doing – the expected gains from labour migration. In addition, the relatively high wage does not attract investors or technology to increase productivity in export sectors. During the Interim Period, Palestinian growth and economic development was not export-led but rather was driven by consumption through higher incomes from workers' remittances from Israeli jobs. The positive consequences of this growth model include higher household incomes and lower poverty when labour can move relatively freely. But the downside – especially during periods of closure – involves uncertainty, income volatility, high unemployment and poverty, uncompetitive domestic wages and substantial vulnerability to external shocks.

The post-Oslo period has been characterised by fluctuating degrees of economic integration between the WBGS and Israel with respect to trade and labour flows. Although the customs union provided preferential Palestinian access to Israeli markets, it effectively limited Palestinian imports to relatively expensive Israeli goods. The net effect restricted domestic Palestinian productivity growth and hindered expansion of export products and markets beyond Israel. Palestinian and Israeli labour market integration produced mixed effects: whereas access to high-paying Israeli jobs increased Palestinian employment and household incomes, it also raised domestic Palestinian wages, dampening labour demand and diminishing Palestinian competitiveness on export markets. Moreover, the uncertain business environment – exacerbated by the closure policy and a weak institutional framework for promoting investment – discouraged investors due to the perceived risks. Together, these policies resulted in a development path of Palestinian economic dependence on Israel.

Modelling trade options

Looking to the future, this analysis asks whether an alternative trade regime would generate better Palestinian economic outcomes than the existing CU. To answer this question, we first need to decide what criteria define 'better economic outcomes'. Higher GDP growth? Higher per capita income? Lower unemployment? More exports? Less dependence on Israel? Lower poverty? This analysis will consider all of these criteria to assess what type of trade regime best meets these objectives and thus could be judged as optimal. The analysis developed in this chapter extends our earlier work in 'Long-term policy options for the Palestinian economy' (World Bank 2002).

We consider four potential trade policies: CU, 'open' NDTR, 'closed' NDTR and FTA. Rather than simply conducting a theoretical exercise, the analysis takes as its point of departure the conditions on the ground in 2003 – for example, income levels, wages, unemployment, prevailing mobility restrictions and the resulting transactions costs – in order to reflect the above-described distortions that severely impacted Palestinian economic performance post-Oslo and will continue to be central.

It is necessary to recognise that although the choice of a future Palestinian trade regime may not be constrained as it was in the past under occupation, other key factors lie outside the decision function of Palestinian policy makers. More specifically, Israeli security policies affect the movement of goods and labour both across borders and within the WBGS itself. This in turn affects economic outcomes through two transmission channels: the demand for Palestinian labour in Israel and the level of transaction costs for traded goods and services. The analysis thus considers a range of scenarios to account for these exogenously determined factors.

To assess optimal trade policy, we develop a recursive dynamic CGE model calibrated to the Palestinian economy. The model combines in a consistent framework the demand and supply conditions on goods and factor markets by describing the economic relations among households, producers, the government and the rest of the world. The model's parameters are drawn from a social accounting matrix for 1998 (based on PCBS data). The CGE model considers seven sectors: agriculture, manufacturing, construction, transport and communications, commerce and tourism, other private services, public services, and two trading partners; Israel and the rest of the world. Economic growth is generated through job creation, capital accumulation in productive activities and productivity gains, the latter depending on the degree of competition, openness and movement restrictions. Exogenous assumptions about population and labour force growth, technical progress, world prices of traded goods and real wage growth in Israel are also needed, and are based on historical evidence from the 1968–2000 period (see Table 2.1). Additional factors that shape future trade and growth outcomes under various policy regimes include transaction costs associated with the movement of goods and services and the magnitude of Palestinian labour flows to Israel (both treated as exogenous).

Modelling capital

Physical capital accumulation, or investment, depends on the availability of savings originating from households, the government and the rest of the world through foreign direct investment and official development assistance. Household savings depend positively on household incomes, government savings depend positively on tax revenues (determined by the tax structure and the level of economic activity) and public expenditures are treated as exogenous. Foreign savings, which consist of investment spending financed by foreign aid and private transfers, are assumed to follow historical paths, particularly with respect to donor aid flows.[10] The model distinguishes between productive and unproductive capital (e.g. residential building); only the former contributes to GDP growth when accumulated. Increased access to external markets is assumed to expand investment opportunities and thus the share of savings invested in productive activities. Empirical studies indicate a positive relationship between investment and trade openness (Levine and Renelt 1992; Wacziarg 2001) and, in this analysis, the ratio of productive investment over savings is modelled as a function of the share of exports in GDP (with an elasticity of one-third). The initial productive capital stock is calibrated in 1998 to match the observed capital stock growth from 1998 to 1999 and the overall elasticity of GDP with respect to capital is fixed at 0.40, equal to the share

Table 2.1 Exogenous assumptions

Annual growth rate 2000–2010	*(%)*
Population	3.5
Labour force	4.4
Exogenous technical progress	0.5
Real public expenditures	2.7
World price of imports	0.0
World price of exports	1.0
Real wage in Israel	1.0
Net foreign savings	3.7

of capital remuneration in total value-added.[11] The implied rate of return to capital (before tax) equals 12.5 per cent in 1998.

Modelling labour

In the model, labour supply is exogenous and aggregate labour demand is equal to the sum of sectoral labour demand determined by sector output and factor costs (both wages and capital). As discussed above, limits on Palestinian labour flows to Israel increase unemployment, lower wages and reduce the probability of finding a job in Israel. The model captures this inverted relationship between wages and unemployment through a Phillips curve specification which also takes account of periods of extreme closure such as during the ongoing intifada.

Modelling productivity growth

A large literature supports the idea that outward orientation favours TFP growth by encouraging technological transfers, enlarging the choice of inputs and reinforcing competitive pressures. Following Dessus *et al.* (1999), an increase in the share of tradable activities in GDP is accompanied by an increase in total factor productivity; international experience is used to calibrate this phenomenon. This assumption is supported by the observed underutilisation of human capital in the WBGS resulting from the distorting effects of Palestinian labour flows to Israel and the one-sided nature of trade relations with Israel and limitations on third party trade. Expanding tradable activities and reducing distorted incentives could enhance the use of available human capital in growth-generating activities. Total factor productivity growth is modelled as the sum of two components:

1. an exogenous trend reflecting exogenous technical progress – assumed low at 0.5 per cent and consistent with historical trends (World Bank 2002);
2. an endogenous component in which TFP is a function of the share of exports in GDP (with an elasticity of 0.1, see Dessus *et al.* 1999).

Additional assumptions

Other factors influencing the evolution of the Palestinian economy are introduced into the model. The nature of Palestinian export opportunities in Israel are treated distinctly from those in the rest of the world. In light of the long-term Palestinian presence in Israeli markets, the close ties with Israeli businesses and consumers, and the significant market shares developed in Israel, the model assumes that Palestinian producers have some market power in Israeli goods markets. But this advantage is counterbalanced by the relatively limited growth prospects of the Israeli market compared to the much larger world market. Palestinian producers do not hold strong positions on international markets, by contrast, and face tough competition to develop new markets; in the event that domestic agents produce goods at competitive prices, however, the prospects for export outlets in the rest of the world are significantly larger than in Israel. With respect to investment, entrepreneurs have a greater capacity to adjust production techniques to new opportunities with the latest vintage of capital relative to already installed capital for which there is little substitution among intermediate inputs, labour and capital.

Last but not least, we assume a progressive political rapprochement between Israel and the WBGS from 2003 onwards, which entails lower transaction costs, greater access to the Israeli labour market and a partial transfer of clearance revenues. By 2005, a Palestinian state is established, creating the possibility for Palestinian policy makers to design a new trade policy. We assume that the transition to statehood will be accompanied by large inflows of capital in the first years following its inception, to provide financial support for creating new public institutions.

Policy scenarios

Sixteen scenarios are constructed to reflect potential future economic relations between the WBGS and Israel. These can be organised in the framework of a 4×4 matrix; for each of four potential trade policy options (CU, 'open' NDTR, 'closed' NDTR and FTA) we consider low and high transactions costs, and low and high Palestinian labour flows to Israel.

Specifically, the CU scenario envisages a continuation of the current trade policy as defined by the Paris Protocol. Under the NDTR, the WBGS adjusts the nature of its trade relationships with both Israel and the rest of the world. In the 'open' NDTR, a 5 per cent tariff rate is imposed on all imports, from all origins, and purchase taxes are eliminated. In the 'closed' version of a NDTR, tariffs and purchase taxes on Israeli goods are set at rates similar to those currently applied to imports from third parties. In addition, the NDTR enables the WBGS to expand its access to export markets, through WTO accession for instance, or simply by initiating trade with countries with which Israel does not trade. We assume a conservative 5 per cent increase in the price at which Palestinian exporters can sell their goods on third parties' markets in the 'open' NDTR scenario, compared to only 2 per cent in the 'closed' version. Another consequence of this departure from the Paris Protocol is the imposition (in both the 'open' and 'closed' versions) of a tariff on Palestinian exports to Israel, which we assume would be similar to the average tariff (differentiated by product) imposed by Israel on imports from the rest of the world. Finally, we assume that an FTA would be used to develop trade relationships with the rest of the world while maintaining preferential relationships with Israel.

For this option we assume that the WBGS would adopt a policy similar to that of an 'open' NDTR for imports from third parties. An FTA would create the need to check the origin of goods flowing between the WBGS and Israel to determine whether they are produced within the FTA (and as such are eligible for tariff exemption) or whether they are re-exports originating from third parties (and thus subject to tariffs). Controlling for origin is modelled by assuming a cost equivalent to 3 per cent of the goods' nominal value, while increased Palestinian exporters' preference for tax exempt Israeli inputs is modelled by augmenting the share of Israeli imports in total imports by 2.5 per cent after controlling for the relative price of Israeli imports relative to imports from the rest of the world.

In reality, controlling for the origin of goods traded between the WBGS and Israel will necessitate establishing a customs administration; this is true for all policy scenarios except the CU. The annual cost of running such an administration is conservatively estimated at US$50 million (Daoud 2000). On the other hand, controlling these flows will lessen the extent of fiscal leakages, which are estimated to cost the WBGS some US$50–100 million a year. Various arrangements could be introduced to control trade between the WBGS and Israel, from fixed customs stations to marking goods to distinguish their origin. Thorough discussion of the various technical possibilities and their fiscal and trade implications goes beyond the scope of this chapter; we simply assume that the associated administrative costs are exactly compensated by lower fiscal leakages.

Transaction costs are extremely high at present and depend to a large extent on the current environment of severe mobility restrictions imposed by Israel. Even during periods of relatively open borders between the WBGS and Israel, transaction costs are relatively important, given the effectively landlocked nature of the Palestinian Territories (there is no port in the Gaza Strip). But it is the externally determined level of security precautions, border closures and rather draconian limits on individuals' movements that determine the cost of transactions. The modelling exercise considers low and high levels of transaction costs. In scenarios with low transaction costs, total factor productivity in the transport and commerce sectors is assumed to be 40 per cent higher than in scenarios with high transaction costs and 20 per cent higher in 2010 compared to 2000. In scenarios with high transaction costs, productivity levels in the transport and commerce sectors are 20 per cent lower in 2010 than in 2000. These cost variations are plausible, evidenced during the second intifada by a 50 per cent decline in productivity levels in these sectors, which led to an increase in their domestic price – as well as the price of goods that use transport and commerce services as inputs – and lower demand for these services. The success of any future export promotion strategies will depend critically on exogenous factors determining the magnitude of transaction costs.

The external environment with respect to labour flows to Israel follows two potential paths in the model. In the first, the share of Palestinian workers in Israel in 2010 is similar to that in 2000. Given that the labour force is projected to grow by approximately 50 per cent during this period, the number of Palestinian workers in Israel would reach approximately 160,000 by the end of 2010 (excluding East Jerusalem). The second potential path assumes that by 2010 only 70,000 workers will commute daily to Israel. Under both scenarios, we assume that Palestinian workers remain confined to low-skill activities in Israel (e.g. construction, agriculture, services) and that their average remuneration grows by 1 per cent a year. The magnitude of labour flows to Israel affects economic outcomes through three channels. The first relates to workers' remittances from Israel: high remittances permit the WBGS to import more rather than develop competitive export industries. The second concerns Palestinian household incomes: higher remittances entail higher incomes and probably higher savings available for investment. The third transmission channel relates directly to the labour market: Palestinian workers commuting to Israel withdraw from the domestic labour market, thus easing pressure on unemployment.

Simulation results

Together, these combinations of trade regime alternatives, high and low transaction costs, and high and low labour flows to Israel represent a range of policy options and varying degrees of cooperation on the political and economic fronts. No particular likelihood is attached to any of these scenarios, given the uncertainty of future directions of the peace negotiations. For each scenario, we report in Table 2.2 the 2010 value of the following outcome indicators: real per capita income, average GDP growth (during 2000–2010), the dependency index, unemployment, the share of exports in GDP and the poverty rate.[12]

The results of the various scenarios should be considered against the backdrop of a baseline scenario that reflects the status quo (i.e. a modified CU, constrained labour flows to Israel and high transaction costs). Figure 2.4 below depicts the future path of GDP and per capita incomes in this baseline scenario. Although we believe that the creation of a Palestinian state will lead to some sort of economic recovery, future economic trends – especially in the near term – reflect the enormous impact of the ongoing intifada, particularly through the destruction of capital stock and lost markets. Moreover, it will take several years, in any scenario, to regain the per capita income and poverty levels that prevailed on the eve of the second intifada. In fact, the most optimistic scenarios explored herein foresee per capita incomes in 2010 only 2 to 3 per cent higher than those in 2000. But this result largely depends on exogenous assumptions regarding capital inflows and productivity, *inter alia*, which are at least partially independent of the choice of trade policy.

Table 2.2 Simulation results

Transaction costs	*Labour flows to Israel*	*CU*	*Open NDTR*	*Closed NDTR*	*FTA*
Real per capita income 2010 (base 100 = 2000)					
1 Low	High	102.0	**103.2**	100.6	100.9
2 Low	Low	94.1	**98.1**	92.7	95.0
3 High	High	**90.1**	90.0	89.2	89.1
4 High	Low	79.6	**81.6**	78.6	79.6
GDp growth 2000–2010					
5 Low	High	4.7%	**4.9%**	4.4%	4.7%
6 Low	Low	5.2%	**5.5%**	4.9%	5.4%
7 High	High	3.4%	3.5%	3.1%	**3.6%**
8 High	Low	3.8%	**4.0%**	3.4%	3.9%
Dependency index 2010 (*)					
9 Low	High	27.4%	26.5%	**24.8%**	26.9%
10 Low	Low	22.1%	20.1%	**19.5%**	21.7%
11 High	High	28.2%	27.7%	**25.5%**	28.7%
12 High	Low	23.2%	21.6%	**20.5%**	23.1%
Unemployment rate 2010 (*)					
13 Low	High	14.1%	**13.9%**	14.0%	14.2%
14 Low	Low	19.5%	**18.2%**	19.7%	19.1%
15 High	High	18.2%	18.4%	**18.1%**	18.7%
16 High	Low	25.6%	**24.8%**	25.7%	25.6%
Exports/GDP 2010 (*)					
17 Low	High	17.4%	**18.0%**	15.2%	17.1%
18 Low	Low	21.9%	**23.1%**	19.4%	22.8%
19 High	High	15.8%	15.9%	13.7%	**16.1%**
20 High	Low	19.9%	**20.7%**	17.5%	20.6%
Poverty rate 2010 (*)					
21 Low	High	28.4%	**27.5%**	29.3%	29.2%
22 Low	Low	33.8%	**31.1%**	34.8%	33.2%
23 High	High	**36.6%**	**36.6%**	37.2%	37.2%
24 High	Low	43.8%	**42.4%**	44.5%	43.8%

Note

*In 2000, the dependency index stood at 25.3 per cent (source: authors' calculation); the unemployment rate was 14.3 per cent (source: PCBS); exports/GDP were 16.0 per cent (source: PCBS) and the poverty rate was 30.7 per cent (source: World Bank).
Figures in bold represent optimal results.

The first result emerging from Table 2.2 is that, *ceteris paribus*, low transaction costs lead to better outcomes with respect to all six indicators compared to high transaction costs. This makes sense given that low transaction costs imply higher total factor productivity in the transport and commerce sectors, which eventually transmits to the whole economy. A more complex result emerges for labour flows to Israel: under all four trade regimes, high labour flows to Israel entail higher per capita income levels and lower poverty and unemployment compared to low labour

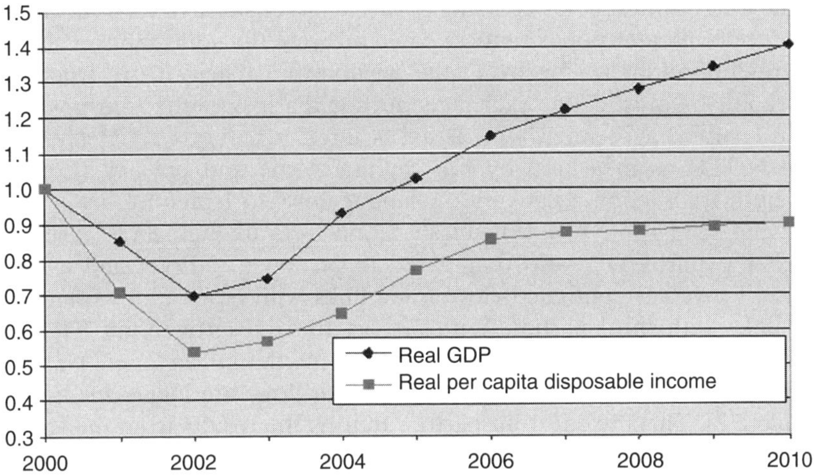

Figure 2.4 GDP and real per capita incomes, 1998–2010, high transactions costs, low labour flows, customs union (authors' calculations).

flows. On the other hand, low labour flows always generate higher GDP growth and exports through lower wages, higher domestic employment and the positive dynamic feedback to total factor productivity. Furthermore, the ratio of GDP to GNP increases in this setting, which leads to a decline in the dependency index.

Examining the results with a view to ranking the preferred trade policy option, we can rule out a 'closed' NDTR, which leads to inferior outcomes with respect to incomes, GDP, exports and poverty. These results emphasise the critical need to develop external outlets for Palestinian economic output, which in turn would contribute to economic growth and higher living standards. The Palestinian economy is too small and poor to rely solely on domestic demand to generate growth. Only two aspects work in favour of a 'closed' NDTR. The first is the lower dependency on Israel, concurrent with reducing trade with all partners as a result of higher barriers to trade. The second concerns unemployment, which is marginally lower than in most other trade policy scenarios when labour flows to Israel are high. This can be explained by the fact that greater openness – under an alternative trade regime such as an 'open' NDTR, for example – entails greater downward pressure on wages (or equivalently a stronger depreciation of the real exchange rate) to remain competitive and finance vital imports. The resulting lower domestic wage means higher unemployment (recall the Phillips curve specification). Although trade liberalisation like that envisaged under an 'open' NDTR requires greater restructuring of the economy with inherent adjustment costs, the reward is far greater in terms of real incomes and wages, as the price of consumer goods declines more rapidly than wages. Higher investment (originating from abroad, the government, or households deciding to save a larger share of their incomes in the face of greater opportunities) could mitigate the adjustment costs of trade liberalisation by improving the economy's capacity to restructure more rapidly. Adjusting the exchange rate could also ease the adjustment.

A free trade agreement with Israel is inferior to both a CU and an 'open' NDTR as measured by per capita income and poverty (except when both transaction costs and low labour flows to Israel are low – see lines 2 and 22 in Table 2.2). When transaction costs are high, an FTA leads to higher export/GDP ratios compared to an 'open' NDTR and a CU because it involves continued close trade links with Israel plus expanded trade links with third parties. With respect to GDP growth, an FTA is marginally superior to a CU but yields lower growth than an 'open' NDTR (except when both transaction costs and labour flows are high – see line 7 in Table 2.2). This mixed result partly confirms the results from the static analysis mentioned above that an FTA is inferior to a CU and an 'open' NDTR because it does not reduce trade diversion and at the same time induces extra costs stemming from the introduction of rules of origin.

As the preceding discussion implies, the simulation results point to no single optimal trade regime with respect to all indicators, but rather, a series of second-best choices in a given environment of externally-determined transaction costs and labour mobility for a particular indicator. The preponderance of best outcomes emerges under an 'open' NDTR, as illustrated by the Table 2.2 results in bold, but in many cases the results across alternative trade policies are close in magnitude.

External factors are central in determining the relative merits of the four trade policies considered. The choice of best trade regime appears to be particularly important when labour flows to Israel and, to a lesser extent, transaction costs are low; the differences among the outcomes of the trade policies are slightly magnified. By contrast, high labour flows to Israel and high transaction costs tend to narrow these differences. This observation is explained by the fact that these two variables each have a direct bearing on trade activity. In an environment of high transaction costs, trade policy does not matter much because its marginal impact is minimal. Similarly with respect to labour flows to Israel, high flows ease the external constraint and reduce the share of exports in GDP and GNP, leading to a more muted impact of trade policies on incomes. Based on these considerations, an open NDTR provides maximum leverage under low transaction costs and low labour flows to Israel. In this particular setting, the impact of trade liberalisation is magnified by the low transaction costs faced by importers and exporters; it is equally favoured by the downward pressure exerted on wages from the restricted access to the Israeli labour market, which makes Palestinian products more competitive on international markets, as reflected in the strong export and GDP performance indicated in lines 6 and 18 in Table 2.2.

Although the open NDTR generally yields superior outcomes, high transaction costs and high labour flows render an open NDTR less attractive since the potential gains from trade liberalisation cannot be fully mobilised, and hence cannot compensate for the reduced access to the Israeli goods market. In this setting, an FTA generates higher GDP and export shares, but a CU performs better with respect to per capita income and unemployment, and no worse with respect to poverty.

The modelling results also suggest that the choice between a CU, open NDTR and FTA ultimately has little impact on Palestinian dependency on Israel, as measured by the share of Palestinian exports of goods and labour to Israel over GNP. Various elements contribute to this result, including the fact that an open NDTR does not reduce the volume of exports to Israel compared to a CU because greater competitiveness compensates for higher tariffs imposed on Palestinian goods in Israel. This result implies that reducing Palestinian dependency on Israel would be better achieved through lower transaction costs, given that exports to third parties rather than to Israel are disfavoured under high transaction costs.

Conclusions

The experience under the Paris Protocol illustrates the degree to which political and economic factors are intertwined; both types of factors need to be addressed in a comprehensive framework. The fact that political pressures from Israeli security concerns imposed severe economic hardship on the Palestinians and threatened newly-gained Palestinian autonomy contributed to the unravelling of the interim agreement. As policy makers look beyond the ongoing hostilities to consider a post-conflict period of Palestinian sovereignty, the future shape and functioning of the Palestinian economy will depend both on the policy framework in place, particularly vis-à-vis major trading partner Israel and, to a large extent, on the nature of the security controls put in place by the two partners.

The simulations of the scenarios developed in this chapter suggest that there is no single optimal trade policy, given that the relative merits of a customs union versus an open non-discriminatory regime versus a free trade area critically depend on the degree of restriction on the movement of goods and people. But an open non-discriminatory trade regime performs best under most circumstances. The simulation exercise is useful for better understanding the range of factors affecting the various trade policies envisaged. Although the interplay of multiple variables produces a complex set of outcomes with both small and large distinctions among the 16 scenarios with respect to the outcome indicators considered, several conclusions emerge. Low transaction costs lead to better outcomes under all four trade options. Low labour flows to Israel lead to higher GDP growth and exports and lower dependency, but at a substantial cost in terms of per capita incomes, unemployment and poverty. A closed NDTR represents an inferior trade policy choice when comparing income, GDP, exports and poverty outcomes. An open NDTR generates the most positive results vis-à-vis the measurement criteria considered herein and provides maximum leverage with low transaction costs and low labour flows to Israel. But high transaction costs and high labour flows render an open NDTR less attractive, as the potential gains from trade liberalisation are not fully mobilised and hence do not offset reduced access to the Israeli goods market. In this setting, an FTA is preferable regarding GDP and export shares, but a CU performs better in terms of per capita income and unemployment.

Striking a balance between Israel's short-term security concerns on the one hand (namely through limiting the influx of Palestinian workers to Israel) and raising Palestinian living standards in the longer run on the other hand, will prove extremely difficult, even in the absence of the various political objectives clamouring on both sides. From Israel's perspective, this analysis suggests certain merits to Israeli efforts to reduce transaction costs which would help Palestinians to reap the benefits of an open non-discriminatory trade regime. For the WBGS, the challenge of balancing autonomy and growth objectives is difficult as well, since growth opportunities will originate either from a resumption of labour flows to Israel or through the adoption of an open non-discriminatory trade regime which will only marginally reduce the vulnerability of the Palestinian economy to external shocks in general, and its dependence on Israel in particular.

Notes

1 The views expressed here are those of the authors and do not necessarily reflect those of the World Bank, its Executive Directors or the countries they represent. The authors are grateful to David Cobham and Nu'man Kanafani for their useful suggestions. The usual disclaimers apply.

2 The trade arrangement between Israel and the Palestinian Territories (WBGS) codified in the Paris Protocol is known as a 'modified' CU because WBGS has access to a limited range of imports from Arab League member countries (goods on lists A1, A2 and B of the Paris Protocol), whose 1998 value amounted to US$35 million, just 1.1 per cent of total Palestinian imports.

3 Figure 2.1 does not indicate the extent to which the income gap between Palestinian and Israeli households has fallen in absolute terms since 1967 because we show per capita income indices rather than levels. There is indeed some uncertainty regarding the difference in per capita income levels between WBGS and Israel at any single point in time. This stems from the fact that, despite the close degree of economic integration and extensive use of the Israeli currency in the Palestinian economy, WBGS and Israel may not necessarily face the same price levels. Most likely, Israeli prices hover around the upper range of prices faced by WBGS residents. Anecdotal evidence and theory both suggest that the price level in WBGS may be lower than in Israel for non-tradable goods. On the other hand, the parallel movement in the price levels of tradable goods in the WBGS and Israel supports the assumption that most consumer

prices in Israel and the WBGS are nearly the same (World Bank 2001). For the sake of illustration, had the per capita income gap (measured with per capita GNP at purchasing power parity) been approximately 1:10 in 1968, as suggested by Naqib (2000), it would have declined to approximately 1:5 in 1980 and rebounded to 1:8 by 2000.

4 See World Bank (2003) for a detailed discussion of the economic impact of the second intifada.

5 To calculate this index we use information on GNP, total exports and the share of Palestinian workers in Israel (source: Palestinian Central Bureau of Statistics) and the wage differential between Palestinian workers in Israel and WBGS (source: Arnon *et al.* 1997). We assume that the share of exports to Israel in total exports remained constant throughout the period, as did the compensation of employees in GDP.

6 See Astrup and Dessus (2001) for a detailed presentation of trade patterns prevailing in WBGS on the eve of the second intifada.

7 This represents the cost of subcontracting customs operations to a private firm, which is about twice as costly as directly establishing and operating five commercial and five passenger stations, but is likely to reduce leakages and revenue losses associated with PA customs personnel's lack of experience and potentially weak enforcement of customs regulations (a universal concern that is mitigated through private contracting). An additional issue is the need for special trading and border arrangements with respect to Jerusalem.

8 A non-discriminatory trade regime implies that a country sets its trade policy unilaterally and provides no preferential access, charging the most favoured nation (MFN) tariff. The MFN principle, which underlies both GATT and the WTO, states that a country will treat all countries equally from the viewpoint of access to its markets, providing no preferential access to any country.

9 If for political reasons the customs union were to remain in effect under a final status agreement, several improvements could be made to counter Palestinian losses, for example by adopting a macro-based revenue sharing formula, and/or direct Israeli compensation of WBGS for the losses it incurs under a CU.

10 Specifically, official development assistance which jumped to US$929 million in 2001 in response to the intifada is assumed to return progressively to historical levels of US$462 million per year from 2007 onwards.

11 Sectoral shares of capital remuneration in GDP are: 0.50 in agriculture, 0.58 in manufacturing, 0.58 in construction, 0.19 in commerce, 0.43 in transport and 0.35 in services. These shares are estimated using a two-step procedure. Capital remuneration in each sector is obtained by the difference between the value added reported in the supply-use table built by PCBS for 1998 and the corresponding labour remuneration extracted from PCBS labour force surveys. This generates an average share of 0.45, which is subsequently adjusted downward to 0.4 to reflect under-accounting of actual labour value added in the following sectors: agriculture, commerce and other private services.

12 The poverty rate is a function of real per capita consumption. The elasticity is assumed to be –4.0, in line with levels observed during the period 1996–1998 (see World Bank 2001).

References

Arnon, A., Luski, I., Spivak, A. and Weinblatt, J. (1997) *The Palestinian Economy: Between Imposed Integration and Voluntary Separation*, Leiden: Brill.

Astrup, C. and Dessus, S. (2001) 'Trade options for the Palestinian economy: some orders of magnitude', MENA working paper series, 21, Washington, DC: World Bank.

Daoud, Y. (2000) 'Revenue and direct cost implications of a policy switch to an FTA', paper prepared for PECDAR, Ramallah, mimeo.

Dessus, S., Fukasaku, K. and Safadi, R. (1999) *Multilateral Tariff Liberalisation and the Developing Countries: A Global Policy Simulation*, Development Centre Policy Brief no. 18, Paris: OECD.

Levine, R. and Renelt, D. (1992) 'A sensitivity analysis of cross-country regressions', *American Economic Review* 82: 942–963.

Naqib, F.M. (2000) 'Economic relations between Palestine and Israel during the occupation era and the period of limited self-rule', working paper 2015, Cairo: Economic Research Forum for the Arab Countries, Iran and Turkey.

Ruppert Bulmer, E. (2003) 'The impact of Israeli border policy on the Palestinian labour market', *Economic Development and Cultural Change* 51: 657–676.

Wacziarg, R. (2001) 'Measuring the dynamic gains from trade', *World Bank Economic Review* 15: 393–429.

World Bank (2001) *Poverty in West Bank and Gaza*, Washington, DC: World Bank.

World Bank (2002) *Long-term Policy Options for the Palestinian Economy*, Washington, DC: World Bank.

World Bank (2003) *27 Months of Intifada, Closures and Palestinian Economic Crisis*, Washington, DC: World Bank.

Discussion

Christopher Adam and Christian Friis Bach

Overview

The creation of an appropriate trade regime is of central importance to any country but particularly to a small open economy such as the putative Palestinian state. This chapter, which analyses the interactions between trade regimes, transactions costs and labour flows, is both insightful and provoking. It illustrates very clearly the tension between the creation of institutions which resonate with aspirations of economic and political sovereignty on the one hand, and the constraints imposed by the reality and inertia of current patterns of economic behaviour on the other.

Stripped to its core, this chapter is concerned with a relatively simple question: which of a small range of alternative trade arrangements best serves the interest of a (sovereign) Palestinian state? Concentrating exclusively on real per capita income – the measure that approximates most closely economists' notion of welfare – three core results emerge. First, in all scenarios the 'closed' non-discriminatory trade regime (NDTR) and the free trade area (FTA) are dominated by the customs union (CU) and 'open' NDTR. In other words, the race is between only two alternatives. Second, when transactions costs are relatively low the open NDTR regime dominates the customs union, and proportionately more so when Israeli demand for Palestinian labour is low. By contrast, when transactions costs are high the customs union is (marginally) preferable in welfare terms. The third point is that virtually all the variation in the results derives from variation *within* each trade regime, for exogenous assumptions about transactions costs and labour flows. Differences *between* trade regimes, controlling for these external characteristics, are extremely small.

It is well-known that the static welfare effects – Harberger's triangles – arising from changes in trade regimes implied by this class of model are often small, particularly when levels of protection are low (as is the case here); the puzzle here is that they are still low despite embodying a range of dynamic spillovers. This suggests one of two possibilities; either the dynamic effects are not powerful or they are but they happen to work in opposite directions. Failing to untangle these effects increases the risk that the wrong conclusions are drawn from this chapter, conclusions that the authors might be reluctant to fully endorse. In particular, there is a risk that the analysis gives the impression that since the difference in outcomes is small, Palestine could, for two pins, choose either. This invites two alternative interpretations. The first is that despite the political imperative, and the earlier evidence from the World Bank, the case for a wholesale redesign of the existing trade regime is difficult to make and hence an optimal strategy would be to work towards improving the functioning of the customs union. But, equally, these results could be interpreted as showing that a unilateral NDTR – even in the most adverse scenario – is no more costly than, and may be slightly advantageous (in welfare terms) to, the existing regime. It is doubtful that either interpretation reflects the true complexity of the situation the authors wish to portray.

Evaluating the model

With any simulation model, the devil is in the detail. Authors are invariably damned if they over-report the model and results, and damned if they don't. This chapter errs on the side of under-reporting: with so much detail hidden, it is unclear whether the differences between the core simulations are 'genuine', in the sense that they are being driven by differences between trade regimes per se rather than by auxiliary assumptions underpinning the model, its closure, or the design of particular experiments. Three specification issues in particular seem to drive the results.

First, the goods market embodies subtle and important assumptions about export market conditions which appear to scale up the costs of trade-diversion in a rather arbitrary way. The model assumes that Palestinian suppliers to Israel enjoy a measure of market power so that they face endogenous and declining terms of trade in the face of increased supply. By contrast, suppliers to the rest of the world (who are price-takers) enjoy an annual exogenous terms of trade *gain* of 1 per cent per annum. Aside from whether this is a reasonable reflection of market conditions facing Palestinian exporters, the more important question is how powerful this effect is. Is it strong enough to reverse the relative rankings of the regimes? What would happen to the results if it was assumed that all exporters were price-takers, regardless of destination? More generally, given what we know about initial trade patterns, a more comprehensive discussion of the assumptions underpinning goods market behaviour would have been welcome.[1]

Second, the characterisation of productivity also appears to lean in favour of the open NDTR. The assumed trend component of productivity growth appears high, but is probably neutral across trade regimes. Less persuasive is the assumption that it is stimulated from *total* export growth. Empirical evidence is divided on what sort of exporting increases productivity (manufacturing and non-traditional exports or traditional exports) or even whether the principal channel is, in fact, via imports. Linking productivity growth to total exports in circumstances where market conditions for all exports are already assumed to be more favourable outside the customs union imparts considerable heft to the open NDTR.

Third, the simulations embody a range of auxiliary assumptions whose contribution to the (very small) differences between the scenarios is difficult to assess but which may be extremely important. One central example illustrates our concern. The open NDTR simulation consists of an 11 per cent point reduction in the average tariff on all imports and the elimination of purchase taxes – which together constitute a rather large trade liberalisation – but then combines this with a 'conservative 5 per cent increase in the price at which Palestinian exporters can sell their goods on third parties' markets in the open NDTR scenario, compared to only 2 per cent in the "closed" version' (page 23). The justification is that an open NDTR makes it possible to negotiate better trade agreements and to enter the WTO. Given that Palestine already enjoys preferential access to the EU market, it is not obvious this would occur. Moreover, the assumption is completely *sui generis,* a feature of the *current* customs union arrangement, but is not intrinsic to the customs union itself. Regardless of realism, and as with our earlier points, it would be useful to know how important this particular term of trade gain is in driving the wedge between the CU and the open NDTR.

Fiscal issues

Issues of revenue sharing are central to any customs union arrangement, especially in settings where parties are unequal. The chapter makes passing reference to the revenue question but ultimately sidesteps it in the simulation model via two complementary assumptions. The first is that any changes in the costs of revenue collection across regimes are self-financing through changes in leakages, and the second is that the government has recourse to a lump sum tax instrument which allows all simulations to be 'revenue neutral'. This is very advantageous if the objective is to quantify the pure trade-diversion effect of a customs union. It is less useful, and possibly even harmful, for characterising the deep trade-offs at issue here since it means not only that there is no pressure on the fiscal authorities to alter distortionary non-trade taxes (either up or down) in response to differential fiscal outcomes, but also that aggregate savings and investment are fully insulated from fiscal effects of trade reform.

Kicking the issue into touch like this draws the debate away from what many would argue is the central issue guiding the choice of trade regimes, namely the practicalities of revenue mobilisation in unequal customs unions. Unless the customs union (or, indeed, a free trade area) is to be rejected out of hand, a fair assessment of alternative trade regimes requires the question of revenue sharing between sovereign states to be addressed. In Europe, for example, the VAT system provides the backbone for an invoice-based revenue sharing system. Where such systems do not exist, the mechanisms for equitable revenue distribution are more problematic. Kanafani (2001) highlights three features of the Paris Protocol system which currently limit the scope for a coherent framework for the efficient working of a customs union: the lack of contiguous borders; Israel's heavy reliance on non-tariff barriers to trade (with Palestine having no redress to international appeal); and serious problems about revenue sharing. The political settlement anticipated in this volume is likely to address the first of these and possibly the second, but not necessarily the third, which reflects a number of structural concerns about the flow of goods and services – the indirect import problem. As such, Palestine may remain in the worst trade regime of them all – trade distortions without the compensating full tariff revenue.

The history of trade relations in Southern Africa may provide some guidance on feasible arrangements between unequal parties. Dating back to 1910, the Southern African Customs Union (SACU) is the oldest existing customs union in the world. Many of the structural features of Israeli–Palestine relations were (and are) present in Southern Africa: the economies are extremely different in size and wealth (South Africa's economy is almost 70 times that of Lesotho's); South Africa accounts for an overwhelming share of total union trade; the small countries, Botswana, Lesotho and Swaziland (BLS) have always had limited access to port facilities (especially at times of South African supported conflict in Angola and Mozambique); and on a number of occasions South Africa used its power to impose highly trade diversionary practices on the SACU.[2]

The revenue sharing formula embodied in the 1969 SACU Agreement was notable for its (successful) attempt to compensate the BLS for the effects of polarising trade-diversion and the loss of (short-run) fiscal discretion, and for the way in which it handled the indirect import problem. For Lesotho and Swaziland in particular this represented a huge benefit to public finance management. It is highly unlikely that the generosity of the 1969 SACU revenue sharing formula could ever apply to a Palestine–Israeli customs union, and indeed it has not survived the renegotiation of the SACU in 2002. However, two features of the new formula are worth noting. The first is that it embodies the principle of basing revenue allocations on national accounts estimates of consumption and production rather than on trade invoices, thereby ensuring that revenues are allocated according to the ultimate rather than initial destination of imports into the common customs area. As it happens, only the excise component is computed in this fashion in the new SACU, but the same mechanism could equally be applied to the customs component of revenue. The second feature is the 'development fund' which consists of a pre-specified share of the revenue pool which is then shared according to the deviation of each individual country's per capita GDP relative to the SACU average. These two features could serve as inspiration for future revenue sharing mechanisms between Israel and Palestine.

Conclusions

Ultimately, choices over trade policy for a new Palestine, and the extent to which it truly reflects Palestinian preferences, will be shaped by the reality of the political settlement. This settlement may nullify some of the options considered in this chapter and may bring other arrangements, for example a customs union with Jordan and Syria, a free trade area with the EU, or an export processing zone, into the frame. Moreover, trade reforms are likely to be incremental, reflecting both the web of preferential arrangements present already in the region, and the limits of political flexibility. Reality is therefore likely to be much more complex than general equilibrium models can accommodate. Nonetheless, when located within this broader political analysis, general equilibrium economic models such as the one developed in this chapter will play an important role in informing this policy debate.

Notes

1 Elasticities of substitution in consumption or transformation in supply are particularly crucial determinants of outcomes. For instance, if trade patterns in the initial equilibrium are highly specialised (as is the case for Palestinian exports), even very large relative price movements lead to only modest changes in trade patterns unless producers' elasticities of transformation are extremely (and possibly unrealistically) large.

2 For example, the imposition of a fuel levy on BLS consumers to finance the pro duction of import-substituting shale-oil production so as to reduce South Africa's dependency on imported oil.

Reference

Kanafani, N. (2001) 'Trade – a catalyst for peace?', *Economic Journal* 111: F276–F290.

3 Alternative currency arrangements

David Cobham[1]

Introduction

There are a number of alternative currency arrangements and monetary frameworks from which a sovereign Palestinian state could choose. The first is a continuation of the status quo, under which three different currencies are used in the WBGS – the new Israeli shekel (NIS), the Jordanian dinar (JD) (used more in the West Bank than in Gaza) and the US dollar (USD) – with the former being used for most transactions, especially retail ones, and the latter two used more for savings deposits and for some durable goods transactions (Hamed 1999); while the Palestinian Monetary Authority supervises the banking system but has no lender of last resort (LOLR) function. A second arrangement would be the creation of a new Palestinian currency, with the currency anchored – either under a currency board or under a fixed but adjustable parity – to the NIS, the JD, the euro or the dollar or, conceivably, some other currency or basket of currencies. A third alternative would be a currency union with Israel, while a fourth would be a currency union with Jordan. Finally, a new currency with a more or less flexible exchange rate and the ability to design and operate an independent monetary policy could be considered.

The question of what currency arrangement would be most suitable for a new Palestinian state is one where direct empirical research is difficult. Some good work has been done on earlier periods (between 1967 and the late 1980s, or for the Oslo years from 1994), but the experience of the last few years (since September 2000) is unlikely to throw much light on future conditions. Moreover, major changes in economic policy and economic development (notably in the direction of trade) can be expected during the first few years of the new state, and the optimal currency arrangement will depend on the characteristics of the Palestinian economy over a more settled longer term. This chapter does not, therefore, present major new empirical work, but it surveys previous contributions, gives some new context for the issue by looking at other comparable economies, provides some new data on the possible anchor currencies and analyses the issues in terms of the optimal monetary framework more broadly understood, with reference to recent research on exchange rate arrangements, central bank independence, monetary policy and monetary integration.

The second part of the chapter examines the currency arrangements which have come to be chosen by other economies which are as small and/or as open as that of the putative Palestinian state; it shows that most have chosen fixed, but not highly fixed, exchange rates, with separate currencies. The following section reviews studies of the amount of seigniorage which could be obtained from the issue of a new Palestinian currency; it suggests the steady state seigniorage gains would not be large. Next we look at attempts to identify the probable trade patterns of the future Palestinian state using gravity models, as a way of identifying the optimal peg for a new currency; we find that the largest share (but not an overwhelmingly large share) of Palestine's trade is likely to be with the European Union. The next section investigates the intrinsic suitability of the various possible anchor currencies; it argues that the euro and the dollar would be acceptable anchors, but not the NIS or the JD. We then identify the criteria which an optimal monetary framework should fulfil, and suggest a specific goal and a strategy for attaining it. Conclusions are then presented.

Currency arrangements in small open economies

As a starting point for the investigation it may be useful to identify the exchange rate regime preferences revealed in the choices made over time by economies comparable to that of an independent Palestinian state, bearing in mind the trend towards a 'polarisation' of exchange rate regimes discussed in, for example, Frankel (1999).[2] Table 3.1 presents some evidence on various relevant groups of countries in terms of the new classification of exchange rate regimes provided by Reinhart and Rogoff (2002), which uses data on the parallel market and other indicators to identify the regimes actually operated, rather than those which governments announce.[3]

Relevant comparators for Palestine would be small and open. A new Palestinian state is likely to have a population of between 3 and 5 million,[4] a GDP (PPP adjusted, 2000 prices) of around US$8–12bn,[5] and international trade (imports plus exports) of at least 90 per cent of GDP.[6] The first row of Table 3.1 presents the exchange rate regimes used in December 2001 by countries that are small in terms of population, where small is defined as below 10 million.[7] Of the 73 countries in the UNDP's *Human Development Report 2002* that fall into this category, 14 per cent were in a currency union or had a currency board, 25 per cent had some other form of fixed rate, 27 per cent had some form of crawling regime and 26 per cent some kind of managed regime, while only 7 per cent were freely floating and one was 'freely falling'. The second row focuses on a subset of these countries; those with populations nearer to the likely population of

Table 3.1 Exchange rate regimes in small open economies

Category	*Number of countries in category*	*Percentage highly fixed*	*Percentage fixed*	*Percentage crawling*	*Percentage managed*	*Percentage floating*	*Percentage free fall*
Small-population 1	73	14	25	27	26	7	1
Small-population 2	35	14	26	20	31	6	3
Small-GDP	48	4	38	27	21	10	0
Highly open	48	17	21	27	27	6	2
Common group	21	5	38	33	19	5	0

Notes
Categories (data from UNDP *Human Development Report* 2002):
small-population 1 = population (2000) ≥0.3 million, ≤10.5 mn;
small-population 2 = population ≥3 mn, ≤7.5 mn;
small-GDP = GDP in PPP US$ (2000) ≤20bn;
highly open = exports + imports >90 per cent of GDP (2000);
common group = countries appearing in each of small-population 1, small-GDP and highly open.
Regimes (data from Reinhart and Rogoff 2002):
highly fixed = no separate legal tender and currency board;
fixed = peg, de facto peg and horizontal band of +/−2 per cent;
crawling = pre-announced crawling peg, pre-announced crawling band of +/−2 per cent, de facto crawling peg, and de facto crawling band of +/−2 per cent;
managed = de facto crawling band of +/− 5 per cent, moving band of +/−2 per cent, managed floating;
floating = freely floating;
free fall = dual market, freely falling.

an independent Palestine, that is between 3 and 7 million; there is a small switch between the crawling and managed regimes, but overall the choice of regimes is not much different. The third row considers size in terms of GDP, with small taken as having a PPP adjusted GDP less than US$20bn; for these 48 countries the percentage with a currency union or board was smaller while the percentage on a fixed rate was higher, and 10 per cent of countries were freely floating. The fourth row reports regimes for 48 countries that were highly open, in the sense that their exports and imports together accounted for 90 per cent or more of GDP; here there were more countries with currency boards or in currency unions (the set included the five smallest members of the Eurozone), rather more on crawling and managed, and less on other fixed pegs, and 6 per cent with free floats. The final row of the table brings together the 21 countries which fit each of the criteria of smallness of population (below 10 million), smallness of GDP, and high degree of openness: of these countries, 5 per cent (Estonia) operated a currency board and 5 per cent (Tajikistan) a free float, and the rest were distributed between fixed (38 per cent), crawling (33 per cent) and managed (19 per cent) regimes.

Table 3.2 gives some more details on this common group of countries, with a view to highlighting any trends over time in the choice of exchange rate regime.[8] It shows for each country the regimes used in successive decades, and the final regime as used in Table 3.1. In the 1960s and early 1970s those countries that existed as separate countries (some were parts of the USSR or of Yugoslavia) were nearly all on a fixed rate, but later, in the 1970s or in the 1980s and 1990s, many experimented with crawling pegs and managed floats and, in a few cases, with free floats. By 2001, however, countries seem to have returned to nearer the fixed end of the spectrum: in 1990 14 per cent of countries had fixed, 21 per cent crawling, 50 per cent managed and 14 per cent free floating rates, but by 2001 those numbers had become 38 per cent (plus 5 per cent highly fixed), 33 per cent, 19 per cent and 5 per cent respectively.[9]

Overall, these findings suggest that, for economies that can be considered broadly comparable to that of an independent Palestine, governments have never been keen on free floating and have become less so over time. There is not much enthusiasm for the other extreme, of a currency union or a currency board, but over time countries have tended to adopt harder pegs.

Studies of seigniorage in Palestine

A pioneering attempt to estimate the scale of seigniorage in the WBGS was made by Hamed and Shaban (1993). They argued that the use of Israeli currency (notes and coin) in the WBGS provided a previously unrecognised 'mechanism of resource transfer from the Palestinians to the Israeli Central Bank' (p. 130). Given that no data were available for

Table 3.2 Evolution of exchange rate regimes in common group

Country	*Population*	*GDP PPP (US$ bn)*	*Openness (trade as % of GDP)*	*1960s*	*1970s*	*1980s*	*1990–2001*	*December 2001*
Congo	3.0	2.5	121	A, C	C, D	D, C	C	C
Cyprus	0.8	15.8	93	A	A, B	B	B, A	A
Equatorial Guinea	0.5	6.9	153	A1	A	B, A	A	A
Estonia	1.4	13.8	172				C, A, A1	A1
Gambia	1.3	2.1	109	A1	A1	D	D, B	B
Guinea-Bissau	1.2	0.9	90	A1	A1, A	A, B	B, A	A
Guyana	0.8	3.0	208	A1, A	A	A, B, C	C, B	B
Honduras	6.4	15.7	98	A	A	A, C	C	C
Jamaica	2.6	9.6	99	A	A	A, B	B	B
Jordan	4.9	19.4	111	A	A	A, C	C, A	A
Kyrgyzstan	4.9	13.3	98				C, B	B
Lesotho	2.0	4.1	116	A1	A1	A	A	A
Macedonia, TFYR	2.0	10.3	107				C, A	A
Malta	0.4	6.7	217	A	A, C	C	C	C
Mauritania	2.7	4.5	98	A	A, B	B, C	C, B	B
Mauritius	1.2	11.9	131	B	B	B	B, A	A
Moldova	4.3	9.0	127				A, C, A	A
Mongolia	2.5	4.3	147				D, B	B
Nicaragua	5.1	12.0	121	A	A	D	D, A, B	B
Swaziland	0.9	4.7	147	A	A, C	C	C	C
Tajikistan	6.1	7.1	166				D, A, D	D

Notes
Regime data from Reinhart and Rogoff (2002):
A1: highly fixed = no separate legal tender and currency board;
A: fixed = peg, de facto peg and horizontal band of +/−2 per cent;
B: crawling = pre-announced crawling peg, pre-announced crawling band of +/−2 per cent, de facto crawling peg, and de facto crawling band of +/−2 per cent;
C: managed = de facto crawling band of +/−5 per cent, moving band of +/−2 per cent, managed floating;
D: floating = freely floating;
E: free fall = dual market, freely falling.

money holdings in the WBGS, they made two estimates: a low estimate which assumed that the ratio of Palestinian NIS currency holdings to GNP was the same as that in Israel; and a high estimate which assumed that, because of the low use of bank deposits in the WBGS (there was essentially no banking system serving the Palestinian population over the period), the ratio of Palestinian currency holdings to GNP was the same as the ratio of Israeli holdings of currency plus demand deposits to GNP. On this basis average seigniorage per year from 1970 to 1987 was 1.6 per cent of Palestinian GNP on the low estimate and 4.2 per cent on the high estimate. These are relatively large numbers; they reflect in part the fact that inflation in Israel (and therefore for the most part in the WBGS as well) averaged 88 per cent per annum over this period.

Arnon and Spivak (1996a; see also chapter 6 of Arnon *et al.* 1997) estimated the seigniorage that might accrue to a Palestinian issuer of currency as part of an evaluation of the introduction of an independent currency. They estimated demand for money (M1) functions for Syria and Egypt, with the inflation rate as the opportunity cost variable (given the absence or constancy of the interest rate), and obtained results for the two countries which were statistically indistinguishable. They made a minor adjustment to the parameter estimates to impose a unitary income elasticity of money demand, and then used the resulting function, with the assumption that the money multiplier was 1.5, to predict the demand for money in the Palestinian economy for different combinations of growth and inflation. They envisaged a long-run share of the new currency in overall money which was inversely related to the inflation rate, and a phased transition towards that long-run share. They then calculated the seigniorage which would accrue to the issuing authority under different growth and inflation scenarios. The maximum seigniorage occurs at an inflation rate of 5 per cent. In this case the average seigniorage over the first five years of transition is 4.6 per cent of GDP, and the long-run steady state seigniorage is 1.2 per cent p.a.

Hamed (1999) produced estimates of NIS seigniorage in the WBGS in the post-Oslo period (1994–1998), in the context of an argument that Israel was continuing to extract resources from the WBGS 'as a result of the failure of the Paris Protocol to include a seigniorage reimbursement provision' (p. 9). He calculated a lower bound estimate on the basis of the assumption used by Hamed and Shaban (1993) for their low estimate, namely that the ratio of Palestinian NIS currency holdings to GNP was the same as that in Israel, but he argued that such an estimate was biased downwards because it took no account of the higher precautionary demand for cash in the WBGS (due to closures and other uncertainties) and the less frequent use of non-cash means of payment in the WBGS. He therefore also calculated an upper bound estimate on the basis of the ratio of outstanding JD currency to GNI in Jordan, which would be biased upwards because it took no account of the use of the JD for cash payments for durable goods in the WBGS. On this basis the average per annum seigniorage was between 0.31 per cent of WBGS GNI (for the lower bound) and 1.68 per cent (for the higher bound).[10]

The most recent attempt to estimate seigniorage is that of Erickson von Allmen and Fischer (2001) who attempt to assess how much seigniorage is foregone by the Palestinian Monetary Authority (PMA) as a result of its not issuing a Palestinian currency and accrues to the central banks of Israel, Jordan and the US instead. Because they have already argued in their paper for a currency board, under which Palestinian currency issues would have to be backed by foreign exchange reserves, they define seigniorage as the interest earnings on those foreign exchange reserves.[11] They calculate the median ratio of currency to GDP for the 100 economies whose income per capita is closest to that of the WBGS, at 5.5 per cent. That is used to generate an estimate of the amount of a new Palestinian currency which would be held, and at an assumed interest rate on the corresponding foreign exchange reserves of 5 per cent this produces an estimate of seigniorage as 0.3 per cent of GDP.

Some interesting comparative data can be found in a Bank of England study of 44 developing countries (Fry *et al.* 1996), which calculated the seigniorage revenue for these countries in each of three subperiods 1979–1983, 1984–1988 and 1989–1993. The authors emphasise the relationship between seigniorage and inflation, and report (p. 38) that central banks operating conservative monetary policies with a fair degree of independence typically produced seigniorage of 0.5 to 1.0 per cent of GDP. In fact, for the 23 (country-subperiod) episodes in their sample in which inflation was ≤5 per cent the average seigniorage was 0.53 per cent of GDP; for the 32 episodes with inflation >5 per cent but ≤10 per cent average seigniorage was 0.96 per cent, and for the 30 episodes of inflation >10 per cent but ≤15 per cent it was 1.27 per cent (calculated from Fry *et al.* 1996, pp. 122, 131).[12]

It is suggested later in this chapter (p. 52) that the Palestinian state needs to aim for price stability in the form of inflation under 5 per cent. The Bank of England study suggests that in that case the steady state seigniorage gains from the existence of a Palestinian currency would be, if anything, smaller than those estimated by Hamed (1999) or Arnon and Spivak (1996a), and closer to those estimated by Erickson von Allmen and Fischer (2001). Even at inflation rates of up to 10 per cent they would not be large, either as a proportion of GDP or as a proportion of the overall expenditure or revenue of a Palestinian government.[13] The transitional gains from the issue of a new currency would be much higher, but it is arguable that the transitional period is one in which the pressure on the Palestinian budget is likely to be less acute, as the result of a foreign aid 'dowry' on the establishment of the new state.

Trade patterns

There is a substantial literature on the appropriate trade regime for a new Palestinian state, focused mainly on the choice between a customs union with Israel, a free trade agreement (FTA) with Israel or a non-discriminatory trade regime (e.g. Kanafani 2001; World Bank 2002; Dessus and Ruppert Bulmer, Chapter 2, this volume). However, this research has little to say about the likely patterns of trade in terms of the destination of exports and the origin of imports, and it is those patterns that are important in considering the appropriate exchange rate regime and the appropriate anchor currency (if any). The alternative technique which has been used by some researchers is that of gravity models of trade, which can be used to generate predictions of the pattern of trade to be expected for a country with the same characteristics as the new state on the basis of the relationships between characteristics and trade patterns for other countries.

The first application of a gravity model in this area was by the World Bank (1993: 45–47 and Annex 3), which used as regressors the logs of GDP and GDP per capita in each country, the log difference in per capita GDP between countries (to capture the Linder effect), the distance between them and the area of each, and dummies for a common border, a common language, being an island, and membership of preferential trade arrangements (ASEAN, EEC, LAFTA). The equations were estimated for 1987–1989 average annual data on 15 middle- to upper-income countries with substantial non-primary exports, and the results then used with data for Israel and the WBGS – the latter under varying assumptions about border, language and trade arrangements – to generate predictions about shares of trade between the WBGS and Israel. The results suggest that the existing concentration of the WBGS's trade with Israel was far above what would be expected on the basis of a common border and 'language' (interpreted as a proxy for a history of persistent economic interaction) and a free trade area, and even further above what would be expected on the basis of a common border only.[14]

Arnon *et al.* (1997, chapter 4) used a simpler model with a limited number of regressors (the log of GDP in each country, the log of the distance between them, a common language dummy, an FTA dummy and the difference in per capita GDP between countries), estimated on 1991 data for 35 countries which included most Middle Eastern countries, some Asian and Latin American countries, leading EU countries, the US and Japan. The results were then used to predict trade between the West Bank, Gaza Strip, Israel and Jordan for 1986–1987 and 1992–1993. When these predictions were set against the actual flows it was found that the predicted WBGS exports to Israel were below actual levels and predicted WBGS imports from Israel were even further below the actual levels; though these 'distortions' were somewhat smaller in 1992–1993 than in

1986–1987. Arnon *et al.* interpreted their findings as implying that the 'captive market' effect – which acts to raise Israeli exports to the WBGS – was stronger than the 'proximity' effect – which acts to raise WBGS exports to Israel. Arnon *et al.* (1996) used the same model but focused more on the potential for trade between these countries in the future; they predicted that trade between a new Palestinian entity and Israel would be much lower (than current levels) even if there was a customs union or free trade agreement between them. They also found that trade between Jordan and a new Palestinian entity, on the other hand, would remain relatively low, even in the case of a trade agreement.

For present purposes a more relevant study is that by Bannister and Erickson von Allmen (2001), which uses at its starting point the model of Al-Atrash and Yousef (2000) and aims to evaluate the potential for trade expansion under a new regime. The model uses additional regressors – population in each country, measures of trade restrictiveness, measures of transportation and transactions costs, and a landlocked dummy, but not GDP per capita in each country or the difference between them – and a larger range of countries (Israel, the WBGS, 18 Arab countries and 43 others that cover over 90 per cent of trade with the Middle East), with data for 1995–1997. Bannister and Erickson von Allmen apply the results of a base run to predict trade flows for the WBGS, and find that WBGS exports to and imports from Israel are well above the predicted levels, while those to and from the rest of the world (mostly the US, European Union and Japan) are below predicted levels. Since these results come from point estimates with no statistical significance attached to them, the authors then re-estimate the model with dummies for WBGS trade with Israel and for WBGS trade with the rest of the world. In this case the coefficient on the former is positive but not significant, while that on the latter is negative and significant.[15] The authors interpret these findings as showing that 'no support can be found for the hypothesis that [Israel and WBGS] overtrade with each other' but the WBGS 'undertrades with the rest of the world' (p. 91).

These findings are somewhat surprising, since on their earlier results WBGS exports are predicted to be lower than actual by $203 million to Israel but higher by $119 million to the EU, by $32 million to the US and by $20 million each to Japan and Egypt, while imports are predicted to be $1552 million lower than actual from Israel, but higher by $285 million from the EU, $181 million from the US and $76 million from Japan: the differences in trade with Israel are very large.[16] Overall, the predicted pattern of trade implies that 32 per cent of WBGS exports and 19 per cent of WBGS imports should be to/from Israel (as against the existing 94 per cent and 86 per cent), 28 per cent of exports (25 per cent excluding the UK) and 38 per cent of imports (32 per cent) to/from the EU, 8 per cent of exports and 18 per cent of imports to/from the US, 5 per cent of exports and 7 per cent of imports to/from Japan, and 5 per cent of exports and 2 per cent of imports to/from Egypt.[17]

What is important here is not the historical issue of the extent to which WBGS trade was distorted by occupation, but the question of how and where Palestine will trade in the future. Bannister and Erickson von Allmen explain their initial results partly in terms of the existence of a currency union between the WBGS and Israel, and recent research has found very large effects on trade patterns from currency unions (see Frankel and Rose 2002; Rose 2000, 2001; Mélitz 2001). Insofar as the existence of a currency union is crucial to, but not allowed for in, these results, they cannot provide useful indications of what trade patterns are likely to develop in an independent Palestinian state, which may well choose another currency arrangement.[18] Even so, their results suggest the largest proportion of its trade – 35 per cent – will be with the EU (30 per cent excluding the UK which may stay outside the Eurozone), 22 per cent with Israel, 15 per cent with the US and 6 per cent with Japan. The greater importance of the EU than the US in trade is a general characteristic of Middle Eastern countries. It is not highlighted in the three main gravity model studies of the region – Al-Atrash and Yousef (2000), Blavy (2001) and Miniesy *et al.* (2002) – all of which group trade with industrialised countries (North America, Europe and Japan) in the same category. However, Frankel and Rose (2002) report that for each of Egypt, Israel and Turkey there is more trade with the Eurozone than with the dollar zone, and hence predict that for each of them there would be much higher gains from joining EMU than from dollarisation.

Anchor currencies

There are four currencies which can be considered as possible anchor currencies under currency board or other arrangements, or even (in the first two cases) as candidates for currency union with a new Palestinian state: the NIS, the JD, the euro and the USD.

To serve as a good anchor, a currency needs first of all to be stable and credible. Stability has two main dimensions: inflation and the exchange rate. Table 3.3 presents some basic data on the *ex post* performance of the possible anchors over recent decades (given the absence of long runs of data on an aggregated basis, some of the Eurozone data is for Germany).[19] On inflation, it is clear that in the past the Eurozone (Germany) has experienced the lowest inflation of the four, followed by the US, then Jordan and lastly Israel; and the four are ranked in more or less the same order in terms of the volatility of inflation. Changes in nominal exchange rates follow broadly the same pattern,[20] while changes in real exchange rates (which are not available for Jordan) have been smaller for Israel (despite the high volatility of nominal exchange rates[21]) than for the US and the Eurozone.

A second criterion for a good anchor currency is that its country and that of the currency which proposes to peg to it should not be subject to

Table 3.3 Stability of potential anchor currencies (*ex post*)

	US – USD		*Eurozone – euro**		*Israel – NIS*		*Jordan – JD*	
	Mean	*s.d.*	*Mean*	*s.d.*	*Mean*	*s.d.*	*Mean*	*s.d.*
Consumer price inflation (%)								
1973–1982	8.8	2.6	5.2	1.4	66.2	39.8	11.6	3.6
1983–1992	3.8	0.9	2.1	1.4	97.7	127.5	7.2	7.6
1993–2002	2.5	0.6	1.9	1.0	7.2	3.9	2.7	1.6
*Change in nominal exchange rates (%)***								
1973–1982	0.7	6.1	−0.6	5.6	—	—	0.3	5.4
1983–1992	−2.7	7.6	1.6	6.0	−30.9	27.0	−5.5	11.8
1993–2002	2.1	4.4	−2.0	4.4	−4.2	6.0	−0.4	0.7
*Change in real exchange rates (%)****								
1973–1982	5.4	5.6	−4.8	6.0	—	—	—	—
1983–1992	−4.0	7.0	2.0	5.1	0.2	5.0	—	—
1993–2002	2.0	4.9	−2.7	4.6	0.4	5.2	—	—

Source: *IFS*.

Notes
*data for inflation are for Germany rather than the Eurozone as a whole;
**effective rates for USD, euro and NIS, rate against USD for Jordan;
***relative normalised unit labour costs for US and Eurozone, relative consumer prices for Israel.

asymmetric shocks. Arnon and Spivak (1996b; see also Arnon *et al.* 1997, chapter 6) used the Bayoumi and Eichengreen (1993) technique to identify transitory (demand) and permanent (supply) shocks in Israel, the West Bank, the Gaza Strip and Jordan over the period 1968–1992. They found that the transitory shocks were generally not well correlated, except between Israel and the West Bank. But the permanent shocks between each of Israel, the WB and the GS were highly correlated, while those between any of these and Jordan were not. These findings are probably explicable in terms of the trade and other restrictions imposed by Israel on the Occupied Territories, and the rupture in trade links between them and Jordan. Whether the economies will continue to experience correlated shocks in the future depends primarily on the extent of changes in trade patterns.

On both these criteria past performance is, of course, not necessarily a good guide to future performance. To shed some light on the latter, Table 3.4 presents some data taken from a recent survey carried out at the Bank of England of the monetary frameworks in some 90 countries (Fry *et al.* 2000). This survey used a wide range of evidence, including both published data and extensive questionnaire answers from the central banks concerned, and it tried to answer questions – e.g. about the focus of monetary policy – in partial and qualitative, rather than all-or-nothing, terms. In the absence of data for the Eurozone, data for Germany – which are sometimes more and sometimes less relevant – are given. The table also provides averages for the industrialised, transition and developing economies included in the study (27, 22 and 44 respectively).[22]

The first section of the table gives assessments of the short and medium-term focus of policy. For the sample as a whole, industrialised countries on average focus heavily on both the exchange rate and inflation, while transition and developing countries put more emphasis on money as well. Israel (classified in this study as an industrialised country) is primarily an inflation targeter, despite its earlier emphasis on exchange rate targets (crucial to the stabilisation plan after the runaway inflation of the mid 1980s). Reinhart and Rogoff (2002, Appendix III) classify Israel, from February 1991, as operating a de facto crawling band around the US dollar, and refer to 'an ever widening band, which was 39.2 per cent as of December 30, 2000'. Jordan has a strong focus on the exchange rate, coupled with some focus on money – for which targets have been announced since 1992 – and less on inflation. Reinhart and Rogoff (2002, Appendix III) classify Jordan as operating a de facto peg to the USD since September 1995. The USA, on the other hand, has no focus on the exchange rate (and is classified by Reinhart and Rogoff as a free floater), but some focus on money (as of 1998; monetary target ranges ceased to be announced from 2000) and some on inflation. Other observers, e.g. Clarida *et al.* (1998) have tended to see the US as an informal inflation targeter. Germany is shown in the table as having a heavy emphasis on money, and

Table 3.4 Monetary framework characteristics

	Israel	*Jordan*	*USA*	*Germany*	*Industrialised*	*Transition*	*Developing*
Short- and medium-term policy focus							
Exchange rate focus	13	63	0	13	44	45	39
Money focus	0	25	25	88	17	34	34
Inflation focus	88	13	19	19	39	44	35
Institutional characteristics							
Independence	66	74	92	96	83	80	65
Accountability	100	75	83	17	71	83	65
Policy explanations	68	60	95	70	72	57	51

Source: Fry *et al.* (2000, Appendix III).

Note
Scores range from a minimum of 0 to a maximum of 100.

a considerable part of that emphasis continues to be present in the 'monetary policy strategy' of the European Central Bank together with a focus on price stability (e.g. Angeloni *et al.* 1999; Issing *et al.* 2001);[23] the Eurozone is also a free floater.

Since different types of policy focus may work efficiently in different circumstances, and their effectiveness may depend heavily on the commitment of the monetary authorities, a more important aspect of whether a currency would be a desirable anchor currency is probably the institutional set-up. The Bank of England study, like those of Grilli *et al.* (1991), Cukierman (1992) and others, classifies the US Federal Reserve and the German Bundesbank as highly independent (and the ECB is usually taken to be even more independent than Germany). The Central Bank of Jordan (CBJ) is less independent than these three but above the average for developing countries, and the Bank of Israel (BoI) is slightly less independent again. On the other hand, the Federal Reserve is given as highly accountable, more so than the CBJ, while the BoI is supremely accountable and the Bundesbank (and, it is generally assumed, similarly the ECB) much less so. Finally, the US Fed gives good explanations of policy, while those of the ECB are open to some criticism,[24] and the BoI and the CBJ lag behind.

Finally, it is useful to consider the business cycles in the four possible anchor countries. Figure 3.1 shows output gaps, derived from a simple regression of quarterly GDP on a linear and quadratic trend, for the Eurozone, the US and Israel. The Eurozone had a pronounced boom in the early 1990s, associated with German reunification, while the US had a deep recession in the early 1980s and a boom in the late 1980s. Since then, however, the cycles in the two have come more into line with each other. Israel, on the other hand, shows a much less smooth, indeed distinctly

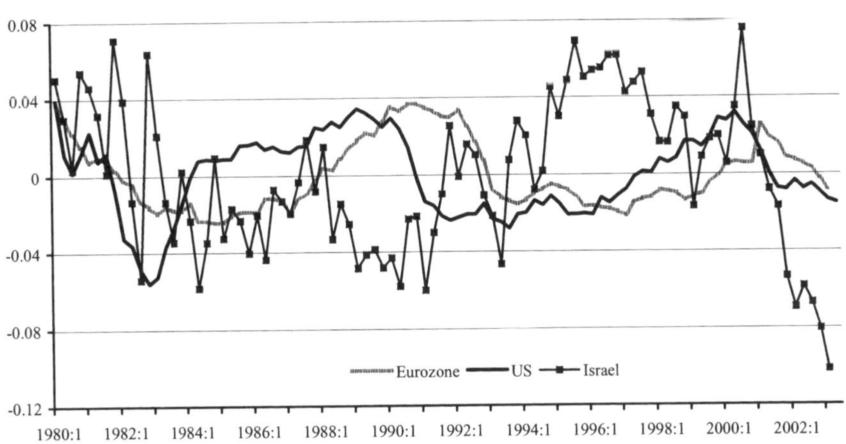

Figure 3.1 Output gaps in Eurozone, US and Israel.

jerky, cycle which is not synchronised with either the Eurozone or the US. This exercise cannot be replicated for Jordan because of the lack of quarterly data, but Figure 3.2 shows the annual growth rates for each of the four countries. Again, Israel's growth is more variable than that of the Eurozone or the US, but Jordan's growth rate is even more so, with extreme outliers in 1989 and 1992.

Overall, it seems clear that the US dollar and the euro have to be considered as acceptable anchors in themselves (that is, without regard to the ship to be anchored). The Israeli NIS has been much less stable in the past, while its relatively low level of central bank independence suggests that it is not possible to be confident that the improvement of recent years will be sustained (and there have been recurring tensions between the central bank and finance minister). Jordan also has a record of some instability, with a large devaluation in 1988–1989, but its central bank is more independent than the developing country average.

Optimal monetary frameworks

An optimal monetary framework should maximise the growth and level of welfare in the economy concerned. In particular, there are four ways in which an ideal framework could contribute to this end. First, it should ensure price stability, understood as inflation of less than 5 per cent.[25] Second, it should facilitate long-run economic growth, by contributing to a stable and predictable macro environment. That implies that it should minimise domestic aggregate demand shocks, which includes preventing conflict between monetary and fiscal policy, and minimise external aggregate demand shocks, by ensuring stability and non-misalignment of the real exchange rate. Third, it should provide a credible commitment to price

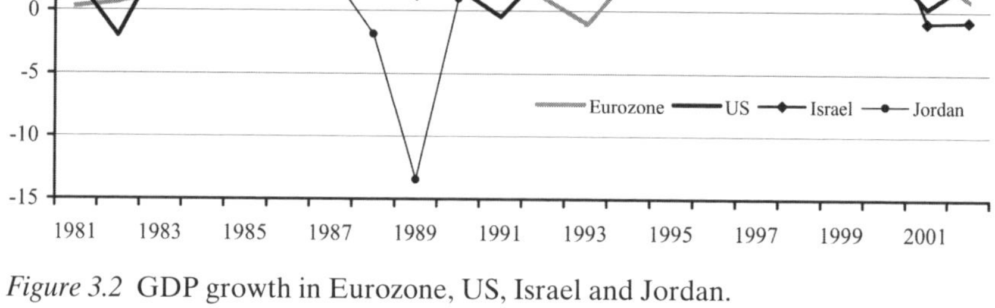

Figure 3.2 GDP growth in Eurozone, US, Israel and Jordan.

stability, in order to minimise the risk premium in long-term interest rates. And fourth, it should provide a framework within which financial stability can be assured, which means, in particular, that there should be some provision for a lender of last resort (LOLR) function.

A new Palestinian state will start from a position in which there is no established central bank with a historical record that could induce credibility, and in which the fiscal policy institutions may be subject to strong political pressures. Such considerations have been widely taken to imply that an independent currency with a floating exchange rate would not be viable, at least in any near future, and that a highly fixed exchange rate operated by a currency board with minimal discretion would be desirable – e.g. Hamed (1999), Naqib (1999) and Erickson von Allmen and Fischer (2001).[26] This would imply a rather 'tougher' regime than those chosen in most cases by comparable (but 'older') economies, as reported earlier (p. 41). There are, of course, some disadvantages as well as advantages associated with currency boards (notably the difficulty of making any LOLR function available), but Williamson (1995) has argued that currency boards are more suitable (and more likely) in small open economies, particularly when they start with low confidence.

However, the central problem here is that a currency board requires a reserve currency to be used as a peg.[27] The earlier implications (pp. 47–52) are that there is no fully satisfactory peg for a Palestinian currency board, or for a more conventional fixed rate regime. On the trade side, the preference must be for a peg to the currency area with which the Palestinian economy does the largest share of its trade, in order to maximise the development of trade and its benefits in terms of growth. At the moment the largest share of WBGS trade is with Israel, but in the future, according to the results of Bannister and Erickson von Allmen (2001), it is likely to be with the EU. However, the share predicted remains, for example, well below the shares of trade that many Eurozone countries have with their currency union partners.[28] On the other hand, it seems likely that Jordan, and to a lesser extent Israel, will also tend to increase their trade with the EU, and that would reduce the risks associated with a peg to the euro.

With respect to the intrinsic characteristics of the possible anchors, the USD and the euro are more attractive anchors because they are much more stable than the NIS and the JD, and this is likely to continue. The fact that cyclical divergences between the US and the Eurozone have become rather smaller over the last decade might indicate that there is less danger of asymmetric shocks from a peg to one or the other, but this convergence has not diminished the fluctuations in the exchange rate between the USD and the euro.

It should also be noted that the introduction of a new Palestinian currency is unlikely to be straightforward or rapid. The status quo in the WBGS involves three different currencies being used and, under the liberal economic arrangements usually envisaged for the new Palestinian state (and with workers continuing to commute to Israel and receiving wages in NIS), it is difficult to see how the comprehensive use of a new currency could be imposed. Its acceptance will have to be earned, as Arnon and Spivak (1996a: 8–10) and Erickson von Allmen and Fischer (2001: 126) have recognised, and in a context of network externalities it is clear that established currencies exert a strong gravitational pull.[29]

In the absence of a peg which is clearly superior to the others, and in a situation where the introduction of a new currency will be far from easy, it might seem sensible to exercise caution; to wait and see how trade patterns develop, and to focus the new state's limited managerial and policy-making resources on other policy areas first. But the importance of currency unions for trade patterns, and the de facto currency union of the status quo, suggest that such caution would act as a drag on the desirable redirection of Palestinian trade flows. Some more decisive action is therefore necessary.

The obvious approach is first to identify the long-run goal, and then to construct short-run policy as a way of moving towards that goal. The evidence presented on p. 47 suggests that the largest share of Palestinian trade will eventually be with the Eurozone, while the next section argues that the euro is intrinsically a suitable anchor currency. The long-run goal should therefore be a (fixed rather than highly fixed) peg to the euro, operated by a central bank which has developed the competence and the credibility to use some discretion in monetary policy (notably to change the exchange rate parity in case of a severe asymmetric shock) and to act as a lender of last resort. That implies the introduction of a new currency, but this should be facilitated by its introduction under a currency board arrangement with an initial peg to the NIS; as the Argentinian example makes clear this will require sound fiscal as well as monetary institutions. Later, when trade patterns have begun to change and the Palestinian Monetary Authority has become more of a central bank, the peg can be switched to the euro,[30] and policy can become gradually less rigid as has happened in countries like Singapore and Hong Kong (Williamson 1995; Naqib 1999). This would eventually enable the central bank to operate some limited discretion for dealing with asymmetric shocks, and to act as a lender of last resort.

Conclusion

The evidence presented in this chapter suggests that a new Palestinian state has initially no alternative but to opt for a relatively hard peg, with a low level of discretion in monetary policy. However, there is no fully satisfactory anchor currency, in terms of both the likely trade flows of Palestine and the intrinsic stability of the anchors. In addition, the introduction of a new currency in the Palestinian context where three external currencies are currently in use is likely to be difficult. However, there are strong reasons – connected not with the seigniorage gains, which are likely to be small, but with the impact on trade patterns – for moving away from the status quo of an informal currency union with Israel. The evidence suggests that in the long-run the Eurozone will become Palestine's most important trading partner, and the euro is a stable and suitable anchor currency. The long-run goal should therefore be a monetary framework with a peg to the euro but some scope for short-run discretion and for the operation of the LOLR function. In the short-run Palestine should move towards this goal via the introduction of a Palestinian currency under a currency board, with a peg initially to the NIS but later to the euro.

Notes

1 I am grateful to Samar Maziad for research assistance on the sections on currency arrangements in small open economies and anchor currencies; and to the Honeyman Trust, the Royal Economic Society and the Carnegie Trust for grants which enabled me to start working in this area.
2 For a wider ranging focus on developing countries see Fischer (2001) and ECB (2003a).
3 Calvo and Reinhart (2002) had shown that in some cases announced regimes did not correspond well to governments' practices.
4 Arnon and Kanafani (Chapter 10, this volume) give the 2001 population of the WBGS as 3.3 million; a large immigration of refugees from Lebanon, Jordan, Syria and elsewhere following a full peace settlement could raise that figure to 4 million or more.
5 Erickson von Allmen and Fischer (2001) give 1999 GDP for the WBGS (not PPP adjusted) as US$4.2bn as against $7.5bn for Jordan. The *Human Development Report 2002* gives Jordanian (Israeli) GDP in 2000 as $8.3bn ($110.4bn) (unadjusted) and $19.4bn ($125.5bn) (PPP adjusted). It seems likely that the WBGS price level is dominated by that of Israel (see Arnon *et al.* 1997: 13–14), which means that the PPP adjustment would make a much smaller difference for the WBGS than for Jordan, though some increase over time from a population influx also needs to be considered.
6 Bannister and Erickson von Allmen (2001) give data showing WBGS trade between 1980 and 1999 mostly in the range 100–120 per cent of GDP. The ratio of imports to GDP might be lower for the new state, but the ratio of exports is likely to be higher.
7 Countries with a population below 0.3 million are excluded as being too small to be useful comparators. Countries whose regimes are not classified by Reinhart and Rogoff are also excluded.
8 The group includes countries with widely differing growth performances, from Cyprus, Equatorial Guinea, Guyana, Malta and Mauritius which had GDP per capita growth 1990–2000 of 3 per cent p.a. or more, to Kyrgyzstan, Moldova and Tajikistan which all had sharply negative growth.
9 Excluding from the later period those countries which did not exist as separate entities in 1990 makes little difference to the comparison.
10 Israeli inflation over this period averaged 9.6 per cent.
11 See Williamson (1995: 20) for the argument that seigniorage should be calculated in terms of the return on the assets backing the currency issue, but that if currency is backed by domestic assets instead of foreign exchange its return might in fact be lower.

12 For the three subperiods Jordan had seigniorage of 2.3, 1.4 and 4.3 per cent respectively, with inflation of 9.1, 2.6 and 11.8 per cent; while Israel had seigniorage of 1.6, 1.6 and 0.5 per cent, with inflation at 118.4, 152.5 and 15.9 per cent. The study's calculation of seigniorage uses the inflation tax (determined by the inflation rate) on the central bank's liabilities in reserve money, but also makes some adjustments for interest payments on bank reserves (see Fry *et al.* 1996: 34).

13 It should be noted that the definition of seigniorage is not straightforward (see, for example, Bofinger 2001, Chapter 11), but the conclusion reached here does not depend on a particular definition.

14 Their results suggest that WBGS imports from and exports to Jordan would be 2.2 and 3.9 per cent of total WBGS imports/exports respectively in the first situation, and 5.8 and 6.4 per cent in the second.

15 The former is 1.45 for imports and 1.36 for exports, with standard errors of 1.25 and 1.27 respectively. The latter is −1.51 for imports and −1.59 for exports, with standard errors of 0.17 in both cases.

16 Since the point estimates are roughly the same for each dummy, the difference in significance must be mainly the result of a difference in the variance of the dummy variables across observations. This will necessarily be higher for the WBGS–rest of world dummy since there are more observations where the dummy is equal to one, while for the WBGS–Israel dummy there is only one such observation. I am indebted to Chris Adam for this point.

17 They also predict almost no change in WBGS imports to or exports from Jordan, at 1.2 per cent and 3.8 per cent respectively.

18 An independent Palestinian state could also choose to open a seaport so that it would no longer be landlocked.

19 Since the European Central Bank (ECB) was modelled partly on the Bundesbank future Eurozone performance is likely to be comparable to past German performance.

20 The data for Jordan's exchange rate are against the USD rather than effective, and the latter – if it were available – would presumably have moved rather more: while the JD's rate against the USD remained at 1.410 from 1997 to 2001, that against the euro went from 1.244 in 1997 to 1.606 in 2000 and 1.576 in 2001 (data from Central Bank of Jordan website).

21 In the mid 1980s this may be a reflection of the stylised fact that purchasing power parity holds more nearly in hyperinflations, but from 1986 it is probably more the result of the crawling band exchange rate regime which was operated.

22 These (unweighted) averages were calculated from the distributions in Tables 4.1–4.6 of Fry *et al.* (2000).

23 Some authors have claimed that the Bundesbank was in practice more of an inflation targeter; see Bofinger (2001: section 9.2). The ECB's 'monetary policy strategy' is changing, albeit slowly, see ECB (2003b).

24 See, for example, Alesina *et al.* (2001) and Begg *et al.* (2002).

25 See Fischer (1994: section 2.3) and Bofinger (2001: section 5.2) for balanced discussions of the evidence on inflation and growth. The inflation targets of major central banks (the Fed, the ECB, the Bank of England, etc.) are around 2–3 per cent, and it is difficult to see what would justify a new Palestinian state having an objective that was significantly higher.

26 An additional argument for fixity is that this might facilitate the avoidance of a Dutch disease problem arising from large (private and official) capital inflows in the first years of the new state.

27 The choice of the appropriate peg seems not to have been widely discussed. Hamed (1999) favours a dollar peg on the grounds of JD and NIS instability, but recognises that this will expose the Palestinian economy to shocks arising

from changes in the exchange rates of its main trading partners against the USD. Naqib (1999) does not seem to identify the appropriate peg for the currency board which he advocates for the short-run, but (in company with Dabbagh 1999) favours currency union with Jordan in the longer run. Erickson von Allmen and Fischer briefly discuss the choice between the NIS, the USD and the euro but present no conclusion.

28 For example, in 1988 – i.e. at a relatively early stage in the process of European monetary integration – the 12 members of the European Community obtained 58 per cent of their imports on average from other members, and exported 60 per cent of their exports to them (Hitiris 1991: 208).

29 This is one reason why European governments opted for the 'institutional' rather than the 'currency competition' approach to monetary union (Gros and Thygesen 1998, Chapter 10).

30 One way of handling this transition would be by fixing to a basket of the NIS and the euro and gradually reducing the weight on the former and increasing that on the latter. The main disadvantage of this proposal is the lower level of transparency (even if the weights are publicly announced).

References

Al-Atrash, A. and Yousef, T. (2000) 'Intra-Arab trade: is it too little?', working paper no. 00/10, IMF.

Alesina, A., Blanchard, O., Galí, J., Giavazzi, F. and Uhlig, H. (2001) *Defining a Macroeconomic Framework for the Euro Area: Monitoring the European Central Bank no. 3*, London: CEPR.

Angeloni, I., Gaspar, V. and Tristani, O. (1999) 'The monetary policy strategy of the ECB: theoretical and empirical foundations', in D. Cobham and G. Zis (eds) *From EMS to EMU*, London: Macmillan.

Arnon, A. and Kanafani, N. (2004) 'Absorbing returnees in a viable Palestinian state: a forward looking macroeconomic perspective', Chapter 10, this volume.

Arnon, A. and Spivak, A. (1996a) 'On the introduction of a Palestinian currency', *Middle East Business and Economic Review* 8 (1): 1–14.

Arnon, A. and Spivak, A. (1996b) 'Monetary integration between the Israeli, Jordanian and Palestinian economies', *Weltwirtschaftliches Archiv* 132: 259–277.

Arnon, A., Spivak, A. and Weinblatt, J. (1996) 'The potential for trade between Israel, the Palestinians and Jordan', *World Economy* 19: 113–134.

Arnon, A., Luski, I., Spivak, A. and Weinblatt, J. (1997) *The Palestinian Economy: Between Imposed Integration and Voluntary Separation*, Leiden: Brill.

Bannister, G. and Erickson von Allmen, U. (2001) 'Palestinian trade: performance, prospects and policy', in R. Valdivieso, U. Erickson von Allmen, G. Bannister, H. Davoodi, F. Fischer, E. Jenkner and M. Said, *West Bank and Gaza: Economic Performance, Prospects and Policies*, Washington, DC: IMF.

Bayoumi, T. and Eichengreen, B. (1993) 'Shocking aspects of European monetary integration', in F. Torres and G. Giavazzi (eds) *Adjustment and Growth in the European Monetary Union*, Cambridge: Cambridge University Press.

Begg, D., Canova, F., De Grauwe, P., Fatás, A. and Lane, P. (2002) *Surviving the Slowdown: Monitoring the European Central Bank no. 4*, London: CEPR.

Blavy, R. (2001) 'Trade in the Mashreq: an empirical examination', working paper no. 01/63, IMF.

Bofinger, P. (2001) *Monetary Policy*, Oxford: Oxford University Press.

Calvo, G. and Reinhart, C. (2002) 'Fear of floating', *Quarterly Journal of Economics* 117: 379–408.

Clarida, R., Galí, J. and Gertler, M. (1998) 'Monetary rules in practice: some international evidence', *European Economic Review* 42: 1033–1067.

Cukierman, A. (1992) *Central Bank Strategy, Credibility and Independence: Theory and Evidence*, Cambridge: MIT Press.

Dabbagh, O. (1999) 'Monetary integration between Jordan and Palestine', Economic Research Forum working paper no. 9934.

Dessus, S. and Ruppert Bulmer, E. (2003) 'The choice of trade regime depends on multiple factors', Chapter 2, this volume.

ECB (2003a) 'Exchange rate regimes for emerging market economies', in *Monthly Bulletin*, February 2003, European Central Bank.

ECB (2003b) 'Evaluation of the ECB's monetary policy strategy', statement by O. Issing on 8 May, available at http://www.ecb.int/key/03/sp030508_2slides.pdf.

Erickson von Allmen, U. and Fischer, F. (2001) 'The choice of future exchange rate regime in the West Bank and Gaza', in R. Valdivieso, U. Erickson von Allmen, G. Bannister, H. Davoodi, F. Fischer, E. Jenkner and M. Said, *West Bank and Gaza: Economic Performance, Prospects and Policies*, Washington, DC: IMF.

Fischer, S. (1994) 'Modern central banking', in F. Capie, C. Goodhart, S. Fischer and N. Schnadt (eds) *The Future of Central Banking*, Cambridge: Cambridge University Press.

Fischer, S. (2001) 'Exchange rate regimes: is the bipolar view correct?', *Finance and Development* 38 (June): 18–21.

Frankel, J. (1999) 'No single currency regime is right for all countries or at all times', *Princeton Essays in International Finance*, no. 215.

Frankel, J. and Rose, A. (2002) 'An estimate of the effect of common currencies on trade and income', *Quarterly Journal of Economics* 117: 437–466.

Fry, M., Goodhart, C. and Almeida, A. (1996) *Central Banking in Developing Countries*, London: Routledge.

Fry, M., Julius, D., Mahadeva, L., Roger, S. and Sterne, G. (2000) 'Key issues in the choice of monetary policy framework', part I of L. Mahadeva and G. Sterne (eds) *Monetary Policy Frameworks in a Global Context*, London: Routledge.

Grilli, V., Masciandaro, D. and Tabellini, G. (1991) 'Political and monetary institutions and public financial policies in the industrial countries', *Economic Policy* no. 13: 342–392.

Gros, D. and Thygesen, N. (1998) *European Monetary Integration*, 2nd edition, Harlow: Addison Wesley Longman.

Hamed, O. (1999) 'Current monetary arrangements between Israel and the West Bank and Gaza Strip and possible alternatives', paper commissioned for the EU.

Hamed, O. and Shaban, R. (1993) 'One-sided customs and monetary union: the case of the West Bank and Gaza Strip', in S. Fischer (ed.) *The Economics of Middle East Peace*, Cambridge: MIT Press.

Hitiris, T. (1991) *European Community Economics*, 2nd edition, Hemel Hempstead: Harvester Wheatsheaf.

Issing, O., Gaspar, V., Angeloni, I. and Tristani, O. (2001) *Monetary Policy in the Euro Area*, Cambridge: Cambridge University Press.

Kanafani, N. (2001) 'Trade – a catalyst for peace', *Economic Journal* 111: F276–290.

Mélitz, J. (2001) 'Geography, trade and currency union', CEPR working paper no. 2987.

Miniesy, R., Nugent, J. and Yousef, T. (2002) 'Intra-regional trade integration in the Middle East: past performance and future potential', forthcoming in H. Hakimian and J. Nugent (eds) *Trade Policy and Economic Integration in the Middle East and North Africa: Economic Boundaries in Flux*, London: RoutledgeCurzon.

Naqib, F. (1999) 'The economics of currency boards: the case of the Palestinian economy in the West Bank and Gaza Strip', paper presented to the sixth annual conference of the ERF, mimeo, University of Waterloo.

Reinhart, C. and Rogoff, K. (2002) 'The modern history of exchange rate arrangements: a reinterpretation', NBER working paper no. 8963.

Rose, A. (2000) 'One market, one money: estimating the effect of common currencies on trade', *Economic Policy* no. 30: 7–45.

Rose, A. (2001) 'Currency unions and trade: the effect is large', *Economic Policy* no. 33: 449–461.

Williamson, J. (1995) *What Role for Currency Boards?*, Washington, DC: Institute for International Economics.

World Bank (1993) *Developing the Occupied Territories: An Investment in Peace, Volume 2: The Economy*, Washington, DC: World Bank.

World Bank (2002) *Long Term Policy Options for the Palestinian Economy*, Washington, DC: World Bank.

Discussion

Chris Allsopp

This is an extremely useful chapter, which goes about as far as it can in discussing the important question of currency arrangements for a future Palestinian state. Its final policy recommendation is a two-stage strategy, starting with a currency board with Israel, and moving later to a relatively hard peg against the euro.

The conclusion follows neatly from a series of stylised facts and some major assumptions.

- The WBGS is at present highly dependent on and integrated into the Israeli economy. The NIS is the most important currency for transactions – no doubt reflecting in part the fact that many Palestinians work in Israel and are paid in the NIS.
- Despite the present high degree of trade with Israel, studies such as those based on gravity models suggest that in the longer term trade with the EU is likely to be more important (and a switch in the direction of trade is surely a political objective as well).
- The NIS has not been stable and is not a suitable 'anchor currency' in the longer term. (The author is careful, of course, not to assume that the past is necessarily a good guide to the future.)
- On monetary policy, the author buys into the conventional view that a nascent Palestinian state would lack credible institutions, and that therefore it would need an extremely 'hard' exchange rate regime initially to provide stability and to act as a 'discipline device' (a currency board).
- Despite these institutional problems, there is an underlying assumption that the new state would need its separate currency. One of the reasons for this is the objective of changing the direction of trade.
- Another major assumption is that a hard peg with the euro would in fact stimulate and facilitate a change in the direction of trade. (Footnote 18 notes that a Palestinian state might choose to open a seaport which might, for a number of reasons, be even more important than the currency arrangements).

The overall line effectively puts together a direction of trade argument (favouring a peg to the euro) with a suitability argument (the euro is a relatively stable and credible anchor currency) together with two monetary regime arguments: the first is that initially a really hard peg is necessary and the second is that in the longer term the monetary policy regime should be more flexible and tied (though more loosely) to the more suitable anchor currency.

In this short comment I concentrate on the monetary regime/exchange rate regime arguments. The question that is not really faced is what kind of a macroeconomic framework a new Palestinian state might be seeking to end up with.

A new Palestinian state would be small and open. (The chapter contains some suggestive material on similar countries, mainly drawn from an IMF study, but the diversity is so great that it really provides no useful guide. The author suggests that there is some tendency towards greater fixity on average but it is hard to draw any conclusions from that.) A useful starting point is to consider what such an economy would look like if it were really part of a common currency area.

Clearly, in that case, there would be no separate monetary policy and no separate exchange rate. In macroeconomic terms, regional adjustment would then depend on flexibility of wages and prices (affecting the real exchange rate relative to other countries/areas) and fiscal policy. By analogy with, say, small countries in the euro area, we can imagine that the fiscal authority raises taxes and determines public expenditure. The fiscal authority can presumably borrow (that is, run a deficit from time to time) subject to solvency constraints. Clearly, the development of the fiscal institutions would be one of the principal challenges for a nascent state. As in other common currency areas, the fiscal authorities should ideally (credibly) guarantee that the fiscal position was 'sustainable' and, subject to that, use fiscal policy to provide some stabilisation against short-term shocks.[1]

Other monetary/exchange rate arrangements can be looked at against this stylised situation. Given the analysis in the chapter, we are particularly interested in two alternatives. The first is a currency board (e.g. with the NIS). The second, for the longer term, is a more independent monetary policy – though still with a 'hard' peg against the euro.

The big question with the currency board proposal is what the advantages are relative to continuing with a de facto currency union with Israel. They do not appear to be great. The 'old' argument for currency boards was that the seigniorage would accrue to the country concerned. Cobham makes an excellent case that seigniorage revenues would be relatively small (for reasonable inflation rates) and that this argument should not be decisive.

The new argument is usually about credibility and 'discipline'. As far as credibility is concerned, this only arises with a separate currency. The discipline argument is usually about fiscal policy. That is a double-edged argument, however, since as Cobham notes, currency boards themselves are not credible unless fiscal policy is under control. A currency board without fiscal discipline (and a means of dealing with insolvent banks and private sector companies) is highly risky. It is difficult to resist the conclusion that economic logic suggests accepting the status quo (it would be much simpler) and concentrating efforts on the development of appropriate economic policy institutions – especially in the fiscal area. Currency boards have the disadvantages of a common currency area, they increase risks of failure, and they have few compensating advantages. A separate currency could be a longer term objective, but for it to be desirable it is necessary to look quite closely at what the advantages might be.

The main advantage of a separate currency put forward in the chapter is that it would allow pegging to the euro rather than the NIS. The potential advantages are:

1 that the euro is more suitable as an anchor;
2 that trade flows would be stimulated.

It is undoubtedly true that the NIS has been unstable in nominal terms. Interestingly, the data suggest that the real exchange rate has been rather stable. There are clearly trade-offs between nominal stability and real exchange rate issues that would need to be considered further. As noted, the main argument for the initial currency board (i.e. establishing a separate currency) is that it would facilitate a change later.

The usual argument for a separate currency is that it facilitates a more independent monetary policy which can help in managing the domestic macroeconomy. With free capital movements, the authorities can control, however, only one of domestic interest rates and the exchange rate. The suggestion in the chapter is that, eventually, the new state should have a relatively fixed exchange rate against the euro. This means that interest rates are not available for managing the domestic economy. The chapter suggests that the objective should be to develop 'the competence and the credibility to use some discretion in monetary policy (notably to change the exchange rate parity in the case of a severe asymmetric shock). This amounts to the proposition that monetary policy should be available to help in changing the real exchange rate – to bring it more in line with fundamentals. This would be a substitute for wage-price flexibility – which indeed is likely to be imperfect. But it is worth recalling that the situation when this is likely to be helpful is when nominal wages and prices are inflexible but where real wages and the real exchange rate can in fact change. In a number of important cases, such exchange rate manipulation would not be helpful. If, for example, real wages are 'high' because of the wage paid in neighbouring countries – especially Israel – this could not be dealt with by exchange rate change. Nor is it likely that 'Dutch disease' problems due to capital inflows could easily be mitigated by the exchange rate regime.[2]

Another argument put forward for an independent currency/monetary policy is that lender of last resort facilities could be developed. This is a complicated issue. In principle, it has little to do with monetary policy (except in so far as central banks quite often perform both roles). Supervisory arrangements for monetary and other institutions are clearly extremely important and would need to be developed. Beyond this, fiscal arrangements are clearly key in dealing with major financial stability problems.

In conclusion, it is natural to think of a new Palestinian state with its own currency. This comment has been sceptical about the suggestion of a currency board with the NIS which could be quite risky. The development of institutions, especially in the fiscal and supervisory areas, is needed anyway and would be needed to support the adoption of a separate currency with or without a currency board. With successful institutional development, a number of options for the monetary and exchange rate arrangements would open up (including, in principle, inflation targeting with a floating exchange rate, or various kinds of fixed or semi-fixed exchange rates). Without the appropriate institutional arrangements, not only would the options be much more limited, but the adoption of particular exchange rate arrangements could be risky.

Notes

1 There is a developing literature which draws on the experience of monetary policy institutions to suggest desirable fiscal policy arrangements (reaction functions) within common currency areas (Wyplosz 2002; Swedish Government 2002).

2 The suggestion in the chapter is that a 'fixed' exchange rate might stop capital inflows causing problems. The likelihood is, however, that domestic wages and prices would adjust.

References

Swedish Government (2002) 'Stabilisation policy in a monetary union: summary of the report', Swedish Government Official Reports SOU 2002: 16, Stockholm, Fritzes Offentliga.

Wyplosz, C. (2002) 'Fiscal policy: institutions versus rules', CEPR discussion paper no. 3238.

4 Budgetary and fiscal policy

Christopher Adam, David Cobham and Nu'man Kanafani

Introduction

Between 1967 and 1994, the budgetary policy of the Israeli administration in the West Bank and Gaza Strip (WBGS) seems to have been much like that of former British colonial regimes. Owen and Pamuk (1998: 52) described the major budgetary principle of colonial economic practice as follows:

> Colonies should pay for themselves without recourse to special financial assistance from the metropolis. This produced pressures for fiscal conservatism including the need to make sure that they balanced their budgets. This, in turn, ensured that, given the fact that the first call on their resources was to spend money on administration and the police, there were usually only small sums left for welfare or public works.

In the WBGS there was little infrastructural spending by the Israeli administration, and health and education services were largely provided by NGOs.

The Palestinian Authority (PA) began to function as a fiscal authority in 1994. Since that time it has substantially increased its tax-gathering capacity, to a point that compares well with other countries in the region. The PA's expenditure has also been substantial and significantly above revenues, but as a result of considerable support by external donors, most of which went to finance capital expenditures which the PA could not fund, the domestic fiscal balance remained moderate. However, it should be emphasised that the PA was starting from scratch as an entirely new administration, and that its operations were subject to a high degree of political and economic turbulence, related in particular to the intensity of closures in 1994–1996 and then the start of the second intifada in September 2000.

The government of a new Palestinian state will inherit the budgetary and fiscal arrangements put in place by the PA. But it will need to move decisively towards a budget that will be self-sustaining at some point in the future. And it will need to cope with particular challenges which arise from the need to overcome the effects of occupation and conflict, to welcome and absorb a large number of returning refugees, and to expand the role of the state to cover a wider range of activities including comprehensive health and education provision, pensions and other social support programmes.

We first examine the PA's budget from 1996 to 2003, highlighting some of the key structural characteristics of the budget and placing it in a regional and international context. We then consider the challenges facing a new Palestinian state in designing a fiscal programme that is consistent with the needs and aspirations of the new state and those it represents. In doing so we focus both on the 'structural' aspects of fiscal policy design – issues of the structure of taxation, public expenditure, debt and the institutions of fiscal management – and on the question of the macroeconomic sustainability of the fiscal stance.

The Palestinian Authority's budget

Overall performance

Tables 4.1(a) and 4.1(b) provide basic data on the PA's budget since 1996, including the planned budget for 2003, where Table 4.1(b) expresses the fiscal position in terms of estimated GDP.[1] The PA began for the first time to raise revenues in its own right in 1994, and achieved remarkable success by increasing revenues from 17.6 per cent of GDP in 1996 (and 8 per cent in 1994) to consistently over 20 per cent of GDP between 1997 and the second intifada in 2000. This is substantially above the average in neighbouring Arab countries (IMF 2003a: 62).

On the expenditure side, the budget is partitioned between the recurrent budget, which was overwhelmingly funded by domestic revenues, and the development budget, a large proportion of which has been donor-financed. Soon after the signing of the Declaration of Principles (DoP) in 1993 an international conference of donor countries was held and pledged $2.4bn to assist the Palestinian reconstruction and development programme (1994–1999). Further contributions increased the total to $3.4bn. The initial understanding between the PA and donors was that funds would not be used for short-term budgetary expenditure after 1994, but would be devoted to long-term public investment, hence the separation between the two budget components. Over time it was anticipated that the PA would make gradually increasing contributions to the development budget. While the Authority was moving in this direction (the recurrent budget deficit was progressively eliminated between 1994 and 1999) the adverse conditions caused by closures and the intifada, and then by Israel's withholding of clearance revenues (see below), necessarily reversed this trend, with all the aid going to support the budget and nothing to capital

Table 4.1a The budget of the PA, 1996–2003, (in NIS m)

	1996	*1997*	*1998*	*1999*	*2000*	*2001*	*2002*	*2003*[1]
Revenue (actual)	*2,059*	*2,785*	*3,300*	*3,898*	*3,829*	*1,148*	*1,574*	*5,057*
1 Domestic revenue	937	1,143	1,233	1,498	1,434	1,148	1,018	1,037
Tax revenue	663	735	865	1026	982	759	640	593
Income tax	168	228	260	310	278	177	145	
VAT	209	268	316	367	393	323	271	
Customs duties	76	75	94	144	98	33	13	
Property tax	3	2	2	6	6	7	4	
Excises	207	162	193	199	207	219	207	
Non-tax revenue	274	408	368	472	452	389	378	444
Transportation fees	72	112	110	117	117	98	51	
Health insurance	40	44	55	83	75	46	64	
Health fees	30	35	39	38	40	33	27	
Others	132	217	164	234	220	212	236	
2 Revenue from clearances[2]	1,124	1,642	2,066	2,400	2,395	1,749	1,620	1,620
Customs duties	226	476	780	1,030	1,013	736	740	
VAT	543	709	777	844	907	708	620	
Petroleum excises	303	371	406	415	371	305	260	
Income tax	13	18	35	26	27	0	0	
Health fees	20	28	35	36	27	0	0	
Other clearances	19	40	33	49	50	0	0	
Actual disbursement	1,122	1,642	2,067	2,400	2,395	0	556	4,020

Expenditure	*3,420*	*3,899*	*4,084*	*4,893*	*4,946*	*4,714*	*4,980*	*6,394*
1 Total current expenditure	2,647	2,994	3,188	3,902	4,891	4,621	4,937	5,198
Wage bill	1,286	1,622	1,774	2,147	2,537	2,862	3,124	3,123
Non-wage	1,361	1,372	1,414	1,755	2,354	1,759	1,813	2,075
Recurrent balance	*−588*	*−209*	*112*	*−4*	*−1,062*	*−3,473*	*−3,363*	*−141*
2 Total capital expenditure	773	905	896	991	55	93	43	1,195
Overall balance	*−1,361*	*−1,114*	*−784*	*−995*	*−1.117*	*−3,566*	*−3,406*	*−1,337*
Total financing	*1,361*	*1,114*	*784*	*995*	*1,117*	*3,566*	*3,406*	*−1,337*
Foreign	1,197	1,043	907	1,014	221	2,238	2,214	3,735
Direct current expenditure	157	20	2	23	0	0	88	
External budget support	267	118	9	0	221	2,238	2,126	2,675
Direct capital expenditure	773	905	896	991	0	0	0	1,060
Domestic								
Expenditure arrears	0	18	288	42	268	978	558	−2,075
Net borrowing (residual)	164	53	−411	−61	628	350	634	−324

Source: adapted from IMF(2003, Table 4.2) and the PA's MoF website (www.mof.gov.ps).

Note
1 planned budget;
2 including payments withheld.

Table 4.1b The budget of the PA, 1996–2002 (in % of GDP)

	1996	*1997*	*1998*	*1999*	*2000*	*2001*	*2002*
Revenue (actual)	*17.6*	*20.1*	*20.4*	*20.8*	*21.1*	*7.2*	*11.2*
1 Domestic revenue	8.0	8.3	7.6	8.0	7.9	7.2	7.2
Tax revenue	5.7	5.3	5.3	5.5	5.4	4.8	4.5
Non-tax revenue	2.3	2.9	2.3	2.5	2.5	2.5	2.7
2 Tax clearances							
Accrual	9.6	11.9	12.8	12.8	13.2	11.0	11.5
Actual	9.6	11.9	12.8	12.8	13.2	0.0	3.9
Expenditure	*29.2*	*28.2*	*25.2*	*26.2*	*27.3*	*29.7*	*35.3*
1 Total current expenditure	22.6	21.6	19.7	20.9	27.0	29.2	35.0
Wage bill	11.0	11.7	11.0	11.5	14.0	18.1	22.2
Non-wage	11.6	9.9	8.7	9.4	13.0	11.1	12.9
Recurrent balance	*−5.0*	*−1.5*	*0.7*	*0.0*	*−5.9*	*−21.9*	*−23.9*
2 Total capital expenditure	6.6	6.5	5.5	5.3	0.3	0.6	0.3
Overall balance	*−11.6*	*−8.1*	*−4.8*	*−5.3*	*−6.2*	*−22.5*	*−24.2*
Total financing	*11.6*	*8.1*	*4.8*	*5.3*	*6.2*	*22.5*	*24.2*
Foreign	10.2	7.5	5.6	5.4	1.2	14.1	15.7
Direct current expenditure	1.3	0.1	0.0	0.1	0.0	0.0	0.6
External budget support	2.3	0.9	0.1	0.0	1.2	14.1	15.1
Direct capital expenditure	6.6	6.5	5.5	5.3	0.0	0.0	0.0
Domestic							
Expenditure arrears	0.0	0.1	1.8	0.2	1.5	6.2	4.0
Net borrowing (residual)	1.4	0.4	−2.5	−0.3	3.5	2.2	4.5
Memorandum items							
GDP (US$m)	3,668	4,009	4,258	4,517	4,442	3,765	2,974
NIS/US$	3.19	3.45	3.8	4.14	4.08	4.21	4.74

Source: see Table 4.1a.

expenditure, a situation which forced the PA to allocate some money itself to finance certain urgently needed capital expenditure.

Over the first five years of its existence, the PA was also remarkably successful in maintaining a tight control on the level of domestic deficit financing. The PA's overall fiscal deficit declined from almost 12 per cent of GDP in 1996 to around 5 per cent in 1999 (or from around 5 per cent of GDP to a position of overall balance when directly foreign-financed expenditures are excluded), and this was accompanied by a sharp reduction in the PA's net domestic deficit (i.e. its direct borrowing from the banking sector). Since then, however, fiscal performance has been severely disrupted by the second intifada (which started in September 2000) and the intensification of the Israeli closure (physical siege) policy. Domestic revenues declined sharply as the result of economic crisis, political turmoil and difficulties in tax collection. Clearance revenues collected by the Israeli tax authorities on behalf of the PA also declined, but more importantly the Israeli government refused to transfer these monies in 2001 and for all except the final month of 2002. By the end of 2002 Israel had transferred only NIS556 million (16 per cent) out of the NIS3,370 million due (see Table 4.1a). At the same time, with the sharp drop in the number of Palestinians working in Israel there was strong pressure on the PA to increase expenditure and alleviate economic hardship. However, expenditure was broadly stabilised, while the large increase in the overall fiscal deficit which emerged was made up by increased external finance – partly from the European Union and partly from the Arab countries – which was now paid directly to the PA and, given the domestic revenue crisis, was increasingly used to fund current instead of capital expenditures. As we discuss later, external developments and the fiscal reforms underpinning the 2003 budget have helped to return the overall fiscal stance to a broadly sustainable position, at least given continued levels of external support.

It is important to stress, however, that the accounts of the PA do not fully reflect the overall fiscal position of the Authority. In particular, the data in Table 4.1 omit some important revenues and expenditures. A large part of actual expenditure in the WBGS on health, education, social services and maintenance and buildings has been carried out by international organisations and foreign financed NGOs. The most important of these is probably the United Nations Relief and Works Agency (UNRWA) which is in charge of the welfare of the refugees and refugee camps in the WBGS. Table 4.2 shows the levels of expenditure by UNRWA in recent years, both in the WBGS and in the refugee camps elsewhere. For 2003, for example, UNRWA's total planned expenditure in the WBGS amounted to about $154 million, or to some 14 per cent of the planned expenditure in the PA budget. On the revenue side, and especially until 2000, certain tax and non-tax revenue flows remained off budget. Between 1995 and mid 2000, a total of approximately $590 million

Table 4.2 UNRWA's regular budget by programme and field (US$000)

	West Bank		*Gaza*		*Total UNRWA**	
	2002	*2003*	*2002*	*2003*	*2002*	*2003*
Education programme	*26,963*	*28,176*	*57,077*	*60,171*	*172,255*	*179,066*
General education	20,506	21,687	53,467	56,452	150,458	156,952
Elementary education	13,416	14,100	32,852	34,477	91,934	95,141
Preparatory education	7,090	7,587	20,615	21,975	56,956	60,017
Secondary education	0	0	0	0	1,568	1,794
Vocational and technical	5,017	5,012	2,122	2,168	13,563	13,715
Teacher education	636	639	0	0	1,097	1,102
Management	804	838	1,488	1,551	7,137	7,297
Health programme	*12,410*	*12,704*	*16,764*	*17,305*	*58,911*	*60,662*
Medical care services	9,394	9,636	11,435	11,924	42,201	43,686
Environmental health	1,738	1,764	3,450	3,468	9,375	9,505
Supplementary feeding	684	698	1,409	1,436	4,320	4,407
Management	594	606	470	477	3,015	3,064
Relief and social services	*4,982*	*5,156*	*11,748*	*12,211*	*33,630*	*34,908*
Relief services	4,106	4,277	10,679	11,140	29,423	30,669
Social services	702	702	868	866	2,770	2,781
Management	174	177	201	205	1,437	1,458
Operational services	*6,456*	*6,514*	*8,311*	*8,393*	*61,422*	*65,916*
Residual	*2,374*	*2,142*	*2,156*	*1,387*	*4,530*	*3,529*
Grand total	*53,185*	*54,692*	*90,056*	*99,467*	*330,748*	*344,081*

Note
*Total in all fields of operations, i.e. Jordan, Syria and Lebanon as well as Geneva headquarters. Ref UNRWA'S website (accessed 3.12.2003).

of excise revenues on tobacco, alcohol and petroleum were diverted into accounts which were neither under the control of the Ministry of Finance nor incorporated in the PA's budget. As the IMF reports, however, most of this revenue – equivalent to around 2.3 per cent of GDP (or 12 per cent of annual PA revenue) per annum – was used for investment in PA commercial operations through the Palestinian Commercial Services Company (PCSC) (IMF 2003a: 88–89). The PA rapidly acquired a number of commercial assets, many of which were in effect awarded monopoly status (notably cement and petroleum), and for several years these activities were not publicly accounted for. Other assets (including, for example, a stake in ORASCOM Telecommunications) were bought or set-up out of diverted tax revenues. The PA's commercial entities, some 67 in total, were highly profitable. The IMF report makes a rough estimate of their profits over the years 1995–2000 at around $300 million, which was also channelled outside the PA budget (IMF 2003a: 89, 91).

In addition, fees and charges levied by some ministries (health, education, car licensing, etc.) were paid directly to the ministries' bank accounts and spent at the discretion of ministers, which reduced the Treasury's ability to control revenues and expenditure (IMF 2003a: 89).

Key features of the PA's fiscal operations

The PA's short, albeit intensive and occasionally dramatic, experience in fiscal matters has revealed a number of bottlenecks and weaknesses. Some of these have now been dealt with in the fiscal reform which accompanied the preparation of the 2003 budget (see below), but others are of a more structural nature and cannot be tackled under the present geopolitical and economic constraints.

Tax structure and fiscal leakages

One of the initial successes of the PA was the creation of a healthy revenue base. Between 1994 and 1999 the PA managed to raise revenue to around 21 per cent of GDP, which is high relative both to other countries in the region and to countries with similar structural characteristics. Although the WBGS is currently classified as a lower-middle-income country its per capita income ($930 per capita) places it in the lowest quartile of the lower-middle-income range,[2] while many of its structural characteristics, such as relatively low levels of industrialisation, openness to trade, and vulnerability to external shocks, mean that its natural comparators consist of low- rather than middle-income countries. Estimates for low-income countries suggest that revenue mobilisation in the late 1990s averaged between 15 and 18 per cent of GDP (see Abed *et al.* 1998; Gupta *et al.* 2002). This level of revenue mobilisation, which is much closer to that enjoyed by middle- or upper-middle-income countries, is all the more striking given that it has been achieved with tax rates that are relatively modest by international standards.

However, these impressive aggregate figures mask the fact that the PA revenue base is disproportionately weighted towards indirect taxes and away from direct income taxes. Indirect taxes (domestic indirect taxes plus taxes on trade) account for nearly 80 per cent of total WBGS revenue, compared to around 50 per cent for Jordan, Lebanon, Morocco and Tunisia, a similar share for all low-income countries, and just over 30 per cent for Israel (IMF 2003a: 66; Adam and Bevan 2003). This structure is not the outcome of an explicit choice over the tax regime but rather reflects the Oslo Agreements which imposed the overall structure of indirect taxes,[3] the relative efficiency of the Israeli clearance and tax-gathering mechanisms, and the effect of the economic and political crisis on the PA's ability to collect income tax.

The high dependence on indirect taxation in general gives rise to a further feature of the budget. Tax revenues accrue to the PA through two channels: domestic direct and indirect tax collection, and tax clearances remitted by Israel. The former are collected by the PA itself, while the latter are collected by Israel on behalf of the Palestinian Authority and refunded via clearance procedures which were agreed upon in the Oslo Accords. The share of clearance revenues in total revenues increased from 54 per cent to 63 per cent between 1996 and 2000, and the degree of fiscal vulnerability associated with the tax clearance system was dramatically illustrated when Israel stopped the transfers in 2001. The tax clearances remitted by Israel to the PA consist of three main flows:

- VAT collected by Israel on goods sold by Israel to the Palestinians (against invoices).
- Customs duties and excise (purchase tax) collected by Israel on goods imported through Israel and specified as destined for the WBGS.
- 75 per cent of the income tax paid by Palestinians working in Israel (and all the taxes paid by Palestinians working in the Israeli settlements).

While the clearance mechanism was technically efficient, it was also a source of disputes (Kanafani 2001). Actual implementation of the system meant that the PA has been losing customs duties on indirect imports, i.e. goods which are re-exported by Israel to the WBGS; purchase taxes on (as well as customs duties on the import content of) Israeli manufactured products sold to the Palestinians; and customs duties, excise taxes and VAT on purchases which are not documented by invoices. Conservative estimates of this fiscal leakage (the revenues which accrue to Israel but are not transferred to the PA) put the figure at somewhere between 3 per cent (Naqib 1996) and 4.2 per cent (Dumas 1999) of GDP.[4]

Arrears and debt

Even after external budget support the PA's budget was running at a small deficit during the relatively 'good' years of the late 1990s, but it reached alarming levels during the crisis years of 2001–2002. The sharp increase in deficit was financed partly by borrowing from domestic banks and partly by the accumulation of payment arrears. With the suspension of clearance transfers from Israel and the deepening fiscal crisis, the PA's fiscal management came to depend on 'forced credit' from the private sector. By the end of 2002 the stock of payment arrears was estimated by the IMF at $531 million, equivalent to around 18 per cent of GDP (or 12 per cent of 2000 GDP, i.e. the level of income prevailing before the sharp crisis-induced collapse in GDP) (IMF 2003a; 77, 95). The PA also borrowed from the commercial banks and from the PMA. Net PA liabilities to domestic commercial banks peaked at the end of 2000, but declined slightly by the end of 2002 to $121 million, or 4 per cent of GDP (IMF 2003a: 77). Although the stock of domestic bank debt was low, it was expensive, with interest rates of 10 per cent on dollar and 15 per cent on NIS loans. Unlike expenditure arrears, however, which contributed to the pressure on the private sector in the WBGS, PA borrowing from the banking system is likely to have had a positive effect on the private sector. The banking system had always (i.e. since 1993) lent out to the private sector only a relatively low proportion of the deposits it took in, and it was even more reluctant to lend under the intifada. Its loans to the PA would not therefore have crowded out loans to the private sector and, by allowing the PA to pay for more of what it was ordering, would have eased the financial pressure on the private sector.

The PA was also accumulating foreign debt. Development expenditure remained almost totally financed by foreign donors, but finance was increasingly in the form of loans rather than grants. The stock of foreign debt stood at about $530 million in mid 1999 (MAS 1999), some 13 per cent of GDP, but increased to $872 million by 2002 (approximately 20 per cent of pre-intifada GDP) (IMF 2003a: 82).

The true scale of the external debt burden is rather difficult to measure. However, most of this debt has been contracted on highly concessional terms and there is a reasonable expectation that a significant proportion would be rescheduled and written-off in due course. Hence, in net present value terms, the true external debt burden is likely to be significantly less than this 20 per cent figure, even accounting for some continued increase over the coming years. This would place a future Palestinian state well below the mean levels of external indebtedness for developing countries as a whole. For example, the latest figures from the OECD, relating to 1999, estimate the nominal average external indebtedness of all developing countries to be approximately 85 per cent of GDP, while Pattillo *et al.* (2002) report that, even after accounting for concessionality, the present value of this external debt is close to 50 per cent.

Public sector employment

The public sector wage bill in the WBGS is relatively high, as a ratio of GDP or of current expenditure, compared to other Arab countries and other comparable countries around the world. The IMF calculated the ratio to GDP, for example, at 15.2 per cent for the WBGS in 2000, as against between 6 and 9 per cent in each of Algeria, Egypt, Israel, Jordan, Lebanon and Syria and around 12 per cent in Morocco and Tunisia in 2001 (IMF 2003a: 92). For lower-middle-income countries as a whole, wages and salaries accounted for approximately 22 per cent of total expenditure during the latter half of the 1990s (somewhat less than 10 per cent of GDP),[5] while Gupta *et al.* (2002) report similar shares for a sample of 39 low-income countries (25 per cent of total expenditure and 7 per cent of GDP). This relatively high ratio for the PA may reflect in part the 2000 fall in GDP; but as Table 4.3 shows, the ratio in 1999, before the crisis, was still 11.6 per cent of GDP, significantly bigger than comparator countries. The evolution of total expenditure is also telling. While in 1996 wage and non-wage expenditures were of comparable size, there was some tendency for the former to rise more rapidly with the increase in public sector employment, which was around 10 per cent at an annual rate from 1997 to 2000; and the growth was in both civil service and security jobs. This phenomenon was largely a response to strong political pressures to increase public sector employment, not least the importance of jobs for returning PLO personnel. However, two things should be noted here. First, the WBGS figure does not include the significant wage bill for people employed by UNRWA. Second, the distribution of new posts was poorly directed: nearly half of public sector workers were employed in the security services, and there continued to be shortages in education, health and the judiciary (Erickson von Allmen 2001: 14).

Table 4.3 The PA's employment and wage bill

	1995	*1999*	*2002*
Employment (1000)	57.0	98.5	124.8
Civil service	32.6	54.1	71.2
Security	24.4	44.4	53.6
Wage bill (mill NIS)	915.9	2,163.5	3,198.0
Civil service	583.3	1,323.5	1,952.5
Security	332.6	840.0	1.245.5
Wage bill as % of GDP	8.6	11.6	22.6

Source: IMF (2003).

Fiscal reforms and the 2003 budget

An attempt was made to deal with some of these weaknesses in the Economic Policy Framework which was introduced in June 2000 in response to growing dissatisfaction among donors. The diversion of revenues was largely ended, but public sector wage employment, which was still only imperfectly controlled by the MoF, continued to rise. There was a sharp squeeze on non-wage spending but a continued, albeit slower, rise in the wage bill: this was largely the result of a conscious decision by the PA to offset, in the way and to the extent that it could, the economic depression associated with the Israeli closures.

A second wave of reforms was initiated in June 2002, partly in response to the deepening political crisis resulting from Israeli incursions into the WBGS. The most important of these reforms were the consolidation of all public revenue – including the profits from PA commercial assets – into a Single Treasury Account; the introduction of stricter controls on spending, with limits on the growth of employment to be properly enforced; increased transparency in the budget; the bringing together of all the PA's commercial assets in the Palestinian Investment Fund, with the introduction of policies to prevent monopolistic practices; and moves to reform existing pension systems (IMF 2003a: 102).

Fundamental to the budget plan for 2003 were an agreement by which the Israeli government resumed the transfer of clearance revenues, including the gradual transfer of the arrears that had built up since January 2001, and expectations of continued external donor support of $535 million for recurrent and $212 million for development expenditure. The budget also envisaged a continuation of the current low level of domestic revenue and a freeze on the wage bill, together with a much needed fillip to non-wage spending which had been cut in the two previous years. The intention was that the transfer of past clearance revenues would be used mainly to reduce the PA's expenditure arrears and repay some bank borrowing, while it was assumed that significant external budgetary support would continue.[6]

Fiscal challenges for a new Palestinian state

A political settlement based on the principles spelt out in the introduction to this volume (an independent and fully sovereign Palestinian state in the WBGS) will change the nature of some of the key features dealt with in the previous section. For example, the state will enjoy greater autonomy over the design of its tax structure and the problems of fiscal leakages will no longer exist, while relationships with external donors may be expected to take on a different character. At the same time, however, the new circumstances of independence and the return of refugees will intensify other problems and bring with them new fiscal challenges as well. In this section we start by considering the macroeconomic constraints within which any future fiscal stance must be defined before turning to a range of structural issues.

Defining a sustainable fiscal stance

A desirable sustainable fiscal stance should have three different attributes:

1 a tax structure which maximises revenue while maintaining tax rates which are stable, progressive, but not excessive;
2 a path for the fiscal deficit which is consistent with stable and low inflation, a moderate debt to income ratio and a path for the domestic interest rate which does not directly threaten short-term macroeconomic performance;
3 a fiscal stance that is counter-cyclical and hence capable of smoothing shocks to private sector consumption.

One of the striking aspects of the short history of the PA has been the remarkable degree of overall fiscal control, at least up to the period of the second intifada, which means that the new state can contemplate the design of a fiscal strategy without having to deal with the latent fiscal and debt crises that plague many low-income countries. As we noted earlier, although the PA's overall budget deficit has been substantial since the mid 1990s, this has principally reflected substantial levels of (highly concessional) external finance. By contrast, the domestic net borrowing requirement (i.e. the overall budget deficit after foreign financing and the accumulation of arrears) remained at relatively low levels between 1996 and 1999, moving from a deficit of 1.4 per cent of GDP in 1996 to a small surplus of 0.3 per cent of GDP in 1999 (Table 4.1b). These deficits, which were significantly lower than the 4 per cent of GDP average for low-income countries as a whole over the same period (IMF 2003b), meant that domestic debt on the eve of the crisis of 2000 was exceptionally low.

The revenue collapse occasioned by the closures of 2000–2002 clearly undercut this performance in a dramatic and debt-augmenting way, but the budget (and out-turn) for 2003 has seen the previous flow position more or less restored, even after the elimination of a significant proportion of the domestic arrears that built up during the period when revenue clearances from Israel were halted. Partly as a result of the speed with which fiscal balance was restored, and partly due to the high level of grant financing received from key international donors, this catastrophic fiscal shock saw external indebtedness rise to only just over 20 per cent of GDP.

While the relatively low level of debt and high revenue mobilisation are clearly of immense value to the putative fiscal regime, they mask a number of structural weaknesses in the fiscal set-up which ultimately limit the scope for active fiscal management. The first is that a significant proportion of tax revenue is raised through taxes which are either internationally negotiated (e.g. customs duties) or where the scope for varying rates is likely to be limited (e.g. VAT). Between 26 and 30 per cent of the PA's revenues during 1998–2000 came from customs duties (either collected directly by the PA or reimbursed by Israel, see Table 4.1a). This is a little higher than the average in low-income countries, but substantially higher than that in lower-middle-income countries (which is about 13 per cent). Customs duties amounted to 6.1 per cent of the WBGS's GDP in 2000, much more than in other Middle Eastern countries (IMF 2003a: 86). These ratios are surprisingly high in the light of the customs union arrangements with Israel, the 'fiscal leakages' already discussed, the interim Association agreement with the EU and a number of free trade arrangements with the Arab countries. It is clear, therefore, that the trade regime to be adopted by the Palestinian state will have significant effects on the PA's fiscal revenues. Customs duties are typically an easy and accessible source of revenues, and many developing countries hesitate to adopt a more rational and ultimately more beneficial trade regime in order to preserve that source of income. In the case of Palestine, however, a more appropriate trade regime (such as the non-discriminatory trade regime, recommended in Chapter 2 of this volume) may actually deliver higher customs revenues than the current customs union arrangements with Israel, thereby holding out the prospect that a future Palestinian government may be able to reduce customs rates without adverse effects on the gross proceeds. Set against this, however, is that whatever new trade regime replaces the Oslo arrangement will require Palestine to put in place a competent administrative structure to manage customs control and customs collections, and the cost of that may turn out to be higher than the fees currently charged by Israel for collecting customs and excises on behalf of the PA.

The relative size of these offsetting effects is difficult to assess (although see World Bank 2002, chapter 2 for a discussion of possible revenue effects), but whatever the change in net revenue yields from trade reforms, it will remain the case that a new Palestine will be heavily dependent on trade-based revenues. Since tariff and duty rates will continue to be constrained by international negotiation and the need to ensure that the trade regime remains competitive, a new Palestinian state is unlikely to find itself with much scope for discretionary changes in taxes.

The second, and certainly the most challenging, feature of the current budget is the size of the government wage bill. The PA figures may well overstate the size of the wage bill if the high level of off-budget expenditure is less labour intensive than that reported in the budget, but even so, and setting aside questions of the optimal composition of public expenditure, the large size of the public sector wage bill presents a serious challenge to efficient fiscal adjustment to adverse revenue shocks, especially in an environment of low inflation where any significant real wage adjustments will require correspondingly large nominal adjustments. Even in circumstances where employment legislation and public sector unions are relatively weak, it is notoriously difficult both to reduce the public sector wage bill when downward adjustment is required, and to oppose pressures to increase it in the face of positive external or revenue shocks, including aid surges. Tanzi (1993), for example, argues that efficiency wage effects are particular severe in public sector employment (since public sector employees are often better placed to switch into secondary employment in response to real wage cuts). The political economy literature, on the other hand, stresses the role of 'voracity effects' where the strength of interest groups can induce inefficiently large responses to positive revenue shocks and inefficiently small responses to negative ones (e.g. Tornell and Lane 1999; Adam and O'Connell 1999).

One implication of this kind of structural rigidity is that, in the face of revenue or interest rate shocks requiring expenditure adjustment, the cost of this adjustment will fall disproportionately on the non-wage component of the budget and, if evidence from elsewhere is any guide, on operations and maintenance expenditure on the public capital stock. The exact pattern of adjustment will depend in large measure on the fungibility of donor- and NGO-funded projects and programmes. If they are non-fungible, a much greater share of the cost of fiscal adjustments will fall on the PA's own non-wage budget.

This, in turn, raises two related issues. The first concerns the nature of the fiscal shocks a Palestinian budget might face, and the second is whether, and to what extent, the budget deficit may be used to smooth public expenditure, and thereby avoid costly non-wage expenditure adjustments.

Revenue and aid volatility

The revenue account is likely to be vulnerable to two sources of volatility. The first arises from the heavy dependence on revenue from tradable goods for which Palestine is, and will continue to be, a price-taker, and is likely to have limited discretion over tax rates. Given the openness of the Palestinian economy and the likelihood that the price elasticity of demand for imports is relatively low, the revenue account is therefore vulnerable to real exchange rate shocks which, unless there is rapid pass-through to public sector wages, will be transmitted rapidly onto either the budget deficit or, again, non-wage expenditure. In these circumstances, given the high non-tradable content of public expenditure, real exchange rate appreciations will tend to be budget worsening.

The second major source of vulnerability arises from the continued dependence of the budget on foreign aid. In the past foreign (concessional) financing of the PA budget has been high and volatile, at 5 per cent of GDP (25 per cent of revenue) in 1998 and 1999, but 16 per cent in 2002 (more than 100 per cent of domestic revenue). In the future it seems likely that foreign aid would peak immediately after a political settlement but would then begin to taper off. Aid can affect the budget in two ways. The first is through traditional 'Dutch disease' channels whereby aid inflows not only stimulate 'voracity effects' on the expenditure account but, to the extent that they induce an appreciation of the real exchange rate, may also reduce the domestic value of trade-based revenues. In the case of Palestine, while these Dutch disease effects may be potentially problematic in the medium-term, the short-run risks seem less severe since the combination of the exchange rate arrangements (discussed in Chapter 3) and the likely supply side effect of returning refugees is likely to mitigate the tendency for the nominal exchange rate to appreciate.

The second, and possibly more difficult, problem is that aid flows tend to be more volatile than domestic revenue (Bulir and Lane 2002). Moreover, and despite the fact that some elements of aid, such as food and emergency relief, are explicitly designed to be counter-cyclical, there is evidence that for most developing countries aid flows are weakly pro-cyclical. This reflects in part the effect of conditional aid programmes and the influence of political standoffs between donors and recipients, and in part the internal disbursement arrangements of donors. But these points mean that the likely continued high levels of aid to Palestine will not necessarily make the fiscal management task easier.

Deficit financing and monetary arrangements

The structural rigidities discussed above are not unique to Palestine, nor are they a defining feature of developing countries. In virtually all countries, international agreements and domestic political considerations limit discretion on revenue, while real wage rigidity and/or high non-distortionary expenditure constrain rapid expenditure adjustment. What matters, though is the extent to which deficit financing can be used to avoid costly tax rate adjustments and to smooth consumption in the face of output or other macroeconomic shocks. It is here that industrialised and developing countries are fundamentally different. Gavin and Perotti (1997) find that for industrialised countries the fiscal balance is strongly pro-cyclical, improving in good times and falling in bad times. Moreover, this pattern is strongly asymmetric so that fiscal deficits increase more in bad times, as expenditures increase, than they decrease in good times. This pattern – which implies a broadly sustainable fiscal stance over the medium-term – is consistent with efficient stabilising or tax-smoothing arguments in general, and with the idea that recessions are politically more costly (and require a more expansionary response) in particular. By contrast, for Latin American countries, they find that the fiscal balance is only very weakly pro-cyclical and that the cost of fiscal adjustment is overwhelmingly borne by expenditure adjustments. Adam and Bevan (2003) extend this analysis, showing that for middle-income developing countries the fiscal balance is broadly acyclical and the full weight of adjustment to output and hence revenue shocks falls on expenditure. In the lower income countries, while this is true for moderate output shocks, there is evidence that fiscal deficits are strongly pro-cyclical in response to adverse output shocks. Taken together, this suggests a pattern of fiscal response composed of either significant expenditure adjustment (in the case of middle-income countries) and/or periodically large fiscal deficits in low-income countries, where the latter are typically financed by arrears accumulation, unsustainable recourse to inflation tax, and debt default.

Given what has been written elsewhere, and the recommendations of Chapter 3, it seems reasonable to assume that the new state will soon introduce a new currency under a currency board arrangement with a peg to the NIS. Assuming that such an arrangement was sufficiently credible, this would strictly limit the government's use of central bank finance, and commercial bank borrowing. There would be some seigniorage but, as argued in Chapter 3, the likely seigniorage revenue at sensible inflation rates would be small. Thus in the short-run the scope for discretionary deficit financing would be heavily circumscribed and all fiscal adjustment would fall on non-wage expenditure. Over the medium-term, however, especially as the domestic debt market developed, there may be scope for shifting the task of short-run fiscal adjustment from expenditure to the deficit. But the need to maintain credible fiscal control will remain a priority.

Traditionally, for a government to 'tie its hands' to a fixed exchange rate or a currency board arrangement has been seen as a means of enforcing discipline. However, Tornell and Velasco (1995) have argued the reverse: by delaying the inflationary consequences of fiscal laxity, a fixed exchange rate regime can actually induce greater opportunism. Gavin and Perotti (1997) find weak evidence in support of this for Latin America, but the only robust evidence on exchange rate regimes and fiscal discipline appears to support the view that 'hard peg' arrangements do seem to foster robust fiscal restraint (Fatás and Rose 2001).

If greater exchange rate flexibility was pursued, the government could look to domestic rule-based mechanisms for fiscal control such as the cash budgets increasingly used in many sub-Saharan African countries. Such rules effectively place spending agencies and government as a whole on a cash-in-advance basis, thereby limiting the growth in reserve money. Aside from proving an effective method for addressing inflation (and domestic arrears) problems, such rules serve to embed day-to-day fiscal management in the culture of public policy and tend to strengthen the hand of central agencies (i.e. the Ministry of Finance) relative to spending agencies. The cost, of course, is that deficit rules necessarily imply a loss of discretion and return the whole burden of fiscal adjustment onto expenditure. Clearly there is a trade-off between credibility and discretion; if discretion is at risk of being abused, the case for rules is stronger.

Both the fiscal structure and the monetary/currency arrangement therefore imply a need for a conservative fiscal policy, such that deficits are kept to low levels even in adverse circumstances. Fiscal policy in the future is therefore likely to be unable to play anything more than the most minimalist role in stabilising employment and output – a position that was tacitly accepted in the 2003 budget.

Fiscal policy choices and structural challenges

Given the macroeconomic constraints on fiscal policy in a new Palestine, it follows that the most obvious challenge lies in maintaining the relatively vigorous growth of public revenues and in controlling and limiting the expansion of expenditure. In the past, the PA has benefited from the efficiency of the Israeli tax authorities in collecting taxes and has itself performed well in securing the documentation for reclaiming the money. In a fully sovereign state the Palestinian tax authority will be in charge of directly collecting the taxes, and this will require new administrative structures and skills, as well as substantial transparency and comprehensive enforcement. And if the PA does not continue to collect at least the same proportion of taxes to GDP as during the Oslo period, the arguments about fiscal leakage will lose much of their force.

Attitudes to paying taxes

It is hardly surprising that an anti-tax culture flourished among the Palestinians during the long years of occupation. People did not see either collective or personal benefits in return for paying taxes and tax evasion was considered as a form of resistance against the occupiers. Prior to 1994, Palestinians were systematically 'over-taxed'. Taxes to the Civil Administration and the Israeli treasury in the 1980s and early 1990s amounted to some 18–24 per cent of GDP. At the same time the level of public expenditure was less than 15 per cent of GDP, which 'is very low compared to other countries and implies a net transfer to the treasury' (UNCTAD 1996: 35).[7] Changing that attitude will be difficult and will take time but it is essential, not only to secure sufficient public revenues to finance the public services, but also to consolidate the democratic foundations of the future Palestinian society. At the same time a successful strategy to change attitudes and to enhance social commitment will require significant accountability, transparency and public participation in decision-making.

Reconstruction and development expenditure

A future independent Palestinian state will confront three major expenditure challenges: the short-run requirement for large reconstruction and development expenditure; the medium-term challenge of responding to the demographic change, including the consequences of absorbing returnees; and the longer-term challenge of funding high quality social services from own resources.

The most pressing challenge will be the need for immediate large-scale infrastructural spending to rebuild facilities destroyed by Israeli military action, to establish an adequate social and physical infrastructure and to reorganise the road network to reintegrate the Palestinian territories. Soon after the signing of the DoP the World Bank designed an emergency assistance programme for the Occupied Palestinian Territories with a total cost of $3.7bn over the five-year period 1994–1998. The Bank estimated that $2.4bn of this would be in the form of public investment, to be financed almost entirely by international donations, while the remaining $1.3bn would come from private capital inflow. These estimates are no longer valid: some of the infrastructural spending was carried out but there has been widespread destruction of public and private properties carried out by the Israeli army during the years of the second intifada. It is unrealistic to assume that the PA would be able to finance a comprehensive reconstruction programme from its own resources. However, it is important that the PA should, from the beginning, devote a share of its revenues to reconstruction and long-term development, not only to emphasise that all expenditure should ultimately be financed from its own resources in the long-run, but also to affirm Palestinian national 'ownership' of the development strategy. The allocation of a modest amount of money to development projects in the PA's 2003 budget is a positive sign in that direction.[8]

As the Palestinian government increasingly contributes directly to the finance, as well as the design and control, of reconstruction and development efforts, the case for an integrated budget incorporating all the activities of the public sector is strengthened. There are some arguments for maintaining a partition between the recurrent budget (predominantly government-financed) and the development programme (predominantly donor-funded), reflecting principally the greater uncertainty over the scale and timing of donor funding. However, as the evidence from highly aid-dependent low-income countries is beginning to suggest, these arguments are outweighed by the gains in terms of the coherence and coordination of public expenditure that derive from integrated frameworks for public expenditure management. Moreover, the same evidence suggests that an inclusive and integrated budgetary framework tends to strengthen the hand of governments relative to donors in ensuring that public expenditure as a whole reflects domestic government priorities rather than those of external donors.[9]

Demographic changes

Public finance is highly sensitive to demographic change, and Palestine is likely to experience significant demographic shifts in the next few years, even without taking the issue of returnees into account. The PCBS's estimates suggest that endogenous population growth in the WBGS will decline to 3.2 per cent by the year 2010 (from about 3.8 per cent in 1999) but labour force growth will outpace that substantially and will reach an annual rate of 4.4 per cent (see Davoodi and Erickson von Allmen 2001). The impact of the resulting significant rise in the share of the labour force in total population could be 'unambiguously positive for fiscal revenues', leading to an increase in fiscal revenues by 1.3 per cent of GDP, according to Jenkner (2001: 100). Obviously, this is subject to the condition that the economy would be able to provide employment and absorb the additional labour force. On the other hand, the same study argues that the demographic impact will be 'less clear for expenditure', but suggests that the reduction in the age-dependency ratio (smaller proportions of people older than 65 and of school children relative to total population) along with stringent expenditure control would reduce expenditure by 1.4 per cent of GDP. Thus, natural demographic change in the WBGS by the year 2010 would lead to fiscal consolidation, reducing the budget deficit by a little less than 3 per cent of GDP.

The same framework was applied by Jenkner to examine the impact of a possible return of 600,000 refugees to the WBGS. She concluded that revenues would rise by a further 0.3 per cent of GDP while expenditure would fall, through a further slight reduction in the age-dependency ratio, by a further 0.3 per cent. Thus, the budget deficit could shrink by a further 0.6 per cent by 2010. The study concluded that 'Immigration may have beneficial macroeconomic and fiscal effects over the medium-term – but only if the economy is able to generate and sustain employment without undue compression in real wages' (Jenkner 2001: 111).[10]

However, as Jenkner points out in several places in her study, her analysis is based on some simple and questionable assumptions: not only that the economy would achieve sufficient growth to absorb the ever expanding labour force (at reasonable real wages), but also that the policy environment in Palestine would be conducive to growth in general and with respect to the tax system and trade regime in particular. Equally important is the implicit assertion that current per capita public expenditures, by the PA or the UNRWA, whether in the form of social services or infrastructural spending, are generally adequate and would be capable of supporting the assumed acceleration of growth in the economy.[11]

Overall, then, there are no inevitable adverse consequences of the demographic shifts which the WBGS are expected to face in the near future. Population increase, and labour force growth in particular, could make it easier to pursue a 'sound' fiscal policy – but this depends crucially on whether the additional labour could be absorbed and on the policy decisions which are made with respect to both revenue collection and public expenditure. The PA's policy decisions could turn the demographic shifts into a fiscal blessing or a fiscal curse.

Public services and social expenditure

Along with the poor state of basic physical infrastructure, the WBGS suffers from limited and deteriorating public services which, in a number of important areas, are worse than in neighbouring Arab countries. Per capita consumption of electricity is substantially lower than in neighbouring countries, as well as the number of doctors per 100,000 inhabitants, fresh water supply and sewerage (only 38 per cent of total households in the WBGS are connected to sewerage networks). Poverty is widespread (20 per cent of households in 1998 were earning less than NIS1460 per month), provision of cultural services is extremely limited, illiteracy is as high as 14 per cent (1997), there is a large number of pupils per class (37.5 pupils per class at the secondary level and 47.7 pupils at the elementary level in the UNRWA schools), and over 40 per cent of the population are without health insurance of any type.[12]

The new Palestinian state is likely to want to assume a significantly wider responsibility for social spending of various kinds, notably education and health, partly to improve the levels of service currently on offer and partly because it will eventually have to take over those services now provided by UNRWA and other NGOs. Actually, about 28 per cent of the students enrolled in basic education in the WBGS were in UNRWA schools in the school year 1999/2000 (MAS 2000). Table 4.2 shows the levels of expenditure by UNRWA in recent years, both in the WBGS and in the refugee camps elsewhere. Assuming that most of the residents of the refugee camps in neighbouring countries will return to the WBGS (see Arnon and Kanafani, Chapter 10 in this volume), then it is not totally unrealistic to suggest that all of this expenditure – some $344 million in 2003 as against $1278 million of expenditure in the PA's budget – will need to be assumed by the PA.

Additional costs will be involved in enhancing the provision, and the quality, of public services. Health and unemployment insurance as well as comprehensive pension schemes are of particular importance here. However, it is possible to design insurance schemes to be self-financing and fiscally neutral (see Sayre and Olmsted, Chapter 7 in this volume), and this will ease a fiscal burden which is already large enough.

The tax system as a policy tool

Alongside their primary role of providing revenues to fund public expenditure, tax systems are often designed to fulfil two other major functions: the redistribution of income between different social groups and the stimulation of growth by mobilising savings and changing the incentive structure to divert investment and consumption in specific directions.

Due to lack of reliable data on household income distribution (see World Bank 2001: 26) we rely instead on the distribution of consumption expenditure. Distribution of consumption reveals poverty more directly than income distribution, but inequality with respect to consumption can also be substantially lower than inequality as measured by the distribution of income. Table 4.4 makes clear that, while average per capita consumption in the West Bank was more than 25 per cent higher than that in Gaza, inequality was almost identical in the two regions in 1998. Average consumption of an individual in the richest quintile is about five times that of a person in the poorest quintile, and the richest 20 per cent of the population undertake about 40 per cent of total consumption.

This is the sort of inequality that a steeply progressive income tax scheme can aim to address. In fact the PA had such a scheme with a high marginal tax rate up to 1999, when it was substantially reformed and replaced by a less progressive system with lower tax rates. Table 4.5 shows the income tax rates and brackets for 1995–1998, and since 1999. While in

Table 4.4 Inequality in Palestine: consumption expenditure per capita by quintile, 1998

Quintile (fifth)	*West Bank*		*Gaza Strip*	
	US$	*Per cent*	*US$*	*Per cent*
Top 20%	3,027	39.0	2,227	39.7
Fourth 20%	1,762	22.7	1,245	22.2
Middle 20%	1,324	17.1	937	16.7
Second 20%	1,007	12.9	727	13.0
Lowest 20%	636	8.2	472	8.4
Average	1,551		1,122	

Source: World Bank (2001).

Table 4.5 Income brackets and tax rates

Pre-reform: 1995–1998		*Post-reform: since 1999*	
Income bracket (NIS)	*Tax rate (%)*	*Income bracket (NIS)*	*Tax rate (%)*
From 1–4,200	5	From 1–27,000	5
From 4,201–10,500	10	From 27,501–66,000	10
From 10,501–16,800	15	From 66,001–110,000	15
From 16,801–29,400	20	From 110,001–above	20
From 29,401–50,400	30		
From 50,401–84,000	35		
From 84,001–147,000	40		
From 147,001 above	48		
Corporate tax:		*Corporate tax:*	
Gaza Strip	37.5	WBGS	20
West Bank	38.5		

Source: Ministry of Finance (cited in Erickson von Allmen 2001).

the former case there were eight brackets with tax rates varying from 5 per cent to 48 per cent, the structure introduced in 1999 has only four brackets and a top rate of 20 per cent. At the same time the corporate tax rate was reduced from 38.5 per cent in the West Bank, and 37.5 per cent in the Gaza Strip, to 20 per cent. This tax reform would appear to have undermined both the pursuit of redistribution and the PA's proceeds from income taxes. But the experience of the past decades, in both developed and developing countries, has demonstrated that high marginal rates have strong negative effects on incentives, and correspond usually with widespread tax evasion and corruption. In addition, a highly progressive income tax system requires for its implementation a highly sophisticated administrative apparatus. Modern conventional wisdom in public finance suggests that a simpler income tax scheme with lower marginal rates leads to higher rather than to lower tax proceeds (as the result of simpler administration, weaker incentives to evade and stronger incentives to earn). Modern thinking in public finance also stresses that a progressive income tax can play only a limited role in bringing about substantial redistribution of income, and that this can be more efficiently achieved via the allocation of public expenditure. Thus the PA's income tax reform does make economic sense and may actually lead to larger tax proceeds. But this also implies that more emphasis should be placed on public expenditure to achieve equity targets.

Redistribution could also be pursued by the imposition of excises and special purchase taxes (and high customs duties) on luxury goods. But the trade-off between equity objectives and maximisation of the tax proceeds is even stronger here than with progressive income taxes: to maximise the proceeds, excise should be imposed on goods with low price elasticity of demand, but these goods are usually income inelastic (since they are consumed also by the poor). The chronic dilemmas between the efficiency, neutrality and equity objectives of the tax system are behind the near-universal tendency to depend increasingly on VAT to finance public expenditure. The main attractions of this indirect tax are its relative simplicity, its low 'excess burden' and its limited distortionary effects. However, VAT is an unambiguously regressive tax, especially when it is set at the same rate on all goods. As already noted, the Paris Protocol required the PA to set VAT at a rate close to Israel's. The main aim behind this was to prevent harmful consequences to the Israeli economy in the absence of a customs border with the WBGS. UNCTAD (1996: 33) had earlier argued forcefully that 'Fifteen per cent is a very high rate for the Palestinian economy in its present state of development. A much lower rate may be considered more appropriate from the viewpoint of equity and growth consideration', while the rates on the newly introduced VAT in Jordan and Lebanon were set at 13 per cent and 10 per cent respectively. Jordan's proceeds from a 13 per cent rate amounted to 8.2 per cent of its GDP in the year 2001, while the 17 per cent rate brought VAT revenues equal to 7.2 per cent of GDP only in the year 2000 in the WBGS and 10.4 per cent in Israel (IMF 2003a: 86). This may be due to the narrow base of the (high) VAT rate in the WBGS, which suggests that it would be possible to reduce the VAT rate without negatively affecting the tax proceeds provided the tax base was expanded (one reason for the narrowness of the tax base in the WBGS is the preponderance of small enterprises which, under the Paris Protocol, are exempted from VAT). On the other hand, the regressive nature of the tax can be eased either by introducing multiple VAT rates (lower on basic staple foods and services) or by exempting these goods and services from VAT altogether. But these measures imply, of course, narrowing the tax base.[13]

The second major function of a tax system is to stimulate growth by mobilising savings and changing the incentive structure to direct investment and consumption in specific directions. However, the idea that higher taxes can increase savings and investment is now subject to serious doubts as governments' propensity to consume has proved to be in many instances much higher than that of the private sector. The PA has deployed the income tax tool to encourage investment. Under the investment promotion law most investment projects benefit from income tax holidays during the first ten years of operation. This explains why almost all of the modest amount of income taxes collected in the WBGS came from individuals rather than from companies. But the experiences of other countries do not show that such tax exemptions substantially encourage corporate investments (Naqib 1996). Many countries also use variation in income tax rates as a tool in their regional development policy, to encourage investment in underprivileged regions.[14] It may be argued that property in general, and real estate in particular, is under-taxed in the WBGS, and that more appropriate taxation here would moderate the strong historic tendency for a substantial amount of domestic investment to be directed towards residential construction. Much will depend here on the future influx of the returnees and the fate of the housing units in the Israeli settlements in the WBGS (see Arnon and Kanafani, Chapter 10 in this volume). What remains certain, however, is that the clash between using the tax structure as incentive instrument and maximising public revenues will remain a major dilemma for policy makers.

Summary and conclusion

In the Oslo period the PA succeeded in creating new budgetary mechanisms where none had previously existed, increasing its revenues to internationally respectable levels, and keeping overall deficits and debt under control, at least up to the start of the second intifada in late 2000. However, the PA relied heavily on indirect taxes to generate revenue, the clearance arrangements were a source of vulnerability (as demonstrated in 2001–2002 when the Israeli government refused to transfer the revenues it collected), the PA's accounts were not comprehensive (some revenues and expenditures were effectively off-budget), and its spending, with respect to public sector employment in particular, was not firmly under control. The overall performance was also heavily dependent on foreign aid, and there was an undesirable split between recurrent and development budgets. The intifada created additional pressures on the budget, and one outcome of these was an intensification of fiscal reform from 2002.

A new Palestinian state, which will inherit its basic budgetary arrangements from the PA, will face a series of new challenges in a variety of areas. It would be hard to change the fiscal structure significantly, even in the medium-term, which means that revenue will continue to be subject to volatility arising from external trade and aid shocks, while expenditure is difficult to adjust. Moreover, the likely monetary and currency arrangements – in the form of a currency board peg to the NIS and later a hard peg to the euro, as discussed in Chapter 3 – will limit the possibility of deficit financing. Hence the fiscal structure, on the one hand, and the likely monetary arrangements, on the other, indicate the need for a conservative fiscal policy, with budget deficits to be kept low even in adverse circumstances. At the same time the new state will need to grapple with the development of public services (and the take-over of those currently provided by UNRWA and other NGOs), the demand for large-scale reconstruction and development, demographic changes and the return of refugees.

Efforts should be made to enhance public revenues through broadening the tax base rather than increasing the tax rates. Equity issues are probably better dealt with via expenditure policy rather than high marginal taxes. Foreign support to the PA's budget, which has been so important, is unlikely to decline abruptly in the early years after the establishment of the new state. Thus, international goodwill, together with compensation from Israel (as argued in Chapter 10), would allow the new authority to spend more than it collects for some years. What is essential, however, is to start planning, from the beginning, to achieve a sustainable fiscal stance in the foreseeable future. The fiscal challenges are not insuperable but the momentum of the reforms, which the PA has already initiated, will need to be maintained and taken further, not least in the areas of transparency and involving the public at large in selecting the priorities and deciding upon their ranking.

Notes

1 GDP estimates for WBGS remain highly tentative. The values used in Table 4.1b are taken from IMF (2003a: 23, Table 2.2).

2 The *World Development Report 2004* (World Bank 2003) defines lower-middle-income countries as those with per capita Gross National Income in 2002 of between \$736 and \$2934, based on the World Bank Atlas Method.

3 The Paris Protocol, the economic agreement within the Oslo Accords, required

the PA to levy VAT at a minimum of 15 per cent compared with the rate in Israel which was then at 17 per cent. Israel increased its VAT rate to 18 per cent in mid 2002, and the PA is generally following the Israeli rate. The Protocol specified also that VAT exemption can be applied only to businesses with annual turnover of less than $12,000.

4 Israel began in 2000 to transfer some purchase tax revenue on Palestinian purchases of Israeli goods, but a methodology put forward by the PA for taking account of the customs duties and purchase tax on indirect imports was rejected by the Israeli government in the summer of 2000 (IMF 2003a: 87).

5 World Development Indicators (2001).

6 Preliminary indications from the monthly reports published on the internet by the MoF (at http://www.mof.gov.ps/reports.htm, accessed 12 January 2004) suggest that both revenues and the wage bill were slightly above plan, and external finance was well below the expected level. The PA was therefore cutting back on non-wage spending, repaying less arrears than hoped, and borrowing from rather than repaying the domestic banking sector.

7 Until 1994 most of the taxes paid by the Palestinians went directly to the Israeli treasury and expenditure by the Civil Administration, the Israeli body which was in charge of running the WBGS, and spending by municipalities was limited to the revenues collected by them (taxes, fees and utility tariffs). The shortfall between the revenues collected by the Civil Administration and the amount of taxes that were actually paid by the Palestinians led to what the World Bank called 'fiscal compression and underfinancing of public sector investment needs'. During the 1970–1990 period, public sector capital expenditure amounted to a mere 3.5 per cent of GDP in the Occupied Territories, which was significantly below the average for developing countries (World Bank 1993 volume 1: 10).

8 There is a 'fungibility' risk here, though: the PA has allocated some resources to urgent development projects because of the lack of foreign aid to finance such projects, but when foreign finance becomes available, the PA might shift those resources back to financing recurrent expenditure.

9 The difficulties of classifying expenditures are well known. For example, expenditure on education and health which are in the recurrent budget could also be considered as investment expenditure which would increase the economy's productive capacity in future.

10 The Jenkner study did not take account of the point that the PA will have to take responsibility for all the services currently provided by the UNRWA, whether for the refugees that are resident in the WBGS or for the 600,000 returning refugees. She made a very rough estimate of these costs, putting them at $394 million per year (some 9 per cent of GDP in 2000), and concluded that 'Obviously, such an expense could not be covered by an improved revenue effort alone but highlights that sustained donor support will be required together with stringent expenditure controls in the PA' (Jenkner 2001: 110).

11 Text books in public finance stress the importance of Wagner's Law according to which the relative weight of the public sector (as a percentage of GDP) tends to increase with the increase in per capita income. As often with these types of trends, it is difficult to establish strictly the line of causality. However, the endogenous growth theory literature argues that long-term growth can depend heavily on the level and nature of public expenditure and the strategy underlying it.

12 For information about the state of the physical infrastructure see Mody (1999). Comprehensive coverage of various social/cultural indicators is available in *MAS Social Monitor* (2000 and 2001).

13 The adoption of multiple VAT rates involves administrative difficulties as well as a higher degree of distortion in relative prices. There is a trade-off between equity (based on the concept of 'ability to pay' and the notion that the richer should pay more) and distortions: the least distorting tax is a 'neutral' tax, a tax which leaves the relative prices of goods and services intact. Lebanon's 10 per cent VAT was introduced in February 2002, but with the exemption of a relatively long list of activities and goods including livestock and raw agricultural products, bread, milk, yoghurt, pasta, baby food, feed, books and newspapers, gas for household consumption, agricultural machinery, medicines, etc. The Lebanese Ministry of Finance expects the 10 per cent VAT to produce revenues equal to 4 per cent of GDP (see the VAT Law, Ministry of Finance, December 2001 at http://www.finance.gov.lb/main/vat/vatlaw_e02.pdf, accessed 1 January 2004.

14 Regional imbalance is apparent in the WBGS, not only between Gaza and the West Bank, as made clear in Table 4.4, but also within each area. About one-half of the poor in Palestine live in three districts: Khan Yunis, Gaza City and Hebron (World Bank 2001: 6).

References

Abed, G. *et al.* (1998) *Fiscal Reforms in Low Income Countries*, IMF occasional paper 160.

Adam, C. and Bevan, D. (2003) 'Staying the course: maintaining fiscal discipline in developing countries' in S. Collins and D. Rodrik (eds) *Brookings Institution Trade Forum 2003*.

Adam, C. and O'Connell, S. (1999) 'Aid, taxation and development in sub-Saharan Africa', *Economics and Politics* 11: 225–254.

Bulir, A. and Lane, T. (2002) 'Aid and Fiscal Management', IMF working paper 02/112.

Davoodi, H. and Erickson von Allmen, U. (2001) 'Demographics and long-term growth in the Palestinian economy', in R. Valdivieso, U. Erickson von Allmen, G. Bannister, H. Davoodi, F. Fischer, E. Jenkner and M. Said (eds) *West Bank and Gaza: Economic Performance, Prospects and Policies*, Washington, DC: IMF.

Dumas, J-P. (1999) 'Fiscal leakage in the West Bank and Gaza Strip', MEDA Team, MEDA Programme, EU Directorate General 1B.

Erickson von Allmen, U. (2001) 'Recent developments in the Palestinian economy', in R. Valdivieso, U. Erickson von Allmen, G. Bannister, H. Davoodi, F. Fischer, E. Jenkner and M. Said, *West Bank and Gaza: Economic Performance, Prospects and Policies*, Washington, DC: International Monetary Fund.

Fatás, A. and Rose, A. (2001) 'Do monetary handcuffs restrain Leviathan? Fiscal policies in extreme exchange rate regimes', IMF Special Papers 47 (special issue): 40–61.

Gavin, M. and Perotti, R. (1997) 'Fiscal Policy in Latin America', NBER Macroeconomics Annual, 11–61.

Gupta, S., Clements, B., Baldacci, E. and Mulas-Granados, C. (2002) 'Expenditure composition, fiscal adjustment and growth in low-income countries', IMF Working Paper 02/77.

International Monetary Fund (2003a) *West Bank and Gaza: Economic Performance and Reform under Conflict Conditions*, Washington, DC: IMF.

International Monetary Fund (2003b) 'Role of the fund in low-income member countries over the medium term – issues paper for discussion' IMF paper SM/03/257.

Jenkner, E. (2001) 'Fiscal policy: the challenges from demographic dynamics and other medium-term developments', in R. Valdivieso, U. Erickson von Allmen, G. Bannister, H. Davoodi, F. Fischer, E. Jenkner and M. Said, *West Bank and Gaza: Economic Performance, Prospects and Policies*, Washington, DC: IMF.

Kanafani, N. (2001) 'Trade – a catalyst for peace', *Economic Journal* 111: F276–F290.

MAS (1999) *MAS Economic Monitor*, no. 5, June, Jerusalem and Ramallah: MAS.

MAS (2000) *MAS Social Monitor*, no. 3, February, Jerusalem and Ramallah: MAS.

MAS (2001) *MAS Social Monitor*, no. 4, May, Jerusalem and Ramallah: MAS.

Mody, A. (1999) 'Infrastructure for growth', in I. Diwan and R. Shaban (eds) *Development Under Adversity: The Palestinian Economy in Transition*, Washington, DC: MAS and the World Bank.

Naqib, F. (1996) *A Preliminary Evaluation of the Tax System in the West Bank and Gaza Strip*, Jerusalem and Ramallah: MAS.

Owen, R. and Pamuk, S. (1998) *A History of Middle East Economies in the Twentieth Century*, London: I.B. Tauris.

Paris Protocol (1994) *Protocol on Economic Relations Between the Government of Israel and the P.L.O., Representing the Palestinian People*, reproduced in the Appendix to Arnon *et al.* (1997) also available at http://www.pna.gov.ps/key_decuments/Protocol_on_Economic_Relations.pdf (accessed 14 January 2004).

Pattillo, C.A., Poirson, H. and Ricci, L. (2002) 'External debt and growth', IMF working paper 02/69.

Tanzi, V. (1993) 'Fiscal issues in adjustment programs', in R. Faini and J. de Melo (eds) *Fiscal Issues in Adjustment in Developing Countries*, London: Macmillan.

Tornell, A. and Lane, P. (1999) 'The voracity effect', *American Economic Review* 89: 22–46.

Tornell, A. and Velasco, A. (1995) 'Fiscal discipline and the choice of exchange rate regime', *European Economic Review* 39: 759–770.

UNCTAD (1996) *Prospects for Sustained Development of the Palestinian Economy: Strategies and Policies for Reconstruction and Development*, Geneva.

UNCTAD (2001) *The Palestinian Economy: Achievements of the Interim Period and Tasks for the Future*, Geneva.

World Bank (1993) *Developing the Occupied Territories – An Investment in Peace*, 6 volumes, Washington, DC: World Bank.

World Bank (2001) *Poverty in the West Bank and Gaza*, Washington, DC: World Bank.

World Bank (2002) *Long Term Policy Options for the Palestinian Economy*, Washington, DC: World Bank.

World Bank (2003) *World Development Report 2004: Making Services Work for Poor People*, Washington, DC: World Bank.

Discussion

Adel Zagha

Adam, Cobham and Kanafani have contributed a comprehensive chapter on which there is limited scope for comment. The book comes out at a critical juncture in Palestinian political development, and it is useful to have a few optimists to remind us that dreams imply challenges, and addressing those challenges is part of the process by which the dream can be realised.

There is no doubt that fiscal viability is a building block in the process of state formation. The authors have pointed out important challenges explicitly and sometimes implicitly. They give insights into the interrelations and interactions between fiscal, monetary and demographic challenges. Of course, they cannot be expected to draw a precise road map by which these challenges can be addressed, but they have been able to point out the advantages and disadvantages of certain trends. As usual, it is left to the political interaction in the Palestinian arena (given the final status agreement with Israel and the donor support) to find the way to equilibrium positions based upon the weights that might be given to the pros and cons of certain actions.

Palestine is going to be a latecomer to the community of national states. Is it going to benefit from this situation and be able to avoid the obvious mistakes of other countries, or is it going to be beset by the traditional problems of developing nations? How can the Palestinians reorganise their fiscal arrangements to help themselves out of the misery of a prolonged occupation and the failure of the Palestinian Authority to lay down the basis for a sustained development path? What is required for them to choose the right mix of policies?

I agree that there will be a 'need for a conservative fiscal policy, with budget deficits to be kept low even in adverse circumstances'. But what is the right mix of public expenditure that would be conducive to sustainable development? Should education and health be marginalised again? Are the security services going to consume Palestinian resources while not creating enough security? Is the maintenance of the infrastructure going to be ignored with the obvious fatal consequences for sustainable development? These questions and some others are not stressed enough in the chapter.

Maybe there was not enough space left for these issues. Maybe it is premature to seek answers for these questions. But we have to realise that it is a matter not just of how much resources the government has at its disposal, but of how these resources are utilised.

Population policy has been very important in the development of successful examples elsewhere in the world, including Egypt and Iran. It is well known that population growth can be a blessing as much as a curse. In a situation where downward wage rigidity is the rule, population growth will tend to have negative consequences including the loss of comparative advantage. I am sure that the majority of returnees will be from the younger generation and will add to fiscal pressures. Even without their return, public expenditure per capita in the areas of health and education is declining to levels which will make it difficult to sustain even the current low standards of education and health over the next ten years. Human resources in the wider sense of the word are increasingly becoming the substitute for the lack of physical capital. When these human resources are ignored what is left? Given the momentum behind population growth, an independent Palestinian state is not going to be viable without the immediate introduction of a comprehensive population policy. This is consistent with the conclusion that 'equity issues are probably better dealt with via expenditure policy rather than high marginal taxes'.

I am totally in agreement with the conclusion about enhancing 'revenues through broadening the tax base rather than increasing the tax rates'. It has also been mentioned that there is great potential for property taxes both to raise revenues and for equity purposes. We are still far from 'taxation with representation'. The need to deepen the democratic culture and democratic processes is widely recognised to be an important factor in the reform of the tax system, and should be emphasised.

Moreover, as explained in Fjeldstad and Zagha (2002), the state formation process in Palestine during the period 1994–2000, in contrast to the European experience, was related not to inter-state war but to insurgency against, or negotiation with, Israeli occupation. This conflict did not contribute to an increase in the tax extracting capacity of the Palestinian National Authority (PNA) as wars did in the West. Although the conflict changed the relations between the new rulers and the ruled, relations of accountability between the PNA and citizens remained weak – perhaps because the government depended only partly on their citizens to mobilise revenues. The authority relied more on foreign aid and taxes on international trade instead. However, given its limited room for manoeuvre, the PNA maximised domestic revenues subject to the constraint of consolidating and maintaining power. In particular, the PNA was constrained by the bargaining powers of interest groups and by international factors in its efforts to mobilise tax revenues. Thus, the PNA used the tax system as a means of enhancing rents from industries and sectors in which the leadership had economic interests and, furthermore, to grant generous tax exemptions to potentially important stakeholders such as professionals and large expatriate capital. In contrast, few tax concessions were given to employees in the formal sector. Thus, the business interests of the minority of expatriate capitalists were more influential than trade unions and the emerging domestically based business associations. How would this trend affect the potential for tax reform in the future? Could the search for rents be transformed into a drive for tax reform? Could tax policy become developmental rather than just the extortion of public resources to the benefit of small influential interest groups?

The issue of the administrative aspect of the budget and fiscal policy in general has been overlooked. We have to acknowledge the very weak administration, especially in the fiscal affairs of the government. Competent administration is essential for a viable Palestinian state. Fiscal reform is not going to be successful if employment policy does not change systematically from a concentration on political loyalty to an emphasis on professional requirements, especially at the low and middle levels of the administration. This should be looked at as a continuous process in which training, education and continuing education programmes need to be developed to tackle this deficiency.

In conclusion, there is a potential for the Palestinians to re-embark on a sustainable path for development. There are many choices available to them. It is up to them to consolidate their fiscal stance, find niches in the world markets to further their integration, and increase their internal resources from a sustainable growing economy.

Reference

Fjeldstad, O-H. and Zagha, A. (2002) 'Between Oslo and al-Aqsa: taxation and state formation in Palestine 1994–2000', CMI report R, 2002: 13, Bergen: Chr. Michelsen Institute.

5 The role of the financial sector

Osama Hamed

Introduction

Following the closure of all banks soon after the Israeli occupation in 1967, there was little formal financial intermediation in the West Bank and Gaza Strip (WBGS) for almost 26 years. The few bank branches that operated in the WBGS in the period 1967–1993 were mainly deposit collection outlets with very little lending. Most savings of WBGS Palestinians in this period were kept as currency holdings or in financial institutions outside the WBGS, particularly in Jordan. Informal finance played a major role in this period. Money changers accepted deposits, arranged currency transfers and extended credit. Non-governmental organisations (NGOs) provided subsidised credit, particularly in the agricultural sector.

After the signing of the Oslo Accords in 1993 the number of banks operating in the WBGS rose sharply and bank deposits increased substantially. A stock exchange was also established during the post-Oslo period. Despite the expansion of bank deposits and the opening of a stock exchange, the Palestinian financial system in the post-Oslo period continued to be rudimentary. Bank lending remained limited. The loan-deposit ratio in the domestic banking system peaked at 40 per cent in September 2000, before declining after the start of the second intifada at the end of that month. The insurance industry has been limited almost exclusively to the automobile sector, which usually does not generate significant investment funds. Pension funds have not represented a significant source of investment funds for the domestic economy either. Pension benefits in the private sector have been limited to a few provident funds that deposit their accumulated funds at commercial banks. The retirement system that covers West Bank government employees has been a pay-as-you-go system. The funded pension schemes that cover Gaza Strip government employees and employees of the United Nations Relief and Works Agency (UNRWA) have not so far been a significant source of investment funds for the local economy. While the UNRWA pension scheme has accumulated several hundred million dollars, all of these funds have been invested abroad. The funds accumulated by the Gaza employees pension scheme were held by the Israeli authorities until the mid 1990s, when they were turned over to the PNA. There have been no indications since then that these funds have been invested directly in the Palestinian economy.

Competition from commercial banks, along with official regulation, severely limited customers' deposits as a source of funds for the informal sector in the post-Oslo period. However, some informal sector lenders, such as wholesalers and large money changers have had access to bank credit in this period, based on collateral or reputation capital. Hence, the informal sector has continued to be a major source of credit.

A permanent political settlement of the Palestinian–Israeli conflict will have far-reaching implications for the Palestinian financial system. It should be expected to result in a significant reduction in political uncertainty, which would in turn induce economic growth. It would most probably include financial compensation for Palestinian refugees, providing an important source of funds for the Palestinian financial system. Finally, a permanent political settlement would very likely result in the dismantlement of UNRWA. This would in turn release several hundred million dollars currently kept in the UNRWA employee pension fund, some of which will no doubt find its way to the Palestinian financial system.

A disproportionate share of economic growth in the period after the permanent settlement would most likely come from new companies because of constraints on existing companies imposed by the Israeli authorities over the years. A possible source of funds for new companies is diaspora Palestinians. Some diaspora Palestinians may limit their involvement in these companies to financial investment, while others may choose more extensive involvement. A potentially effective mechanism for involving diaspora Palestinians in building and nurturing new companies is the venture capital fund.

The Palestinian financial system in the post-permanent settlement period will most likely be dominated by commercial banks. A corporate bond market does not exist at the present time and cannot be expected to develop until proper conditions are created for the emergence of a public debt market. Based on the experience of other Arab countries, we should not expect the emergence of a significant life insurance industry due to cultural reasons. While pension funds may one day become an important source of investment funds, this should not be expected to be the case in the near future because of financial and institutional constraints. The creation of new companies and increased demand for the shares of existing companies, induced by an expected reduction in political uncertainty, will undoubtedly stimulate the equity market. However, the experience of other developing countries indicates that the growth potential of the equity market is limited.

The deposit base of the banking system will no doubt expand in the post-permanent settlement period. Some increase in bank lending should also be expected due to the reduction of political uncertainty. However, the loan-deposit ratio of the domestic banking system cannot be expected to reach the level of neighbouring countries unless mechanisms are put in place to increase the availability of collateral. Furthermore, a significant increase in bank lending will require expanding the bank supervisory capacity of the Palestinian monetary authority.

The informal financial sector will continue to play a significant role in the Palestinian economy after a permanent settlement. It will provide services to segments of the credit market usually ignored by the formal sector because of high transaction costs, such as small short-term loans. The informal sector will also provide start-up capital to new companies, and could be used to channel credit subsidies to the poor.

This chapter first surveys recent developments in the Palestinian banking system, and explores possible changes in the banking system in the post-settlement period, including policy options to stimulate bank lending. It goes on to examine current conditions of the equity market and its potential in channelling investment funds into the Palestinian economy. Finally, it looks at the role of informal finance in the Palestinian economy.

Commercial banks

The Oslo period

The WBGS banking sector expanded substantially in the Oslo period, following 26 years of severe Israeli restrictions.[1] By the end of September 2000, which marked the beginning of the intifada, there were 21 banks and 128 bank branches in the WBGS, compared to 2 and 13, respectively, at the end of 1993.[2] Most bank branches that opened in the post-Oslo period belonged to banks chartered in Jordan.[3]

By the end of September 2000, total deposits in the WBGS banking system stood at $3,721 million, compared with $219 million at the end of 1993. More than two-thirds of these deposits were at Jordanian bank branches. The shares of current accounts, savings accounts, and time deposits in WBGS deposits at the end of September 2000 are shown in Figure 5.1.

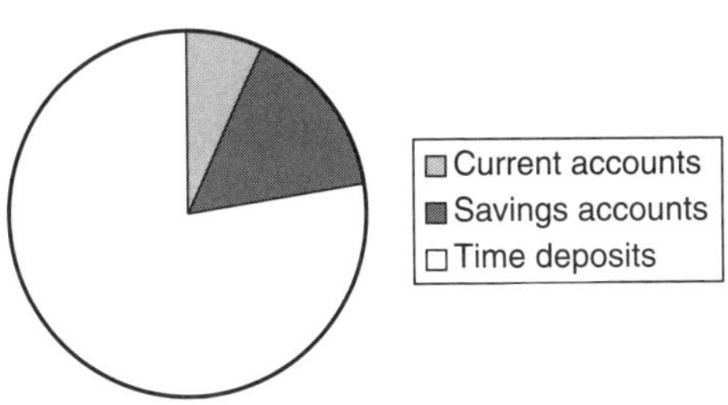

Figure 5.1 Distribution of deposits by type, September 2000 (source: PMA data).

Bank deposits during the direct occupation period were denominated exclusively in the new Israeli shekel (NIS) in the Gaza Strip, and in NIS as well as the Jordanian dinar in the West Bank. Accounts in other currencies were not allowed. The NIS was the main medium of exchange in both the West Bank and the Gaza Strip in this period. The currency composition of bank deposits in the Gaza Strip as well as the West Bank changed drastically in the Oslo period, despite continued use of the NIS as the main medium of exchange. In the Gaza Strip, a rapid dollarisation of bank deposits took hold soon after Israel relinquished its supervisory authority over the banking system in 1994.[4] In the West Bank, where the Jordanian dinar had been the main store of value during the direct occupation period, the dollarisation was more gradual (Figure 5.2).

Bank lending during the Oslo period did not keep pace with deposit growth and most of the loans were in the form of overdraft facilities, thus limiting the role of banks as financial intermediaries. At the end of September 2000, total outstanding loans for the WBGS banking system were $1,507.2 million, which translates into a loan-deposit ratio of 40.5 per cent. This ratio is substantially lower than comparable ratios in neighbouring countries.[5] Of total loans at the end of September 2000, 59.6 per cent were in overdraft facilities.

The intifada period

Despite frequent severe restrictions during the intifada, the Palestinian banking system has made amazing efforts to ensure customers' access to their deposits. To avoid disruptions during periods of severe travel restrictions, banks have provided their out-of-town employees with living accommodation within walking distance from bank premises. To deal with unexpected changes in withdrawal patterns, they have increased their cash holdings substantially. By the end of 2002, the cash-deposit ratio for the WBGS banking system was 4.7 per cent, compared to 2.6 per cent at the

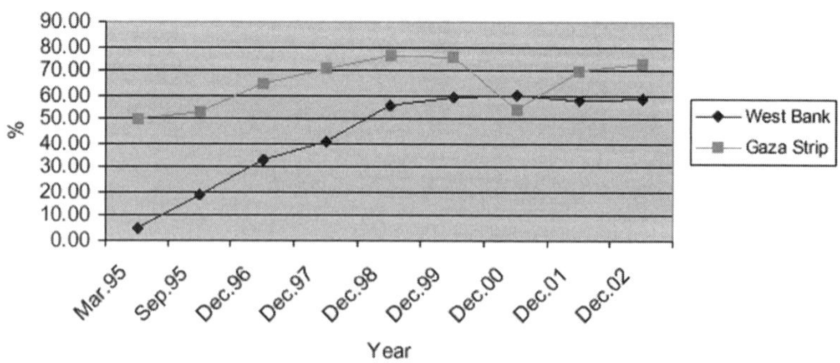

Figure 5.2 Share of the dollar in bank deposits, 1995–2002 (source: 1995 data from Hamed (1995), all other data from PMA).

end of September 2000. Such measures have been instrumental in maintaining public confidence in the banking system.

While anecdotal evidence indicates a sharp increase in bank loan default rates, and official statistics show a substantial decline in bank lending, a bank panic has so far been avoided and the decrease in bank deposits has been limited. Total deposits in the Palestinian banking system have not declined as sharply as overall economic activity during the intifada period, decreasing by only 8.5 per cent in the period September 2000–December 2002. One possible explanation for the limited drop in bank deposits is an increase in precautionary savings by households that were able to maintain their pre-intifada income levels, such as government employees and recipients of transfers from relatives abroad. Another possible explanation is the closing of bank accounts in Israeli banks that belonged to Palestinian workers in Israel and the transferring of the funds from these accounts to WBGS banks.[6] Total outstanding loans decreased by 36.5 per cent in the period September 2000–December 2002. If we add to that the increase in loan non-payment, which is not reflected in outstanding loan figures, the result is a substantial drop in new bank credit.

There has been no significant change in the distribution of WBGS bank deposits between current accounts, saving accounts and time deposits during the intifada (Figure 5.3). The currency composition of bank deposits has not changed significantly during the intifada either (Figure 5.2).

Future challenges and prospects

The main challenges facing the Palestinian banking system in the post-permanent settlement period are increasing lending, expanding bank supervisory capacity and dealing with the dominant role played by banks chartered in Jordan. Addressing the issue of Jordanian banks becomes particularly important once a Palestinian currency is introduced because

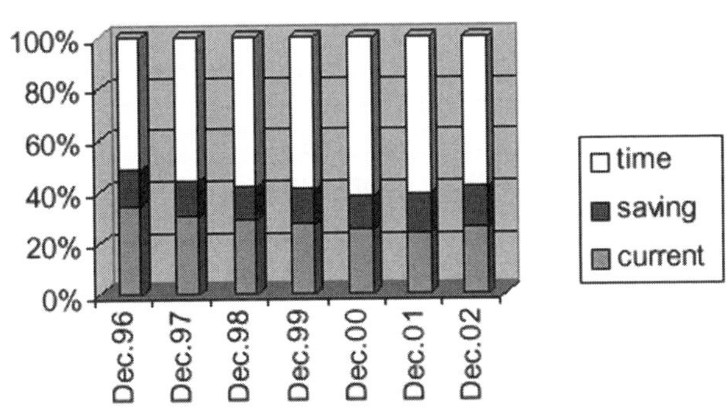

Figure 5.3 Shares of current accounts, savings accounts and time deposits in total WBGS bank deposits, 1996–2002 (source: PMA data).

of its implications for monetary stability. Some increase in bank lending can be expected as a result of reduced political uncertainty following a permanent political settlement. A further increase in bank lending can be achieved by putting in place mechanisms to increase the availability of suitable collateral. One area where such a mechanism can lead to a significant increase in bank lending is land registration. Significant expansion of bank credit, however, requires expanding the bank supervisory capacity of the Palestinian Monetary Authority, which is currently limited.

A permanent political settlement should be expected to substantially reduce political uncertainty which, in the post-Oslo period, severely limited investment and economic growth. In addition, assuming that the political settlement produces a sovereign Palestinian state with control over its borders, Palestinian companies will have direct access to international markets, thus eliminating a major constraint to growth in trade-dependent industries in the Oslo period. A permanent settlement should also be expected to end Israeli-imposed restrictions on the movements of people and goods between the different regions of the WBGS that segmented the Palestinian market and limited economic growth.

Economic growth induced by a reduction in political uncertainty, along with reduced precautionary demand for cash, resulting from decreased uncertainty, will no doubt increase the deposit base of the WBGS banking system. The decrease in uncertainty will most likely increase the average maturity of bank deposits and will make it easier for bank managers to predict customer withdrawal patterns, hence increasing the lending capacity of the banking system. Finally, decreased political uncertainty will enhance the value of the balance sheets of private firms as predictors of future cash flow and profits, thus facilitating risk assessment and bank credit to these firms.

One area where government action can increase the availability of suitable collateral significantly is land registration. At the present time, 70 per cent of land in the West Bank, and around 10 per cent in the Gaza Strip, are not properly registered. Additionally, some of the land that is properly registered cannot be used as collateral for bank loans because of ownership fragmentation. The main reason for such fragmentation is the difficulty in dividing the estates of many of the people who have died since 1967, due to the displacement of a large number of Palestinians from the WBGS after the 1967 war and the subsequent emigration of many others to different parts of the world.

Resuming the land registration process that has been frozen by Israel since 1967 should be a high priority for the Palestinian government in the post-permanent settlement period.[7] A judiciary process should also be put in place to deal with land fragmentation. Implementing these measures will go a long way towards facilitating bank lending because land represents the most valuable asset owned by most WBGS Palestinians.

Bank regulation and supervision in the WBGS falls within the responsibility of the PMA, which was established in 1994. Like other PNA institutions, the PMA is currently overstaffed by political appointees, many of whom lack the technical skills necessary for bank regulation and supervision. The lack of sufficient supervisory capacity has not been detrimental, so far, to the safety and stability of the banking system, due to limited lending and the fact that most deposits are at banks chartered in Jordan, and therefore supervised by the Central Bank of Jordan.

In the post-permanent settlement period, bank lending is expected to increase significantly, and overdependence on Jordanian banks may not be a desirable option (see below). In such an environment, expanding the supervisory capacity of the PMA becomes essential for the safety and stability of the domestic banking system.

Unless the Palestinian state created as part of the permanent political settlement enters into a monetary union with Jordan, continued domination of the Palestinian banking system by Jordanian bank branches may cause serious disruptions to the Palestinian economy. Such domination will make it difficult for a Palestinian inter-bank market to develop because of the tendency of foreign bank branches to depend on their head offices as a source of liquidity. This will in turn make it extremely difficult for the PMA to influence domestic money supply, which may become an important monetary policy issue once bank lending increases significantly and a Palestinian currency is issued. In addition, if the US dollar continues to account for a large share of bank deposits, the Palestinian banking system, and hence the Palestinian economy, will be vulnerable if Jordan suffers a foreign exchange crisis. Finally, current arrangements for Jordanian bank branches leave WBGS depositors unprotected in cases of bankruptcies.[8]

To deal with these problems, at the very least, Jordanian bank branches should be converted to subsidiaries.[9] The PMA may also have to find ways to strengthen the role of locally chartered banks in the domestic banking system. However, such measures should be taken only after the PMA builds sufficient supervisory capacity.

The Equity market

The stock exchange

The Palestinian Securities Exchange (PSE) was established in 1997 by a private company, Palestine Investment and Development Corporation (PADICO), and continues to be owned and run by the same company. The PSE has so far been self-regulated. 24 companies are currently listed on the PSE, some of which were established in the post-Oslo period and were listed soon after they opened for business. The PSE market capitalisation at the end of 2002 was $638 million.

By 2000, the annual turnover ratio at the PSE reached 23.4 per cent, a level comparable to stock markets in neighbouring countries (Table 5.1). The turnover ratio, however, has declined considerably since then because of the intifada (Figure 5.4).

Prices at the PSE have been volatile, with volatility driven mainly by political factors. In the PSE's first three years of operation, the Jerusalem Index, which measures the overall performance of the PSE, showed an increasing trend. The trend has reversed since the intifada.

Public confidence is essential to the effectiveness of a stock exchange in channelling long-term investment funds into an economy. To maintain public confidence, stock exchanges tend to limit listing to companies that have been in business for a number of years and have a track record of profitability and sound financial management. So far, having a track record has not been a precondition for being listed on the Palestinian Stock Exchange. Some people may justify the continuation of this practice by the fact that two of the companies that were listed without track records (PALTEL and PADICO) have been very successful and have been the most widely traded on the PSE. However, a closer examination will show

Table 5.1 Stock exchange data for selected Middle Eastern countries, 1999

Country	*Market capitalisation as percentage of GDP*	*Annual turnover ratio in %*
Jordan	72.2	9.4
Egypt	36.8	31.6
Lebanon	—	9.3
Israel	29.8	63.3
WBGS	20.1	20.8

Source: Standard and Poor's (2001).

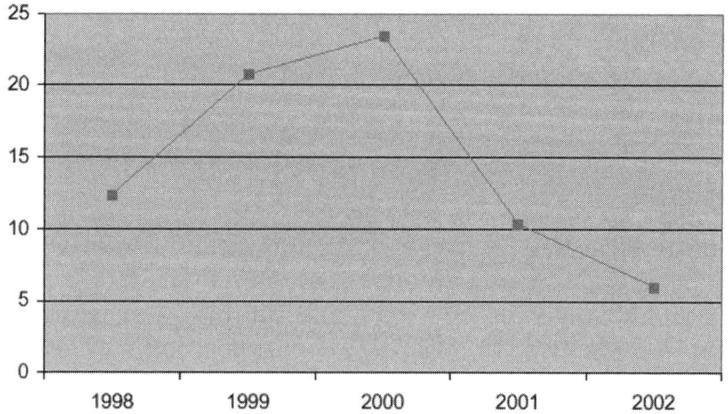

Figure 5.4 Annual turnover ratio at the PSE, 1998–2002 (%) (source: PSE data).

that one of these companies (PALTEL) owes its success to its monopoly status in the telecommunications sector. The other (PADICO) is a highly capitalised holding company backed by a group of Palestinian diaspora billionaires. It is highly unlikely that many newly formed companies in the post-permanent settlement period will have the advantages enjoyed by these two companies. Listing companies without a track record should, therefore, be discontinued. Otherwise, it may undermine public confidence in the exchange. To avoid a conflict of interest and increase public confidence in the PSE, PADICO should also end its exclusive ownership of the PSE. A government regulatory framework for the PSE, which has been lacking so far, should be put in place. Such a framework should include strict auditing standards, clear insider trading rules and timely corporate reporting.

Increasing public confidence in the PSE will improve the prospect of venture capital funds as a potentially important source of investment funds in the post-permanent settlement period. It will do so by providing venture capital funds with an exit mechanism (the IPO) for their temporary investment in high risk companies, thus increasing the likelihood of such investment.

Venture capital as a potential source of funds

The venture capital fund is a financial intermediary that invests mainly in new companies with high growth potential. Unlike other financial intermediaries, the involvement of the venture capital fund in its target company is not limited to providing funds. It also helps run the sponsored company for a limited period of time, typically seven to ten years. During this period, representatives of the venture capital fund sit on the company's board, facilitate its access to further capital and new markets, and help recruit key managerial personnel. In return, the venture capital fund receives an equity stake in the company that is later cashed out through a buyout or an IPO. The main sources of funds for venture capital are usually wealthy individuals, pension funds, and other institutional investors. While most successful examples of venture capital funds in recent years (such as Silicon Valley in the US) were in high technology sectors, there is no reason why venture capital funds cannot play a similar role in other high growth sectors, and they have done so in some countries.

Venture capital funds have recently begun to play an important role in some newly industrialised and developing countries. The most successful so far, Israel and Taiwan, have been countries that have been able to draw on their expatriate communities as a source of funds and technical expertise.[10] In Israel, venture capital funds invested mainly in high technology companies with links to Silicon Valley. The Israeli venture capital fund industry, which was initially heavily subsidised by the government, raised a large share of its funds from American Jews and Israelis living in the US.

It also depended on the same groups in establishing links with the US venture capital industry and high technology companies in Silicon Valley. In Taiwan, venture capital funds have been involved mainly with companies that manufacture goods for high technology US companies. While the Taiwanese raised most of their funds locally, they relied extensively on Chinese Americans in obtaining US manufacturing contracts for their sponsored companies. Expatriate Indians are also playing an important role in the evolving Indian venture capital industry.

The Palestinian economy has a great growth potential in the post-permanent settlement period. Unlike other developing countries, capital does not represent a significant constraint to economic growth. Based on 2002 data, the domestic banking system alone can inject an additional $1,787 million into the Palestinian economy if its loan-deposit ratio reaches Jordan's 80 per cent level, which is not an unrealistic possibility. The expected disbursement of funds held by the UNRWA pension fund will add several hundred million dollars. Substantial funds should also be expected to flow into the Palestinian economy through refugee compensation schemes and investments by diaspora Palestinians. In view of the enormous Palestinian investment in education in the last 50 years, the high technology sector could be a significant contributor to economic growth in the new Palestinian state.

The growth potential of existing Palestinian companies in the WBGS is limited because of constraints imposed on them by the Israeli occupation authorities over the years. Hence, much of the growth potential in the permanent settlement period is expected to come from new companies, providing fertile ground for a venture capital industry. International organisations, such as the IFC, should play an important role in launching the Palestinian venture capital fund industry by providing seed funds and technical expertise, as they did in other newly industrialised and developing countries. As in Israel, Taiwan and India, diaspora Palestinians should be expected to play a leading role in the venture capital industry and be a major source of capital and technical know-how.

The informal financial sector

The informal financial sector was the main provider of financial services in the WBGS in the period 1967–1993. Competition from commercial banks, along with government regulation, limited the range of financial services provided by the informal sector during the post-Oslo period. The markets for services such as money transfers, cheque cashing and customer deposits were taken over almost completely by commercial banks. The informal sector, however, continued to be a major source of credit because of limited lending by commercial banks.[11] Providers of informal sector financial services in the WBGS since 1967 include family and friends, money changers, wholesalers, retailers and NGOs.

As in other developing countries, borrowing from family and friends has been an important source of funds in the WBGS, especially for groups with high income fluctuations. In a 1996 MAS survey, almost 27 per cent of WBGS adults reported borrowing from family and friends. In the 1990s, such borrowing was particularly common among workers in Israel, whose income was quite erratic in this period due to frequent Israeli closures. Borrowing from family and friends has also been an important source of start-up funds for small firms.

Buying goods on credit from the local store has been a long-standing tradition in the WBGS. Such credit is usually provided for a month but is often extended for a longer period. Since 1967, store credit has been initially denominated in NIS but converted to Jordanian dinars or US dollars if extended beyond a month, because these two currencies have been perceived to be more stable than the NIS.

Wholesale credit has also been very common in the WBGS. It is usually provided to retailers for two to three months and has, in recent years, been backed by post-dated cheques. A large share of wholesale credit provided in the post-Oslo period has been financed by loans obtained from commercial banks, where wholesalers have had an easier access to credit because of ownership of reputational capital and/or assets acceptable as bank loan collateral.

The main activity of money changers – money changing – has been commonly used in the WBGS since 1967 because most WBGS households have used one currency (the NIS) as a medium of exchange and another currency (the US dollar or the Jordanian dinar) as a store of value. As part of the process of providing money changing services, money changers collected valuable information about customers' income and spending patterns, enabling them to reduce the risk and transaction cost of other financial services, such as credit, cheque cashing and money transfers. Hence, money changers handled most money transfers between the WBGS and the rest of the world (except for Israel) in this period. They were also a major source of credit, which was financed until the early 1990s either from their own funds or by interest paying deposits collected from customers.

The substantial expansion of the WBGS banking system in the 1990s resulted in a sharp decline in customer deposits held by money changers, and dried up demand for other money changer services, such as money transfers and cheque cashing services. A 1997 set of regulations enacted by the PNA curtailed deposits held by money changers even further. The regulations required money changers to refrain from accepting customer deposits and providing credit, and stipulated that each money changer should have a minimum capital of $50,000. They even specified the minimum office space to be maintained by the money changer. Despite the 1997 ban, money changers continued to be an important source of credit in the WBGS. With the dwindling of customer deposits due to competition from commercial banks and the government ban, credit extended by money changers has been financed mainly through their own funds and loans obtained from commercial banks.

The credit provided by money changers since 1967 has not been limited to the small short-term loans traditionally provided by informal sector lenders. Money changers have often provided relatively large loans to business borrowers who could not obtain bank loans because of the lack of suitable collateral. A small money changer's loan to a regular customer is usually provided without collateral, requiring only the presence of two witnesses. Larger loans are normally backed by collateral. The most common form of collateral for such a loan in recent years has been the post-dated cheque. The interest rate on money changers' loans ranges between 6 and 10 per cent a month, depending on the maturity of the loan and the creditworthiness of the customer.

Non-government organisations began providing credit in the WBGS in the 1980s and have been financed since then mainly by foreign donors. NGO loans extended in the 1980s and early 1990s were mostly to the agricultural sector and were either interest-free or offered at interest rates substantially below market rates. Most of these loans were not backed by physical collateral, requiring only third party guarantees. The default rate on loans extended in this period was very high, reaching 60 per cent at some NGOs.

By the mid 1990s, NGO lending strategies began to go through major changes. To reduce their default rates, some NGOs began requiring physical collateral. Others instituted lending programmes that use group solidarity lending mechanisms. Under these mechanisms, which have been used successfully in many developing countries, the group assumes collective responsibility for all loans obtained by members. Such responsibility motivates members of the group to screen out high risk individuals and put peer pressure on borrowers to avoid default. The two NGOs that set up solidarity based lending programmes in the WBGS (Save the Children and UNRWA) have reported very low default rates (below 2 per cent up to 1997).

Future prospects

The informal financial sector is expected to continue to play an important role in the Palestinian economy in the post-permanent settlement period. This will most probably be the case even after bank lending increases significantly, reaching a level comparable to that in neighbouring countries. One area where the informal sector should be expected to play an important role is providing small short-term loans, because lower transaction costs give them a comparative advantage over commercial banks in this market. The informal sector should also be expected to play an important role in channelling credit subsidies to the poor. Loans from family and friends will remain an important source of start-up funds for small companies.

Government authorities should not constrain the informal sector by unnecessary regulations. Some regulations, such as prohibiting the acceptance of customers' deposits and requiring NGOs that use public or donor funds to account for the use of these funds, are unavoidable. However, more intrusive regulations, such as the 1997 regulations that put severe restrictions on money changers, should be avoided. Evidence from developing countries shows that government regulation of the informal sector has been ineffective and even counterproductive, and should be minimised.

Notes

1 Israeli restrictions during this period included a closure of all banks operating in the WBGS on the eve of the 1967 Israeli occupation and a ban on non-Israeli banks that lasted until 1986, when the Bank of Palestine won an Israeli court case to reopen one of its branches in the Gaza Strip. Soon after that a Jordanian bank (Cairo Amman Bank) was allowed to reopen one of its branches in the West Bank.

2 The 1993 figure does not include Israeli banks, which catered mainly to Israeli settlements.

3 Jordanian branches accounted for 11 of the banks and 67 of the bank branches that operated in the WBGS on the eve of the intifada. Only two other banks (a British bank and an Egyptian bank) operated in the WBGS at the time.

4 The Bank of Israel relinquished its bank supervisory role in the Gaza Strip immediately after the PNA was established in 1994. The relinquishing of Israeli bank supervisory authority in the West Bank was gradual and was not completed until the end of 1995.

5 In Jordan, for example, the loan-deposit ratio is currently around 80 per cent.

6 I am grateful to Sébastien Dessus for bringing this to my attention.

7 The purpose of this suspension became obvious when the Israeli occupation authorities began confiscating some of the land that was not properly registered in order to build Israeli settlements.

8 A 1986 agreement between the Bank of Israel and the Central Bank of Jordan that allowed the opening of Jordanian bank branches in the WBGS included a guarantee from the Central Bank of Jordan for depositors at Jordanian banks operating in the WBGS. This agreement expired when the Bank of Israel relinquished its supervisory role over WBGS banks. As far as I know, the PMA has not yet obtained a similar guarantee from the Central Bank of Jordan.

9 This is not the prevailing view in the literature (see Clarke *et al.* 2003 for a survey). However, the prevailing view is based on studies of highly capitalised banks based in industrialised countries that have limited foreign operations. In contrast, Jordanian banks have limited capital and WBGS deposits account for a large share of total deposits at many of these banks.

10 The material on the role of venture capital funds in India, Israel and Taiwan draws heavily on Dossani and Kenney (2002). Other sources on venture capital funds in developing countries include Green (1991) and Sagari (1992).

11 The material on the informal sector in the post-Oslo period is based on Hamed (1998).

References

Clarke, G., Cull, R., Martinez Peria, M. and Sánchez, S. (2003) 'Foreign bank entry: experience, implications for developing economies and agenda for future research', *World Bank Research Observer* 18: 25–60.

Dossani, R. and Kenney, M. (2002) 'Creating an environment for venture capital in India', *World Development* 30: 227–53.

Green, M.B. (1991) *Venture Capital: International Comparisons*, London and New York: Routledge.

Hamed, O. (1998) *Informal Finance and Lending NGOs in the West Bank and Gaza Strip*, Ramallah: Palestine Economic Policy Research Institute (MAS).

Hamed, O. and Khano, M. (1995) *Palestinian Banking Sector: Statistical Review*, Ramallah: Palestine Economic Policy Research Institute (MAS).

Sagari, S. (1992) *Venture Capital: Lessons from the Developed World for the Developing Countries*, Washington, DC: World Bank.

Standard and Poor's (2001) *Emerging Stock Markets Fact Book*, Washington, DC: International Finance Corporation.

Discussion

Andy Mullineux

In this very interesting chapter, the financial sector in the West Bank and the Gaza Strip (WBGS) in each of three periods since the 1967 Israeli occupation is assessed, and prospects for the post-settlement period are considered.

The formal financial sector was largely closed down from 1967 to 1993 and the informal financial sector thrived. From 1993 to 2000 there was a fairly rapid development of the formal sector in which foreign banks (mainly Jordan-based Arab banks) opened branches and a stock exchange was established, whilst the informal sector was repressed by restrictive legislation. This period gives an insight into what might be possible in a post-settlement period. Projecting forward from that period Hamed forms expectations and makes policy recommendations, relating to: the removal of at least some restrictions on the informal sector; the use of expected compensation and UNRWA pension funds (e.g. for house building in the case of the former), with a warning of the need to avoid 'bubbles' and inflationary pressure; land registration (important to provide collateral); increasing bank supervisory capacity; dealing with the 'problem' of Jordanian bank domination; the role of venture funds; and strengthening the stock exchange.

There are a number of lessons that can be learnt from the numerous financial sector reform programmes in other developing countries and in Central and Eastern European and other 'transition' and 'emerging market' countries in the past decade or so.

One of the most important of these is that banks are, and are likely to remain for some time, the most important financial institutions because of asymmetric information problems. For capital markets to thrive a much more sophisticated financial system is required with supporting legal, reporting, accounting and auditing infrastructure. Less developed economies lack the expertise and struggle even to staff their central banks with skilled and experienced supervisors, as Hamed implicitly observes.

Hamed is perhaps overly optimistic about the role venture capital will play, relative to banks and the informal sector, in the early post-settlement period. One can see a role for informal private equity sponsorship by 'business angels', perhaps drawn from the diaspora, but it is notoriously difficult to develop a fully fledged venture fund industry and to do so will naturally take time. Venture funds tend to look for relatively large investment opportunities. In the early post-settlement days these are likely to be in relatively short supply. Smaller 'growth enterprises' seeking external funding will normally look to the banking sector to supply it. Furthermore, for venture capital to thrive there must be an 'exit' for the investors, and suitable exit routes are usually 'Initial Public Offerings' (IPOs) on specialist stock exchanges, which themselves only thrive in the presence of a well functioning 'senior' stock exchange. In my view the short- to medium-term focus should be on the development of a well functioning banking sector, leaving the development of the capital market to the medium- to long-term and considering whether a regional rather than national stock market might be appropriate. That having been said, it is well known that asymmetric information can lead to adverse selection and induce credit rationing (Stiglitz and Weiss 1981). Further, even in developed financial systems (including the UK and the US) the urban poor are faced with financial exclusion, and informal sector institutions (money lenders and pawn brokers, credit unions, community development finance institutions) voluntarily step in to plug the gaps. Governments can encourage this in various ways and can favour the 'not for profit' institutions with tax concessions and other special schemes whilst legislating against 'usury' and heavy-handed debt collection practices.

Rural banking is even more problematic. Agricultural cooperative banks have worked well in Europe (e.g. France) and elsewhere (Japan), but have faced problems in Africa (Tanzania). Mobile commercial bank branches can have a role to play (South Africa). Specialist microfinance banks have been successful (Grameen Bank, Bangladesh) and so have NGO microfinance schemes (BRAC, Bangladesh). Cooperative banks (e.g. Raiffeissen banks in Austria and Switzerland) have also been very successful in urban areas, supporting artisans and others, and credit unions are popular in many countries (e.g. US and Ireland). There is thus plenty of experience to draw upon in plugging the gaps, but the prime objective should be to create a well functioning commercial banking system, with as few gaps as possible. A thriving informal banking sector is part of the answer in that it proves that providing financial services to the relatively poor is potentially profitable and also provides competition to the commercial banks.

A key lesson from previous restructurings is that conditions have to be created in which commercial banks are willing to lend, rather than just take deposits and invest them in government and central bank debt securities or elsewhere. Commercial banks should also be encouraged to lend with due consideration of the risks involved whilst providing adequately for losses and holding sufficient capital and liquid reserves. Hence good regulation and supervision is essential, especially if rapid expansion of bank lending can be expected.

The South-East Asian and other recent financial crises have made it clear that the monetary and exchange rate context is also important for financial stability. We will not rehearse the debates concerning whether small open economies should float or fix, and whether in the latter case a currency union might be desirable; and also what level of capital controls might be appropriate, as these are considered in detail in Chapter 3. Questions such as the following are, however, clearly of great importance in setting the context in which financial sector restructuring will take place: should the WBGS simply fully dollarise, or should it form a currency union based on the Jordanian dinar, or even 'dinarise'? What are the implications of these alternatives for the dominance of Jordan-based banks in the WBGS?

Compensation payments could be used to increase the supply of housing, as Hamed suggests, and, along with UNWRA funds, they could also be used to provide the basis of a funded national pension scheme (much as privatisation income was used in Poland). An increase in housing supply and ownership would in turn stimulate bank lending by providing a collateral base.

As Hamed notes, progress would have to be preceded by land registration and the resolution of competing claims. The latter requires a well functioning judiciary to resolve the disputes and the process takes time, as the resolution of conflicting claims in East Germany has demonstrated. It is also well known that banks will not lend if they can not get their money back. Collateral is no good if the lenders cannot get title to the pledged assets (as is currently the case in Thailand). Well functioning bankruptcy laws are an essential part of the financial architecture and, again, take time to put in place. The credibility of the central bank, which is likely to remain responsible for both monetary and financial stability, including supervision, will also take time to build. A separate supervisory agency is probably inappropriate until a higher level of financial sector development has been achieved, given the likely shortage of suitably trained staff.

To underpin financial stability, a risk-related deposit insurance scheme, with a comprehensive coverage, is likely to be required. Hamed alludes to the need for deposit insurance in discussing what to do about Jordan-based bank domination, noting that since 1994 deposits have essentially been unprotected. The banks operating in Jordan should be required to contribute to a state-run deposit insurance scheme and to pay premia related to the risks to which they are exposing deposits. But they should only be admitted to the scheme (and be allowed to operate) if they meet internationally recognised capital adequacy, provisioning and liquidity standards *inter alia*. Such an approach has been adopted by the Bosnian monetary authorities.

With regard to the role of foreign banks in emerging financial markets, it is now widely accepted that they bring in much needed skills and that small countries are unlikely to be able to foster 'national champions' able to compete in the increasingly global market. Central and Eastern European states have seen a progressive increase in foreign bank market share, none more so than Estonia where the foreign banks dominate the market, and a similar trend is evident in a number of East and South-East Asian countries following post-1997-crisis restructuring.

To encourage banks to lend, particularly to small and medium sized urban and rural enterprises, loan guarantee schemes, under which the state absorbs some of the default risk, are clearly required. This was evident in Germany under post-war reconstruction and most European countries (including the UK), the US and Japan operate such schemes. They are often combined with the provision of pre- and post-loan training and advice to reduce failure rates. The aim is in part to coax the banks into lending in sectors in which they have little experience, so that they learn how to do it and make a profit in the process. The generosity of the guarantee schemes can then be scaled back. This is the short-term solution. It should only be open to insured banks that fully comply with a regulatory and supervisory system that is based on internationally accepted best practice.

Whilst the commercial banks are re-learning to lend, the informal sector will continue to have an important role to play. As bank learning and land registration progresses, home ownership becomes more widespread, and well functioning bankruptcy laws are established, the reliance on loan guarantees can be scaled back. As banks and their supervisors gain credibility, the deposit insurance coverage can also be scaled back (especially for larger depositors).

In the medium-term venture funds (many of them operated by banks) will take over the financing of the larger 'growth SMEs', the more so as the capital market develops to provide an exit route for them. Strict reporting requirements and good regulatory and corporate governance systems, underpinned by effective auditing, will accelerate the development of the capital markets as providers of equity and debt (bond) finance. The introduction of pension funds will also stimulate the development of capital markets. Commercial banks will need to develop investment banking skills to retain the business of their most creditworthy clients.

Reference

Stiglitz, J.E. and Weiss, A. (1981) 'Credit rationing in markets with imperfect information', *American Economic Review* 71: 393–410.

6 Company law and corporate governance in Palestine

Clare Woodcraft and Khaled Islaih[1]

Introduction: institutionalising corporate governance in a sovereign state

Investment and corporate governance

Since the collapse of global giants such as Enron and World Com, corporate governance and specifically company law have come under immense scrutiny throughout the world but most notably in the more sophisticated financial markets of the west. The high profile demise of certain US corporates, in what is a highly regulated and developed industrial market, clearly demonstrated how swiftly investor confidence can dissipate if legislation is weak.

Company law is now being revisited globally with a view to overhauling the current system of checks and balances that governs corporate behaviour. Developing nations seeking to introduce new, or update old, corporate legislation clearly face an unprecedented opportunity to fast-track the domestic drive to achieve international best practice standards by monitoring global developments.

In the West Bank and Gaza Strip (WBGS), where a draft company law awaits ratification, where legal reform is being posited as a key condition for future peace negotiations, and where, in a sovereign environment, international investment would be critical for the reconstruction process, understanding the global context of corporate good governance is paramount. Since in the global investment arena corporate governance is increasingly a key risk factor taken into consideration during the decision-making process, a sovereign Palestine must ensure that local legislation is consonant with global norms (Bradley 2003).

Understanding global developments

The US Sarbanes-Oxley ruling which came into law in July 2002 requires that CEOs and CFOs, including those of foreign companies, be required to certify at regular intervals that their reports and financial statements contain no untruths and omit no material facts. It also aimed to ban subsidised personal loans to top executives and prompt disclosure on share dealings to repay company loans. Most importantly, it proposed to toughen the audit process such that accountants rotate the audit partner overseeing a firm's accountants and that auditors can no longer sell certain non-audit services to audit clients.

In September 2001, the European Commission set up a group of high level company law experts with a mandate, in part, to provide the Commission with recommendations for a modern regulatory European company law framework. One of the overriding goals seems to have been that of achieving simplicity and indeed one of the core elements of the mandate of the group was to consider the possible simplification of corporate rules in light of the earlier SLIM (Simpler Legislation for the Internal Market 1999) report on the Second Company Law Directive of December 1976 on the formation and capital maintenance of a public limited liability company.

Underlying the overall reform process – which was well underway even prior to the US corporate and accounting scandals – is a series of goals: to encourage enterprise and competitiveness; to preserve the benefits of the company form; to modernise, rationalise and simplify company law; to focus on core company law issues and to encourage the adoption of good practice in company management.[2]

Broadly speaking, the primary aim is to encourage shareholders to exercise effective and responsible influence over companies by promoting transparency of information available while trying to minimise the costs and disruption to business.[3] Ultimately the aim is to ensure that investor confidence is maintained and, as a result, investment flows secured. For Palestine, where internal capital will be insufficient in a sovereign environment to reconstruct the national economy, effective legislation that nurtures the confidence of both external and internal investors is critical.

The lack of an effective legal and regulatory environment is one of the key impediments to sustained growth in developing economies and notably to investment promotion (Gray 1997). The WBGS is no exception and has the additional burden of high political risk to add to an underdeveloped and highly fragmented legal system. Indeed, one of the primary concerns currently related to economic development is the urgent need to address the legal and regulatory framework.

As the World Bank (n.d.) points out in a recent document yet to be formally released, 'Prior to the current crisis, political risk was not perceived as the greatest obstacle to investment: rather, investors cited the lack of a well-regulated domestic economy'. The Bank goes on to note that, 'while the PA has come a long way in creating the legal and regulatory foundations for a market economy . . . challenges remain'.

Moreover, the report notes that while this problem has been recognised for a long time:

> when discussing policy reform and investment promotion in Palestine, officials and civil servants tend to interpret this in terms of incentives to attract foreign investment only i.e. tax liberalisation, incentives, privatisation of government owned assets. Rarely do they consider the improvement of domestic procedures, despite the fact that this is one area where foreign investors have consistently pointed to weaknesses. Experience from other developing regions suggests that while many have implemented a comprehensive system of incentives for privatisation there is generally too much emphasis on tax holidays at the expense of general simplification of the regulatory regime,[4]

and, one might argue, at the expense of the effectiveness of company law and its enforcement.

Corporate governance in the aggregate

This chapter will focus on company law but within the context of corporate good governance as a much broader concept and company law as the main legislative component thereof. Corporate governance has been innumerably defined and deconstructed but a recent report published by UNCTAD (Mallin 2003) offers a useful summary of what the varying interpretations incorporate:

- systems of control within the company
- relationships between the company's board, shareholders and stakeholders
- the company being managed in the interests of the shareholders and stakeholders
- greater transparency and accountability to enable users of corporate information to determine whether the business is being managed in a way that they consider appropriate.

According to the OECD, corporate good governance is about the 'set of relationships between a company's board, its shareholders and other stakeholders. It also provides the structure through which the objectives of the company are set and the means of attaining those objectives, and monitoring performance, are determined'.[5]

It is important to acknowledge that corporate governance is not necessarily directly related to illegalities per se. Issues connected to executive pay, for example, occur legally: disproportionate salary structures can exist within the legal framework (*The Economist* 2003c). In the WBGS, business practices are very specific to the hostile operating environment that has emerged. These practices are often well entrenched and may override legislation and the ability to enforce it if they are not considered prior to the ratification of new laws.

Corporate governance in a sovereign Palestine

The aim of this chapter is not to define a new form or structure for legislation in a sovereign environment. Instead, the aim is to offer a guideline for ensuring that existing draft legislation is not simply adopted wholesale but instead carefully honed, or indeed redrafted, in line with the existing reality and in line with the economic opportunities that would emerge with sovereignty. Moreover, the chapter does not attempt to project a regional model for corporate governance. All too often the region fails to institutionalise a system that can integrate with global norms because the focus is on harmonising already distorted regional legacy systems rather than creating new ones that can build international economic relationships. (Such is broadly the case in the WBGS at the moment where there is more interest in harmonising legislation in line with regional norms than building *ab initio*.)

Instead, the chapter looks at the prospects for sound corporate governance within a sovereign Palestinian state in the light of the historical and existing institutional factors that have shaped local business practices. Specifically it will look at company law – variously described as 'the greatest single discovery of modern times',[6] 'the legal basis for one of the most important institutions organising our economy'[7] and 'a vehicle for growth . . . [and] a key indicator of our national competitiveness – weighed up by potential investors'.[8] It will examine how company law, as one tool of corporate governance, can serve to streamline these practices and provide a level playing field to promote domestic and foreign investment within a sovereign state.

The current legal reality in Palestine

A legacy of fragmentation

In the WBGS, the legislation that has governed private sector activity for the past eight decades has been fragmented and non-indigenous and the product of two different authorities. The first is the Ottoman Empire that ruled from 1516 to 1917 and ended after 400 years with the British occupation of Jerusalem in 1917. This British Mandate was effective in the Gaza Strip through the Companies Ordinance no. 18 of 1929. The second is Jordanian rule, which was effective in the West Bank and governed private sector activity through Companies Law no. 12, 1964. The latter is a combination of the law effective in the Gaza Strip at that time and the Syrian Trade Law no. 149 of 1949, which was based on the French legal code.

After the 1967 war, Israeli forces occupied the WBGS, including East Jerusalem, and proclaimed full control of legislative, executive and judicial powers of what then became known as the Occupied Territories. After the promulgation of Military Order 947 of 1981 all legal and administrative powers were transferred to the newly established Civil Administration. Since occupation, the Israeli military courts and military committees retained complete jurisdiction over certain criminal matters, all land disputes, taxes, natural resources and fiscal matters. Since 1967, there have been more than 2,500 military orders issued in the WBGS as well as many others that have never been published.

Since 1994 and pursuant to the Declaration of Principles on Interim Self-Government Arrangements in 1993 (commonly referred to as the Oslo I Agreement), one of the major challenges facing the Palestinian Authority (PA) has been the unification and harmonisation of the various elements of the legal system in the WBGS. The inherent lack of cohesion in this system has served to undermine its ability to create a private sector legal code that is adhered to and that can promote a positive investment climate. However, over and above the structural flaws in the legislation, Israeli occupation of Palestinian territory (and the associated trade structure distortions), the more recent co-option of the private sector on the part of the PA and the ongoing level of political turmoil and uncertainty as now embodied in the second Palestinian intifada have largely nullified the legal system's influence as a determining force in economic activity. The intensity of these factors, coupled with the weakness of the Palestinian judicial system and the dominance of Israeli military forces, has meant that private sector behaviour is guided by 'realpolitik' and the practical and changing daily reality of commercial activity rather than by a judicial code.

This is not to say that commercial activity is undertaken in a legislative void. There are two different company laws being implemented in Palestine, which nominally govern company registration for public limited, private limited and foreign companies and limited partnerships and which, *de jure*, control the behaviour and activity of private sector commercial entities within the domestic economy.

Existing legislative framework

The existing company law varies little from its neighbouring counterparts and, in particular, Jordanian and Egyptian law. Partnerships comprise limited partnerships in addition to general partnerships. General partners are personally responsible for debts and liabilities of the company while limited partners are only responsible for the size of their share in the company and cannot be part of management. Private limited companies carry moral independent responsibility, partners have limited responsibility and shares are not offered for exchange. Public limited companies have moral independent responsibility and since shares are offered for exchange they play a major role in channelling savings into investments.

Presently there is no separate bankruptcy law in Palestine. Bankruptcy regulations are part of the Jordanian Trade Law of 1966 presently implemented in the West Bank, and the draft Palestinian Trade Law refers to bankruptcy regulations. However, the Ministry of National Economy wants to remove bankruptcy regulations and put them in a separate law – this issue is still under discussion.

Corporate bankruptcy is executed through the court system. However, the relevant company laws provide the option only for voluntary and involuntary liquidation. In both cases, a receiver must be appointed. The procedures are time consuming and can take over three years to be completed. Moreover, there are no business reorganisation or restructuring options under the existing legal framework.

In the WBGS, there is a now a draft Companies and Partnerships Law that is significantly more progressive in this respect and provides for the reorganisation and restructuring of the company and offers the creditors compromise agreements. However, there is still an urgent need within the WBGS to improve and accelerate court procedures for bankruptcy and liquidation.

Draft legislation

The Companies and Partnerships draft law was to have been enacted in 1999 and was developed by the Palestinian Ministry of Economy and Trade and by the Adam Smith Institute, International Division. While this document is considered by the legal community in the WBGS as a sound starting point and certainly in line with international standards of the time, the dynamics of the domestic environment coupled with the dynamics of global economic developments mean that it too must be revisited and redefined in line with new variables and the changing operational environment.

The draft company law, which is based on British, Australian and New Zealand legislation, has yet to be presented to the Palestinian Legislative Council (PLC) and does go some way towards resolving the structural distortions currently inherent in the legislative system in that it harmonises the registration and incorporation process as well as applying uniform fees to both the West Bank and Gaza. It also eliminates existing requirements for par value of the share and stated capital, and simplifies the incorporation procedures.

Critically, the new law eliminates duplication and simplifies procedures for local and foreign companies. It establishes the Ministry of Economy and Trade as the single regulator and ensures that all business entities register with the Company Controller who sets a flat fee for incorporation. The draft legislation also recognises pre-incorporation contracts, gives shareholders pre-emptive rights, allows for the redemption of shares, defines the rights and obligations of secured creditors, provides protection for minority shareholders' rights and requires high disclosure standards. It also introduces clear measures for solvency tests, offers recklessness and negligence rules and clarifies the rules for distribution of dividends.

Broadly speaking, the draft company law replicates international standards and requirements although it has incorporated special procedures for Palestine-specific issues such as the Company Controller's responsibilities, which have been largely reduced to those of Company Registrar. It also takes into consideration the structural specifics of the Palestinian market, especially regarding issues related to the Palestinian diaspora, the need to re-unify legislation and the need to place the responsibility for company registration with the Ministry of Economy instead of the Ministry of Justice (as was the case in Gaza due to Egyptian law influences). However, in the main it considers historical and status quo issues rather than what might be and the level of sophistication that may occur once sovereignty is achieved.

While the enforcement of the existing draft law would go a long way towards offsetting the fragmentation of Palestinian company law, the law itself still tends to focus on the registration aspects of corporate behaviour rather than the operational ones. The inevitable structural and institutional growth that will accompany full sovereign jurisdiction must be fully taken into consideration, given that the evolution of the private sector may outpace that of its governing legislative code.

In general, there is no overriding consensus among the legal community in the WBGS regarding the existing draft company law, primarily because it has yet to be finalised and, more importantly, has only been subject to limited public debate and scrutiny.

Jordan as a role model

There is an inevitable temptation when considering Palestinian development challenges to draw upon the experience of sovereign neighbours, notably Jordan. It is often suggested that Jordan's legislative framework should be adopted wholesale in a sovereign Palestinian environment. However, this argument is weakened by two main points.

First, Jordanian legislation is itself relatively traditional and in many cases has grown in an ad hoc way out of an externally imposed and alien legal system (mainly British). While the 1997 Jordanian Company Law is considered a vast improvement over the 1964 version, it is still considered less than progressive by the Palestinian legal community and in need of updating. Palestinian lawyers argue that it is weak when considering modern commercial transactions and notably securities transactions, accounting standards, corporate governance, the role of the courts, the role of the registrar/controller and mergers and acquisitions.

Moreover, it is argued that the Jordanian model of a Company Controller is too rigid to be consistent with liberal market norms and requires overly close supervision of companies that might be considered intrusive and counterproductive. While the Palestinian draft also incorporates a Company Controller, it has a much more liberal mandate than that of Jordan.

Second, Jordan is still struggling to move its private sector away from traditional areas of activity and into a more knowledge-based, hi-tech paradigm and its legislation has tended to focus very much on the existing structure of commercial incorporations rather than develop a more progressive option that can promote high-growth, non-traditional private sector activity (Ayyoub 2002).

Palestinian lawyers argue that a sovereign Palestine would require more advanced benchmarks than those available in neighbouring countries such as Jordan and Egypt. Indeed, some even go so far as suggesting that a sovereign Palestine could provide a legislative role model for the region as a whole since the ongoing process of drafting new legislation is based on advanced and modern securities and insurance laws.

A maturing market and evolving legislation

The PA has not ignored the value of legislation in attracting investment and notably foreign investment.[9] In 1998, the Law on the Encouragement of Investment in Palestine was ratified providing a comprehensive structure to:

> achieve the development objectives and priorities in Palestine by increasing investment through the establishment of an institution responsible for encouraging and promoting investment in Palestine; the provision of guarantees to all investors and investments operating in Palestine; the granting of incentives to investors and the provision of an appropriate environment for encouraging investment in Palestine.[10]

The PA has also developed supporting draft legislation including the Court Formation Law (no. 15, 2001), the Civil and Commercial Procedures Law (2001), the Arbitration Law (no. 2, 2000) and produced plans to establish commercial courts. Palestinian regulators have assigned a particular significance to the court law, which they rightly see as the fundamental pillar of legal independence and enforcement and which provides for the establishment of courts at all levels.

The Civil and Commercial Procedures Law deals with international courts and allows a Palestinian with no residency in Palestine, in addition to foreigners with residency, to be prosecuted. The Arbitration Law allows parties to resolve disputes by using arbitration, taking into account international agreements to which Palestine is signatory. This law has important implications for the private sector in the area of international trade. If a Palestinian company had a dispute with an international company then both parties could solve the disputes using international arbitration.

In reality there is a strong trend within Palestinian society to strengthen the legal system, particularly in areas such as court organisation, human resources and support for the Attorney General's Department to be able to enforce court resolutions – currently this is a particularly significant problem. However, all of these efforts focus mainly on overhauling fundamentally flawed historical legislation rather than on introducing modern, progressive legislation that pre-empts the governance implications of rapid economic growth.

The current operational reality

Distortionary economic links

Legislation that governs private sector commercial activity cannot be effective if it fails to acknowledge the structural specifics of the operating environment. In the WBGS, occupation has created a very unique and distinct operating environment that has conditioned private sector commercial activity in line with the de facto operating environment rather than the *de jure* legislative one.

Since 1967, the economic outlook for WBGS, including the performance of the private sector, has been affected by economic links with the larger and more dynamic Israeli economy. In 1968, Israel developed an economic strategy towards Palestine through its military orders which not only provided the legislative framework for the Civil Administration, but also served to restrict Palestinian social and economic life. These orders enabled Israel to exploit Palestinian economic resources to serve its economic and political interests in the 'administered territories'.

The application of this strategy allowed Israel to integrate Palestinian markets into its own and to ensure that the economic activities of the WBGS were fully dependent on Israel. This inevitably led to major structural distortions within the Palestinian economy in addition to labour market imbalances (Naqib 2002) and created a highly skewed operating environment.

Uncertainty and investment decline

These distortions, and the coping strategies that emerged among the Palestinian private sector, had a major impact on the way business is conducted in the WBGS. They also had a major impact on the way business relationships were fostered and secured given that the risks associated with doing business in Palestine were not simply those associated with a regular market.

Indeed, they were directly linked to the unpredictable and erratic implementation and enforcement of Israeli military orders which demanded that the Palestinian private sector constantly operate with a high level of acumen and in crisis management mode. Contingency planning is highly entrenched in the Palestinian business sector since being able to plan long-term or strategically is virtually impossible given the highly politicised operating environment and the inability on the part of private sector companies to influence this environment at any level.

This operating environment critically affected the investment climate. Ultimately, Israeli regulatory restrictions combined with political uncertainty have limited private investments in productive sectors and channelled such investments into residential construction and housing projects. In addition, there have been reductions in critical investments in human resources and technology, thereby compromising the sector's level of competitiveness (Naqib 2002).

Corporate size and structure

The competitiveness of the private sector has also been affected by its size and structure. Throughout the occupation, Palestinian private firms have tended to be small with more than 60 per cent of firms employing less than four workers and most having sole proprietorship. For instance, in the West Bank 67 per cent of industrial registered firms were sole proprietorships with less than 3 per cent public shareholding companies. The smaller size firms with simple organisational forms reflect the impact of the existing regulatory environment on investors' attitudes. Thereby, investors tended to invest mostly in family-based micro-enterprises that required less interaction with the Israeli Civil Administration (World Bank 1993: volume 3, 53).

The onset of the Oslo process saw the creation of much larger corporate entities driven by new-found optimism in the prospect of a peace dividend and hence potential economies of scale. However, in reality, the private sector has remained small-scale and dominated by sole proprietors (Table 6.1). Data supplied by UNSCO demonstrates that the process of company registration has been declining in the past few years with the total number of registered firms falling to 550 in 2002 from a high of 846 in 1999 (Table 6.2).

The small-scale nature of the private sector has largely defined the operational norms in the WBGS, notably financing structures. Palestinian companies and family-owned firms still rely heavily on informal equity in the form of savings and funds from relatives and business associates. According to a Private Sector Needs Assessment Industrial Sector Survey produced by the Palestinian Federation of Industries (PFI) and the Palestine Trade Centre (Paltrade), within the industrial sector prime sources of finance are mainly self or family with 73.4 per cent of firms using self-financing and 34.2 per cent family financing. According to the report, 'only 4.7 per cent reported tapping on money lenders for financing and 16.3 per cent from banks' (Table 6.3). The report also notes that West Bank firms make greater use of bank financing than Gazan firms although it is more limited there (Paltrade 2002).

Table 6.1 Private sector establishments, 2002

Economic activity	*Unlimited liability*	*Limited liability*	*Limited shares*	*Public share holding Co.*	*Share-holding Co.*	*Limited partnership*	*General partnership*	*De facto company*	*Sole proprietor*
Agriculture	0	0	0	0	4	9	16	147	5,876
Mining	0	0	0	0	12	1	9	24	287
Manufacturing	1	1	13	5	433	84	211	1,009	12,437
Utilities	0	0	3	0	61	5	12	104	675
Construction	0	1	2	4	106	10	16	35	310
Wholesale	0	7	3	1	440	110	316	1,865	35,612
Hospitality	1	0	0	0	19	4	17	127	2,405
Transport/comm	0	0	0	2	55	7	15	47	492
Finance	0	0	0	16	24	2	10	23	323
Real estate	0	0	1	2	101	24	49	160	2,230
Education	0	0	0	0	15	5	6	35	970
Health	0	0	0	1	10	4	9	39	2,280
Other	0	0	0	0	8	10	20	78	2,752
Total WBGS	2	9	22	31	1,288	275	706	3,693	66,649

Source: Palestinian Central Bureau of Statistics (PCBS).

Table 6.2 Company registration in West Bank and Gaza, 1997–2002

Legal status	*1997*	*1998*	*1999*	*2000*	*2001*	*2002*
Private limited	761	550	831	776	639	548
Public limited	4	2	4	2	3	0
Foreign	0	0	11	11	5	2
Total	765	552	846	789	647	550

Source: UNSCO reports on the Palestinian economy, various editions.

Given the significant reduction in risk that a sovereign framework would bring, it is fair to assume that the formalisation of the Palestinian private sector would be rapid and have significant implications for finance. Formal financial institutions in a sovereign jurisdiction would inevitably find lending to private firms more viable than is currently the case and hence the dependence on informal equity may decline although the growth of new corporates would offset this decline. Moreover, the number of listed companies would increase with the emergence of full macro-economic jurisdiction (and associated policy tools) thereby bringing further structure to private sector activity and further importance to the formal capital market.

The organised capital market as a structuring force

The Oslo years saw the establishment of the Palestinian Securities Exchange (PSE) and the formal listing of Palestinian companies. Since it was incorporated as a private shareholding company in 1995, it has established a fully electronic exchange and depository with trading, settlement and clearing systems provided by international expertise and has gone some way towards providing a structure for corporate governance.

It has established clear listing requirements and a regulatory framework. At least 50 per cent of a listed firm's subscribed capital must be paid-up; subscribed capital must exceed $750,000; the number of outstanding common shares must exceed 100,000; the company must have at least 100 shareholders and at least 25 per cent of the common stock must be offered to the public through a public offering of shares. Throughout the duration of their listing, companies are required to maintain at least 25 per cent of their outstanding shares with the public, a minimum of 100 shareholders of $100 or more of shares at par value and equity of not less than 50 per cent of the subscribed capital.

In a sovereign environment, the PSE could serve not only to encourage the formalisation of the structure of the private sector and encourage a broadening of its ownership base but also to facilitate and maximise the repatriation of long-term investment capital.

In general, the PSE is well structured as a self-regulating organisation

Table 6.3 Sources of finance for Palestinian industry (%)

Sources	*West Bank and Gaza*		*West Bank*		*Gaza*	
	Fixed assets	*Working capital*	*Fixed assets*	*Working capital*	*Fixed assets*	*Working capital*
Self	73.36	73.50	70.42	72.17	74.30	73.46
Family	34.15	34.02	32.39	30.66	34.88	35.80
Money lenders	4.69	5.45	4.23	3.77	4.94	6.48
Banks	16.32	17.48	21.60	21.70	12.65	14.51

Source: PalTrade.

Note
Firms might have more than one source at the same time and so numbers may not add to 100%.

that calls for global standards in terms of registration and trading and is overseen by a board of eight directors. It offers protection against insider trading, price manipulation and fraud, and aims to ensure prompt, wide and extensive dissemination of market data and company information and to assure liquidity in all securities through market making services. However, the PSE remains small with only 24 listed companies and a market capitalisation of just over $1bn (Table 6.4).

Private sector survey

Against this background, the findings of the World Bank Business Environment Survey (WBES) conducted in mid 2000 (prior to the second intifada that started in September 2000) constitute a highly indicative assessment of how the post-Oslo environment and the lack of PA jurisdiction over sovereign economic policy tools brought a whole new level of operating challenges.

The results of the WBES suggest that the main constraints identified by participant firms in the survey were high levels of policy instability and uncertainty, corruption, inflation, the exchange rate and taxes and regulation. In contrast, the constraints recorded in the 1996 survey were mainly basic services and infrastructure access. Nearly 80 per cent of WBES respondents in 2000 identified policy instability and uncertainty as the main constraint to business operations and expansion. Participants associated the risks and uncertainty with various factors, including ambiguity surrounding the final status economic arrangement with Israel. Moreover, 70 per cent of respondents reported that Israeli security measures constituted the biggest regulatory and administrative burden. As for the rule of law, WBES participant investors ranked the courts and judiciary lowest among other public institutions in terms of the quality of services (Sewell 2001).

In 2001, the Centre for Private Sector Development (CPSD) carried out a survey on the state of the private sector to assess the impact of the Israeli measures imposed since September 2000 and the role of the PA institutions. According to the main findings 37 per cent of respondents thought that the PA's commitment to a genuine market economy was poor. 52 per cent of respondents ranked PA institutions as having no clear mission. 37 per cent of respondents thought that the level of intervention in private sector activity was excessive. 78 per cent thought that the PA's monopolistic behaviour had a serious impact. As for the judicial system, 33 per cent believed that the system was slow in settling disputes, 41 per cent thought it was not fair and 39 per cent gave a negative rating for its ability to implement the resolutions (CPSD 2001).

The domestic private sector has absorbed much of the economic crisis associated with the intifada since September 2000. The intensification of Israeli-imposed closures, curfews and military operations and the

Table 6.4 Palestine Securities Exchange – listed companies

	Company	*Trading currency*	*Capital*	*% capital paid*	*Nominal share price*	*Status*
1	Arab Concrete Products Co. Ltd	JD	660,000	100	1	Active
2	Arab Hotels Co.	JD	6,916,488	100	1	Active
3	Arab Islamic Bank	$	21,000,000	100	1	Active
4	Arab Insurance Est.	JD	869,400	100	1	Active
5	Arab Co. for Paint Products	JD	1,500,000	100	1	Active
6	Arab Investors Co.	JD	9,452,328	100	1	Active
7	Arab Real Estate Establishments Co.	JD	948,890	100	1	Active
8	Arab Care Medical Services	JD	10,000,000	100	1	Suspended
9	Beit Al Mal Holdings	JD	10,000,000	100	1	Active
10	Gaza Ahliea Insurance Co.	$	5,512,500	100	1	Active
11	Grand Park Hotel & Resorts	JD	1,150,000	100	1	Suspended
12	Jerusalem Cigarette Co.	JD	7,000,000	100	1	Active
13	Jerusalem Pharmaceutical Co.	JD	1,000,000	100	1	Active
14	National Insurance Co.	JD	3,850,000	100	1	Active
15	Palestine Development & Investment Co.	$	172,132,000	100	1	Active
16	Palestine Telecommunication Co.	JD	67,500,000	100	1	Active
17	Palestine Cement Co.	JD	3,908,988	100	1	Suspended
18	Palestine International Bank	JD	11,903,201	100	1	Active
19	Palestine Investment Bank	$	20,000,000	100	1	Active
20	Palestine Investment & Development Co.	JD	5,307,001	100	1	Active
21	Palestine Real Estate Investment	JD	15,000,000	100	1	Active
22	Al Quds Bank for Development & Investment	$	20,000,000	100	1	Active
23	Vegetable Oil Industries Company Ltd	JD	3,000,000	100	1	Active
24	Arab Palestinian Shopping Center	JD	4,500,000	100	1	Active

heightened risk have reduced investment. According to World Bank estimates the volume of private investment declined from US$1.25bn in 1999 to only US$50 million in 2002. Destruction of physical infrastructure and the accelerated depreciation of capital assets have significantly affected the capacity of the Palestinian economy and its ability to recover rapidly from recession (World Bank 2003).

Institutional fragmentation

Private sector performance has been further impaired by the weak performance of legal institutions which were significantly affected over the last three years by Israel's occupation policies. The severe closure measures restricted the functioning of the high court and the Diwan al-Fatwa wa al-Tashri'a (the legislative drafting committee). As a result, judges, employees, attorneys, clients and witnesses have had restricted access to the workplace.

Moreover, judicial institutions were directly targeted during 'Operation Defensive Shield' with Israeli soldiers breaking into the Palestinian Court of Appeals in Ramallah and damaging files, looting private law firms and human rights NGOs. The activity of the Palestinian Legislative Council (PLC) was also undermined by restrictions on movements although teleconferences were held to facilitate meetings in some circumstances.

Continued Israeli military attacks on the Palestinian security services have undermined the ability of Palestinian society to police and govern itself. Targeted institutions included prisons, office complexes, forensic laboratories and military courts, so that even if criminals are captured there is no place to incarcerate them (Bolding 2002).

This catalogue of examples serves to emphasise that the Palestinian private sector operating environment has been radically and structurally affected at all levels in such a way that corporate behaviour is very case-specific, difficult to predict, ad hoc and not based on any kind of long-term strategic planning. Moving to a sovereign environment will inevitably relieve the current challenges to private sector activity. It will not, however, remove the entrenched and distorted behavioural patterns that have emerged over the decades: reluctance to invest, lack of confidence in the business environment, short-term contingency planning rather than long-term strategic investment and lack of confidence in the ruling authorities.

The IT sector as a case study

Growth under adversity

The impressive growth of the Palestinian information technology (IT) sector over the past seven years offers a useful insight into the extent to which private sector growth is conditioned by the operating environment and how the institutional structure of any one sector may be skewed by the legacy of occupation. In a sovereign Palestinian state, effective legislation, regulation and enforcement can help standardise and institutionalise best practices. However, it cannot annul the deviant patterns of corporate behaviour that have emerged through occupation and conflict.

The growth of the IT sector in the WBGS and the nature of the associated business practices clearly represent responses to the operational reality on the ground rather than organic growth in the demand for IT services and products. As a result, the sector has grown in a manner that may not necessarily bode well for competitiveness in a sovereign environment and one which may not withstand the onslaught of international competition that sovereignty would bring.

However, it has nurtured the Palestinian entrepreneurial spirit and attracted western-educated professionals who openly call for the adoption of international best practices in terms of the operating environment and notably the legislative framework. As such it merits special consideration and demonstrates the need for forthcoming legislation to consider sector specifics, the very small-scale nature of the Palestinian private sector and how company law could support rather than hinder in this respect.

The Palestinian IT sector is comprised largely of a young, dynamic and well-educated entrepreneurial class with a strong de facto voice and a very clear understanding that effective legislation can facilitate rather than undermine development. This class very quickly demonstrated its ability to organise itself, notably through the creation of the Palestinian IT Association (PITA),[11] set up in 1999.

According to estimates by the Palestine Trade Center, the IT industry in the WBGS has expanded by more than 25–30 per cent per year since 1997 such that IT has been Palestine's fastest growing industry. While official statistics for the year 2000 suggest that IT has made only a limited quantitative contribution to the domestic economy,[12] they show that it comprises 63 firms operating in computer-related activities and employing over 206 employees with a total output of some US$3 million. It also hosts 126 firms engaged in telecommunication activities employing 2,375 workers and with US$88 million in value-added.

In the middle of the last decade, the accelerated annual increase in local demand for IT products and services fuelled the growth in this industry. The creation of Palestinian national institutions created increased demand for IT products and notably for Arabic software. The establishment of modern government offices required procurement of office equipment including computers and networks to exchange information. The establishment of a private telecommunications company (PALTEL) also expanded Palestinian access to communication services.

Moving online as a coping strategy

Since the outset of the latest intifada in September 2000 and, unlike other Palestinian business sectors, IT businesses have sustained their growth. Palestinian institutions and enterprises have relied heavily on internet communication and video conferencing to get around closures and other Israeli-imposed movement restrictions and maintain day-to-day business operations. For example, the prominent Birzeit University developed an electronic utility called Ritaj (Arabic for 'gate') to facilitate interactions between faculties and students. Much of this was due to the efforts of PALTEL, which managed to maintain fully operational services despite the conflict environment.

The sector has witnessed rapid growth in infrastructure. According to PALTEL statistics, the number of phone lines rose from 222,200 in 1999 to more than 292,000 lines in 2001 while the number of localities connected to the company's network increased from 345 in 1999 to 460 localities at the end of 2001. Thus the expansion of the company's network facilitated a tangible transfer to online operations within the Palestinian business community.

According to Palestine's Internet Society, internet penetration has risen to over 6 per cent. Similarly, the volume of internet services including the number of leased lines, websites and internet cafes increased by 50 per cent during the current intifada. Service prices in Palestine, however, remain among the highest in the region due to the absence of competition.[13]

Internet penetration is expected to rise markedly over the next two years. PALTEL has launched a new campaign called 'Net Forever' to increase internet usage and penetration in Palestine. The service aims to meet the needs of heavy internet users in homes and businesses. The company offers service subscribers separate internet lines at a fixed monthly rate. More recently, PALTEL launched, jointly with the Arab Bank, a local internet service provider and a Ramallah-based computer hardware retailer to facilitate and enhance Palestinians' access to the virtual world.

The success of Palestinian IT companies has gone beyond domestic borders to reach regional markets, with some successful export projects to GCC countries. Industry insiders acknowledge that at the outset the industry received little more than sympathetic attention, but having demonstrated the high quality of its products, competitive prices and professional support and customer care, it has seen the growth of real business opportunities with Gulf companies.[14] Through regular Palestinian participation at GITEX, a global IT exhibition held in the UAE every year, PITA has opened a branch office in Dubai's Internet City to serve the interests of member companies in the Gulf region.

Market expansion in the Gulf region has also been accompanied by important technical achievements. The collective efforts of the Palestinian internet community have resulted in the assignment of PS as a Palestinian internet domain. Earlier this year Palestine's internet chapter of the global internet society (ISOC) was established. The mission of Palestine's chapter is to link Palestinian internet professionals and users throughout the Palestinian diaspora in the hope of creating a tangible venue where Palestinian professionals around the world can contribute to the advancement of internet applications in Palestine.

Governing the sector

Importantly, on the regulatory front, the local IT community representing public and private institutions has been actively involved in supporting the growth of the industry by promoting the use of modern technologies and advocating the creation of an enabling regulatory environment. A telecommunications law is currently under review and takes into account new aspects of the telecommunication business and the Ministry of Economy and Trade has completed a draft e-commerce law. The ministry is also now working very closely with various stakeholders to draft an intellectual property of copyrights law. Serious discussions are also underway aimed at reducing tariffs to make internet access more affordable to smaller firms and Palestinian families.

The existing capacity and future potential of this industry are indicative of the growth of the private sector as a whole in a future sovereign environment. While it has followed the high growth path of the IT industry globally, the sector's total contribution to GDP for 2000 was not more than 3 per cent. Moreover, many of the behavioural norms of this sector are entirely a product of the distortions of the local market rather than a response to indigenous organic growth in demand. However, it has emerged as a defiant and vocal sector within the corporate environment in the WBGS and highlights the private sector's ability to fast-track technology adoption and support the development of effective legislation.

Company law for Palestine

Entrepreneurial voice

A key ingredient of a well-functioning legal system in a market economy is the demand from market participants. 'The demand for legal and institutional reform that arises from economic liberalization is as critical to legal reform as the supply of good laws and functioning legal institutions', according to Gray (1997: 15). The Palestinian IT sector is a case in point, where young, well-educated professionals are calling for the rapid introduction of relevant legislation cognisant of the need to structure the future growth of their industry. As Gray points out, 'The best formal legal systems operate only at the margin, leaving most standards in a society to be internalized and "self-enforced" by society itself'.

The review process in the UK has adopted this approach and when Margaret Beckett launched the Company Law Review in March 1998 she said at the time that she wanted it to be 'an open and fully consultative process'. Analysts suggest that while the process has been very time consuming, this was due to the consultation process and will contribute to the success of the final outcome.

While building local consensus the PA must also keep in mind regional legal reform in addition to that of its neighbouring trading bloc, the EU. Without this it risks creating a non-integrated legislative norm that will later face the problems of harmonisation as currently being witnessed in the EU and indeed in the Middle East as a whole. Importing wholesale western legislation carries high risks in terms of applicability, and the ability to adapt alien legislation to local prevailing norms is critical.[15] However, ensuring the local relevance of new legislation should not negate the need to consider global integration.

The body of knowledge and understanding emerging from the global review of corporate governance, which can serve to guide any emerging market on key components of legislation, has highlighted specific areas. Some of these may seem more relevant in the sophisticated financial and capital market sectors of the west. However, the rapid economic growth that would ensue in a sovereign environment and the inevitable evolution of the corporate sector and associated finance needs mean that Palestine should envisage these challenges as a very real part of its future growth.

To follow this argument through, future corporate governance legislation should consider, in particular: auditing and accounting standards; the relationship with accounting and audit firms; the role and duties of the CEO and CFO; financial incentives for staff; the cost of adhering to new legislation; creating a culture of transparency; the adaptability of legislation and its ability to evolve in line with the operating environment and disclosure standards and norms.

In developing economies it is often considered wise that company law should involve the setting up of a Corporate Law Authority, which would be responsible for the implementation of the registration process, arbitration and tasks other than legal adjudication which would facilitate the implementation of the company law. This is all the more important in the case of Palestine given that the transition process from the existing laws, which seem incomplete, to a new company law administration will require education and support. A good legal framework, especially in a rapidly changing corporate landscape, should comprehend the unification of laws in the region and within the World Trade Organisation set-up. This implies that the company law would need to be forward-looking to ensure that frequent changes or conflicts with wider commercial unions or international agreements do not occur.

Accounting rules are also relatively standard and the acceptance and implementation of the International Accounting Standards (IAS) is considered on a global basis to be more than adequate for proper financial disclosure. The adoption of IAS will also automatically bode well for the auditing profession.

Disclosure

Disclosure, it is believed, can be a powerful and relatively cheap way of both increasing accountability and bringing about desired corporate behaviour. Disclosure is most appropriate in areas such as a company's dealings with its directors, substantial shareholders and related parties. It should normally be left to a company's articles to determine which sort of dealing is prohibited, which needs shareholder consent and which needs board consent only, though the content of a listed company's articles would in turn be affected by the requirements of the relevant listing authority.

Using technology to facilitate disclosure is a common recommendation. In Palestine, use of the web has proven a tangible and reliable way of facilitating the disclosure of information in an environment where physical access is difficult and indeed, as the case study on IT demonstrates, the growth of this sector is setting new norms in terms of governance. Technology should be incorporated carefully, however, and should not isolate individuals without access to it. Shareholders should be free to use the traditional means of communication if they wish.

Moreover, legislators need to consider cost implications. Since communication by electronic means is easy and very fast, there is a possible danger that certain companies may become targets of pressure groups and be bombarded by requisitions, which can result in companies incurring very considerable expense and irrecoverable diversion of management time. In an area where incomes have fallen rapidly in the past few years, changes in the law or regulation must take into consideration the cost and other disadvantages for the efficient operation of business. Care should be taken not to over-regulate, especially in a country that is struggling to establish its competitiveness, since this will put companies at a disadvantage.

Board compensation

The role and remuneration of board members is a critical component of the global discourse and has resulted in some areas of broad consensus. The remuneration of individual board members should be disclosed, particularly if it is linked to the share price performance. Shareholders should have the opportunity to express their view on the principles and limits of board remuneration. It would not normally be appropriate, however, for shareholders' consent to be required in relation to an individual's remuneration package. Normally shareholders do not have adequate information (or, in most cases, experience) to be able to judge the remuneration package the company should pay an executive or officer and the requirement for shareholder consent might inhibit the recruiting process for senior positions.

Boards combine a strategic purpose and a monitoring role. However, it is critical that shareholders do not allow strategic purpose to outweigh the board's duties to its beneficiaries, which would be the case if non-independent directors are allowed to control executive remuneration or auditing, for example. In this respect, independent directors should be empowered to counterbalance the unity of the board and the power of the CEO.

Incentives

Global analysis now also suggests that companies would do well to avoid providing pensions for their employees. This not only exposes them to risk, as the large pension fund deficits of today demonstrate, but also creates a conflict of interests with fund managers and shareholders. Tax breaks can encourage companies to offer such schemes and push employees to keep their pension plans heavily invested in the firm's shares but, as Enron clearly demonstrated, these incentives should be abolished.

Monitoring bodies should not be appointed by or become dependent upon those they monitor and as such auditors should not also perform consultancy business for the firm they audit. Auditing firms should also be changed regularly. Moreover, investors themselves need to acknowledge the value of good corporate governance and its implications for long-term financial sustainability. As *The Economist* (2002) points out:

> It was investors, with their relentless hunt for double digit earnings growth, who encouraged executive fiddling in the final years of the stock market bubble. If the market comes to admire honesty, transparency and good corporate governance, executives will rush to acquire those characteristics. Even in morality, the market rules, in the end.
>
> (*The Economist* 2002)

Company law has to be able to evolve especially in Palestine where on a daily basis the situation changes and where even in a post-conflict situation, the institutional structure of the country will likely take many years to mature. As Hewitt notes of UK company law:

> it was largely created in the nineteenth century. But what was a source of competitive advantage to us then, is now a source of competitive

disadvantage. The law has got out of date and become encrusted with all sorts of amendments and case law. It needs to reflect the huge change we have seen in our economy since Victorian times. Back then, Rowland Hill had just introduced the Penny Post. Now we've got emails, the Internet, text messaging, faxing, computerized bookkeeping and so on.

(2002: 6)

Conclusion: global norms with local credence

Company law as a component

Global experience demonstrates quite clearly that in many countries the mere existence of a company law is not sufficient as economic activity encompasses a vast segment of the legal environment. Thus the presence of laws covering trusts, patents, copyright, trademark registration, foreign investment protection, representation, arbitration, securities markets and other aspects need to be either separately framed or covered comprehensively within the legal system. In a sovereign environment, investment laws alone and specific investment incentives will be insufficient to offset the perception that, notwithstanding the political risk factor, Palestine is poorly regulated.

Local lawyers point out that the legal and regulatory framework as it exists today remains a challenge for both the businessman and for the investor. 'To simply identify which law applies to which business and how to interpret the law is an arduous task. At the same time many of the protections often found in a transparent "rule of law" are still lacking in Palestine'.[16] As in the rest of the world, simplification will prove essential.

Institutional capacity

Inevitably, legislative reform is ineffective if institutional capacity is weak. Developing credible governance institutions across the board is critical for the PA. As local lawyers point out, no amount of draft laws in Palestine will help while 'institutional capacity to implement is lacking ... public governance is weak and interagency/inter-ministerial coordination is limited'.[17] Already the body of draft legislation that exists in Palestine suffers from a lack of coordination between the various ministries and institutions and a lack of regulations that can make enforcement effective.

Moreover, the PLC is dealing with separate laws rather than a series of laws, which contributes to conflicts and contradictions, especially in the absence of regulations and forms. There is a huge need to draft regulations and develop procedures to implement the new laws correctly. In addition, new law provisions should be explained to civil servants in training sessions and other outreach activities to create a common understanding of these provisions and avoid any human error.

The PA must also ensure that the huge distortions in all governing frameworks and the highly entrenched informal relationship structures are acknowledged and addressed in forthcoming legislation. As Gray points out:

> There is a growing literature on informal product and credit markets in developing and transition countries that shows the importance of reputation and family or ethnic networks as screening devices in selecting reliable partners in the absence of formal contract-enforcement institutions.
>
> (1997: 14)

These informal mechanisms dominate in many emerging markets such that enforcing new structures may be difficult if they are not acknowledged:

> Complex or long-term contracts are likely to be relatively scarce in this environment and new firms without family or ethnic connections may find it impossible to break into the contracting network. This in turn carries a risk in that a shortage of new firms and new people means a dearth of new ideas and entrepreneurship and the inability to enter into long-term contracts can inhibit the adoption and development of complex technologies. Additionally illegal (often violent) enforcement mechanisms may substitute for legal ones.
>
> (Gray 1997: 14)

In a sovereign environment, legislators must consider the possibility of rapid growth and hence rapid corporate development and corporate finance. They should not dismiss the possibility that local Palestinian firms will choose to follow a similar path to some of their western counterparts in a situation of rapid growth, rapidly rising returns and disproportionately fast growth in shareholder voice and demands.

Legislation in a sovereign Palestine must acknowledge the historical distortions of the local market, how these will impact future growth and, at the same time, take into consideration the global best practices emerging from more developed markets. In this way, the legal system in Palestine will effectively oversee those aspects of business that have emerged from years of occupation and conflict while at the same time ensuring a link to the global system, competitive practices and sound prospects for long-term growth.

Notes

1 The authors would like to acknowledge the support and assistance of several individuals. They would like to thank specifically Ms Hiba Husseini, a Palestinian Jerusalem-based lawyer for her consistent insights into the changing legal environment in Palestine and Ms Maha Sbeih, also a Palestinian lawyer, for her comments and advice. We also wish to thank Mr Anwer Sher who has been a business consultant in the Middle East for over 20 years and offered useful insights into the regional operating environment. Finally, we are indebted to all of the sources based inside and outside Palestine who provided insights and information on the legal and operational nature of the Palestinian economy and their thoughts on the prospects for sound corporate governance and associated legislation.

2 The case for reform is very different from that in Palestine. In many cases, new corporate governance paradigms are emerging from the push of institutional investors who form a very small component of investors in Palestine. Institutional shareholders have been taking a tough line with corporates that overly reward their CEO while the company flounders, with the most recent examples in the UK where investors protested pay rises at Reuters, Shell and EMI. Similarly, in the US, General Electric and Hewlett Packard have come under attack. (see http://www.entemp.ie/cr/EU-Developments.htm, accessed November 2003).

3 Company law is particularly important for small companies. They are the engines of growth especially in Palestine where they employ 75–80 per cent of the workforce. According to Hewitt:

> Around 88% of all 'novel innovators' (firms introducing a technologically new or improved product to market) are SMEs. And the cost of bad company legislation can have a huge impact on SMEs and the wider economy. An unnecessary burden of £100 a company a year costs our business sector £150 million a year. We need to look rigorously at regulation and ensure we only keep that regulation which is vital to confidence.
>
> (2002: 7–8)

According to *The Economist* (2003a):

> The Sarbanes-Oxley act, passed in the wake of accounting scandals at Enron and other firms, introduced a slew of new regulations, that raised compliance costs – such as the right of the board of directors to hire independent advisers, paid for out of company coffers. Estimates of the additional costs for a public company range from a conservative $1 million to $3 million, depending on the size of the firm.

4 The World Bank (forthcoming) also notes that in Estonia significant progress was made in terms of attracting FDI not just through its Association agreement with the EU (which Jordan has used to a similar end), but also by *inter alia*, repealing the Foreign Investment Law and instead relying on Company and Securities Law and related legislation to govern all investment without distinguishing between foreign and domestic investment.

5 OECD (1998), cited in Mallin (2003).

6 Nicholas Murray Butler, the president of Columbia University in 1911, cited in Hewitt (2002: 5).

7 John Monks, Secretary of the UK Trades Union Congress, cited in Hewitt (2002: 5).

8 Hewitt (2002: 5).

9 The West Bank and Gaza Investment Guarantee Trust Fund was created in cooperation with the PNA by the Multilateral Investment Guarantee Agency (MIGA). The Trust Fund provides eligible foreign investors with guarantees against major political risk concerns such as expropriation, war and civil disturbance in member countries. The Trust Fund aims to direct investment to Palestine and contribute to the reintegration of its areas into the world economy.

10 Excerpt from an unofficial translation of the Law on the Encouragement of Investment in Palestine, Law no. (28), of 1998. http://www.met.gov.ps/english/law/investment.pdf.

11 The Palestinian Information Technology Association (PITA) was founded in early 1999 in Ramallah, Palestine as a membership-based organisation for locally registered companies in the IT sector. The association represents approximately 69 companies from various sub-sectors including hardware distributors, software development firms, office automation vendors, Internet service providers, telecommunications, IT consulting, IT training and related businesses.

12 Growth rates are according to estimates acquired from the Palestine Trade Center and the Palestine Investment Promotion Agency.

13 Muwatin (2003).

14 Murad Tahboub, CEO Asal Technologies, has signed dealership agreements with partners in the UAE and in Saudi Arabia.

15 Peruvian economist Hernando de Soto points out that importing a legal system carries big risks. In post-war Japan, General MacArthur oversaw the introduction of American corporate law, including the old Glass-Steagall Act that separated investment banking from commercial banking and although this proved relatively successful initially the Japanese industrial sector subsequently developed in a very different direction. It is often more effective to go with the grain of local legal practice – formal or, more often, informal – than to adopt an alien 'first-best' model (*The Economist* 2003b).

16 Conversations with Hiba Husseini, practicing attorney of Husseini and Dajani, Attorneys and Counsellors at Law

17 Conversation with Hiba Husseini, see note 16.

References

Ayyoub, T. (2002) 'Companies Law amendment welcomed by some, others call for additional changes', *Jordan Times*, May 9.

Bolding, G. (2002) 'The impact of Israel's ongoing military incursions into Palestinian areas A: a naked assault on the rule of law in Palestine', working paper, Birzeit University Institute of Law.

Bradley, N. (2003) 'Corporate governance: a risk worth measuring?' in UNCTAD, *Selected Issues in Corporate Governance: Regional and Country Experiences*, New York and Geneva: UNCTAD.

Centre for Private Sector Development (CPSD) (2001) *State of the Private Sector: Survey of West Bank and Gaza Strip*, October, Nablus: CPSD.

The Economist (2002) 'I swear: oaths are only a small step in the business of cleaning up American companies', *The Economist*, 17 August.

The Economist (2003a) 'Corporate finance: a (going) private matter', *The Economist*, 22 March.

The Economist (2003b) 'Special report: rebuilding Iraq', *The Economist*, 19 April.

The Economist (2003c) 'A survey of capitalism and democracy', *The Economist*, 28 June.

Government of Palestine, Ministry of Economy and Trade, Adam Smith Institute, International Division, Companies and Partnerships Law, draft, 1999.

Gray, C. (1997) 'Reforming legal systems in developing and transition countries', *Finance and Development*, 14–16 September.

Hewitt, P. (2002) Speech at conference on 'Using Law to Promote Competitiveness and Enterprise: Will Corporate Law Reform Deliver?', Cambridge, July, http://www.law.cam.ac.uk/cccl/Keynote_speech.pdf.

Mallin, C. (2003) 'The relationship between corporate governance, transparency and financial disclosure' in UNCTAD, *Selected Issues in Corporate Governance: Regional and Country Experiences*, New York and Geneva: UNCTAD.

Muwatin (2003) 'The Internet in Palestine', *Parliamentary Horizons*, volume 7, no. 5: 9, Ramallah: Muwatin (Palestinian Institute for the Study of Democracy).

Naqib, F. (2002) 'Economic aspects of the Palestinian–Israeli conflict: the collapse of the Oslo Accord', DP2000/100, Helsinki: World Institute for Development Economics Research.

OECD (1998) *Global Corporate Governance Principles*, Paris: OECD.

Paltrade (2002) 'Private sector needs assessment: industrial sector survey', Palestinian Federation of Industries (PFI), Palestine Trade Centre (Paltrade), in cooperation with Market Access Program, DAI.

Sewell, D. (2001) 'Governance and the business environment in West Bank and Gaza', working paper 23, Social and Economic Development Group, MENA Region, World Bank.

World Bank (1993), *Developing the Occupied Territories: An Investment in Peace*, 6 volumes, Washington, DC: World Bank.

World Bank (2003) 'Twenty-seven months of intifada, closures and Palestinian economic crisis, an assessment', May, Washington, DC: World Bank.

World Bank (n.d.) 'A strategy for private sector development in West Bank and Gaza: from crisis to sustainable growth', unpublished draft document.

Discussion

Oren Sussman

In a book published some 70 years ago, Berle and Means (1932) make a striking observation: that among the US's biggest and most successful companies, ownership is often separated from control, that is, managers rather than owners have effective control over companies. The observation is puzzling: if private property is the basic concept on which the whole capitalist system rests, and if the US is capitalism's paradigmatic and most successful example, then how come, in its very core, private ownership vanishes? Much of the modern thinking about business organisation may be perceived as an attempt to resolve the Berle and Means puzzle. Some have tried to uncover the mechanisms through which owners may regain control, for example when a company is taken over; see Manne (1965) and a flood of papers since then. Some have argued that bureaucracy, rather than ownership, is the basic building block of capitalism; see Marschak and Radner (1972). Yet others have argued that the separation of ownership and control is an aberration from which capitalism is bound to revert; see Jensen (1989). Though Jensen's predictions were obviously premature, they might materialise in the future in response to some spectacular corporate revolution.

As often happens, intellectually puzzling phenomena attract attention disproportionately to their market share. Even within the Anglo-Saxon world the vast majority of companies are not affected by the problem for the simple reason that they are not listed. Outside the Anglo-Saxon world, say in Germany or Japan, owners and bankers (not managers) are the leading players. In emerging markets, equity markets are often underdeveloped. And all over the world, debt rather than equity is the dominant instrument for financing new investments; see Mayer (1988). The recent corporate governance reforms might be relevant to a relatively small number of firms, but for most emerging markets the new thinking is probably irrelevant.

Palestine is a case in point. According to Table 6.1, 92 per cent of businesses have one owner only. We do not know how many of the remaining 8 per cent of businesses actually have dispersed ownership. According to Table 6.3, 16–17 per cent of firms in the WBGS report that they manage to get some bank funding (though we do not know what size that funding is). When financial constraints are that binding, equity must play a very limited role in corporate finance and corporate governance is hardly an issue. Legally defining the limits of managerial power may actually relax a non-binding constraint.

That, however, does not imply that the law does not matter. Evidently, businesses in the WBGS suffer from an extreme shortage of capital. The most likely source of funding is bank credit. In order to operate, banks need to register, and sometimes to seize, collateral. The law has to make sure that these simple, albeit crucial, instruments operate efficiently. In a society where the bureaucracy and the justice system hardly function, this is not a trivial objective to achieve. The several references in the chapter to corruption highlight the point.

It may be argued that preparing the ground for future developments may be a good idea. This argument, however, has several limitations. First, as shown above, the separation of ownership and control is not a universal phenomenon. Possibly, the Palestinian economy may not develop in that direction or the phenomenon may be modified by the time Palestine gets developed enough. Why spend scarce current resources on a future need with uncertain realisation? Second, it is doubtful whether Palestine has sufficient administrative resources to restructure both debt and equity markets simultaneously. If, indeed, the two reforms have to be prioritised, then the debt market should probably come first. It would absorb less resources and generate more funding to the business sector.

A related question is the relationship between Palestine's corporate law and Jordan's. Given the number of Palestinian professionals (accountants, lawyers, bankers etc.) trained in Jordan, the Jordanian origin of the Palestinian system and the extensive business relations between the two countries, adopting the Jordanian law must be less costly than drafting an original law (or even 'copying' some 'advanced' western law). Yet the authors rule that possibility out on the grounds that the Jordanian law is not sophisticated enough. However, in several international comparisons, Jordan seems to perform quite well; cf. La Porta *et al.* (1998). Possibly, the Jordanian system works relatively well because it focuses on the basic rather than on the sophisticated. A financial system need not be sophisticated; it should suit the economy that it is serving. And in that respect, focusing a whole law reform on corporate governance of companies with a separation of ownership and control may be counterproductive.

References

Berle, A.A. and Means, G.C. (1932) *The Modern Corporation and Private Property*, New York: Macmillan.

Jensen, M.C. (1989) 'Eclipse of the public corporation', *Harvard Business Review* 67: 61–75.

La Porta, R., Lopez-de-Silanes, F., Shleifer, A. and Vishny, R.W. (1998) 'Law and finance', *Journal of Political Economy* 106: 1113–1155.

Manne, H.G. (1965) 'Mergers and the market for corporate control', *Journal of Political Economy* 73: 110–120.

Marschak, J. and Radner, R. (1972) *The Economic Theory of Teams*, New Haven: Yale University Press.

Mayer, C. (1988) 'New issues in corporate finance', *European Economic Review* 32: 1167–1189.

7 Structuring a pension scheme for a future Palestinian state

Edward A. Sayre and Jennifer C. Olmsted

Introduction

The economic situation facing Palestinians in the West Bank and Gaza Strip is particularly dismal at the moment. Poverty rates have risen dramatically, in part due to intolerable unemployment rates. While the Palestinian Authority (PA) has, on the one hand, been attempting to build its institutional capacity, the pressure of dealing with the al-Aqsa intifada and the Israeli reaction to it has meant plans to develop a more comprehensive set of institutions have been postponed. As the current situation has acutely shown, one of the biggest gaps in institution building remains in the area of social security. No basic law governing pensions, unemployment insurance and disability insurance exists to date. The lack of a formal social security system not only increases economic uncertainty for the elderly, but also deprives Palestinian workers in Israel of contributions to the Israeli Social Insurance owed to them.

While a number of factors need to be addressed in order to assure a strong state-sponsored social safety net in the future, in this chapter we focus primarily on the question of how to develop a sustainable pension system for Palestinian workers, acknowledging the fact that one of the most pressing problems at the moment is actually unemployment and poverty among both the working and non-working poor. While unemployment and the resulting poverty have admittedly been acute in recent years, the high unemployment rate will, one hopes, be temporary and certainly is not a problem that can be addressed through internal funding. Thus we argue that the current crisis should be addressed by the international community in the form of food assistance and employment creation programmes. This strategy has already in part been implemented, but must be redoubled.

In addition to there being a need to address the current crisis, at least three areas of policy remain relating to labour/economic security that need to be addressed: the development of an unemployment insurance scheme, the expansion of the existing poverty programmes and the establishment of a sustainable pension plan. The objective of such social security programmes is to provide support for those who are unable to support themselves, either because of chronic economic problems such as disabilities, or because of temporary problems which may occur as a result of exposure to a single or multiple risks. Individuals, households and communities who are exposed to multiple risks, may need to fall back on state-provided safety nets, with the poor typically being more vulnerable because of both increased risks and fewer endowments (World Bank n.d.: vi).

In order to reduce economic risks, or at least temper the impact of risks on individuals and their families, researchers need a better understanding of who is likely to suffer from these risks and how individuals, in particular the poor, protect themselves from such risks. Also, it would be helpful to examine how these risks may change over time. In the context of the Palestinians it is worthwhile to examine:

1 the general economic situation facing Palestinians;
2 existing formal and informal safety nets;
3 current and projected labour force participation patterns.

By examining these, we can address the question of whether there is a need for a more comprehensive safety net and what form that safety net should take.

While conceding that the development of an unemployment programme is also an extremely important goal, the main objective of this chapter is to contribute to the discussion on the need to establish a pension scheme in Palestine. Our contribution focuses on three areas that have not received sufficient attention in previous proposals. First, there has been insufficient attention paid to both the informal sector and the importance of the safety net for women. Second, some proposals have encouraged very high levels of social protection without acknowledging the potentially negative consequences for the labour market. Third, the recent economic devastation experienced in the WBGS has demonstrated the great degree of vulnerability due to variability in economic outcomes. Any pension scheme must be explicitly flexible in order to deal with a variety of unforeseen contingencies. We present an outline of a basic pension plan that we believe addresses these sometimes competing issues in a way that provides a fair level of social insurance.

Existing economic conditions

In order to evaluate the appropriateness of alternative pension schemes, one must first understand the fundamental features of the Palestinian labour market, with a particular focus on poverty and employment patterns. The administration of any pension scheme depends heavily not only on the level of both current and projected labour force participation, but also on the type of employment options available to workers. Designing a pension scheme is greatly complicated if the participation is informal. At the other end of the spectrum, pensions for public sector workers are very easy to implement, but the public sector is unlikely to encompass the majority of workers. More generally, any attempt to structure a formal social security system in the context of the Palestinian economy needs to address high rates of poverty, low labour force participation rates and high levels of informal employment.

Poverty

According to a recent World Bank publication (2001), one in four Palestinians was poor in 1998. The authors of this report classify this as a high level of poverty and also note that since the increased conflict during 2000 (which continued through most of 2003), poverty rates have likely risen significantly. The World Bank (2002: 31) estimates that by the end of 2001 '40 to 50 per cent of the population had fallen below the poverty line'. Similarly, UNSCO (2002) estimated that by 2002, poverty levels had reached 60 per cent, with Gaza suffering poverty rates of 70 per cent and the West Bank having slightly lower rates of poverty, at 55 per cent.

Poverty is an extremely serious problem in the WBGS, with some groups being more acutely affected by it than others. For instance, the World Bank (2001) study suggests that 32 per cent of households headed by individuals over 65 are in poverty, as compared to 25 per cent in the general population. Female-headed households are also at higher risk. Poverty rates vary considerably between Gaza and the West Bank, with families in the former being far more vulnerable (38 versus 16 per cent respectively). A substantial number of Palestinians can also be categorised as 'working poor'. While households with non-working heads did have higher poverty rates (33 per cent), the poverty rate among working household heads was still 20 per cent. At particular risk among the employed are the self-employed.

While many of the poor are those who have difficulty accessing the labour market because of certain personal characteristics, in the context of the WBGS, particularly in recent years, unemployment has been a major factor contributing to high levels of poverty. Unemployment rates among Palestinians rose to an alarmingly high level, particularly during 2002, when Israeli closures were in place. UNSCO (2002: 7) points out that even official (ILO) measures of unemployment suggest a rise from 28.9 (an already high level) to 33.6 per cent during the first part of 2002.

Protecting Palestinians from economic hardship

Given the high levels of poverty and the vulnerability of certain groups, particularly the unemployed, children, women and the elderly, there is an urgent need not only to examine existing safety nets, but also to begin planning for a more comprehensive safety net in the region. A number of different programmes exist in Palestine, which address poverty. It is important to distinguish between employment creation programmes, such as public sector employment and public works, and more direct methods of helping the poor, including food rations and cash programmes. Substantial employment creation programmes exist in Palestine, and in fact much of the aid in recent years has gone toward programmes to stem unemployment caused by restrictions on employment imposed by Israel (UNSCO 2002 and World Bank 2002). Increased employment creation programmes have been funded by UN monies and by international donors, who had previously been funnelling funds into infrastructure development. Additional programmes to address the extremely high levels of poverty, including rising hunger, were also implemented in 2002, with the UN expanding its mandate considerably, as it began distributing food to far more households than previously (World Bank 2002). While these programmes have lessened the impact of closures, they remain stopgap measures and cannot be considered long-term strategies for addressing poverty and unemployment.

Existing, more structured poverty programmes are administered by the PA, the UN and various religious organisations.[1] Most of these programmes focus on providing assistance to individuals whose access to labour markets may be limited, including widows, orphans and the elderly (PA and Zakat) or to more destitute segments of the refugee population (UN Relief and Works Agency or UNRWA). Researchers and policy makers are only just beginning to get some idea of the extent of coverage under various safety net programmes. Data reported in Heiburg and Ovensen (1993) for 1992, before the Ministry of Social Affairs (MSA) began providing poverty assistance, suggested that 9 per cent of families reported receiving some form of welfare. More current statistics suggest that only 30 per cent of poor households are obtaining some form of cash assistance (World Bank 2001). The study by Hilal and El-Malki (1997) found that formal forms of assistance supported only 3 per cent of women and less than 2 per cent of men.

As the *Palestine Poverty Report* (1998) notes, few if any programmes address poverty among households with working heads, who may suffer from intermittent unemployment or low wages. As the report also notes, pensions remain scarce in Palestine, in part due to the lack of a government sector during over 50 years of military occupation. Although the PA study does not provide numbers, Heiberg and Ovensen (1992) indicate that 3 per cent of Palestinians surveyed were collecting a pension in 1992, while 14 per cent of Jordanians (a comparable population) surveyed around the same time said that they received a government-provided pension or social security (Hanssen-Bauer *et al.* 1998). Olmsted (forthcoming) found that pension rates were higher among Bethlehem-area residents, with 20 per cent of those who identified themselves as retired reporting that they were receiving retirement income. This discrepancy in coverage rates across regions points to one of the issues that must be addressed in designing a comprehensive social safety net. Numbers for the Bethlehem area are probably high because of the proximity to Jerusalem and the number of formal sector positions that have been available in this area historically. More generally, workers in urban areas, and particularly areas near economic centres, where a higher concentration of public sector and formal sector work is located, have greater access to pensions.

Data presented in the *Palestine Poverty Report* (1998: 41) also suggest that the elderly are particularly vulnerable to poverty. Because pensions are limited, the elderly rely primarily on kin, their own labour, or the limited existing relief programmes, for economic survival. Although those without kin are often among the most vulnerable, increasing poverty among the general population has also meant that even elderly with kin may be unable to rely on their relatives for continuing support. In particular, sharp increases in poverty in Gaza do not bode well for an effective family-based safety net. Hilal and El-Malki (1997) conclude that, for a number of reasons, the informal safety net is not adequate for addressing the needs of a growing portion of the population.

Hilal and El-Malki (1997) and Olmsted (forthcoming) discuss the current, primarily informal, safety net that exists in Palestine and note that household structure is one important factor related to the informal safety net. In general the informal safety net is likely to work better in the context of an extended family household structure, since larger households facilitate risk pooling more readily and the elderly in particular are more likely to find support if they are surrounded by kin.

Thus, one question to be raised is whether the extended family household prevails in the region. A number of recent surveys suggest that the nuclear family structure is increasingly replacing the more extended one. PCBS data indicate that in the West Bank and Gaza 2.6 per cent of the Palestinian population now live in one-person households, with another 14 per cent living in two to three person households. Similarly, Khawaja (2001: 48) reports that only about 25 per cent of households in the West Bank and Gaza are extended. The ratio is also considerably higher in Gaza (20 per cent) than in the West Bank (30 per cent), where extended families are more common in the south. It would appear that the prevalence of the nuclear family is growing.

Khawaja (2001) and Olmsted (forthcoming) find that, while nuclear households are on the rise, the elderly still predominantly live with their children, and particularly their sons, within the context of an extended family household. Data from the FAFO survey (Khawaja 2001) suggest that about 50 per cent of the elderly live in extended families. Hilal and El-Malki (1997: 64) come to a slightly different conclusion in their report on informal safety nets in Palestine. They argue that 'a majority of the elderly do not belong to extended families'. They reach this conclusion after finding that the majority of elderly men and women live in households containing fewer than five individuals. At the same time they concur that the majority of the elderly rely on their children (primarily sons) for support. One of the most interesting and telling findings from this survey is that although the majority of the elderly live with at least some kin, a surprising number of the elderly also live alone (7.3 per cent in West Bank, 4.9 per cent in Gaza). This is particularly true of women (12 per cent in West Bank and 8 per cent in Gaza). So one particularly vulnerable group may be elderly women, most of whom still rely on their spouses and children for support, but who may also increasingly be living alone and thus have less access to economic resources. Of course the causality may also go in the opposite direction – with elderly women who now have more resources at their disposal opting to live alone. Alternatively, both these circumstances could be occurring simultaneously, with some older individuals or couples who are comfortably well off opting to live alone, while others who are alone face considerable economic hardship (see Olmsted, forthcoming, for further discussion on this point.)

Employment conditions

Although evidence suggests that employment does not eliminate poverty, labour market participation remains a primary means for gaining access to financial resources. Labour market participation thereby reduces poverty in the short-run, and also allows resources to be saved, either for retirement or as a precaution against the event of an economic downturn. Non-participation due to non-market responsibilities, disability or infirmity creates a gap in economic resources that a pension and/or social security system can help fill.

In order to get a better sense of the existing labour patterns, we examine recent data from the Palestinian Central Bureau of Statistics (PCBS) Labour Force Survey.[2] The first and most striking feature of the labour force is that it is marked by very low labour force participation, resulting from a fairly young population and an extremely low female labour force participation rate. The average age in the West Bank and Gaza Strip (WBGS) is only 16½ years (PCBS 2003) and the female labour force participation rate is only 12 per cent. Low female participation combined with a young population results in an overall labour force participation rate (among those over the age of 15) of only 40.5 per cent for the 1995–2001 period. These participation rates vary not only by sex, but also by region. While the labour force participation rate for women in the West Bank is 14 per cent, it is only 8 per cent in the Gaza Strip. Likewise, men in the West Bank have a participation rate of 71 per cent compared to 63 per cent in the Gaza Strip.[3]

As Figure 7.1 panels (a) and (b) indicate, for men, life cycle considerations are the greatest reason for non-participation in the labour force. Men in the prime working age of 25 to 44 years have participation rates generally above 90 per cent with men aged 45–54 having slightly lower participation rates around 83 per cent.[4] The participation rate drops to near 50 per cent for 55–64 year olds and falls all the way to 20 per cent for those over 65.

However, evidence suggests that for men, non-participation in the labour force is more strongly determined by inability to work due to age and infirmity, than retirement. This is verified by surveys completed by Hilal and El-Malki (1997: 63), who show that only 17 per cent of men over the age of 60 claimed to be retired while 54 per cent of these men were categorised as out of work.

For women, labour force participation for any age group rarely exceeds 20 per cent, but life cycle effects also clearly exist. Figure 7.1 panels (c) and (d) show female labour force participation rates in the West Bank and Gaza Strip, by age group. Women aged 25 to 54 generally have participation rates ranging from 15 to 23 per cent in the West Bank and 7 to 20 per cent in the Gaza Strip. For older women, the participation rate falls from 5 to 15 per cent for 55 to 64 year olds and below 5 per cent for those over 65.

Low labour force participation does not necessarily imply economic hardship. For instance, if individuals have access to other resources, then low labour force participation does not imply poverty. One measure of access to other resources is education level. In general, those having more schooling will have greater access to economic resources and therefore, if participation rates are lowest among the more educated, one can conclude that non-participation is less of a concern. However, looking at Figure 7.2 panels (a) to (d), one can see that those with the most schooling also have the highest rates of labour force participation. For men, those with 16 or more years of schooling have participation rates generally between 80 and 90 per cent, while those with less than 12 years of schooling have rates of less than 70 per cent. For women, the effect of education on participation rates is even more dramatic. Women with 12 years of schooling or less generally have participation rates near or below 10 per cent. For those with 13–15 years of schooling their participation rates are near 30 to 40 per cent, and those with 16 or more years have participation rates as high as 60 to 70 per cent.[5] Clearly, those Palestinians who have the least access to other economic resources are often the same ones who are likely to be out of the workforce.

Informal sector[6]

Another critical issue is the degree to which the employment that does exist is in the formal or informal sector. Traditional social security plans depend heavily upon the administrative capacity of the tax collecting

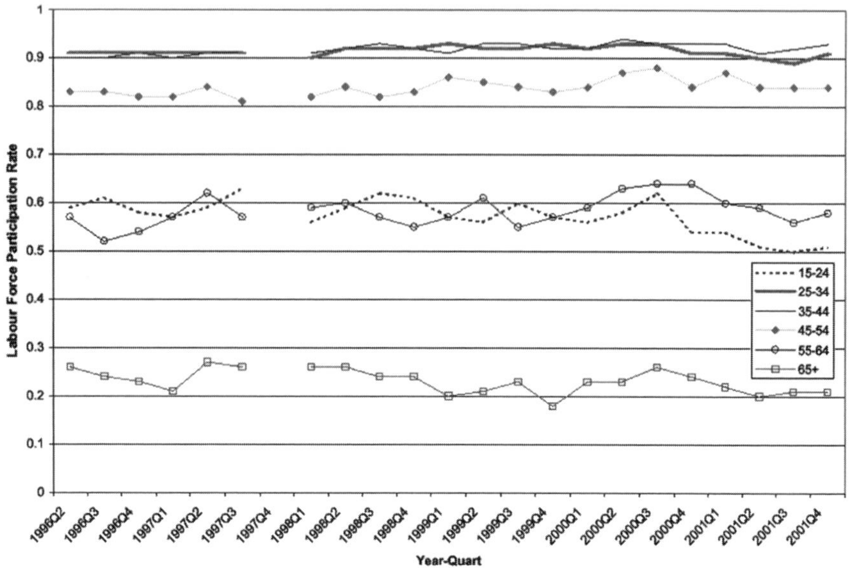

Figure 7.1a Male labour force participation in the West Bank by age group.

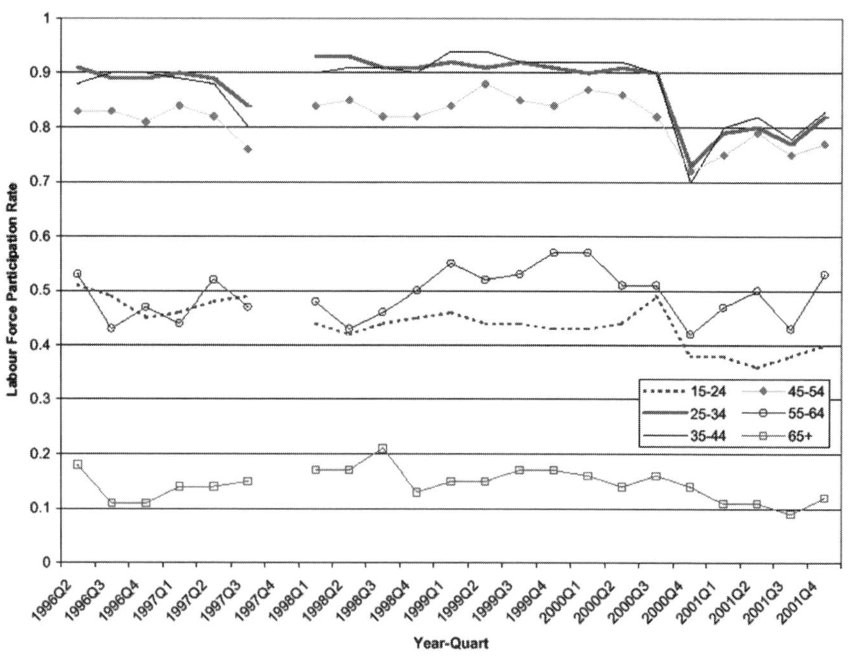

Figure 7.1b Male labour force participation in the Gaza Strip by age group.

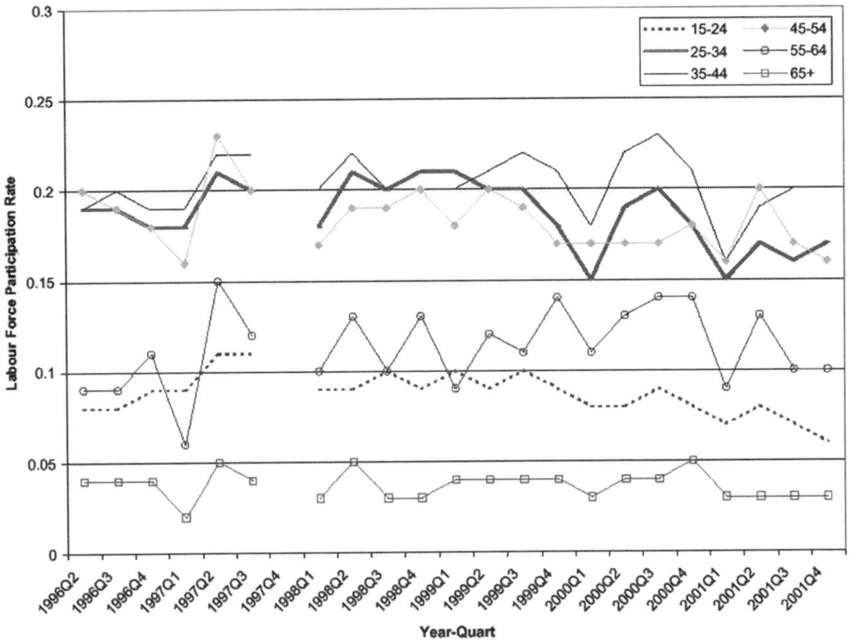

Figure 7.1c Female labour force participation in the West Bank by age group.

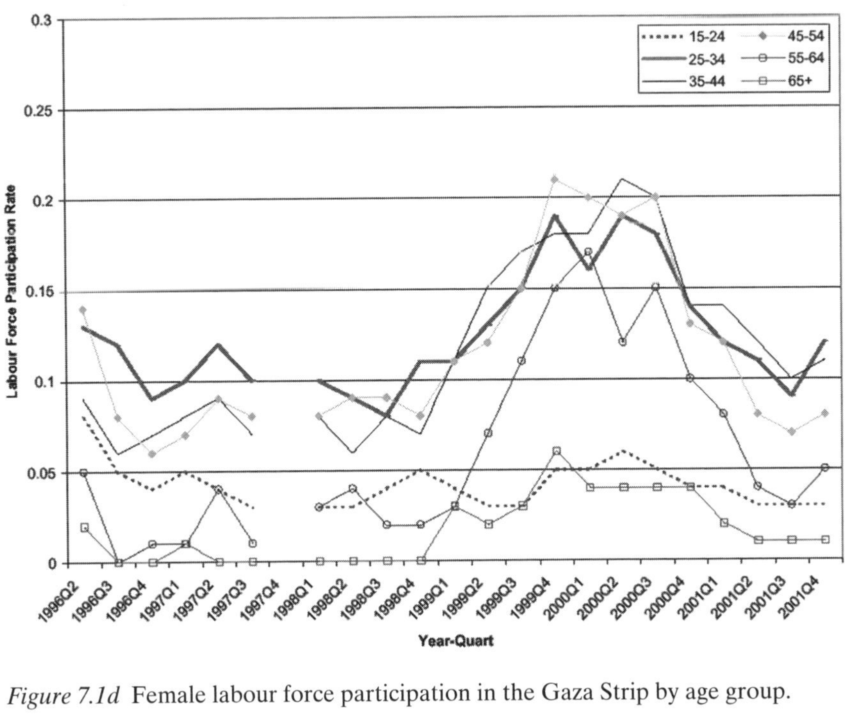

Figure 7.1d Female labour force participation in the Gaza Strip by age group.

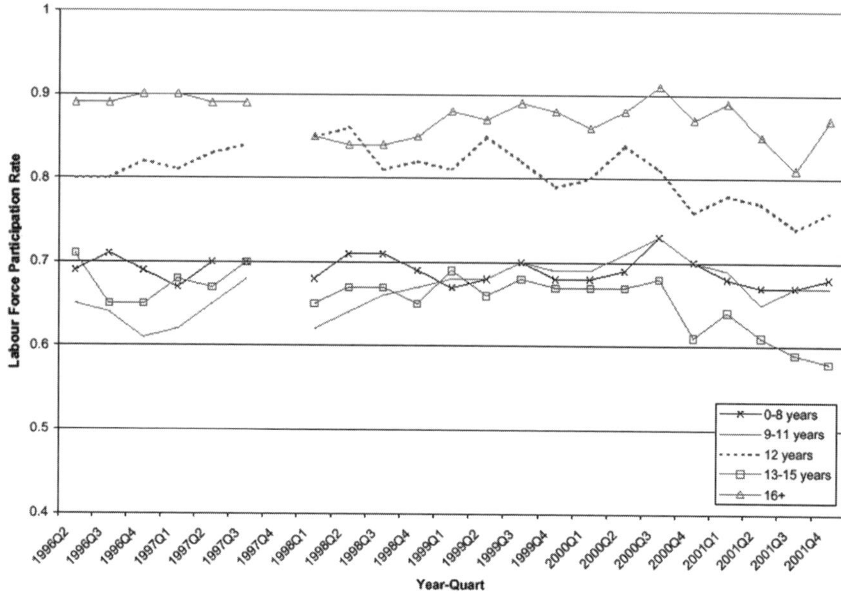

Figure 7.2a Male labour force participation in the West Bank by education level.

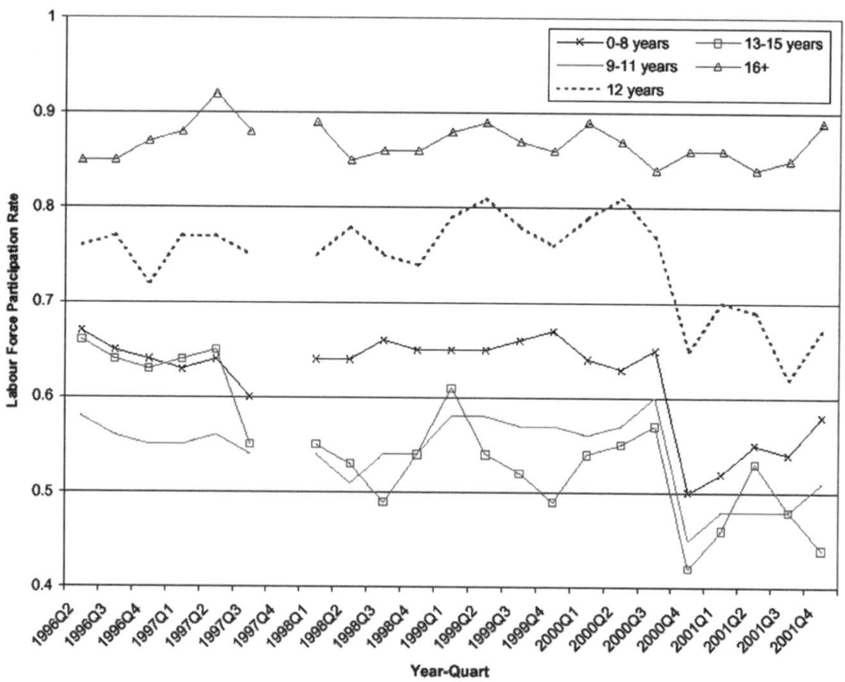

Figure 7.2b Male labour force participation in the Gaza Strip by education level.

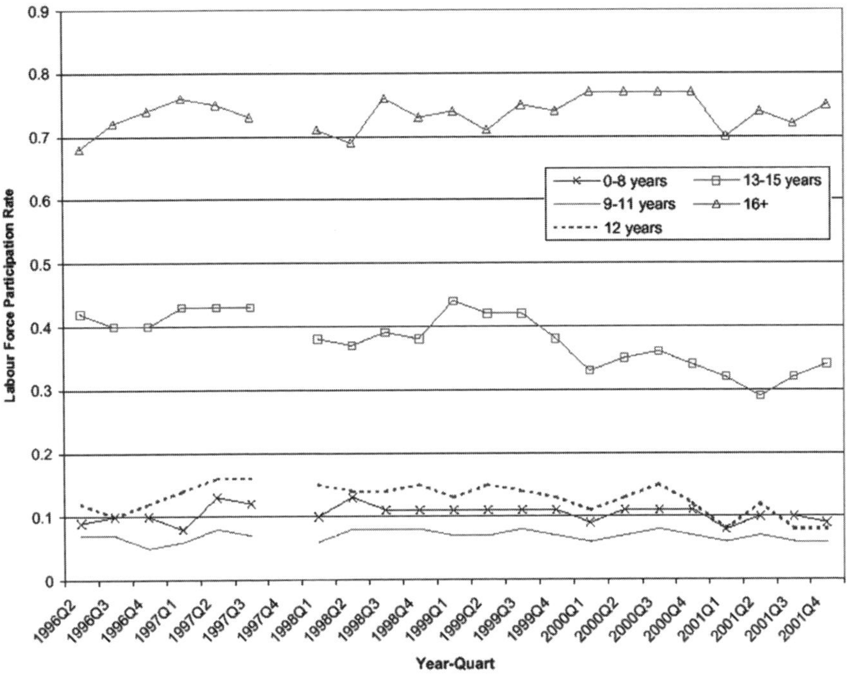

Figure 7.2c Female labour force participation in the West Bank by education level.

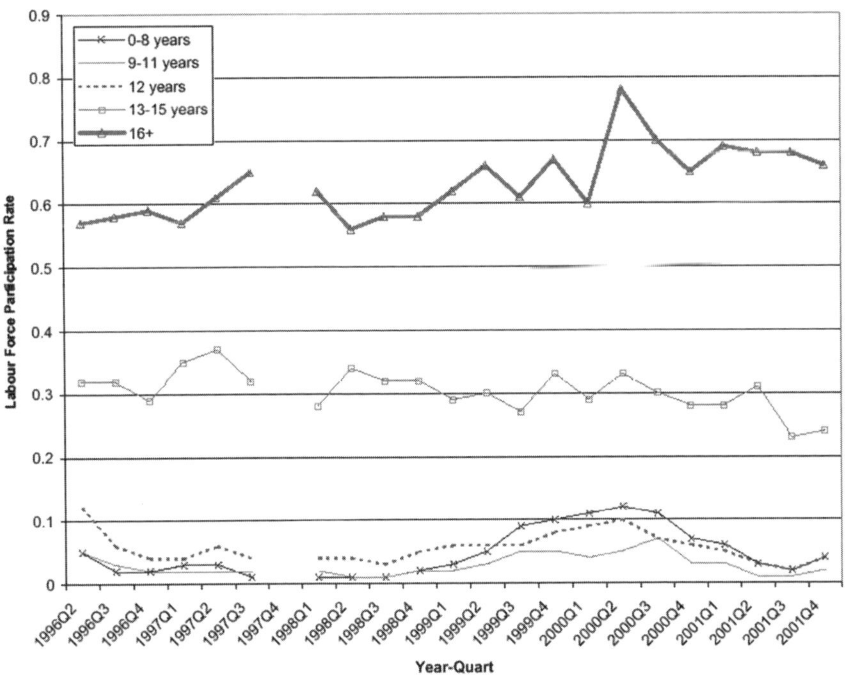

Figure 7.2d Female labour force participation in the Gaza Strip by education level.

authorities, and although the Palestinian Authority has greatly increased its tax collection capacity (see Fischer *et al.* 2001), the effectiveness of a pension scheme will be limited by the size of the informal sector. Informal workers will be less likely to pay income tax and therefore will be less likely to pay into and be able to receive benefits from a funded system of individual accounts. Thus, a plan funded with payroll taxes will be underfunded in a region where the informal sector dominates.

Informal sector employment has been defined in a number of different ways. One definition simply involves defining those who are working in sectors that are not regulated by the state as informal workers (Bernasek 1999). While this definition may be fairly accurate, few data sources categorise workers in this way. Instead, researchers generally rely on the following to determine whether a person is an informal sector worker: whether a person owns or works for an enterprise that is defined as small and thus may be exempt from certain labour regulations; whether a person has no fixed employer and/or no fixed contract; whether a person provides unpaid labour to the running of a business (usually in the form of family labour).

Unfortunately, PCBS data do not include information on all of these categories, making it difficult to estimate the number of informal sector workers in the Palestinian economy. The PCBS labour force survey does provide some variables that can be used to identify at least a portion of informal sector workers. One form of informal sector work involves unpaid family members who make up 10 per cent of all workers. Another category of informal workers are those who claim to be 'on their own account'. These workers may be considered to be in the informal sector because of the very small size of their enterprises.[7] This category of workers comprises another 20 per cent of all workers. While some sole proprietors may have greater access to material resources through their ownership rights, very few of them currently save in a formal pension plan. According to Hilal and El-Malki (1997: 62) only 7 per cent of the self-employed participate in a pension fund, compared to 44 per cent of wage earners and employees.

Finally, those who work as day labourers, who are likely to be categorised as employees but who do not have a fixed employer should also be included as informal sector workers. One category in the PCBS data that may include some day labourers is workers categorised as irregular workers in the private sector. Over the entire time period, these workers represent 5 per cent of employed workers in the West Bank and $1\frac{1}{2}$ per cent of employed workers in the Gaza Strip. Thus, including these three categories of workers yields a conservative estimate of the informal sector of the Palestinian economy of approximately 35 per cent of all workers.

This estimate almost certainly underestimates the extent of the informal sector, for a number of reasons. First, the data do not allow us to distinguish between formal and informal sector employers and wageworkers.

Even among those categorised as employers, a considerable number may also be considered to be informal, if the size of their establishments is small. The average establishment size in the Palestinian economy is very small, suggesting that many private sector employees should also be categorised as informal workers. The average number of workers employed by the 54,467 establishments included in the 1997 PCBS establishment census was 3.5, with agriculture (which contains the vast majority of establishments) having an average size of fewer than two workers. In addition, it is likely that a certain amount of informal sector activity is not even captured in statistics, which may underestimate family labour contributions, particularly those provided by women and children, who may not be perceived as being employed. It should also be noted that some sectors as well as some regions have much higher rates of informal employment and therefore will be more difficult to include in any pension scheme. Data presented in Hilal and El-Malki (1997), for example, suggest that there is considerable variation in levels of formality across regions. They find that between 48.5 (Central and Northern Gaza) and 76.4 (West Bank towns) per cent of workers report having 'steady work', suggesting that the other 51.5 and 23.4 per cent are in the informal sector (temporary and day labour).[8]

Being in a rural area in particular may lead to higher levels of informality. In fact, the agricultural sector (comprising 13 per cent of the labour force, see Table 7.1) will be the most difficult one to include in such a scheme. 42 per cent of agricultural workers are unpaid family members. Another relatively large sector in the Palestinian economy where informal employment may be more widespread is in the commerce, hotels and restaurants sector. In that sector, 11 per cent of workers are classified as unpaid family members. In addition, many wageworkers in both these sectors would probably fit into the category of informal sector workers, particularly in agriculture. Likewise, more than a third of agricultural, transport and commerce (hotels, shops and restaurant) workers claim to be sole proprietors. While some of the transport and commerce workers could be more easily incorporated into a pension scheme, because of membership in voluntary associations and unions, coverage will not be

Table 7.1 Occupational distribution of Palestinian workers, 1995 to 2001

	Percentage of employed workers
Agriculture	13.5
Manufacturing	13.9
Construction	21.5
Commerce, hotels and restaurants	15.4
Transport, storage and communication	4.3
Services	31.5

Source: Authors' calculations based upon PCBS labour force survey micro-data, 1995 to 2001.

universal. For these workers, the cost of enforcing a mandatory scheme and collecting the appropriate taxes and contributions will be much more difficult than for those who are regular employees at established enterprises.

Labour legislation

Palestinians in the West Bank and Gaza are, at least in theory, covered under various sets of laws that provide them with a certain level of social protection as workers. Two different sets of legislation are relevant in addressing labour protection in the context of the Palestinians, since a substantial portion of Palestinians continue to work in Israel and thus may come under Israeli rather than Palestinian law as workers.

Bar-On (1996) outlines the various protections offered under Israeli law. Sickness, work injury, and maternity leave benefits, as well as certain conditions related to termination and retirement have been mandated under Israeli law for quite some time. But, as Bar-On points out, Palestinian workers who work in Israel do not receive the same benefits as Israelis, because they are not residents. Despite paying fully into the Israeli insurance system, they can make no claims against those payments. The Paris Protocol of 1994 set out to normalise economic relations between the Palestinian Authority and the Israeli government. Unfortunately, this protocol failed, at least in the short-run, to improve upon the redistribution from Palestinian workers who are paying full Israeli insurance taxes, but are unable to receive full benefits.

In order to improve the protection of workers in the WBGS, in May of 2001 Yasser Arafat unveiled the new Palestinian Labour Law. This law was designed to make uniform the different legal institutions surrounding employment, as well as to officially remove the regulations imposed by the Israeli military authority concerning work arrangements. The law did not address the crucial issue of pensions and the overall social safety net. It did, however, expand and codify workers' rights in several important ways. It established the legal working week as being 45 hours long. It set the conditions for overtime pay as being a maximum of 12 hours per week and the rate of overtime pay as time and a half. It also provided standards concerning the number of sick days, vacation time and leave for educational reasons.

While a number of legislative changes have increased the level of protection and benefits available to Palestinian workers in recent years, few studies of take-up rates are available. Bar-on, through an informal survey of a small number of enterprises in the 1990s, provides some insights into this question, suggesting that even the limited protections available to Palestinian workers in the 1990s were not widely enforced. Although recent laws have strengthened Palestinians' labour rights, given the level of informality that remains in the Palestinian economy, and the fact that workers at present have very little bargaining power because of high rates of unemployment, it is highly unlikely that many workers actually receive many of the benefits now mandated by law.

Existing proposals for a Palestinian pension scheme

Before introducing our suggested pension scheme, we will briefly review previous proposals. Table 7.2 summarises the key features of plans suggested by Freeman *et al.* (1994), Hilal *et al.* (1998) and Loewe (2000). The key elements of the Freeman *et al.* (1994) plan include centralised public control, full funding through work-based individual accounts, and coverage for the risks of old age and work-related disability.[9] Benefits are directly tied to contributions and interest earnings on those contributions.[10] The authors suggest low contribution rates, at first, in order not to decrease current consumption dramatically. Yet the authors predict that with fairly high growth rates in income resulting from the settlement of Palestinian–Israeli hostilities, contribution rates could increase. While the fund would be designed to assist in the cases of old age and disability, there could also be provisions allowing for qualified deductions, such as paying for college tuition and residential housing.

Hilal *et al.* (1998) propose a pension scheme as part of a comprehensive social security plan that includes pensions, health insurance, worker disability insurance and an income maintenance programme for poor households. Unlike the Freeman *et al.* (1994) proposal the Hilal *et al.* (1998) plan is decentralised, consisting of many individual plans offered through the workplace. Decentralisation allows for co-existence between the government programme and current pensions offered by private employers and NGOs. All employers are mandated to offer several pension options to workers, and with compulsory enrolment. Though mandatory, compliance is encouraged through tax incentives for contributions.

Loewe (2000) proposes a pension scheme that includes both a fully-funded component and a pay-as-you-go (PAYG) component. The reason for a hybrid scheme lies in the specific institutional features of the Palestinian economy. While economists agree that a work-based, funded scheme is more efficient, the elderly poor are an immediate concern, and a small PAYG component immediately ameliorates some elderly poverty. Loewe's scheme also includes a role for both private insurers and the state. Private insurance companies provide the funded portion of the plan and, by doing so, minimise political interference involved in the administration of the plan. Private insurers are potentially less susceptible to corruption, which might involve funnelling money from pensions into companies owned either by the government or by individuals in the government. While the private sector is responsible for the funded portion, the public sector would still administer the PAYG component. Loewe suggests that a contribution rate of 11 to 13 per cent of earnings

Table 7.2 Basic characteristics of previous pension proposals

Characteristics of plan	*Freeman* et al. *(1994)*	*Hilal* et al. *(1998)*	*Loewe (2000)*
Funding	Fully funded	Fully funded	Both fully funded and PAYG
Private or public	Public[a]	Private	Private and public
Centralisation	Centralised[a]	Decentralised	Decentralised
Tax/contribution rates	N/A[b]	10% from employees 12.5% from employers[c]	11% to 13% for those earning more than $650 per year
Israel workers	Either transfer the past balances to a general fund or to an individual fund in the name of the Palestinian worker. Future payments will follow same pattern (p. 86)	No specific provision	No specific provision
Eligibility	Work-based but some separate social assistance needs to be established	Work-based but emphasis is put on further development of social assistance	Universal and work-based. Current elderly immediately benefit from PAYG system.
Disbursements	Can use some of it for other qualified expenses including housing and children's education	Early withdrawal is penalised. No specific provision for funding other spending	No specific discussion
Types of risks covered	Low income in old age. Work related accidents	Old age. Work accidents are covered under a separate insurance fund	Old age

Notes

a Freeman *et al.* (1994) state that 'We recommend . . . establishment of a Palestinian "provident fund" as exists in Singapore'. The authors' discussion of their plan is similar to the original formulation of the Singapore Central Provident Fund that was centralised and public. Beginning in 1986, the CPF began liberalising in a number of ways that involve more private involvement and decentralisation.

b Although Freeman *et al.* do not state a specific tax rate, they do refer to the Singapore provident fund. The contribution rates are 20 per cent paid by employees and another 16 per cent paid by the employers.

c Hilal *et al.* do not make suggestions of the contribution rate for all workers, but in general seem to want to expand the pension plan currently covering Gaza workers. The contribution percentages listed in the table reflect those currently paid for Gazan governmental workers.

would provide for both the funded portion (9 per cent) and the current elderly through the PAYG portion (2 to 4 per cent).

While each of the three proposals has positive attributes that are worth keeping, each is also deficient in some regard. The deficiencies range from simply not foreseeing the events since September 2000 to the omission of specific provisions that target particularly vulnerable groups. While most of this discussion will centre on characteristics of plans that are listed in Table 7.2, it is useful to discuss two elements that are not found there. First, none of the programmes sufficiently attempts to specifically cover elderly women. Loewe (2000) bases his contribution rate on providing for a family with two members, but goes no further. The extremely low labour force participation rate of women in WBGS (10 per cent) implies that the type of employer-provided coverage encouraged in Freeman *et al.* (1994) and Hilal *et al.* (1998) will not guarantee income stability for elderly women.

Second, each of the provisions would be very difficult to provide to informal workers. These workers are not included in a system proposed by Hilal *et al.* (1998) where each employer offers a menu of choices to his employees. The possibility of not covering 30 to 50 per cent of the workers would substantially decrease the effectiveness of a fully-funded plan. For this reason, some type of universal coverage based upon PAYG is important.

The proposal by Hilal *et al.* (1998) also recommends the implementation of very high contribution rates, which could be problematic. Under their scheme, workers contribute 10 per cent of their gross pay to the pension plan, and the employer contributes an additional 12.5 per cent. Because this policy is fully funded, it requires a higher contribution rate than would a PAYG system that takes advantage of the relative youth of the Palestinian workforce. Furthermore, these high contribution rates are only part of the comprehensive social safety net advocated by the authors. In addition to high pension contributions, payroll taxes must be collected for unemployment, health and worker disability insurance, as well as income support for the poor, resulting in total taxes and contributions rising above 50 per cent of gross pay. Such high payroll taxes though may, as pointed out by Mitchell (2000), encourage informal sector employment, as both employees and employers seek to avoid the high taxes.

An alternative to existing proposals

Risks covered

A comprehensive social security system should cover risks that lead to poverty. The benefits associated with covering these risks include health insurance, maternity leave, disability, retirement, insurance for widows and orphans and unemployment insurance. Maternity, sick, vacation and hajj leaves are included in the 2001 Labour Law, obviating any additional protection. Additionally, the Palestinian Authority has instituted a fairly broad subsidy programme for health care. Thus, the main risks currently uncovered by the social safety net are old age, disability and unemployment.

We propose a social security plan that provides retirement, survivor and disability benefits. The universal portion of the plan should be available to those over 65 and to those who have suffered the loss of a main provider through death. The work-based portion should be available to those who reach the retirement age, their survivors and those who have sustained a disability preventing them from further employment. Also, the work-based component would be available to cover expenses during a period of prolonged unemployment.

State-provided unemployment insurance is currently much more difficult to implement than other aspects of social security, and we do not propose such a plan. Unemployment in the WBGS is largely a function of the political situation and not as much a function of decisions by individual employers or industries. As such, it is primarily the responsibility of the international community to provide stopgap unemployment assistance. With a permanent settlement of hostilities, a comprehensive unemployment compensation plan could be enacted. Because of efficiency and moral hazard issues, this plan should be experience-rated where employers that are more likely to dismiss workers pay larger premiums than those with less volatile employment patterns. This provision would imply that Israeli employers would pay higher premiums than employers in Palestine.

Eligibility and coverage

A fundamental question to be addressed in designing a social security plan is whether benefits are guaranteed to all eligible citizens (universal) or only to those who pay into the system (work-based). A universal plan will provide benefits to all those who meet specific eligibility criteria, while a work-based programme will only provide money to those who paid into the system through payroll taxes or individual accounts. While a universal plan guarantees against consumption falling below a specific level, a work-based plan is more efficient and encourages formal sector employment. Under a universal plan, workers are able to avoid paying into the system if they work informally, but are still guaranteed benefits. Conversely, a work-based plan encourages workers to seek formal employment to gain access to the pension system.

Our suggestion is for a pension scheme that consists of both a universal component, giving benefits to everyone over 65, and a work-based component, available only to those who make contributions. This hybrid programme (similar to Loewe's proposal) provides a minimum level of consumption for all elderly people, while still encouraging formal employment. The level of universal benefits will be kept low, thereby providing significant additional benefits to joining the work-based plan.

Funding

Because our proposed pension scheme includes both universal and worker-based components, two different financing mechanisms are used. The universal component is to be financed from payroll taxes rather than from general revenues. Payroll taxes are more acceptable to workers, partly because the tax can be seen as closely tied to a benefit that they themselves will later receive.

The work-based portion of the pension scheme should be funded through mandatory minimum contributions from both the employee and the employer. The specific level of contributions could vary, but a system of 4 per cent paid by the employee and an additional 4 per cent paid by the employer would be sufficient to guarantee two people an income above the poverty line, given reasonable assumptions about labour market conditions (see below). Voluntary contributions above the mandated 4 per cent by the employee are encouraged by allowing the contributions to be tax deductible and by allowing earnings to be tax deferred.

Informal sector workers

It is difficult to design a programme that sufficiently guarantees all informal sector workers an old age pension. However, a decentralised system involving non-governmental organisations (NGOs) and labour unions could include many informal workers without an excessive administrative burden. Currently, some NGOs and professional associations provide members who are sole proprietors with pension plans (Hilal *et al.* 1998). Many of the 20 per cent of workers who are sole proprietors are eligible for these types of plans. Plans organised by voluntary membership or union membership could be responsible for providing information and collecting contributions. The contribution rate may need to be adjusted because there would be nothing coming from the employers. Each individual would be mandated to contribute 8 to 10 per cent of his or her salary to his or her pension. A survey of NGOs by Hamed and Al-Botmeh (1997) showed that, of the 34 NGOs that offered pension plans, the average contribution was 8 per cent of the employee's salary.

The implementation of a pension scheme for the informal sector would be difficult, but not excessively so. Already there are numerous NGOs in the WBGS that organise the informal sector. Relief organisations and women's cooperatives provide an institutional structure that could be used to implement this programme. Informal workers have been provided with pension plans in other countries. For example, Indian beedi workers are eligible for pension and disability benefits (Jain 1999).

Women

Elderly women throughout the world tend to suffer higher rates of poverty than other groups. This is due to a number of factors. One such factor is that the design of most pension programmes tends to disadvantage women (Ghilarducci 1999 and Heisel 1996) due to their connection to market-based work. While women generally do more work than men when one counts household production, women are likely to be excluded from market work-based pension programmes.

Palestinian women are no exception to this problem. While time-use studies suggest that Palestinian women work upwards of 60 hours (Heiburg and Ovensen 1993: 213), women's labour force participation rates remain low. Globally women are also more likely to suffer poverty in old age, because of their higher longevity. Again, Palestinian women are no exception, with an average life expectancy at birth of 74 compared to 70 years for men (PCBS 2003).

The design of our suggested pension plan attempts to take into account both women's greater life expectancy and their considerably lower labour force participation rates. By proposing a plan that includes both a universal component guaranteed to all elderly, and survivor benefits for women, we hope to minimise the gender bias associated with most pension schemes. A further benefit to the plan we propose is that by implementing a work-based pension programme for informal sector workers, more women will be contributing to this scheme.

Summary of plan's suggestions

The comprehensive pension plan that we suggest conforms to the specific needs of the Palestinian labour market. It provides universal coverage for citizens over 65 and a work-based scheme to encourage savings for all labour market participants. The revenue collected for the universal portion is from payroll taxes, implying that while only formal sector workers are paying, all workers can benefit. A larger portion of the pension scheme involves individual accounts provided by financial institutions and insurance companies through employers. Tax treatment of the individual accounts will encourage delaying withdrawal until age 60. These individual accounts can vary by type of assets held (guaranteed securities, equity, bonds) and by provision of benefits. Since this portion is a defined contribution plan, the benefits can be administered as an annuity or as a transfer of the account to the beneficiary and survivors.

Note that we are suggesting two different ages for 'retirement'. While workers can begin drawing down their individual accounts at age 60, it is not until 65 that workers will become eligible for the universal portion. These two retirement ages are based upon the following reasons. First, 60 is the retirement age for public sector workers in the West Bank and Gaza.

Therefore, the system of individual accounts is compatible with the institutions that already exist. Second, based upon the authors' calculations from PCBS data, fewer than one-third of workers aged 60–64 are not working due to age or illness, while 80 per cent of those over the age of 65 are non-participants due to age. By having two retirement ages, the universal pension would not encourage early retirement by those who are still fit for work.

The pension agency implementing this programme will be independent of other branches of the government, but will work closely with the Ministry of Finance, Ministry of Social Affairs and Ministry of Labour. The agency will be in charge of the design and supervision of the programme, but the individual accounts will be outside of the agency's control. The agency will provide the regulatory framework within which insurance companies and financial institutions must work, but will not make decisions concerning where the money is invested. In addition to the employer–employee coverage that is going to focus primarily on formal workers, the agency should also establish funds that will help provide pension plans for the informal workers through NGOs and trade unions.

Projection of pension benefits under different economic conditions

We will now describe how different contribution rates and labour market conditions will affect the ability of the pension scheme to protect elderly income. We assume the following baseline conditions for key parameters. Following Loewe (2000) the real interest rate paid on pensions is set at 2.4 per cent. Average earnings are calculated from 1999 PCBS labour force data: West Bank workers earn $5,000 per year and Gazans earn $3,750. Taking these earnings as mean earnings over all working years and using the return to a year of experience of 1.3 per cent (estimated from the authors' regression analysis), we derive an earnings profile for the average worker. We also assume no economic growth. In other words, we assume that average real earnings remain the same as those today. Unemployment affects this hypothetical average worker in an average way, such that a 10 per cent unemployment rate implies that he or she is unemployed for 10 per cent of his or her working years. An average of 10 years of schooling implies that each worker has 44 potential work years. With a 10 per cent unemployment rate, this worker will only be employed for 40 years. Using this basic framework, we present below three sets of projections, which we designate the 'optimistic', 'average' and 'pessimistic' scenarios. Under the optimistic scenario, the unemployment rate is 10 per cent. Under the average scenario, the unemployment is 18 per cent, the average rate estimated during the years 1995 to 2001. Under the pessimistic scenario, we assume an unemployment rate of 25 per cent.

Figures 7.3a to 7.3c present projections for yearly benefits paid from the

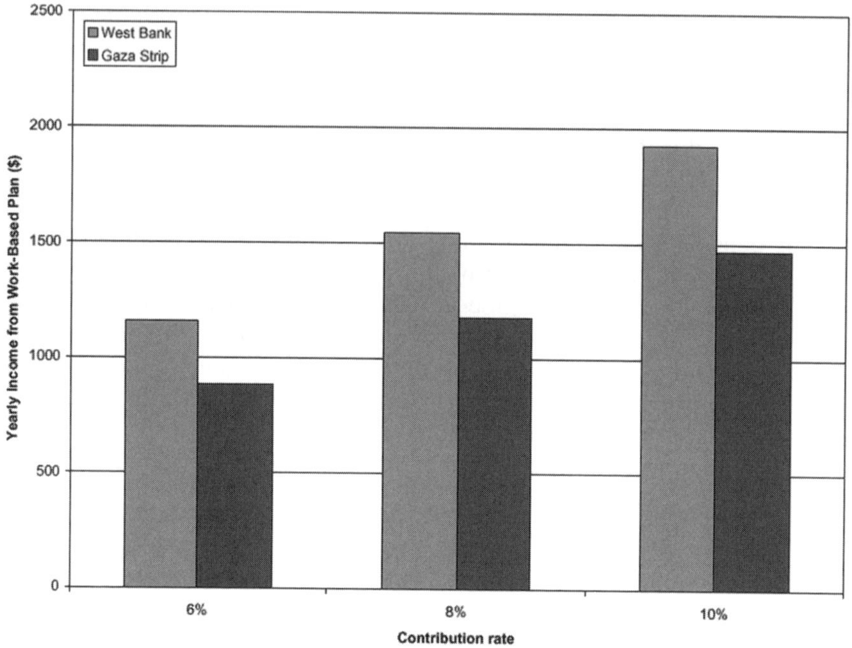

Figure 7.3a Projected consumption under optimistic scenario (10% unemployment).

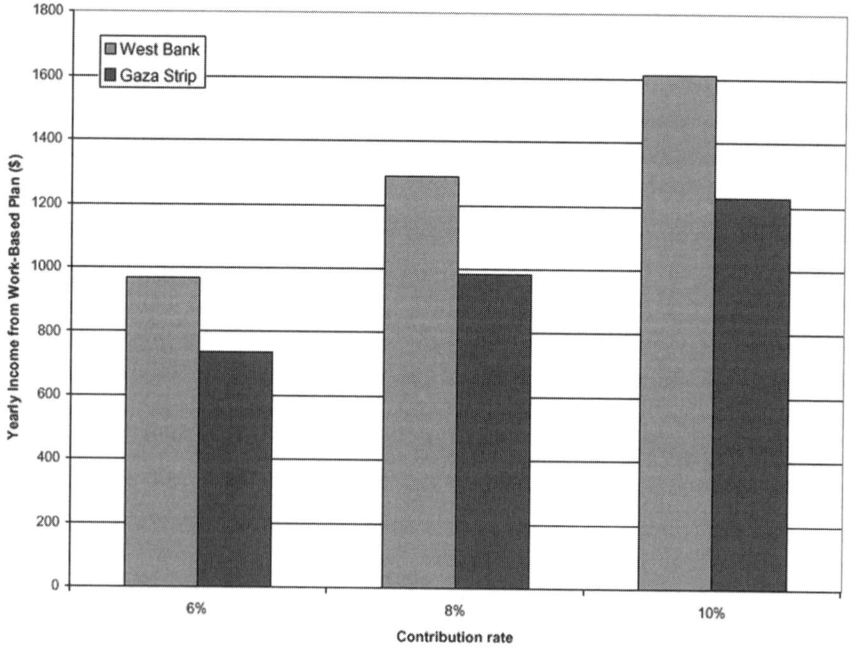

Figure 7.3b Projected consumption under average scenario (18% unemployment).

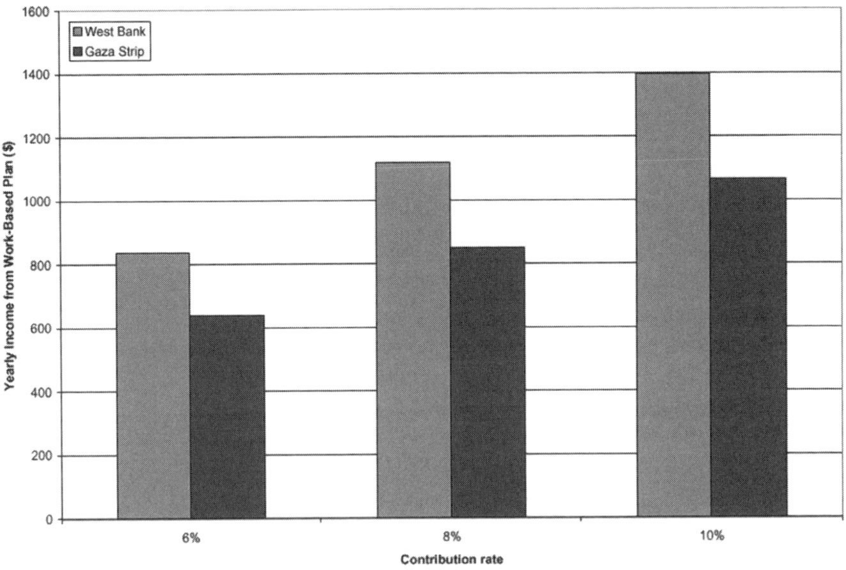

Figure 7.3c Projected consumption under pessimistic scenario (25% unemployment).

fully funded portion of the pension scheme. In these projections, we assume that both members of an elderly couple reach their life expectancy at age 60. While life expectancy at birth has been calculated by the PCBS in their demographic studies, we needed to use life expectancy at age 60 to estimate the number of years that pensioners would draw from their accounts. We used the orphanhood data reported in PCBS (1997) to calculate life expectancy at age 60 separately for WB and GS men and women. This estimation yielded a life expectancy at age 60 of 18 additional years for men from the Gaza Strip and 21 additional years for Gazan women. For Palestinians in the West Bank, women can expect to live 22 years after they turn 60, while men can expect 19 more years.

Note the following caveats concerning these projections. First, we assume that there is only one worker in the family. If the spouse also contributes to an individual account, the amount available for consumption would increase. Second, we have not included the PAYG portion in this calculation. These calculations, therefore, assess the ability of the work-based, funded portion of the pension scheme to be a viable source of income. Third, participation in the informal sector would decrease the amount of retirement income available. Fourth, if these accounts were available for other risks, including temporary disability or unemployment insurance, then the amount available to the elderly would be lower. Finally, economy-wide risks, such as inflation or financial crises, could also lead to lower retirement income.

Under the optimistic scenario (Figure 7.3a), the low contribution rate of 6 per cent does not guarantee consumption above the World Bank poverty line of $2 per day for residents of the West Bank or the Gaza Strip. With an 8 per cent contribution rate, West Bankers, with their significantly higher wages, consume above the poverty line, but Gazans will not. Meeting poverty line consumption under the average scenario (Figure 7.3b) is only possible for West Bankers who contribute 10 per cent per year. And under the pessimistic scenario of 25 per cent unemployment (Figure 7.3c), not even the highest rate of contribution allows a Palestinian couple to consume more than $2 per day from these individual accounts.

We now add in the universal component. To project the contribution from the PAYG component, we assume that half of all workers are informally employed and do not pay payroll taxes. We also assume that 20 per cent of tax revenue goes toward administrative costs. Figures 7.4a to 7.4b show total pension benefits from the universal and funded portions for workers turning 65 in the years from 2007 to 2057. For the funded portion, we assume an 8 per cent contribution rate and an 18 per cent unemployment rate. Assuming that the plan is fully implemented in 2007, individuals turning 65 that year will only benefit from the universal portion. Likewise, those who turn 65 in 2012 will turn 60 in the first year of implementation, and only benefit from the universal plan. Those who turn 65 in 2017 will be able to contribute to their individual plans for the last five working years, while those who retire in 2022 will have 10 years of contributions, and so on. Under these conditions, as individuals contribute at younger and younger ages, the size of their individual accounts grows until we reach those who turn 65 in 2057, who will have contributed for their entire working lives.

The universal component also grows, but this is due to demographic changes. Using population data from the PCBS, we estimate projections of the relative sizes of the working age population and 65 plus population. Due to Palestinians' relative youth, the real value of the PAYG benefit triples from $209 in 2007 to $680 in 2057. The relative sizes of retiree and working age populations, however, are dependent upon factors that are extremely difficult to predict. The return of refugees,[11] an accelerated demographic transition to lower birth rates, and an increase in the formality of the labour market will all dramatically change the level of funds flowing into this programme and make the programme more or less feasible. Thus we provide our projections with a certain amount of caution. However, we do feel that we can draw two conclusions with a fair amount of certainty. First, given the relatively higher wages in the West Bank, a universal scheme is vital in redistributing income across the population of the West Bank and Gaza Strip. Only with a universal component can elderly Gazans be assured of getting above the poverty line consumption rate of $2 per day. A second conclusion is that the relative size of the PAYG portion may allow for some use of these funds for purposes other

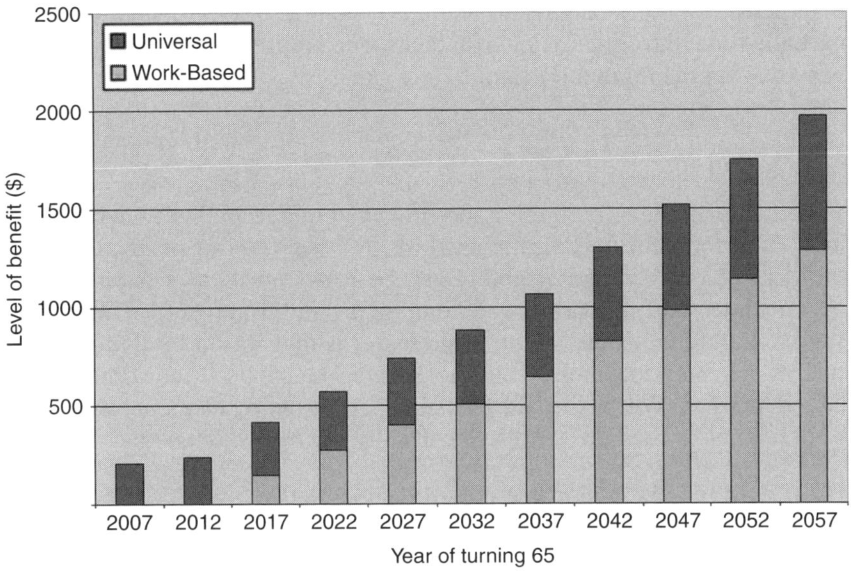

Figure 7.4a Total projected benefits for workers in the West Bank.

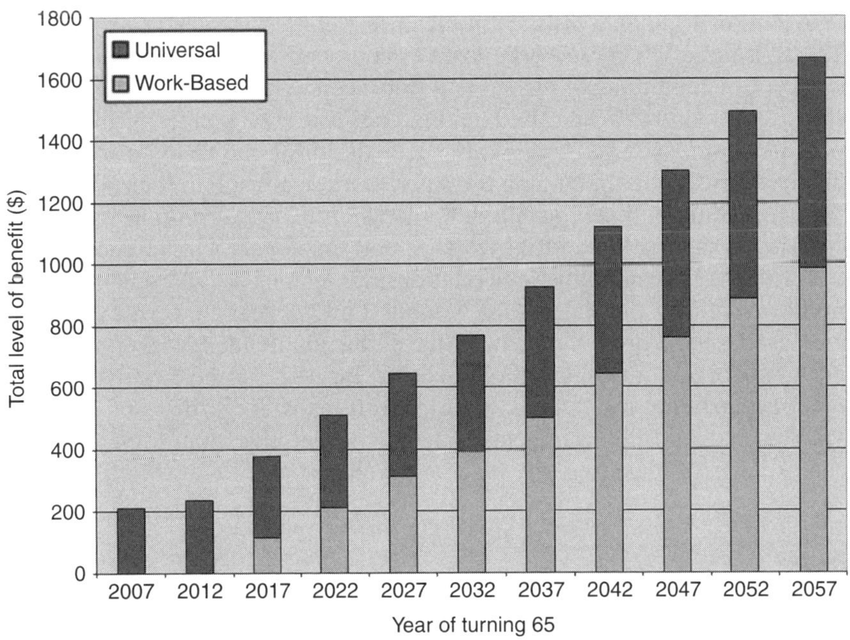

Figure 7.4b Total projected benefits for workers in the Gaza Strip.

than pensions. For example, an unemployment insurance benefit could be partially funded from these payroll taxes, once retirees begin to draw more heavily from the funded portion.

Conclusion

This chapter has explored the issues involved in developing a social security system for a future Palestinian state. A basic level of protection from the risks of old age and disability can be provided by a pension scheme that includes both a work-based component and a universal component. We have outlined some of the basic features that would be important in such a scheme, accounting for the specific elements of the Palestinian labour market. We have paid particular attention to elements that have been missing in previous works. Specifically, we have discussed:

1 how to include the informal sector and women;
2 how volatility will affect the viability of any scheme;
3 why a scheme must not place too high a payroll tax burden on employers.

We are hopeful that a scheme that explicitly considers these elements will help provide a guaranteed income to Palestinians throughout their old age.

Additional benefits also accrue from a well-designed pension scheme. Through these schemes, workers are encouraged to save in formal capital markets, making funding available to businesses and increasing the capital stock of a country. While the banking and insurance sectors of the Palestinian economy showed remarkable growth during the Oslo period, other financial institutions, including the stock market, are still in their formative stages. Additionally, by developing a pension plan based upon individual contributions, it is hoped that workers and employers will be encouraged to formalise their employment relationship, leading to additional protections covered by the Palestinian Labour Law. A real concern exists that increased social protection could have the unintended consequence of pushing workers into the informal sector, but this can be largely avoided by not depending too heavily upon payroll taxes. Regardless of the final scheme and its funding mechanism, it is imperative that some form of comprehensive social security plan be developed soon.

Notes

1 Islam stipulates that those who can afford to do so should donate a percentage of their income to Muslim organisations in the form of Zakat, which is then redistributed to the needy. Christian organisations also provide some poverty assistance.

2 Each PCBS labour survey contains approximately 23,000 individuals, with slightly more males than females. For the entire 1995–2001 period, the data used here include 276,000 men and 269,000 women. Since most households are surveyed in several different rounds, the number of unique observations is only one-third to one-quarter of the above figures. Approximately 30 per cent of the sample is from Gaza and the rest is from the West Bank, excluding the portion of Jerusalem annexed by Israel in 1967. The PCBS has allowed dissemination of labour force micro-data for survey rounds from September–October 1995 to October–December 2001. The labour force data are acknowledged as being systematically and effectively collected, using internationally accepted survey methodology. However, from quarter to quarter, some variation occurs because of difficulty in movement caused by Israeli restrictions, so the focus in this section will be on general trends rather than quarter-by-quarter variations. These data are taken at the household level, often with one member of the family answering questions for all other family members aged 15 years and older.

3 Rates are lower for Gaza in part due to the sharper decrease in labour force participation in the Gaza Strip after the outbreak of the al-Aqsa intifada in September 2000.

4 This very high labour force participation rate for prime aged men is consistent with very few individuals claiming to be disabled. According to the PCBS Health Survey from 1997, only 2.3 per cent of men and 1.8 per cent of women claimed to be disabled (Hilal *et al.* 1998).

5 Olmsted's (2001) regression analysis of Palestinian women's labour force participation suggests that education has a non-linear effect.

6 Because labour force surveys are likely to underestimate in many cases the extent of the informal sector, studies that aim in particular to quantify the extent of and conditions within the informal sector are needed. As was noted by Esim and Kuttab (2002), few studies have explicitly studied the Palestinian informal sector. They also note that the few studies that have been written have focused on women's informal sector activity, in contrast to the more general literature on informal activity which, according to Bernasek (1999), has focused primarily on men.

7 If the workers also had employees, then they would be considered 'employers' and not 'on own account', so these enterprises have only a single worker.

8 Estimates of the informal sector for other parts of the Middle East and North Africa suggest similar trends, with over 40 per cent of jobs often being in the informal sector (World Bank, forthcoming.)

9 Most of our description is based on Freeman *et al.* (1994) suggesting a plan similar to the Central Provident Fund in Singapore.

10 The two general categories of plan that we will discuss are work-based, fully funded programmes and those that are universal in coverage and funded through a pay-as-you-go (PAYG) mechanism. Throughout this chapter we will use the term 'work-based' to describe a plan that is funded by contributions by a worker who then becomes eligible for benefits based upon his or her contribution to the pension fund. These types of plans are also referred to as defined contribution plans. While there are nuances that demarcate these different terms, we will use them interchangeably in this chapter. A PAYG plan, on the other hand, is one in which payments to current retirees are made from revenue collected from current workers. Our plan includes a *universal* PAYG portion, which does not require the retiree to show a work history in order to collect benefits; she merely needs to meet the age requirement.

11 It should be noted that a massive return of elderly Palestinians who are currently in the diaspora would put a considerable burden on any WBGS pension

plan. It would be unreasonable to expect the modest plan we are proposing to be able to accommodate such a large increase in recipients. Again it seems that assuring the economic well-being of diaspora Palestinians should be addressed by the international community and/or some form of reparations.

References

Bar-On, A. (1996) 'Social security programmes in the West Bank and Gaza Strip: challenges for the new Palestine', *Journal of Social Policy* 25(1): 63–81.

Bernasek, A. (1999) 'Informal sector', in J. Peterson and M. Lewis (eds) *The Elgar Companion to Feminist Economics*, Cheltenham: Elgar.

Esim, S. and Kuttab, E. (2002) 'Women's informal employment in Palestine: securing a livelihood against all odds', Washington, DC: International Centre for Research on Women, mimeo.

Fischer, S., Alonso-Gamo, P. and Erickson von Allmen, U. (2001) 'Economic developments in the West Bank and Gaza since Olso', *The Economic Journal* 111: F254–F275.

Freeman, R., Abu-Shokor, A., El-Ahmad, A.Q. and Kilnov, R. (1994) 'Palestinian–Israeli–Jordanian labour mobility: the current situation and issues for a peaceful future', in S. Fischer, L.J. Hausman, A.D. Karasik and T.C. Schelling (eds) *Securing Peace in the Middle East*, Cambridge: MIT.

Ghilarducci, T. (1999) 'Pensions and old age retirement', in J. Peterson and M. Lewis (eds) *The Elgar Companion to Feminist Economics*, Cheltenham: Elgar.

Hamed, O. and al-Botmeh, S. (1997) *The Workplace as a Source of Pension Benefits and Health Insurance in the West Bank and Gaza Strip*, Jerusalem: Palestinian Economic Policy Research Institute (MAS).

Hanssen-Bauer, J., Pedersen, J. and Tiltnes, A. (eds) (1998) *Jordanian Society: Living Conditions in the Hashemite Kingdom of Jordan*, FAFO Report 253, Oslo.

Heiberg, M. and Ovensen, G. (1993) *Palestinian Society in Gaza, West Bank and Arab Jerusalem: A Survey of Living Conditions*, FAFO Report 151, Oslo.

Heisel, M. (1996) 'Challenges to Social Security for women: case illustrations of Turkey and Egypt', in J. Midgley and M. Tracy (eds) *Challenges to Social Security: An International Exploration*, Westport: Auburn House.

Hilal, J. and El-Malki, M. (1997) *Informal Social Support System (non-institutionalized) in the West Bank and Gaza Strip*, Jerusalem: Palestinian Economic Policy Research Institute (MAS).

Hilal, J., El-Malki, M., Shalabi, Y. and Ladadweh, L. (1998) *Towards a Social Security System in the West Bank and Gaza Strip*, Jerusalem: Palestinian Economic Policy Research Institute (MAS).

Jain, S. (1999) 'Basic Social Security in India', in W. van Ginneken (ed.) *Social Security for the Excluded Majority*, Geneva: International Labour Office.

Khawaja, M. (2001) 'Family and household', in J. Pedersen, S. Randall and M. Khawaja (eds) *Growing Fast: The Palestinian Population in the West Bank and Gaza Strip*, FAFO Report 353, FAFO Institute for Applied Social Science, Norway: Centraltrykkeriet AS.

Loewe, M. (2000) 'Protecting the old in a young economy: old age insurance in the West Bank and Gaza Strip', *International Social Security Review* 53(3): 59–82.

Mitchell, O. (2000) 'Building an environment for pension reform in developing countries', in Z. Bodie and E.P. Davis (eds) *The Foundations of Pension Finance*, London: Edward Elgar.

Olmsted, J. (2001) 'Men's work/women's work: employment, wages and occupational segregation in Bethlehem', in M. Cinar (ed.) *The Economics of Women and Work in the Middle East and North Africa*, volume 4 of Research in Middle East Economics, Amsterdam: JAI Press: 151–174.

Olmsted, J. (forthcoming) 'Gender, ageing and the evolving patriarchal contract', *Feminist Economics*.

Palestinian Central Bureau of Statistics (2003) *Demographic Indicators in the Palestinian Territory (1997–2003)*, last accessed 13 August 2003, http://www.pcbs.org/english/populati/dem97_03/table_01.htm.

Palestinian National Authority (1998) *Palestine Poverty Report: Poverty in Palestine*, National Commission for Poverty Alleviation, Palestinian Poverty Eradication Commission.

United Nations Special Co-ordinator (UNSCO) (2002) *The Impact of Closure and Other Mobility Restrictions on Palestinian Productive Activities*, October, accessed 1 August 2003, http://www.un.org/News/dh/mideast/econ-report-final.pdf.

World Bank (no date) 'Social protection sector strategy: from safety net to springboard', The World Bank, Social Protection Sector, accessed 1 August 2003, http://wbln0018.worldbank.org/HDNet/hddocs.nsf/2d5135ecbf351de6852566a90069b8b6/1628e080eb4593a78525681c0070a518/$FILE/complete.pdf.

World Bank (2001) *Poverty in the West Bank and Gaza*, Washington, DC: World Bank.

World Bank (2002) *Fifteen Months – Intifada, Closures and Palestinian Economic Crisis: An Assessment*, March, Washington, DC: World Bank.

World Bank (forthcoming) *Unlocking the Employment Potential in the Middle East and North Africa: Toward a New Social Contract*, Washington, DC: World Bank.

Discussion

Felix FitzRoy

This chapter provides a useful overview of labour market and social problems in the area, followed by policy suggestions for a comprehensive pension plan. As in most developing countries there are serious problems of poverty, unemployment, non-participation and informal employment, particularly among women, the less qualified, and the elderly. Most of the latter are supported in extended families and have no pension claims. However, nuclear families are becoming more prevalent, raising the need for a public safety net. There is considerable regional inequality in all these indicators. UN and other donors have been mainly responsible for existing programmes to alleviate the currently worsening poverty situation.

While the most educated men (over 16 years of education) have the highest labour force participation rate, those with 13–15 years education have the lowest, e.g. much lower than men with 12 years of education. This surprising fact may not be unique to Palestine, but the only explanation offered is that this group may contain more discouraged workers. In view of its relevance for education and employment policy, this question deserves more study.

The main focus of the prescriptive part of the chapter is on old-age pensions and disability benefits. The authors argue that unemployment benefits should not be included in the social security programme, because unemployment 'is largely a function of the political situation', so that experience rating would impose large exogenous costs on employers. However, this is not an argument against providing support for the apparently large numbers of unemployed (18 per cent) from general tax revenues. It is not made clear what proportion of these unemployed – and the large proportion of inactive – really work (at least part-time) in the informal sector. If most of them do, then benefits may be unnecessary, but if many do not, particularly older men with family responsibilities who are less likely to be supported by extended families but not yet eligible for pensions, then benefits for them are no less important than supporting the elderly. The US system of experience rating may well be unsuitable for Palestine, but again this is not an argument against unemployment insurance, but rather a good reason for adopting a European-style benefit system.

Another problem is that payroll taxes and employer contributions are emphasised as more acceptable to workers with no mention of their negative effect on labour demand and employment. With inward investment likely to be a top policy priority for development and job creation, the burden of taxation on capital should be minimised, and barriers to entrepreneurship and new firm start-ups removed rather than extended.

The large informal sector raises various problems for implementation of any kind of welfare system, and these are discussed in detail with reference to the support of the elderly by a comprehensive as well as a work-based pension. It would have been natural to include some discussion of unemployment benefits as part of the necessary social safety net, but this is neglected, together with consideration of general equilibrium feedback such as the effect of payroll and other taxes on employment and investment.

Discussion

Radwan Shaban

This chapter reviews the issues surrounding the consideration of a pension scheme by a future Palestinian state, makes a specific proposal, and provides some simulation of aspects of the proposal's impact. The chapter is very well-written, and provides a solid policy think-piece that is grounded in analysis of labour markets and poverty. I have been asked to provide comments on the poverty linkage to the proposed pension scheme.

The chapter provides a nice overview of the poverty and labour market situation to support its recommendations. In particular, the poverty risk increases for a household that is headed by a female, someone older than 65 years, or a self-employed person engaged in the informal labour market. Moreover, the coverage of the existing poverty programme is inadequate, as only 30 per cent of poor households obtain some form of cash assistance. In addition, the traditional safety net, such as the family, does not work effectively for all individuals. For purposes of the chapter, it would also be important to identify the risk of falling into poverty by age, particularly for older people, whether they are heads of household or not.

In proposing a pension scheme, it is important to specify its objectives. In addition to insurance against old age (disability and long-term unemployment), the authors' proposal has an anti-poverty objective for the old. Given the two objectives, it is reasonable and natural for the chapter to provide two instruments:

1 a defined-benefit universal coverage that guarantees a minimum (but low) income level for all old people, which is paid for by a payroll tax;
2 a work-based defined-contribution pension to be paid for by employees and employers.

A benefit of the proposed scheme is that it acknowledges the needs of older women, who make up the majority of old people but would mostly be unable to benefit from a work-based pension scheme given their very low labour force participation rate. Under the proposal, old women would benefit from the universal coverage offered to all those older than 65 years.

Given that the universal benefit is not tied to contributions, it would seem unfair to make these payments to wealthier old people, particularly those who may not have contributed to the pension scheme.

Another major concern is whether the pension scheme is the best instrument of addressing the needs of old women (and men) who may not have been able to benefit from a work-based pension scheme. Perhaps the safety net, with its poverty focus, is the better instrument for addressing these needs. Indeed, government social assistance provides aid to the needy who are unable to work, with a sizeable fraction of the benefits going to households headed by females or old people. The coverage of these benefits may not be as universal as the chapter's proposal. But improving the coverage of the existing poverty-targeted social assistance needs to be seriously considered. The benefits and costs of the proposed universal benefit component of the pensions scheme will need to be weighed against the benefits and costs of improving the targeting of the existing social safety net.

8 Strategies for economic development, the role of Gaza and the future of the refugee camps

Eduardo Anselmo de Castro and Chris Jensen-Butler

Introduction

The spatial structure of the Palestinian economy is at the very core of the Palestinian problem. Territorial expansion, territorial control, transport links, closures, the control of water and the right to return are illustrations of the fundamentally spatial nature of the problem. The aim of this chapter is to examine the interrelationships in the Palestinian economy between economic growth and development, concentration of economic activity, spatial economic structure and the future conditions for some of the least privileged Palestinians, those living in the refugee camps. Specific features of Palestinian society and the economy are examined, using the economic theory of agglomeration and increasing returns, and somewhat untraditional conclusions concerning a potential Palestinian development trajectory are drawn.

A further set of conclusions concerns the refugee camps in Palestine. Given this theoretical foundation, a number of the characteristics of both the refugee camps and the refugee population could, in principle, become an asset for development. In other words, many problems generated by the process of integration of refugees and refugee camps could be transformed into opportunities, if appropriate policies are adopted.

The arguments presented rest upon a number of key political and economic assumptions concerning the future development of the Palestinian economy in the context of a sovereign Palestinian state. These are discussed in an earlier chapter, and for the purposes of this study are taken as given.

The recent evolution of the Palestinian economy

The Oslo Agreement of 1993 laid the foundations for optimism concerning future economic performance in Palestine. This was followed by the Paris Protocol in 1994 and by the Interim Agreement (Oslo II) in 1995. The Paris Protocol essentially consolidated the existing customs union between the Palestinian territories and Israel with a common external tariff, free mobility of labour and the establishment of a monetary authority (Cobham 2001). These arrangements did not work as intended for various political and institutional reasons, including an insecure economic and political climate, restrictions on labour mobility imposed by the Israelis, and the complexity and deficiencies of the trade arrangements established (Kanafani 2001).

Between 1994 and 2000 economic performance was disappointing, with substantial swings in real GDP growth (8.5 per cent in 1994, −3.2 per cent in 1996, 6 per cent in 1999 and 1.5 per cent in 2000, last quarter), and there were also substantial swings in unemployment (23.8 per cent in 1996, 10 per cent in early 2000) (S. Fischer *et al.* 2001). As economic growth was weak and the population grew rapidly, real GNI per capita was 10 per cent lower in 1999 than in 1993 (Cobham 2001). The IMF had expected real per capita GNI to grow by 0.8 per cent in the year 2000, but revised its estimate to −8.3 per cent in December 2000 after the start of the second intifada (S. Fischer *et al.* 2001). The population growth rate was very high in the 1990s, at 5.1 per cent per annum (Davoodi and Erickson von Allmen 2001), though it is expected that fertility rates will fall, as Palestine moves through the demographic transition, whilst on the other hand immigration to a sovereign Palestinian state will certainly increase. The Ministry of Planning and International Cooperation (MoPIC 1998a) forecasts that the Palestinian population will grow from the 2.9 million living in the West Bank and Gaza in 1998 to 4.9 million by 2010, of which 3.0 million are expected to live in the West Bank and 1.9 million in Gaza. Natural growth is expected to account for about two-thirds of this increase.

Since September 2000 the Palestinian economy has gone into severe depression. The United Nations Conference on Trade and Development estimates that there were direct losses to the economy between October 2000 and March 2002 equivalent to 40 per cent of 1999 GNI, that in late 2002 over 67 per cent of Palestinian households lived under the poverty line of $350 per month and that unemployment was around 30 per cent. All parts of the economy are in a partial collapse described by UNCTAD as a cycle of de-development, compounded by physical destruction of buildings, infrastructure and agriculture by the Israelis (UNCTAD 2002). Clearly the present situation is atypical, which is why the 1990s is a more reasonable point of departure for the themes of the present chapter.

S. Fischer *et al.* (2001), F. Fischer *et al.* (2001) and PNA (2001) explain Palestine's poor economic performance in the 1990s, despite substantial foreign aid donations, in relation to a number of features of the Palestinian economy and society. These include Israeli restrictions and closures which raised transaction costs, transport costs and uncertainty, slow progress in institution building, and poor governance and financial management, creating an unfavourable climate for investment. The United Nations Special Coordinator's Office (UNSCO 2001) has documented the substantial and negative effects of closures on the Palestinian economy.

The structure of the Palestine economy is generally agreed to be distorted by its relationship with the Israeli economy (Bannister and Erickson von Allmen 2001; Arnon and Weinblatt 2001). There is a structural trade deficit, with the Israelis treating the Palestinian economy as a captive market and limiting Palestinian exports to both Israel and the outside world. The dependence of the Palestinian economy on employment of Palestinians inside Israel is considerable. Arnon and Weinblatt (2001) provide documentary evidence indicating that Israel recognised an obligation of care for the welfare of the inhabitants of the Gaza Strip, but that priority was to be given to increasing incomes by inserting more wage earners into the Israeli economy. An important consequence of this policy has been that no priority was given to the promotion of local entrepreneurship and local business development. On the contrary, such initiatives were generally discouraged. Arnon and Weinblatt argue that the principal explanation for the continuation of these relations of dependency under the Paris Protocol of 1994 is to be sought in the theory of incomplete contracts in the context of substantial asymmetries in power relations. This in turn indicates the importance of transaction costs for the Palestinian economy in inhibiting investment and trade. The potential role of agglomerations in reducing transaction costs is discussed later (F. Fischer *et al.* 2001).

These distortions translate into the industrial structure (UNSCO 2001). Agriculture represented 35 per cent of Palestinian GDP in 1990, but fell dramatically to 7 per cent by 2000. Low productivity in family-based agriculture is compensated for by employment of household members in Israel. Growth in manufacturing has not been strong, a common characteristic for middle income countries, with manufacturing's share of GDP reaching 16 per cent in 2000. The main industries represented are traditional: textiles, clothing and leather together comprising 35 per cent of industrial employment. Food processing, plastics, pharmaceuticals and soap are also represented. Services' share of GDP in 2000 was 54 per cent, the more important sectors being wholesaling, retailing and transport. Public services had a 12 per cent share of GDP and public administration and defence 10 per cent. Banking and financial intermediation has been growing rapidly though it still accounts for only 3 per cent of GDP. Finally, the construction sector's share of GDP was 10 per cent, but its surprising 22 per cent share of total employment means that there is low productivity in the sector. The service and construction sectors are dominated by small and medium-sized firms which had substantial employment growth in the period 1998–1999 (UNSCO 2000). Arnon *et al.* (1997) make the point that the industrial structure of the Palestinian economy was transformed in the period 1969–1993 from that of an underdeveloped country to that of a middle-income economy in World Bank terminology, and this process has continued since. Productivity differences between the Palestinian territories and Israel also narrowed in the same period.

The spatial structure of the Palestinian economy

There is a growing awareness amongst economists that spatial structure and economic growth are intimately related (see, for example, Fujita *et al.* 1999). This is certainly the case in Palestine where territorial issues, as well as the fact that Palestine is a territorially divided and partly landlocked state, are fundamental to the operation of the economy. Spatial structures and differences are also central to the following discussion of Palestinian development strategy and the future of the refugee camps.

The West Bank has an area of 5,800 square kilometres and was estimated in 2000 to have a population of around 1.9 million (PNA 2001), and a population density of 344 persons/square kilometre. Gaza had a population of about 1.15 million located in 365 square kilometres, having a population density of 3,151 persons/square kilometre. One further demographic feature of relevance is the Palestinian diaspora. In 2000 it was estimated that 5.2 million Palestinians lived outside the Palestinian territories, of which about 1 million were in Israel. Whilst Jordan had about half of the remainder, there are important Palestinian communities throughout the Arab world. Annual population growth in Palestine was expected to reach 5.4 per cent in 2000. Future forecasts of return migration suggest up to 700,000 return migrants by 2010, mainly refugees in the diaspora, though this depends upon the creation of a Palestinian state (PNA 2001).

In relation to the arguments developed in the following, certain features of the urban system are significant. Gaza is essentially one high density urban agglomeration of over one million inhabitants, with a bipolar centre structure. The West Bank has a more traditional and geographically spread settlement hierarchy. In 1998 about 34 per cent of the West Bank population lived in settlements of less than 5,000 inhabitants, 36 per cent in settlements of between 5,000 and 100,000 inhabitants and 30 per cent in the three main urban areas: Nablus (131,000 in 1998), Jerusalem (242,000) and Hebron (106,000). There is no major urban agglomeration in the West Bank.

Finally, there are the illegal Israeli settlements in Palestinian territory. There were 172,000 Israeli settlers in East Jerusalem in 2000, and 220,000 in the rest of the West Bank and 7,000 in the Gaza Strip in September 2002.[1] It is assumed that a negotiated settlement will result in the release of much of this housing stock to become housing units for the Palestinian population, which typically has larger families than the Israeli population.

Refugees and refugee camps

According to the United Nations Relief and Works Agency for Palestine Refugees in the Near East (UNRWA),[2] in March 2003 there were 901,092 refugees living in Gaza (85 per cent of the population of Gaza) and 647,919 living in the West Bank (32 per cent of the population). In June

2000, 473,000 or 53 per cent of the refugees in Gaza were living in camps, of which there are eight. In the West Bank 157,000 or 27 per cent of the refugees are living in camps, of which there are 19, spread throughout the region from Jenin in the north to Hebron in the south, with some relative concentration on the Ramallah–Jerusalem–Bethlehem axis. This means that both in absolute and relative terms the camps are more important for housing refugees in Gaza than in the West Bank. The average camp size in Gaza is about 56,500 refugees, whilst in the West Bank it is only 9,000. It is also clear that the population of Gaza consists largely of refugees, which is not the case in the West Bank. There are substantial Palestinian refugee populations living in Jordan, Lebanon and Syria. In these three countries, out of 2.5 million Palestinian refugees, about 635,000 live in camps.

The refugee camps are the responsibility of UNRWA, which also owns the land upon which they are located and provides basic services and medical care as well as shelters, now mainly made of concrete or mud bricks. In physical terms, living conditions in the camps are poorer than outside, housing units are smaller and of poorer quality, and sanitation and water supply is of a low standard. According to UN Resolution 194, refugees who choose not to return are entitled to compensation.

Some additional features of the camps should be noted. They are localities with very high population densities, and in the case of Gaza they have substantial populations. They are also highly interactive environments. In this sense they are true agglomerations, particularly in Gaza. They have strong social networks and sometimes strong economic networks. Interpersonal relations of trust, cooperation, shared risk taking and a common culture and language, key elements of what is termed social capital (Putnam 1993), are well-developed. This has arisen in part from a collective response to hardship and in part from resistance to occupation, where the camps play a significant role. Refugees living outside of the camps are, however, often better established economically and integrated locally. Nevertheless, though few reliable data exist on the issue, it has been suggested that there may be moderately high rates of home ownership in the refugee camps in Gaza and the West Bank where perhaps as many as 47 per cent of families in the camps own their own houses, though not, in general, the land.[3]

Long-term economic and spatial policy

The main elements of long-term economic and spatial policy for economic development in Palestine are discussed in the following.

Economic policy and planning

There are a number of policy proposals and plans for long-term economic development. The Palestinian Development Plan 1999–2003[4] outlines the basic principles for economic development of Palestine:

1 an economy which is market-based and private sector driven;
2 open markets and improved market access;
3 priority to be given to development of human resources;
4 development of tourism;
5 integration into a multilateral trading system;
6 improvement of competitiveness through technological progress.

These aims are re-echoed in a paper written by three authors associated with the IMF (S. Fischer *et al.* 2001). The immediate goals, they argue, are restoration of growth and recovery of lost output arising from recent turmoil and closures. In the medium-term, the goals are growth in per capita income and reduction of unemployment in the context of a rapidly growing labour force. Growth rates of 7 per cent per year are, because of demographics, needed to absorb the flow of new workers alone, which, it is argued, can be attained by investment and greater output growth. In the long-term, four factors are identified as important for long-run growth:

1 the rule of law, governance and quality of institutions, to build trust and credibility;
2 fiscal policy, to ensure a budget surplus, mainly through improvements in tax administration;
3 free flow of goods and people between the two parts of Palestine, between Palestine and Israel, and with the rest of the world;
4 public investment in infrastructure.

The policy proposals for the economy as a whole, as described above, will strengthen the performance of the Palestinian economy. Competition, improved access to markets, free trade and aid for investment are fairly standard ingredients in policies for economic development. However, some initial reservations can perhaps be made.

There is only limited consideration of present and future sources of comparative advantage in the Palestinian economy. Reinforcement and exploitation of comparative advantage is the best means of reducing productivity gaps at the international level (Castro and Jensen-Butler 2002). Whilst more traditional approaches to economic development will usually raise incomes in absolute terms, they do not necessarily close income or productivity gaps.

This suggests that it is important to consider the future and potential of the Palestinian economy in relation to the global economic environment and the transition to what has become known as the knowledge-based economy, an example of which is Israel. Elimination of inefficiency and reduction of dependency on the Israeli economy are corollaries to this approach.

Spatial policy and planning

Spatial policy and planning is an element of economic policy and planning which economists have tended to ignore. However, there are signs that this is changing and, as noted above, there is a growing awareness that the spatial structure of an economy is closely related to its economic performance. Furthermore, economic policy and planning in Palestine must necessarily address territorial issues directly.

The Palestinian Authority's Ministry of Planning and International Cooperation has produced a number of physical and spatial plans of which *National Policies for Physical Development* and the *Regional Plans* (MoPIC 1998a and 1998b) are among the more important. The guiding principle of these planning proposals is balanced regional and local development. On the West Bank, a hierarchy of urban centres is proposed, with balanced growth of urban and rural populations and development of both peripheral and more central areas. Balanced development of agriculture, industry and tourism, as well as preservation of the natural and cultural heritage is also to be pursued. The concept of balanced development is even present in the plans for Gaza. Preservation of natural resources and the coastline together with urban development; parallel development of agriculture and industry; sustainable management of natural resources, and relocation of population to the West Bank to avoid overcrowding, are all elements of the Gaza regional plan.

Planning for refugees

It is estimated that by 2010 700,000 refugees will return to Palestine from the diaspora and it is assumed that these returnees will mainly be those who are currently living in camps abroad (MoPIC 1998a). It is probable that richer and better educated Palestinians in the diaspora will be less likely to return, unless Palestinian society and economy are transformed, and this is the type of returnee that would add valuable capital and skills to the Palestinian economy (Sayre and Olmsted 1999). There are general proposals concerning preparation for this return migration, but concrete proposals for their integration into the Palestinian economy are less well developed, other than the West Bank being suggested as the obvious destination.

Strategies outlined by MoPIC (1998a) for dealing with refugee camps inside Palestine are twofold: a short-term strategy for rehabilitation, raising standards of dwellings and services, and a long-term strategy based upon redevelopment of the camps and/or urban integration. Rapid population growth associated with return of refugees, and preservation of agriculture, the environment and amenity constitutes an area of potential conflict. There is, however, little attempt to address the future of the refugee camps in an overall development strategy where refugees and refugee camps are treated as a potential resource.

A long-term perspective for the development of Palestine

Two features characterise recent positive economic performance in richer countries: a transition to a knowledge-based economy where innovation is centre stage (Acs *et al.* 2002) and the ability to operate in global markets, not least through the application of information and communications technology (Jorgenson 2001). The long-term vision of economic development in Palestine presented here is based upon identification of components of competitive advantage in the knowledge-based economy in a global context and examination of these components and their potential in the context of the Palestinian economy.

In economic theory, comparative advantage was traditionally considered to be based upon productive resources which are inherently immobile, such as the natural resource endowment or an immobile labour force with specific skills. In the knowledge-based economy the key element of competitive advantage is reinforcement and creation of locationally specific and immobile positive externalities, related to information and to knowledge generation and, not least, creativity. This in turn is related to the economic advantages of agglomeration and the development of institutions, typically in agglomerations, which favour the development of knowledge-based activities. The Palestinian economy has some potential to generate and take advantage of such external economies, providing an opportunity to close the productivity gap in relation to more advanced economies.

These externalities can be grouped into two main categories; economies of localisation and economies of urbanisation (Henderson 1986; Glaeser *et al.* 1992). *Economies of localisation* arise from agglomeration of firms and support institutions within a restricted and linked set of industries, creating a downward sloping industry supply curve for that agglomeration. The supply curve is the average cost rather than the marginal cost curve, as the average cost curve lies permanently above the marginal cost curve. These supply curves can be either static (a one-off gain) or dynamic (where the gains are cumulative). It is customary to distinguish between pecuniary external economies which operate through the market, and technological external economies which are untraded.

Economies of localisation require a permanent interaction between firms organised along value-chains and between firms and support institutions. They arise for a number of reasons including:

1 the benefits of skilled labour pooling;
2 scale economies for suppliers of intermediate inputs;
3 access to specialised infrastructure, services and institutional support;
4 spread of selected information about relevant markets and technologies;
5 sharing a common pool of knowledge that generates technological spillovers (a pure technological externality);
6 the existence and development of informal and formal networks permitting rapid transmission and development of new knowledge.

Technical progress as the key to per capita income growth is now at the core of growth theory (Grossman and Helpman 1991). Furthermore, knowledge spillovers are increasingly identified as important elements in regional and local economic performance and capacity to innovate (Audretsch and Feldman 1996). Spillover effects appear to be geographically differentiated and spatially concentrated, constituting an agglomeration economy (Jaffe 1989; Acs *et al.* 1994; Acs 2002). In order to generate or reinforce such economies of localisation, Palestine would have to choose a pattern of industrial specialisation which can take advantage of the specific local natural or human endowments, or of institutional factors which constitute the basis for exploitation of external economies in the globalised knowledge economy. It is here where some of the characteristics of the camps are relevant.

In other words, a number of industrial clusters based upon identification of localisation economies could be developed, each with a critical mass. They could either form separate industrial districts or overlap spatially in big urban centres and they could, in principle, be based upon either modern knowledge-based products or production in more traditional industries, where knowledge-driven change and innovation is applied. Clusters appear with increasing frequency in industrial policy throughout advanced economies (OECD 2001).

Economies of urbanisation are generated when industrial clusters overlap spatially and when they interact, creating synergies. Economies of urbanisation are externalities which affect a wide range of industries. They appear as industry cost curves similar to those related to localisation economies, except that it is the size of output in the (urban) region, rather than the geographically concentrated output of a specific industry which is on the horizontal axis. In addition to the same factors creating economies of localisation, they also arise from:

1 the availability and variety of business services;
2 a large labour reserve with a variety of skills;
3 a well-developed infrastructure and knowledge base;
4 scale and scope economies in supply of intermediate goods;
5 scale economies in public service provision.

Knowledge spillovers here occur between industries as well as within. The role of the city as a gateway to external information networks (Granovetter 1973) is also a source of advantage. Because they act on a larger scale than localisation economies, urbanisation economies require a greater critical mass of population and economic activity. At the same time, they are a major source of comparative advantage.

Three related aspects of these externalities associated with agglomeration are commonly identified in the literature. The first aspect is that externalities are inherently spatial, they affect some areas (typically agglomerations) whilst they are absent in others. Second, the institutional features of an economy are given a more prominent role than is the case with neo-classical approaches to growth and development, where there is little room for scale and agglomeration economies anyway. Third, it is frequently argued that social capital enhances the positive effects of these externalities. Social capital (Putnam 1993; Baron *et al.* 2000) includes such elements as trust, norms of cooperation, shared risk-taking, associational activity and social networks. The presence of substantial social capital appears to be positively associated with innovative capacity and economic performance. The underlying explanation is that social capital constitutes a partial compensation for the incompleteness of contracts. It is interesting to note that these elements of social capital are characteristics of Palestinian society both outside and especially within refugee camps in Palestine. Knack and Keefer (1997) have measured the economic effects of social capital at national level using international comparisons based upon international data sets on cultural values. They conclude that trust and civic cooperation do have significant positive impacts on aggregate economic activity, though this is especially significant in poorer countries which have less developed formal institutions, such as property rights or enforcement of contracts. Keefer and Knack (1997), in another paper, conclude that quasi-permanent institutional differences, related to social capital, are central to the explanation of permanent productivity gaps between countries. Social capital is also related to the concept of tacit knowledge, which, unlike codified knowledge, requires a common set of cultural, social and linguistic norms for its transfer. Tacit knowledge seems to play a central role in innovation (Smulders and van de Klundert 1995).

The knowledge-based economy and associated positive externalities are the elements upon which the following analysis of the strengths and weaknesses of the Palestinian economy and the development perspectives are based. These two elements also provide a framework for discussion of the future of the refugees and the camps.

Determinants of competitiveness in the knowledge-based society: a framework for analysis

The determinants of competitiveness in the knowledge-based society can be grouped into two main categories. The first refers to the characteristics of individual agents whilst the second comprises the externalities that reflect the advantages arising from the interaction between agents. These interactions depend not only on the agents' characteristics, but also on the institutional environment. Competitiveness, which can be represented by levels or changes in labour productivity, is related both to individual agents and to externalities. An obvious criticism of this approach is that no account is taken of investment and capital growth, represented by increases in the capital-labour ratio. However, the core of the argument presented is that comparative advantage does not build upon mobile and tradable resources such as investment in physical capital. Rather, the specific characteristics of individual agents and the nature of the externalities arising from their interaction constitute the basis for comparative advantage in the knowledge-based global economy (Castro and Jensen-Butler 2002). Growth in the capital-labour ratio is of course an important determinant of productivity, but it depends fundamentally on domestic saving levels and on capital inflows (which can be in the form of foreign aid). As such, investment is, in principle, available to any country or region which saves sufficiently or which can attract foreign investment. The basic framework for the following analysis is presented in Figure 8.1.

Characteristics of agents

Individuals

Competitiveness is enhanced where individuals have a high level of knowledge, strong technical skills, well-developed entrepreneurial ability and social and interactive skills which lead to cooperative behaviour, promoting trust and risk-sharing and involving a high networking capacity.

Palestinians have a general level of education significantly higher than that of most of the neighbouring states and most Arab and Muslim countries.[5] About 4.5 per cent of the population of the Palestinian territories over 10 years of age hold a degree (bachelor level or higher). Gross enrolment ratios in tertiary education are at reasonable levels.[6] Moreover, Palestine is a good example of equal education levels for men and women, which is a key factor in raising the average level of labour skills.

The service and construction sectors are well represented in the Palestinian economy, and there is a strong presence of small and medium-sized firms and entrepreneurs. In 1998–1999 new firm registrations increased by 38 per cent (UNSCO 2000), though this fell with the renewal of conflicts in 2000 (UNSCO 2001). This entrepreneurial feature of the Palestinian

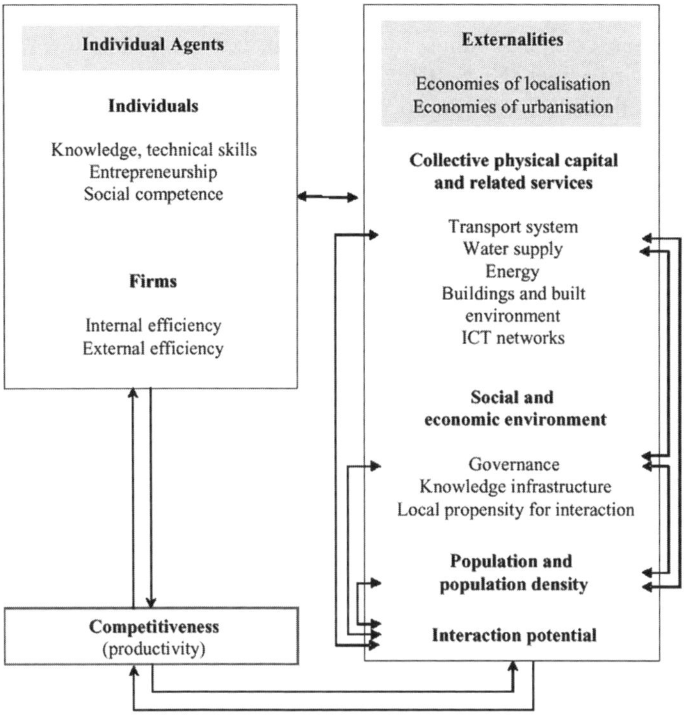

Figure 8.1 Determinants of competitiveness.

economy should be developed, efforts being directed at the quality of entrepreneurial ability and skills.

As noted above, the recent history of Palestine has, at the individual level, created relations of trust, strongly cooperative social behaviour, risk sharing and a high individual networking capacity. This type of social capital is well represented in the refugee camps and these characteristics favour the future development of entrepreneurial capacities, networking and a further strengthening of social capital. Notably, social capital tends to reduce transaction costs. It also means that education, at all levels, especially tertiary level, should be a major policy priority. Ugland (2003) documents the importance of social and family networks for social and economic life within Palestinian refugee camps in Lebanon where networks are stronger in the camps than in other refugee gatherings.

Firms

Competitiveness is enhanced when firms are internally efficient, involving all technical and organisational requirements for the optimisation of the internal operations of the firm. It also involves the capacity to adapt to, and to anticipate, changes in the external world through learning and innovation. Thus, competitiveness also involves external efficiency, related to the capacity to select the best business partners, to optimise both contracts and the flow of information concerning interaction with partners, and to react to the results of a permanent benchmarking exercise. External efficiency is strongly related to the capacity to use information and communication technology (ICT) as well as to the connection to dense social and economic networks.

The Palestinian economy is underperforming, which is a consequence of the low level of efficiency of firms, among other factors. This appears to be related to low levels of investment, weak managerial structures, distortionary subcontracting arrangements with Israeli firms and an unsafe and insecure business environment which raises transaction costs substantially. Improving the internal efficiency of Palestinian enterprises, for example through consultancy and technical assistance, including developing the use of ICT, is an important policy issue. Closely related to this is the need for improvement of entrepreneurial capacity, fully using the existent reserves of social capital. Harnessing the reserves of social capital and using them to enhance the efficiency of Palestinian firms is a major challenge for the Palestinian economy. Efficiency increases are important for firms to be able to take advantage of economies of agglomeration and access to finance for these purposes is a key issue.

UNRWA already runs a number of programmes providing finance for small-scale and non-traditional enterprises in Gaza and the West Bank.[7] The programmes appear to have been successful: since 1994 loans have totalled $61 million spread over 50,282 loans with very low default rates. Extension of this scheme and greater direction and emphasis in terms of use of new technology and learning would be a valuable policy component.

Externalities

There are four main relevant categories here.

The endowment of collective physical capital and services related to its use

Collective physical capital typically has strong public good characteristics, rendering it in effect a positive externality. Collective physical capital includes the following four elements.

First, the transport system, including infrastructure, which is a key factor contributing to economic efficiency and reduction of transaction costs. Second, water and energy supply, which are critical for future development. In Palestine water is a strategic resource, largely out of the control of the Palestinian Authority. Third, ICT networks, including the provision of broadband infrastructure, are key factors enhancing local competitiveness in the global knowledge economy. The weak development in Palestine of this fundamental infrastructure constitutes a barrier to the development of a knowledge-based economy.[8] However, infrastructure provision is in itself not a sufficient condition for take-up of ICT-based services (Castro and Jensen-Butler 2003)

Fourth, improvement of buildings and the built environment, including the refugee camps, which involves provision of high quality housing and replacement of sub-standard housing as well as environmental improvements. These improvements are essential to attract well-qualified human resources and for provision of office space.

Palestine has a large population of refugees living in camps, a fast growing domestic population, the prospect of inward migration from the diaspora, combined with the existence of a poorly built environment. These factors will place substantial pressures on the housing market. At the same time Palestine has one of the most important historical heritages in the world. There is an urgent need for a major programme of urban renewal and urban growth requiring large-scale financial resources, which will in turn place strong pressure on the historical heritage and natural environment. However, the existence of a large population with few property rights with respect to the land, and the land made available by future transformation or even closure of refugee camps (mainly in Gaza) presents an opportunity to embark upon large-scale housing and office development programmes of high quality, with good and innovative urban design and an innovative development process. Resources coming from international aid, from the diaspora and from compensation given to refugees for giving up property rights in Israel can be important sources of finance. Home ownership (as distinct from land ownership) in the camps is a potential source of capital for development of small-scale enterprises. The Palestinian construction sector is, as noted above, large, and the multiplier effects of activity in this sector are substantial.

An additional factor affecting housing supply will be the vacation of illegal Israeli housing in Palestine. Whilst this will increase supply, there are substantial location problems, as this housing was not planned in relation to the structure and development of the Palestinian economy.

The nature of the social and economic environment

The presence of efficient economic agents and a good endowment of physical capital are not sufficient conditions for economic efficiency. The positive externalities arising from the spatial agglomeration of economic agents must be combined with the externalities generated by the institutional characteristics of the environment which are essential to generate and attract qualified human resources, to minimise transaction costs and to generate knowledge spillovers. There are three main components.

First, good governance is a positive externality which is essential for promotion of investment (PNA 2001). It involves:

1 the existence of a secure environment, with low levels of criminality;
2 an efficient legal framework for enforcing contracts;
3 efficiency in administration;
4 transparency, arising from an intense exchange of information and a low level of corruption;
5 pro-active attitudes of public authorities to the support of the economy;
6 availability of financial resources, in particular venture capital.

The cohesiveness of Palestinian society is an important asset which can be used to create stronger governance. Long-term political instability usually reinforces negative factors such as mistrust of administration, inefficient and non-transparent bureaucracy and an administration which tends to over-value political issues and disregard economic and social policies (Keefer and Knack 1997; S. Fischer *et al.* 2001; F. Fischer *et al.* 2001). It appears that the Palestinian Authority is now adopting a more proactive role in relation to governance issues and economic development.

Second, a high quality of the knowledge infrastructure constitutes a positive externality. This includes:

1 tertiary level education providing an increased supply of qualified labour, which also promotes knowledge spillovers;
2 research institutions promoting public R&D and supplying technical and scientific support to firms;
3 promotion of private sector R&D and specialised consultancy services;
4 an institutional framework favouring knowledge spillovers, including incubators and social mechanisms promoting labour circulation and information exchange.

Whilst Palestinians have a relatively high level of general education, the proportion of the population aged 10 years and above holding a university degree is 4.5 per cent.[9] This is not so weak by international standards,[10] but should clearly be increased, with greater emphasis on science and technical disciplines, as well as the strengthening of technical and vocational training. However, R&D activities are not well developed and the productive system has a low capacity to absorb the available technical and scientific expertise. With eight universities and a population of three million, there is a basis on which to build.

Third, a strong local propensity for social and economic interaction constitutes a positive externality. This propensity depends upon a number of factors:

1. the existence of an integrated set of industries, business services and support institutions, organised along value chains;
2. social norms and mechanisms favouring cooperative and risk-sharing behaviour;
3. the existence of high levels of trust between economic actors;
4. strong entrepreneurship;
5. organisations promoting internal (local, regional or national) channels of communication, such as industrial and professional associations or business and social networks;
6. external channels of communication, providing gateways to the outside world such as chambers of commerce, diplomatic and other state-controlled international links as well as professional, academic and cultural networks.

Khawaja and Tiltnes (2002) provide evidence from Palestinian refugee camps in Jordan indicating that entrepreneurship and innovative activity is substantially higher in the camps than amongst refugees outside of the camps. 30 per cent of households in the camps have some experience of self-employment and average income levels are higher in the camps. Entrepreneurship is related to educational background and income level, and the principal constraints to development of enterprise based upon self-employment are limited access to credit and poor infrastructure. The importance of social and family networks in supporting economic and social structures in Palestinian refugee camps in Lebanon has also been documented by Ugland (2003).

Palestine has a high level of dependence on the Israeli economy, arising either from labour intensive sub-contracting relations or from widespread commuting by Palestinian workers to Israel where they are a source of cheap labour. As a consequence, the Palestinian economy is weakly integrated, with little capacity to develop clusters based on an ability to profit from economies of specialisation and localisation. This negative situation is partly compensated for by a social and cultural environment with a good potential to develop an interactive network economy involving a culture of cooperative behaviour, based upon strong internal social networks. This in turn favours the emergence of an economy based on intense exchanges of information and a developed capacity to connect to external networks. These connections can take place through a number of channels, including the Palestinian diaspora, the Arabic language and the widespread sympathy for the Palestinian cause, in particular, but not exclusively, in the Muslim world, which in itself constitutes social capital. Not least, connections arise through an excellent geographical location, on the border between Europe and the Middle East, the advantage of which can be reinforced if cooperation with Israel improves. Palestine can become an excellent economic and cultural platform at the interface between Arab, European and Jewish networks; a potentially key position in the information and knowledge society.

Population and population density

Most of the externalities which influence economic performance are heavily dependent upon economies of scale and economies of scope. Collective physical capital and services related to its use exhibit substantial economies of scale. The bigger the size of a local or regional economy the more efficient is the division of labour between different elements of the production system. Most of the components of knowledge infrastructure are also highly sensitive to economies of scale.

A high population density lowers the cost of almost all public and private services demanded by individuals and households, which are essential elements of quality of life and key factors for attraction of qualified labour. However, a high population density also creates negative externalities, such as congestion and pollution. The balance between positive and negative externalities defines optimal values (or reasonable intervals) for the size of an agglomeration and the density of population. This optimal balance, the achievement of which clearly requires state intervention, varies with the economic and spatial profile of specialisation of regions or localities. Areas with concentrations of agriculture, natural resources and certain types of tourism require low densities, whilst areas specialised in modern industries and services take advantage of high densities as long as territorial planning, environmental policies and transportation systems can prevent congestion, pollution and other negative externalities.

A high density of population and a large absolute population size, particularly in Gaza, favour the reinforcement of economies of localisation and economies of urbanisation. The camps provide initial agglomerations of population upon which to build, which, in the case of Gaza, would be a major urban agglomeration. In the West Bank they can, in some cases, provide additional sources of labour and social capital in smaller agglomerations where industrial clusters can be developed. Given appropriate incentives, some of their population will probably relocate to Gaza, which might also be a destination for returning refugees. A high population density, as noted above, also raises problems of congestion and is a threat to cultural heritage and the natural environment. Therefore, a careful policy and strong planning framework directed to the maximum exploitation of economies of specialisation and urbanisation and the minimisation of environmental damage is necessary.

Interaction potential

In a globalised knowledge-based society, economic efficiency is strongly dependent upon the intensity and variety of interactions between economic and social agents. For a given level of propensity for social and economic interaction, the actual level of interaction inside a region varies positively with the size of this region. The greater the population, the number of productive activities and consumer services, the greater is the number of opportunities to interact. Clearly, cultural and linguistic homogeneity and strong social capital reinforce interaction. On the other hand, the level of interaction with the outside world varies with accessibility to that external world, both in physical and cultural terms. This can be expressed by the following equation, based on the concept of interaction potential (Castro and Jensen-Butler 2003):

$$H_i = \sum_j \frac{P_j}{(D_{ij}C_{ij})^{\phi}}$$

Where:

H_i is the interaction potential of region i;
P_j is the population of region j;
D_{ij} is the physical distance between regions i and j;
C_{ij} is the cultural and political distance between regions i and j. This distance depends on whether both regions share the same language, similar cultural values (religion, etc.) or are separated by political, administrative or other barriers;
ϕ is a parameter representing the propensity for social and economic interaction.

As noted above, Palestine has a high interaction potential with the external world and its transformation into an effective asset should be a principal policy issue. Another aspect of this potential is that, as noted above, richer and well-educated Palestinians living in the diaspora will be less likely to return unless there is rapid growth and transformation of the Palestinian economy and society. If this occurs, then C_{ij} becomes smaller for this group and the potential for entering a cumulative process where growth attracts rich migrants with capital and skills, is present.

The combination of individual characteristics of the agents with the various types of externalities determines the competitiveness of the economic system, as shown in Figure 8.1. In this figure the arrows indicate some of the more important interactions between the basic elements.

A general framework for development

The economy of Palestine has sufficiently strong institutional features to permit formulation of an optimistic long-term vision and policy where Palestine becomes a relatively developed knowledge-based economy, able to develop strong specialisation and agglomeration economies. A substantial social capital is a sound base for permanent innovative activity and knowledge spillovers. When combined with strong connections to external networks and potential high levels of external interaction, there are prospects for transforming Palestine into a competitive, globalised economy.

The main characteristics of such an economy are:

1 high level of education and qualification in the labour force;
2 well-developed entrepreneurial capacity;
3 extensive social and economic networking;
4 strong links with external networks;
5 abundant and relatively skilled labour;
6 existence of substantial social capital;
7 potential for agglomeration;
8 balance between a developed, modern economy and the preservation of a unique cultural and historical heritage and a sensitive natural environment.

Palestine, compared with many middle-income countries, has advantages in relation to most of these characteristics. Furthermore, the refugee camps represent a potential resource in this context.

A cluster-based strategy

Types of cluster

Different approaches to cluster development can be initiated simultaneously. First, planning and development of a number of industrial clusters based upon traditional industrial sectors, such as food, textiles and clothing, leather and shoes, wood and furniture and ceramics can be undertaken in locations where there is some initial advantage and a strong presence of the industry, and where the perspectives for development of high value-added activities within the industry have the greatest potential. This implies the presence of institutions which are likely to promote innovation and productivity in the industry, the existence of a skilled industry-specific labour force and a strong entrepreneurial tradition in the sector.

Second, the question of developing sub-contracting relationships with Israel on the basis of a more equal partnership is also related to cluster development. There are clear advantages for both parties from a more equal and adjacent dual economy. Whilst still profiting from relatively cheap labour, this sub-contracting would enable Israel to compete in labour-intensive, design-intensive, high quality goods and in fashion-led consumer goods which are facing strong competitive pressure from the developing economies. Palestine can develop similar market niches where competitiveness arises from the combination of strong product innovation, marketing and technological capacity with relatively inexpensive factors of production. Examples might include furniture, textiles and clothing, footwear, jewellery and food products. A more equal sub-contracting relationship would involve two-way flows of ideas, innovation and labour, including highly qualified labour.

Third, one or more clusters could be developed around ICT-based services directed especially at the Arab World. These services could be based upon such activities as:

- development of software adapted to the Arabic language and to the specific needs of Arab societies;
- development of internet sites and portals directed to the Arab market with good links to the English language internet sites and services;
- supplying a very large potential market of hundreds of millions of consumers demanding internet contents adapted to Arab culture and specific needs, using the Arabic language and alphabet.

In many cases, this market can be extended to the Muslim world, even using national languages. Furthermore, the linguistic abilities of Palestinians also provide opportunities to develop ICT-based services where linguistic interfaces are required: in publishing, translation, international reservations and other secretarial services.

Fourth, only one cluster should emerge as a major financial centre. If Palestine succeeds in creating a safe and stable economic environment, there are good conditions for the development of a financial centre specialised in the interface between different cultures and societies. Palestinians, particularly in the diaspora, have developed financial skills and connections to the global financial world which are an important asset. However, there are already several centres, such as the Arab Gulf States and the Lebanon, which are serious competitors. The success of Palestine on this trajectory depends on the capacity to cooperate and find complementarities with these centres, rather than trying to out-compete them. Success in this field will attract Palestinians from the diaspora who have both capital and skills, and a process of cumulative growth could be established.

Finally, university-based R&D clusters can be developed. The role of universities as agents promoting strong R&D based innovation activity is well documented (Acs *et al.* 1992; Mansfield 1995). There is also an important and associated human capital dimension. A strong university system will not only serve the Palestinian population but will also provide an alternative university option for the Arab world. Palestine can become a centre for those Arabs who want a more cosmopolitan academic environment but who cannot afford to study in countries such as the US and the UK. This centre can be developed in an enlightened Arab and Muslim culture, with a low degree of governmental control and of influence from the more traditional elements in Arab and Muslim society.

Clusters and the refugee camps

As noted above, in relation to clusters, the camps have a number of potential contributions. First, they represent substantial population concentrations, indicating the potential for realising agglomeration advantage. This is particularly true in the case of Gaza. Second, in many cases they are located close to an existing major settlement – Ramallah, Nablus, Jerusalem, Bethlehem and Hebron – so that economic development initiatives directed at the camps can encompass the adjacent urban economy. Third, they are the locus of dense and well-developed social and economic networks compatible with modern smaller scale production using just-in-time methods. Fourth, they have substantial social capital, in the form of trust and risk-sharing, together with some entrepreneurial advantage. Translating these potential advantages into real productive advantage is a major challenge.

The future of the refugee camps viewed in a broader framework

The quality of the infrastructure and housing in the camps requires urgent attention. The World Bank favours a piecemeal market-based approach to upgrading housing and infrastructure in refugee camps, rather than a centrally planned exercise (World Bank 2003). Three development options are examined:

1 *in situ* upgrading of housing, services and infrastructure in typical refugee camps, as some refugees, it is argued, will choose to remain;
2 new extensions to existing villages and urban areas, where there is infrastructure in place;
3 building new urban areas.

The study reveals, perhaps unsurprisingly, that upgrading is the least costly alternative, in terms of improvement of physical infrastructure, social infrastructure and housing, and that building new urban areas for relocation of refugees is the most costly alternative, with extensions lying in between.

The World Bank approach is problematic in a number of respects. First, there is little consideration given to the future of the camps in relation to economic activity creating income and employment for their present-day residents. The quantity and quality of housing planned for the camps must ultimately be dependent upon the development of the local and regional economy. Second, comprehensive planning schemes are rejected and the preferred approach to financing development of the camps is '*providing lump-sum payments and allowing individuals to build their own units. This would be more welfare enhancing*' (World Bank 2003: 19). This view ignores the well-established research results indicating the existence of strong externality effects, both positive and negative, associated with housing markets and housing development. This means that, in relation to housing and urban development, markets are inefficient (Bailey 1959; King and Mieszkowski 1973; Kain and Quigley 1970, 1974). Creation of positive externalities and control or elimination of negative externalities are key elements in rapid development trajectories involving substantial construction activity. Third, housing is almost certainly a merit good, implying that the exercise of individual preferences in acquisition of housing will lead to sub-optimal resource allocation, as consumers do not appreciate its true value.

Finally, when redevelopment of the camps is advocated in a free market framework, one of the policy implications associated with development of clusters is provision of subsidies to firms in the decreasing cost industry associated with the cluster. The rationale for this type of subsidy is that it increases welfare. The supply curve for decreasing cost industries is the downward-sloping average cost curve, rather than the downward-sloping marginal cost curve, which is permanently below the average cost curve. Marginal cost pricing would, therefore, result in losses to any new firm locating in the cluster which means that society benefits from subsidising the expansion of an industry and output that has localisation economies (Mier 1993; Stull and Madden 1990). There is, therefore, a role for local and regional economic policy to promote cluster development and creation. This policy should include measures and subsidies directed at raising the quality of housing and infrastructure in the camps, linking these developments to the creation of a cluster based upon localisation economies.

What is important, however, is that the massive physical reconstruction involved in reconstruction and renovation of the camps be undertaken primarily by the Palestinian construction sector itself as the multiplier effects of an increase in demand for civil construction are large. This implies a substantial need for learning, labour training, innovation and technical change in this sector, which in turn suggests that the construction sector itself could be at the core of one industrial cluster.

Clusters and territorial strategy

The promotion and reinforcement of localisation and urbanisation economies requires the development of urban agglomerations, with a degree of sectoral specialisation. Careful choice of target industries in relation to clusters based upon localisation economies can be made for the major West Bank towns, taking into account their current industrial mix and competitive advantage. The development of large economic and demographic centres in the West Bank, in itself perhaps unrealistic, creates problems such as starting an uncontrolled process of urban sprawl, which will threaten the development of agriculture and tourism and seriously damage the natural environment. Rapid demographic growth in the West Bank will also increase competition between the urban and agricultural uses of water.

These effects would be partly offset by occupation of vacated Israeli settlements in the West Bank. However, the problem with the location and nature of these settlements is that they were never designed to be integrated with the Palestinian economy; they function essentially as commuter settlements for Israel. On balance it is better to plan for moderate growth of West Bank cities which, in addition to industrial clusters, could be centres of the tourist industry as well as relatively small-scale, environmentally friendly industries and service centres.

East Jerusalem is the future capital city. It is also a symbol of the new state, a religious centre, an historical and cultural heritage centre and a centre for tourism, and it will probably become the main educa-tional centre of Palestine. These functions are not compatible with the development of a large and rapidly growing financial and industrial centre. Jerusalem is not well suited for the role of a big metropolis absorbing most of the population growth. Thus, the (Arab) Jerusalem Metropolitan Area should be planned as a large non-metropolitan city with a reasonable population limit, of perhaps around half a million inhabitants. However, one possible choice of cluster-based development in Jerusalem is an ICT cluster, given the relative concentration of universities. An ICT cluster would be more compatible with the nature of the urban region than a cluster based upon manufacturing industry.

Palestine already has a largely ignored proto-metropolis in Gaza. The population of the West Bank is now around 1.9 million inhabitants and Gaza, which is essentially a single urban area, has 1.15 million inhabitants. The expected population of Palestine in 2010 is about 5 million. Some of the extra 2–2.5 million inhabitants would locate in Gaza if the economic incentives related to a growing urban agglomeration develop. These include rising wage levels, amenities, new housing and a range of elements creating positive external benefits associated with a metropolitan area. This would be the future Gaza Metropolitan Area.

Glaeser *et al.* (1992) conclude that modern and dynamic sectors can take advantage of urban agglomeration economies, whilst traditional industrial sectors can take advantage of localisation economies. Gaza has substantial potential for metropolitan development which could allow it to become the economic and financial centre of Palestine, thus creating a major urban area where the positive externalities associated with agglomeration have a real chance to grow. These urban advantages of Gaza are numerous.

First, transport links are potentially excellent. There is direct access to the sea, Gaza being the only place where a big port, handling most of Palestinian trade, can be developed and where there is an international airport. Second, unlike West Bank cities, the problem of lack of water can be solved with a large-scale desalination facility. Third, accessibility to Egypt, a major trading partner of the future Palestinian state, is very good. Fourth, a substantial part of its population is now resident in high-density refugee camps, which need to be transformed fundamentally in any case. The Gaza camps could be transformed into new urban areas and centres within a single agglomeration. There are good prospects for development of large-scale, carefully planned and innovative urban schemes. Fifth, the institutional features of the refugee camps referred to above will be an important contribution to reinforcement of the positive urban externalities. Finally, a well-advertised process of building a new city, based upon international competitions, would attract international architects and urban planners as well as development capital from both international aid and the private sector. The Palestinian construction sector, already large, would enter into a rapid learning process, incorporating and generating innovation in construction and urban planning, itself knowledge which can be exported.

As the agglomeration advantages of Gaza grow, the Metropolitan Area will become more attractive as a destination for refugees from the West Bank, reducing in turn the problems of urban sprawl and increasing pressures on arable land in that part of Palestine.

This pattern of development would result in a dual urban system, with Jerusalem as the political and cultural capital and Gaza Metropolitan Area as the financial and industrial capital. There are many examples of the success of dual cities: Washington/New York, Madrid/Barcelona, Rome/Milan, Beijing/Shanghai and Edinburgh/Glasgow. With a population of up to 2.5 million inhabitants and a density of 6,500 inhabitants per square kilometre, it would be necessary to sacrifice agricultural land, whilst the beaches and the areas which are nature reserves could be preserved. This could be regarded as the price of saving agriculture in the West Bank. This population density compares favourably with Cairo (23,100) and Shanghai (16,300) or the city of Lisbon (6,670).

In Gaza, agricultural land, refugee camps and land released by urban renewal projects must be carefully allocated to different functions:

1 high density, high quality service centres;
2 industrial parks, specialised in labour intensive, low density manufacturing;
3 residential centres, where a relatively high density of population must be combined with the existence of sufficient green areas and amenities, though some of the goals of balance referred to above would have to be relinquished.

The Gaza Metropolitan Area should not be developed in a piecemeal fashion, as recommended by the World Bank, which would result in a disorganised cluster of several cities and suburbs. Instead, it should be planned as a single metropolitan area, with a coherent settlement pattern.

In parallel with urban development in Gaza, a proactive policy stimulating investment in the financial and ICT sectors is essential. Hi-tech industrial development would also be typical target sectors for this industrial cluster. The social capital constituted by international sympathy, the perception of Palestine as a key factor of stability in the Arab world, the revenues coming from oil in Arab states, and foreign aid, among other factors, constitute resources for the Gaza project, opening a window of opportunity which Palestinians could exploit.

A Gaza Metropolitan Area Development Strategy is fundamentally a disequilibrium strategy, based upon increasing returns. As such, there is an inherent tension in relation to Palestinian aims, policies and ambitions for the West Bank. On the other hand, Gaza may well be the biggest single potential asset possessed by the Palestinian state.

Palestinian economic development, agglomeration and the refugee camps

The central theme of this chapter is that economic development, spatial structure and the future of the refugee camps in Palestine are inextricably linked. The more traditional proposals for a Palestinian economic development strategy, such as access to markets, increased flexibility, competition, free trade and aid for increased investment are, of course, important for generation of growth. They do not, however, directly address the question of comparative advantage and productivity gaps.

The potential that the Palestinian economy has for creating conditions which will generate comparative advantage in the knowledge-based globalised economy have been examined and the nature of the positive externalities, associated with agglomeration, have been outlined. A number of characteristics of the Palestinian economy and society can be viewed as resources if Palestine is to move in that direction. These include a relatively well-educated labour force, substantial social capital, the presence of many entrepreneurs, a potential major agglomeration, Gaza, and a high interactive capacity with the outside world, particularly the Arab world.

The realisation of this potential requires a development policy with a strong spatial component, building on increasing returns and the advantages of agglomeration. Gaza, already having a metropolitan population, is a proto-metropolis whose full development potential has largely remained unrecognised.

This is not an easy policy to develop, as it assumes a degree of disequilibrium, rather than balanced growth, upon which Palestinian development policy has generally rested. In particular there would probably be tensions over the location of investment in the West Bank as opposed to Gaza. Also, the refugee camps have a role to play in this scenario as they have important components of social capital. In Gaza, they constitute the very basis of a new major agglomeration. In the West Bank they can provide the foundation for development of more limited industrial clusters based upon localisation economies.

This approach turns a number of seemingly well-established principles on their heads. Balance in policy and planning is replaced by some deliberate disequilibria. Markets alone will not result in optimal solutions in a world based upon agglomeration economies where there are strong positive externalities. The development process will itself create negative externalities which will overwhelm any Coasian mechanism of negotiation. Furthermore, this development process will scarcely be smooth, as critical mass, take-off and cumulative growth processes are important. Palestine is one of the few middle-income countries that have real potential to make this transition.

Notes

1 Information from Foundation for Middle East Peace (available at HTTP://www.fmep.org/reports/2003/v13n6.html#7) and the Israeli Central Bureau of Statistics (available at HTTP://www.cbs.gov.il/population/new_2003/tab_1.pdf) (both accessed 14 January 2004).
2 A useful source of information on Palestinian refugees is the UNRWA homepage, available at HTTP:/www.un.org/unrwa (accessed 5 August 2003) Also, the Palestinian Refugee Research Net provides information and bibliographic material, available at HTTP://www.arts.mcgill.ca/mep/prrn/prfront.htm (accessed 5 August 2003).
3 Israeli Press report, *Maariv*, 14 July 2003.
4 Available at HTTP://www.palestine-pdp.org/pdp/pdp2000 (accessed 5 August 2003).
5 The UNDP (United Nations Development Programme) Human Development Report gives the Occupied Palestinian Territories (OPT) an Education Index of 0.85 for 2001, which can be compared with 0.99 for the UK, 0.93 for Israel, 0.86 for Jordan, 0.73 for UAE, 0.71 for Saudi Arabia, 0.77 for Turkey, 0.63 for Egypt, 0.83 for Lebanon and 0.82 for middle-income countries. The index is based upon literacy rates and combined primary, secondary and tertiary enrolment ratios. Available at HTTP://www.undp.org, (accessed 5 August 2003).
6 Gross enrolment ratios in tertiary education in 2000/2001 were 29 per cent for the OPT, Jordan 29 per cent, Lebanon 42 per cent, Saudi Arabia 22 per cent,

Iraq 14 per cent, Turkey 24 per cent, UAE 12 per cent, Israel 53 per cent and the UK 60 per cent.

7 The four programmes are:

1 Small-scale enterprises;
2 Micro-enterprises;
3 Solidarity Group Lending (to women);
4 Consumer Lending.

Available at HTTP://www.un.org/unwra/programmes (accessed 5 August 2003).

8 The UNDP Human Development Report gives for 2001 the number of internet users per 1,000 people in the Occupied Palestinian Territories as 18.2 which compares unfavourably with Lebanon (77.6), Jordan (45.2), Turkey (60.4) UAE (314.8), but is better than Egypt (9.3) and Saudi Arabia (13.4). For middle-income countries the figure is 36.8, for Israel 276.6 and for the UK 329.6. For cellular subscribers per 1,000 people the figures are OPT 91, Lebanon 229, Jordan 167, Turkey 295, UAE 616, Egypt 43, Saudi Arabia 113, middle income countries 128, Israel 907, UK 770. Available at HTTP://www.undp.org (accessed 5 August 2003).

9 First Palestinian Census (1997).

10 The percentage of the population of 25–64 years old with a university level educational attainment in 2000 was: Austria 6 per cent, Italy 9 per cent, Portugal 7 per cent, Turkey 8 per cent, UK 17 per cent, USA 27 per cent (OECD Science and Technology Based Scoreboard 2001 – Towards a Knowledge-Based Economy, OECD, Paris, (2000), available at HTTP://www1.oecd.org/publications/e-book/92-2001-04-1-2987/A.8.htm (accessed 5 August 2003)). Note that the populations being compared with Palestine (10 years and over) are not the same.

References

Acs, Z. (2002) *Innovation and the Growth of Cities*, Cheltenham: Elgar.

Acs, Z., Audretsch, D. and Feldman F. (1992) ‘Real effects of academic research: comment’, *American Economic Review* 82: 363–367.

Acs, Z., Audretsch, D. and Feldman, F. (1994) ‘R&D spillovers and recipient firm size’, *Review of Economics and Statistics* 76: 336–340.

Acs, Z., de Groot, H. and Nijkamp, P. (2002) *The Emergence of the Knowledge Economy*, Berlin: Springer.

Arnon, A. and Weinblatt, J. (2001) ‘Sovereignty and economic development: the case of Israel and Palestine’, *Economic Journal* 111: F291–F308.

Arnon, A., Luski, I., Spivak, A. and Weinblatt, J. (1997) *The Palestinian Economy*, Leiden: Brill.

Audretsch, D. and Feldman, M. (1996) ‘Knowledge spillovers and the geography of innovation and production’, *American Economic Review* 86: 630–640.

Bailey, M. (1959) ‘Note on the economics of residential zoning and urban renewal’, *Land Economics* 35: 288–292.

Bannister, G. and Erickson von Allmen, U. (2001) ‘Palestinian trade: performance, prospects and policy’, in R. Valdivieso, U. Erickson von Allmen, G. Bannister, H. Davoodi, F. Fischer, E. Jenkner and M. Said (eds) *West Bank and Gaza: Economic Performance, Prospects and Policies*, Washington, DC: IMF.

Baron, S., Field, J. and Schuller, T. (eds) (2000) *Social Capital: Critical Perspectives*, Oxford: Oxford University Press.

Castro, E. and Jensen-Butler, C. (2002) 'Regional economic inequality, growth theory and technological change', manuscript, Department of Economics, University of St Andrews, UK.

Castro, E. and Jensen-Butler, C. (2003) 'Demand for information and communication technology-based services and regional economic development', *Papers in Regional Science* 82: 27–50.

Cobham, D. (2001) 'Economic aspects of the Israeli–Palestinian conflict: introduction', *Economic Journal* 111: F249–F253.

Davoodi, H. and Erickson von Allmen, U. (2001) 'Demographics and long-term growth in the Palestinian economy', in R. Valdivieso, U. Erickson von Allmen, G. Bannister, H. Davoodi, F. Fischer, E. Jenkner and M. Said (eds) *West Bank and Gaza: Economic Performance, Prospects and Policies*, Washington, DC: IMF.

Fischer, F., Said, M. and Valdivieso, R. (2001) 'Transaction costs in the Palestinian economy: a microeconomic perspective', in R. Valdivieso, U. Erickson von Allmen, G. Bannister, H. Davoodi, F. Fischer, E. Jenkner and M. Said (eds) *West Bank and Gaza: Economic Performance, Prospects and Policies*, Washington, DC: IMF.

Fischer, S., Alonso-Gamo, P. and Erickson von Allmen, U. (2001) 'Economic developments in the West Bank and Gaza since Oslo', *Economic Journal* 111: F254–F275.

Fujita, M., Krugman, P. and Venables, A. (1999) *The Spatial Economy*, Cambridge: MIT Press.

Glaeser, E., Kallal, H., Scheinkman, J. and Shleifer, A. (1992) 'Growth in cities', *Journal of Political Economy* 100: 1126–1152.

Granovetter, M. (1973) 'The strength of weak ties', *American Journal of Sociology* 78: 1360–1380.

Grossman, G. and Helpman, E. (1991) *Innovation and Growth in the Global Economy*, Cambridge: MIT Press.

Henderson, V. (1986) 'Efficiency of resource usage and city size', *Journal of Urban Economics* 19: 47–70.

Jaffe, A. (1989) 'Real effects of academic research', *American Economic Review* 79: 957–970.

Jorgenson, D. (2001) 'Information technology and the US economy', *American Economic Review* 91: 1–32.

Kain, J. and Quigley, J. (1970) 'Evaluating the quality of the residential environment', *Environment and Planning* 2: 23–32.

Kain, J. and Quigley, J. (1974) 'Housing market discrimination, home ownership and savings behaviour', *American Economic Review* 62: 263–277.

Kanafani, N. (2001) 'Trade – a catalyst for peace?', *Economic Journal* 111: F276–F290.

Keefer, P. and Knack, S. (1997) 'Why don't poor countries catch up? A cross-national test of an institutional explanation', *Economic Inquiry* 35: 590–602.

Khawaja, M. and Tiltnes, A. (eds) (2002) 'On the margins. Migration and living conditions of Palestinian camp refugees in Jordan', Oslo: FAFO, Institute for Applied Social Science.

King, A. and Mieszkowski, P. (1973) 'Racial discrimination, segregation and the price of housing', *Journal of Political Economy* 18: 590–606.

Knack, S. and Keefer, P. (1997) 'Does social capital have an economic payoff? A cross-country investigation' *Quarterly Journal of Economics* 112: 1251–1288.

Mansfield, E. (1995) 'Academic Research underlying industrial innovations: sources, characteristics, and financing', *Review of Economics and Statistics* 77: 55–65.

Mier, R. (1993) *Social Justice and Local Development Policy*, Newbury Park, Chicago: Sage.

MoPIC (1998a) *National Policies for Physical Development*, East Jerusalem: Ministry of Planning and International Cooperation, Palestine National Authority.

MoPIC (1998b) *The Regional Plan for the West Bank Governates*, East Jerusalem: Ministry of Planning and International Cooperation, Palestine National Authority.

OECD (2001) *Innovative Clusters: Drivers of National Innovation Systems*, Paris: OECD.

PNA (2001) *Information Note on the Economy of the Occupied Palestinian Territory (West Bank and Gaza)*, Palestinian National Authority, Ministry of Economy and Trade, prepared for the United Nations Conference on Less Developed Countries, Brussels, Belgium, May 2001.

Putnam, R. (1993) *Making Democracy Work*, New Jersey: Princeton University Press.

Sayre, E. and Olmsted, J. (1999) 'Economics of Palestinian return migration' *Middle East Report* 212 – Fall 1999.

Smulders, S. and van de Klundert, T. (1995) 'Imperfect competition, concentration and growth with firm-specific R&D', *European Economic Review*, 39: 139–160.

Stull, W. and Madden, J. (1990) *Post-industrial Philadelphia*, Philadelphia: University of Pennsylvania Press.

Ugland, O. (ed.) (2003) *Difficult Past, Uncertain Future. Living Conditions among Palestinian Refugees in Camps and Gatherings in Lebanon*, Oslo: FAFO, Institute for Applied Social Science.

UNCTAD (2002) *Report on UNCTAD's Assistance to the Palestinian People*, Geneva: Secretariat, United Nations Conference on Trade and Development.

UNSCO (2000) *Report on the Palestinian Economy. With a Special Report on Palestinian Merchandise Trade*, Gaza: Office of the United Nations Special Coordinator.

UNSCO (2001) *Report on the Palestinian Economy*, Gaza: Office of the United Nations Special Coordinator.

World Bank (2003) *Housing and Infrastructure. Scenarios for Refugees and Displaced Persons*, Washington, DC: World Bank (Paper presented at the Stocktaking Conference on Palestinian Refugee Research, Ottowa, Canada, 17–20 June 2003).

Discussion

Leila Farsakh

By concentrating on two issues central to the Palestinian economy, refugees and urban agglomerations, this chapter provides a valuable and original contribution to the literature on the Palestinian economy. Eduardo de Castro and Chris Jensen-Butler propose a strategy for growth that sees refugees, both as individuals and as factors of urban density, as an asset rather than a liability. In their view, the long-term sources of Palestinian growth do not lie simply in expanding trade relations, good governance and sound fiscal policy, as the World Bank and IMF have recommended. Growth also requires a strategy to reduce productivity gaps at the international level, and to transform the economy into a knowledge-based economy. The key factors for such a transformation are skills, social capital and externalities of localisation as well as of agglomeration. Both refugees and urban agglomerations, such as Gaza City, are valuable resources that would make such a transformation possible, especially when accompanied by the right policy framework.

The reason why refugees and Gaza can play such a developmental role hinges on the theory of economic clusters and social capital on which the authors rely. Palestinian refugees tend to be spatially concentrated, have relatively high skill levels, especially by middle-income country standards, and have shown entrepreneurship skills, be it in the Occupied Territories or in the diaspora. They have developed rich social capital, due to localisation externalities which help reduce transaction costs while fostering strong links and trust relations between firms and people. Gaza City, meanwhile, offers various externalities of agglomeration. Its high population density, while a concern for environmental reasons, offers great potential for industrial and service oriented clusters. Developing its housing market would have a strong multiplier effect on the rest of the economy.

While enriching as a perspective, the chapter leaves a number of questions unanswered. First, it remains speculative, due to the absence of enough detailed data on refugees. The authors do not always clearly distinguish between refugees and returnees, nor do they distinguish the skill distributions of Palestinians according to social and settlement background. They also fail to account for the difference in skill and education levels between refugees in the Occupied Territories and those in Lebanon or other diaspora areas. It is thus difficult to be sure that the return of refugees to a crowded place such as the Gaza Strip would be an asset, rather than a liability. Even without counting those who wish to return, the economic contribution that refugees could make cannot be abstracted from the present demographic pressures and labour market constraints. The chapter does not give enough attention to the challenge of employment creation in the WBGS, especially given the high population growth rates, unemployment levels and continuous reliance on the Israeli labour market, which is particularly important for refugees (see Farsakh 2004). The economic contribution of refugees cannot simply depend on the development of the housing sector in the camps, which could be highly speculative. Developments in the labour, industrial and financial markets need to be incorporated into the analysis.

Second, the chapter makes a distinction between the Gaza Strip and the West Bank that is problematic. The authors fail to give enough credit to the role of West Bank cities in creating a number of industrial and service oriented clusters that use and rely on refugee labour and skills. Nablus, for example, has been developing a dynamic financial cluster, and, together with Hebron, has provided various industrial clusters built in the proximity of refugee camps. Meanwhile, not only Jerusalem but also Ramallah have been working on developing ICT and R&D clusters. In the chapter there is an emphasis on developing only Gaza City into 'a metropolitan area' while allowing for 'moderate growth of West Bank cities'. While moderate urban growth is undoubtedly beneficial, it is not clear why Gaza should be the only metropolis or why it should resettle the majority of the refugees. The Occupied Territories are not such a large place, and social capital can develop between cities rather than relying on single, large, heavily populated urban centres, especially once transportation problems are resolved.

Third, the authors, while aware of the importance of the territorial question, do not consider its various dimensions and its wider economic implications. The role of refugees and urban agglomerates in development cannot be abstracted from the way the Israeli–Palestinian conflict is going to be resolved, and from the boundaries that the Palestinian state will be given. The success of a cluster-based strategy will depend not only on the identification of the right sectors or right forms of state intervention. It will depend above all on clear territorial boundaries between Israel and the Occupied Territories as well as free access between Palestinian areas themselves and to the outside world. The economic externalities of localisation and agglomeration will be lost without a resolution of basic territorial issues (such as ports, borders, crossing points etc.) which affect transaction costs as well as economic growth. Moreover, it is not obvious that the integration of Israeli settlements into the Palestinian economy cannot contribute to the development and accommodation of refugees.

Contrary to the authors' argument, the settlements are in fact connected to the Palestinian economy, via the workers they employ, the land they use and the goods they exchange (Farsakh 2004). Settlements are built in the proximity, if not on the land, of neighbouring Palestinian villages and refugee camps. Despite the intensity of closure policies in the 1990s, over 30,000 Palestinians, or one-third of all Palestinians employed in the Israeli economy, have been working in the settlements.

Reference

Farsakh, L. (2004) 'Palestinian labour mobility and the redefinition of economic boundaries between Israel and the West Bank and Gaza Strip', in H. Hakimian and J. Nugent (eds) *Trade Policy and Economic Integration in the Middle East and North Africa*, London: RoutledgeCurzon.

9 Foreign aid strategy

Anne Le More[1]

International assistance to the Palestinian people did not begin with the Oslo peace process. The United Nations involvement, for instance, goes back to the early 1950s with the establishment of the United Nations Relief and Works Agency for Palestine Refugees in the Near East (UNRWA), and many donors, such as the European Commission (EC) and USAID, started their support in the years following the 1967 occupation of the West Bank and Gaza Strip (WBGS). However, it is only over the last decade that aid to the occupied Palestinian territory has become so wide-ranging and substantial: by the beginning of 2002, US$6.5bn had been committed and some US$4.4bn disbursed. At US$195 per person per annum, this represents one of the highest levels of per capita official development assistance in the world, highlighting the political importance assigned to the resolution of the Palestinian–Israeli conflict.[2]

Assistance to the Palestinian people: rationale, scope and composition

Oslo and the intifada years

Aid to the WBGS in the decade following the signing of the Oslo Agreement, and thus its system of management and coordination, has been inextricably linked to the Middle East peace process, with the Palestinian–Israeli Declaration of Principles of 13 September 1993, providing both the prime rationale and the political framework for international efforts. Official assistance has not been targeted solely at the promotion of ‘economic development and welfare’, which is the received definition of what constitutes the principal objective of foreign aid.[3] It has also had an explicit political aim: sustaining peace.

On one level, these two aims have been seen as intertwined. At the time of the first donor conference, which took place in Washington, DC in October 1993, a couple of weeks after the signing of the Oslo Agreement, an optimistic functionalist conception dominated thinking on the economic aspects of peace in the Middle East. According to this approach, economic development and increased regional cooperation would strengthen and consolidate peace through 'spillover' effects.[4] Aid, through contributing to economic growth and through job creation via the implementation of donor-funded projects, would also contribute to sustaining Palestinian political stability and the momentum of the peace process by creating tangible and rapid improvements in basic infrastructure as well as in the living conditions and employment opportunities of the Palestinian population. Finally, the motivations for aid in the context of the Israeli–Palestinian peace process have gone further than 'peace through development', a third priority being to build viable and effective Palestinian institutions so as to lay the foundations for a future Palestinian state.

These three facets – sustaining peace, supporting economic and social development, and building viable Palestinian institutions – have remained at the core of donor intervention over the last decade, even if the beginning of the intifada, the intensification of the conflict, the large-scale Israeli military incursions into Palestinian cities and their intermittent reoccupation added a fourth emergency/humanitarian dimension to donor activities.

Although the rationale for aid to the Palestinians has arguably not changed over the last ten years, the composition of donor assistance, on the other hand, has shifted. This was true even prior to the beginning of the intifada. For instance, while in 1994–1995, 33 per cent of aid disbursements went to transitional and budget support for the Palestinian National Authority (PNA), this declined to 20 per cent in 1996–1997 and to less than 4 per cent in 1998–1999. Similarly, a marked decline is also noticeable in the proportion of resources allocated to human resources and social development on the one hand and institutional development on the other, from 33 per cent in 1994–1995 to 21 per cent by 1998–1999 for the former and from 20 per cent to 13 per cent for the latter over the same period. Support for infrastructure development, however, increased from 19 per cent to 39 per cent of donor support (World Bank and Japan 2000). Over the first five years of the Oslo process, donor disbursements averaged US$464 million per year, although they fell almost 20 per cent between 1996 and 1999. Aid as a share of Palestinian GDP declined over this period from 18 per cent in 1994 to 10 per cent in both 1998 and 1999 (Khan 2003: 4). As of the end of 1999, loans accounted for 10 per cent of cumulative donor disbursement (World Bank and Japan 2000: 18–21).

Since the end of 2000, the allocation of aid has changed even more drastically. The emphasis in donor work has increasingly been directed towards mitigating the impact of the severe economic crisis in the WBGS, resulting from an ever tighter closure regime imposed by Israel on the occupied Palestinian territories.[5] After some years in the late 1990s in which aid was progressively channelled into longer-term socio-economic programmes, the intifada led to a return to the kind of assistance, such as budgetary support and employment generation that characterised the first couple of years of the peace process.

Overall, disbursements rose considerably as compared to the pre-intifada years, as follows: US$482 million in 1999, US$549 million in 2000, US$929 million in 2001 and US$1000 million in 2002. But according to the World Bank, the ratio between development and emergency aid, in commitment terms, which had been approximately 7:1 in favour of development assistance in 2000, had shifted by 2002 to 5:1 in favour of emergency assistance. Furthermore, 'although overall commitments increased by 57 per cent in the period, development assistance declined by 70 per cent (while emergency assistance increased by a factor of 10)'. Indeed, in 2002, out of more than US$1000 million disbursed to the WBGS, 81 per cent (US$829 million) of donor disbursements went to all forms of emergency assistance, including 50 per cent (US$519 million) to budget support to the PNA. From 10 per cent in 1999, aid in 2003 represented approximately 41 per cent of Palestinian GDP (World Bank 2003).

There also has been a shift in the source of contributions. While the European Union (including the EC and EU member states) has remained the largest donor to the WBGS over the last decade and the United States has also been a major donor throughout, the Arab League has become a substantial player only since 2001.[6] By 2002, it accounted for 30.8 per cent of all disbursements, while the EC and EU member states accounted for some 35–40 per cent and the US for 18.9 per cent.[7]

Aid following the establishment of a viable Palestinian state[8]

The rationale for foreign aid following the establishment of a viable Palestinian state is unlikely to be radically different to that of the first decade following Oslo. Its composition, at least at the outset, may also be expected to be very similar to that which characterised the intifada years. This is so for three main reasons.

First, assistance will obviously no longer be directly linked to the peace process and the creation of a Palestinian state, but the idea that economic development will consolidate peace is likely to remain prevalent, and so will the significance of strengthening the institutional capacity of the Palestinian government and state structure.

Second, given the high political stakes involved and the importance of the Palestinian–Israeli context, the new Palestinian state should receive significant aid inflows, especially if international assistance finances a compensation scheme for refugees and the rehabilitation of camps. Donors are likely to desire to remain involved and highly visible, at least for a period after its creation.

Finally, the socio-economic and humanitarian situation has become so abysmal in recent years that even if the single most important cause for the economic crisis is removed, i.e. Israeli closures and restrictions on the movement of Palestinian goods and people, it will take some years for the economic situation to stabilise at its 2000 level, not to mention to return to its 1993 level. In June 2000, after two years of economic recovery and modest growth, the World Bank nonetheless estimated that if the growth rates were sustained, it would take a decade before real Palestinian GNP/capita reached its 1993 level (World Bank and Japan 2000). In March 2002, after a year and a half of severe recession (with per capita real income declining by 12 per cent for 2000 as a whole, and by a further 19 per cent in 2001), it was estimated that average per capita real income was 30 per cent below what it was when the Gaza–Jericho Agreement was signed in 1994 (World Bank 2002). According to the 2003 United Nations Conference on Trade and Development (UNCTAD) report, 'in real terms, in the last three years the Palestinian economy has forgone all the growth it had achieved in the preceding 15 years, with real GDP today below its 1986 level' (UNCTAD 2003: 5).

So with 60 per cent of the Palestinian population estimated as living below the poverty line in 2003 – against 21 per cent on the eve of the intifada – how many years will be needed for the economic situation to stabilise at a reasonably sound level?[9] One can only speculate on this point: incomes could potentially recover faster if political stability was restored, closure was lifted and an open trade regime was actively supported. Nevertheless, relief assistance is likely to continue to constitute a large proportion of donor support for some years, even in the context of a favourable political arrangement and even if, under the circumstances of a new, post-intifada rehabilitation phase, humanitarian assistance declines rapidly and relief aid has to be integrated into a longer-term development vision and strategy.[10] This seems all the more likely as it is now estimated that after three years of continuous decline, the occupied Palestinian territory has been transformed into a 'war-torn economy', exhibiting most of the salient characteristics of many war/conflict economies. This has some important implications for future donor assistance. As has been observed:

> the next 'post-conflict' policy/aid package will be qualitatively different than those that accompanied previous recoveries from shocks and upheaval... The coming phase of economic rehabilitation and 'peace-building' in the region cannot simply take as its goal a return to the pre-2000 situation, whose shortcomings paved the way for events witnessed since. While still needed, humanitarian and relief assistance should no longer be addressed in isolation from development assistance.
>
> (UNCTAD 2003: 4–5)

There will, of course, be some differences between the situation which prevailed over the Oslo decade and that characterising the advent of an independent and sovereign Palestinian state. First, as the intifada years have been marked by acute violence, destruction and conflict and as experience of foreign assistance to war-torn societies in the 1990s has revealed, aid strategy in a new post-conflict phase will need to address additional economic and social issues. In particular, assistance will need to be specifically targeted at the poorest and most vulnerable and marginalised sections of the Palestinian population so as to provide them with a stake and ensure that no key groups (such as the young, refugees, women) are ignored and that potential 'spoilers' (such as the security forces) are neutralised. These are issues to which not much attention has been paid in the 1990s and early 2000s, but which will require serious thinking and strategic prioritisation in the first years following the establishment of a state.

Second, the aid management system will no longer be so intimately linked to a trilateral political process. This means that Israel will no longer be such a relevant third party in most aspects of the aid relationship and donors might be less influenced by political considerations and the constant need to balance the government of Israel (GoI) and the PNA. In other words, although foreign aid is always a highly political enterprise, assistance to the Palestinian people should nonetheless become less politicised once a sovereign independent Palestinian state exists. This may give donors and aid agencies more room for manoeuvre in devising their broad strategic orientations, as the development process will no longer need to be brought directly into the service of bilateral political negotiations.

Finally, the aid environment should be less constraining. In accordance with our working assumption of the creation of a state, most of the project implementation difficulties and impediments on donor activities linked to the damage to donor projects by the Israeli army and to Israeli military occupation, settlement expansion, closure policy, territorial fragmentation of the WBGS, and more recently the construction of the Wall will be less, or no longer, relevant.[11] The degree to which this is the case, however, will largely depend on the content of the final status agreement and the precise attributes of the new sovereign Palestinian state: issues of frontiers, international border crossings, transit, etc. may still remain problematic and hamper the work of the donor community and its Palestinian partners, not to mention the detrimental effects this may continue to have on the living conditions of the Palestinian population as a whole.

However, despite these three main differences, the management of foreign aid is likely to build on existing structures and lessons learned in the past. It is therefore useful first to review the experience of the last decade so as to inform our reflections on a credible Palestinian foreign aid strategy for the future.

Aid management 1993/1994–2003: a donor-driven process

The aid coordination setting

The system for aid management that developed during the Oslo period was fashioned by the objectives mentioned above as well as the realities on the ground. The coordination arrangements which have emerged are elaborate and complex, reflecting the intricacy of the political context and the highly sensitive nature of the conflict, the need to balance competing American and European positions, the unusually large number of donors, UN agencies, other multilateral organisations and NGOs present in the field and aspiring to high visibility, a willingness for rapid disbursement of funds so as to deliver on the 'peace dividend' of the agreement as well as the uncertain, evolving and severely constrained status of the main recipient institution, the PNA (Lister and Venäläinen 1999; Lister and Le More 2003). As the Declaration of Principles provided both the objective and the political framework for the aid effort, the aid coordination structure also rapidly came to embody a trilateral process, with the government of Israel becoming a full actor in the 'triangular partnership' which developed at both the capital and local levels between the donor community, the PNA and the GoI, rather than being simply a donor in a mainly bilateral donor–Palestinian relationship.

At the donor capitals' level, two main bodies were established to provide general direction to the aid effort. Overall strategic supervision of donor assistance was assigned to the Ad Hoc Liaison Committee (AHLC), a high-level group of key political donors established following a meeting of its founders in November 1993. Its principal mandate has been setting the policy framework and development priorities for the WBGS relevant to all donors and aid institutions.[12] A Consultative Group (CG) mechanism was also established and functioned up until 1999, dealing with the actual coordination of donor programmes, aid mobilisation and broad based discussion between the PNA and all its multilateral and bilateral donors. Consultative Groups are a World Bank instrument at the capital level not unique to the WBGS but used in many aid-recipient countries as an all-donor forum to pledge funds and to discuss policy options and particular project activities.

At the local level, three main coordination bodies were set up in the 1990s. The Joint Liaison Committee (JLC) was established to address problems in donor-recipient and tripartite relations. This included issues related to the implementation of the Tripartite Action Plan (TAP) on Revenues, Expenditures and Donor Funding for the Palestinian Authority. This plan, which was signed in April 1995, set out different obligations to be fulfilled by both parties as well as the donor community.[13] To deal specifically with issues constraining donor project implementation, the JLC also established a Task Force on Project Implementation (TFPI) in

1997. While the JLC acted as a local counterpart for the AHLC, the Local Aid Coordination Committee (LACC) was created in 1994 to mirror the CG and has been open to all bilateral and multilateral donors active in the Occupied Territories. Representatives of the PA and UN agencies attend as observers, although since the beginning of the intifada many LACC meetings have been 'informal', i.e. donor-only with no Palestinian representation. The meetings serve as a forum for regular coordination at the operational level.[14] About a dozen Sector Working Groups (SWGs) were established in 1995 as a substructure under the LACC to cover the different fields of donor involvement such as infrastructure, the productive sector, the social sector and institution building.

Since the beginning of the intifada, the JLC, LACC and TFPI have continued to function (although the JLC ceased to meet after June 2002). In addition, two new coordination bodies were set up at the local level. The Task Force on Palestinian Reform, which was established by the 'Quartet' and meets at both the capital and local levels, monitors and supports the implementation of Palestinian civil reforms and provides guidance to the international donor community in its support of the Palestinian reform agenda.[15] Technical and sectoral monitoring activities are delegated to seven Reform Support Groups (RSGs) covering the following fields: financial accountability, local government, market economy, ministerial and civil service reform, the judiciary, elections and civil society.[16] In order to develop and update a coherent donor strategy for dealing with the deteriorating socio-economic and humanitarian emergency and to consider relevant policy options, the Humanitarian and Emergency Policy Group (HEPG) was also established in December 2002.[17] One important difference between the Oslo and intifada arrangements is that the new forums are donor-only coordination bodies whereas the mechanisms set up during the 1990s were explicitly trilateral. This shift in part reflects the deterioration in Israeli–Palestinian bilateral negotiations and the emergency situation in the occupied Palestinian territory, which meant that in order to continue to operate donors had to be able to exclude both parties, or at least to work within a more bilateral donor–Palestinian framework.

All along however, and as a diagram of overlapping memberships of the aid bodies would clearly reveal, the international development agenda for the WBGS has been largely determined by a five-member exclusive club composed of the 'co-chairs' of the LACC (Norway, UNSCO, World Bank), plus the US and EC/EU, with some additional donors or institutions gravitating around and joining in, according to the topic under consideration. For instance, the IMF plays a major role in discussions related to fiscal or budgetary matters. Similarly, UN relief agencies such as UNRWA, OCHA and WFP, the ICRC and INGOs are involved when expertise is required on issues related to the humanitarian and emergency situation. The existence of this 'inner circle' has helped to ensure a high degree of strategic focus and shared vision in the donor community, although at times it has created resentment among those smaller donors or international organisations which felt excluded. It also highlights the primacy of politics in the Palestinian development process. As has been pointed out, the persons and institutions most involved in foreign assistance to the Palestinians have also been the ones with responsibility for the diplomatic and political aspects of the peace process (Hooper 1999: 67).[18]

This interconnectedness of the development and diplomatic facets of the peace process with a strong core of key actors has also resulted in coordination forums themselves becoming a political centre of gravity, thereby also contributing to a balancing of the interests of major actors and in particular those of the US and the EU, the World Bank and the UN. The co-chairs have consistently worked behind the scenes, often engaged in shuttle diplomacy back and forth between the US and the EU in the formulation of a policy consensus concerning aid priorities. As noted by Hooper (1999: 79):

> the forums even provided a certain diplomatic balance to the wholly unbalanced relationship between the PLO/PA and Israel on matters relating to the Palestinian economy. (This was because donors generally shared the concerns of the Palestinians over Israeli measures that adversely affected the Palestinian economy).

Constraints upon the aid management system

Aid management in the WBGS has faced unusual constraints.

1 The economic and political environment for aid has been exceptionally difficult and unpredictable, constantly evolving according to the ebbs and flows of the peace process.
2 Second, the PNA has not only had to develop its administrative institutions from scratch but it has also never been a sovereign state, and lacks such critical state attributes as control over its borders, foreign policy, currency, fiscal and monetary policy, and natural resources. While there was an initial tendency among donors to treat the WBGS as a 'normal', sovereign country, Israel has progressively had to be brought into the Palestinian development equation, partly because much Palestinian trade was with and through Israel and strictly regulated by the Paris Economic Protocol. As has been pointed out:

> many of the characteristics of the Palestinian Authority could be described as characteristics of a client state (of Israel). This was reflected in the agreements the PLO signed at Oslo, in the Paris Protocol, and other treaties. These allowed Israel not only to restrict the defence capacities of the PNA, but also to determine

> its international trade, ensure its fiscal dependence on taxes collected from Palestinians by Israel, control its international borders and internal checkpoints for an indefinite period and so on.
> (Khan 2003: 4)

That Israel was a relevant third party in most aspects of the aid relationship imposed critical limitations on the PNA's room for manoeuvre (especially since the territories remained so economically dependent on Israel), on donor work and policies and on the effectiveness of the aid disbursed.

3 There have been significant donor constraints, such as division and competition among donors and the lack of harmonisation of procedures. Above all, it can be argued that donors have been limited in their actions by political considerations and 'the peace process imperative', i.e. the need to keep the peace process alive at all cost. In effect, and for most of the decade, this has meant that donors have been unwilling to put pressure both on the GoI to reverse its detrimental policies of closure, settlement expansion, land confiscation and annexation, destruction of property, institutional damage and reoccupation of Palestinian areas, and on the PNA to develop into a democratic, transparent and accountable government, no matter how injurious these two developments were to the Palestinian population, the peace process or donors' assistance itself.
4 Finally, other constraints have had to do with the intricate nature of the interim agreement, the jurisdictional complexities arising from the division of the WBGS into areas A, B, and C, the fact that Israel remained the controlling authority in the occupied Palestinian territory, and the myriad of project implementation difficulties arising from Israeli restrictions on the freedom of movement of goods and people, which proved particularly constraining for the travel of the international community's Palestinian counterparts in a situation where PNA bodies were already divided between the West Bank and Gaza and donor offices were variously located in Gaza, Ramallah, Jerusalem or Tel Aviv.

A donor-centred aid framework

Perhaps the single most important feature of the foreign aid framework as it has developed over the last decade is that it has been, and remains to date, a very top-down and donor-driven process. Donors, and in particular the 'inner circle', have tended to dominate most processes of coordination, policy discussion, agenda setting and information-sharing. This is problematic in terms of donor accountability to both the PNA and the Palestinian population at large. As we shall discuss further, this is in part the result of the PNA's weak performance in coordinating and managing foreign assistance, as well as of the constraints and peculiarity of the circumstances under which it operates, not least the emergency situation it has faced since the beginning of the intifada. Moreover, unlike the overwhelming majority of sovereign countries around the world which receive foreign aid, the PNA has had neither legal nor functional autonomy.

However, this can also be explained by the fact that donors in general find it difficult to relinquish control even if best practice guidelines emphasise the responsibility of the recipient government for the coordination and management of aid and the design and implementation of policies. This is all the more so in a context like Palestine's which is so high profile politically and a perpetual locus for turf battles and donor competition for influence and grand visibility.

The aid framework has been donor-led throughout, but this was accentuated with the beginning of the intifada and in particular following the Israeli reoccupation of the West Bank. Between the end of 2000 and the spring of 2003, the PNA ceased to be formally involved in aid forums and, as mentioned, the new coordination mechanisms created by the donor community in 2002 to deal specifically with the emergency situation, the humanitarian crisis and the new Palestinian reform agenda were explicitly donor-only. This marginalisation of the PNA was particularly acute at the central level as donors increasingly channelled their assistance through international organisations and NGOs, as well as directly through local government Palestinian authorities. As mentioned in a recent report on aid management and coordination during the intifada:

> Emergency responses have kept the PA in being but its capacity has been eroded. This has happened directly through physical damage, closures and movement restrictions, and so forth – but also indirectly, through the increasing tendency to bypass PA institutions in the planning and delivery of aid and aid-funded services. Donors are not to blame for the direct damage, but they do share responsibility for the erosion that results from bypassing the PA and setting up alternative mechanisms. The PA also bears responsibility for its own lack of strategic direction and discipline, which has made donor leadership in resource allocation and prioritization as inevitable as it is undesirable.
>
> (Lister and Le More 2003: 20)

In effect, the complexity of an ever evolving situation on the ground, the extreme level of political uncertainty regarding the future (will the PNA still exist tomorrow?), the constant, time-consuming and quasi-real-time need to adapt and cope with changes, mean that it became easier for donors and international organisations just to get on with the job rather than risk huge delays or even total blockage by devoting too much time to coordination and consultation with their Palestinian counterparts. In this respect, the PNA's poor performance in the 1990s did not help to convince donors that they should devote extra time and energy, in an already unusually difficult and unpredictable environment, to ensure greater Palestinian initiative and participation in their own development process.

Palestinian weaknesses

The PNA, born under a continuing occupation and lacking many of the fundamental powers of a state, has never been a typical 'recipient government' and its capacity to fulfil its desired roles has been further weakened since the beginning of the intifada. However, specific Palestinian weaknesses also explain why the Authority failed to exert more leadership over donors in the past. They also indicate areas on which a Palestinian government may want to focus in the future in order to improve aid management and to regain 'ownership' of the development process.

No clear Palestinian development strategy; weak resource management system and monitoring mechanisms

As the PNA was being established, it was inevitable that donors would take the lead initially in aid coordination, planning and monitoring. However, it was hoped that the Authority would progressively develop the capacity to present coherent and realistic plans supported by a disciplined budget and expenditure management system. Such expectations were disappointed for three main reasons.

First, the PNA has never really articulated a strategy for development, partly because of the weakness of the relevant ministers in the period up to 2002, and partly because the leadership, much more interested in the political agenda, treated development strategy as residual – priority was given to paying the salaries of the Authority's employees. This preoccupation stemmed from the perceived political need to compensate for declining income and rising unemployment resulting from the Israeli closure policy and the lack of Palestinian labour mobility. It also highlights the importance placed on patronage as a way to buy political stability.[19] This, compounded by the lack of a sound implementation and budgetary framework and problems of coordination and communication between PNA institutions, meant that line ministries, to whom development was left, had little incentive to put forward clear priorities and to follow official central channels in their dealing with donors. Most sector plans remained shopping lists which ignored the resources available, implementation capacity and sustainability, thus leaving it up to donors to lead the prioritisation process on a bilateral basis. There was thus no overall development vision, no overall policy goals and no real strategic allocation of resources to sectors; instead aid allocation remained driven by a fragmented project approach. With the exception of a few dynamic sectors such as health, education or employment generation, Sector Working Groups (SWGs) remained inefficient. Some progress was made towards a medium-term planning system with the Palestinian Development Plan 1999–2003. However, the plan was never backed up by an adequate budget and, in any case, became obsolete with the beginning of the intifada.

Second, for most of the decade, there was only a tenuous link between recurrent and capital budgets. Donor funds did not pass through PNA accounts, so capital expenditure was neither monitored nor allocated through the regular government channels. This resulted in discrepancies between Palestinian expenditure proposals and actual resources available (Lister and Venäläinen 1999).While international assistance has been tightly monitored by the donor countries and funding institutions, the domestic revenues of the PNA have lacked transparency. This, coupled with poor financial management, has left the PNA open to accusations of misappropriation of funds and corruption, especially with regard to the period 1994–1996.[20] An increased burden was also placed on the PNA's weak resource management system by donors' relatively poor harmonisation of operations and procedures. It is important to note, however, that major progress was achieved in 2002–2003 in the financial field, notably with the establishment of a single treasury account and the unification of the payroll under the control of the Ministry of Finance, increased transparency in salary payments of PNA civil servants, including those of some working in the security apparatus, and greater control over the PA's commercial operations, which were brought largely under the control of the Palestinian Investment Fund, leading to a significant increase of the budget.

Finally, PNA tracking of the funds pledged and disbursed by donors has also been less than adequate. A quarterly aid reporting system was created within MoPIC but it remained cumbersome and was ended in 2000 (Lister and Le More 2003). A new project was initiated by the Ministry of Finance in the summer of 2003 with the support of the IMF, to collect data on development assistance to the Palestinian public sector. It is too early to ascertain whether this initiative will be successful but the database has so far been conceived mainly as an internal exercise to consolidate the development budget with the current budget, so a comprehensive monitoring of donor funds still remains to be established by the Ministry of Planning.

Very poor internal coordination between and within ministries

From the outset, there was considerable confusion and rivalry among PNA ministries and institutions regarding their respective responsibilities for aid management and coordination. In addition to a predictable tendency for Palestinian line agencies to seek direct relationships with donors, there was a lot of overlap in the perceived roles of the Ministry of Planning and International Cooperation (MoPIC) and the Palestinian Economic Council for Development and Reconstruction (PECDAR).

Furthermore, the lack of integration and poor communication between the planning and aid management wings of MoPIC and the further rivalries within MoPIC between the departments located in Ramallah and those operating from Gaza City proved particularly problematic. Until it was split into two separate ministries (Ministry of Planning and Ministry of Foreign Affairs) in May 2003, MoPIC remained a divided and dysfunctional institution which had lost the confidence of the donors. The fact that for much of the decade there was considerable friction between the Ministers of Planning and Finance may also explain why links between the budget process and the capital expenditure proposals for donor support were almost non-existent. Furthermore, the confusion about the respective responsibilities in aid management of the various PNA ministries may explain concerns about the duplication of requests from the PNA and overlaps among donors.

Foreign aid strategy for a viable Palestinian state: independence and ownership in a context of high aid dependency

As made clear in the previous section, the inclination has been for donors to explain their tendency to act on their own, especially since the beginning of the intifada, by the difficult circumstances (problems in the peace process, Israeli occupation and closure policy, poor PA performance and absence of autonomy, etc.), instead of acknowledging that these circumstances, far from justifying such a donor-driven aid system, should in fact lead the international community to recognise that it is incumbent upon it to encourage greater Palestinian participation in the aid effort. In the process, the Palestinians' already fragile national planning and aid management capacities were further undermined. As perceptively observed by Rex Brynen:

> blame [for weak PNA participation in shaping donor, and hence development, priorities] is often placed on the institutional damage wrought by the intifada, closure, and Israeli incursions; a dysfunctional MOPIC; the failure of PA institutions to communicate; or the weak state of PA planning. Of course, weaknesses in the PA do account for a major part of the problem, and have made it easy for donors to justify taking the path of least resistance in project design and partnerships. However, since the purpose of donor assistance is to redress local weaknesses and build local capacities, there are limits to which donors should feel justified in using 'weak Palestinian capacities' as a justification for circumventing Palestinian national institutions.
>
> (Brynen 2003: 8–9)

The principal challenge for a future Palestinian government will thus be to find ways to reconcile high aid dependency with newly acquired political independence and regain 'ownership' of the development process.[21] It will need to break with the pattern of a donor-driven aid framework and assume the lead in formulating a coherent and comprehensive development strategy. As seen, the past record of a PNA-led process is not encouraging, but many of the problems were also linked to the continuation of the Israeli occupation and the fact that the PNA was not a sovereign state. With the establishment of a viable, independent Palestinian state, there is some scope to assert Palestinian leadership and foster a new type of relationship between the Palestinian government and the donor community, based on real partnership and sustained dialogue. The geopolitical importance of Palestine in any Middle Eastern peace framework is a clear asset which will give any Palestinian government some leverage over donors, even if the country is highly aid dependent. Agencies will continue to seek programmes of assistance to the Palestinian people and will accordingly need to spend the budget allocated to this purpose.[22]

There are three main areas upon which the new Palestinian government will need to focus.

Developing a clear strategic vision for the economic and social development of the Palestinian state, managing aid as an integral part of overall resource management and returning to long-term planning

The Palestinian government will need to develop a clear statement of what aid is needed for, based on a global strategic vision for the long-term economic and social development of the Palestinian state. This entails both an economic strategy for recovery, poverty reduction and long-term economic development and a comprehensive plan for furthering and deepening institutional reform. The new Palestinian government will need to take the lead in strategy formulation, budgeting and expenditure prioritisation so that clearly-defined Palestinian priorities form the basis for the donor–Palestinian relationship.

Its planning and prioritisation capacity thus needs strengthening in key line ministries as well as at the central level, with a focus on building upwards from the budget line imposed by the Ministry of Finance. A strong link will need to be established between capital and recurrent expenditures so as to manage foreign aid as an integral part of the overall resource management system.[23] This has the advantage of enabling a highly aid-dependent government, such as the Palestinian government, to allocate all of its resources in accordance with its policy objectives, thus retaining ownership of the process. But this also implies a high level of trust between donors and recipient concerning overall policy objectives but also the efficiency and effectiveness of the government itself, including its fiduciary standards. Developing a good strategic development framework also means close cooperation between the ministries of Planning, Finance and Economy. These three ministries already work well on an informal basis but need to strengthen their collaboration so as to agree on a common strategic framework and create an efficient way to monitor and audit it; in effect this means activating the economic sub-committee of the Cabinet.

On the reform side, this means a political willingness to establish a strong parliamentary democracy based on a genuine separation of powers between the executive, legislative and judiciary branches of government, good governance, the rule of law, transparency and accountability. This in turn implies an empowered Cabinet working closely with the relevant line ministries to develop, implement and monitor a wide-ranging reform programme concerned not only with structural reforms (i.e. those related to technocratic and administrative changes) but also with broader societal aspects essential to the establishment of a modern Palestinian state (i.e. its religious, cultural, educational, gender and other individual attributes). As hinted above, in the narrower context of aid coordination, reform is all the more important as it is a prerequisite for the proper management of donor funds within the overall management of Palestinian resources.

In the area of development planning, the government could build on a process which started recently with the Quick Intervention Investment Programme (QIIP) presented to the donor community in July 2003 by the new Ministry of Planning. Although the QIIP had a short-term strategic focus, it is disciplined and features projects selected on the basis of a four-point strategy for economic recovery covering the following areas: humanitarian and social assistance; reconstruction and repair of public infrastructure; private sector support (including agriculture) and support for the PNA budget. The QIIP has been considered by many within the donor community as the best planning document produced by the PNA so far. It marked a noticeable improvement in terms of the process as well, since the plan was drafted by the relevant PNA ministries in close collaboration with international institutions, in particular the World Bank and the IMF.

At the time of the writing of this chapter, an Economic Recovery Strategy for 2004 was also expected to be presented to donors at the capital-level AHLC meeting scheduled for December 2003 in Rome. This will embody a set of recovery-oriented policies intended to get the economy as close as possible back to its position before the recent decline started during the last three months of 2000. This should provide the basis for the 2004 donor response. In the future, and in the context of the establishment of a state, Palestinian governments will need to develop a longer-term strategy based on a sector-wide approach and covering a few years, in the same spirit although not the same format as the Palestinian Development Plan produced in the late 1990s. For planning and budgetary purposes, and also for Palestinians to exercise leadership over donors, it will also be crucial that the government establish an efficient database management system to track donor flows.

Ensuring greater Palestinian participation in the aid coordination process

Despite its weaknesses, the existing aid coordination and management structure provides a strong platform to build on. However, it needs to become less dominated by donors and less biased to the short-term. As mentioned, the Palestinian government should play a central role in shaping priorities, and a systematic and meaningful dialogue with donors should be established.

Greater Palestinian participation in aid coordination will entail actively steering the process by calling for and chairing meetings, proposing agendas and being in close contact (if not directly engaging) with the secretariats of aid bodies such as the LACC or the TFPR. In this respect, several initiatives could be undertaken. Rex Brynen has suggested some interesting ones. For instance, 'the LACC might establish a subgroup of "friends of MOP", tasked by the broader donor community to work with MOP and other ministries to revitalize aid cooperation'. A permanent PA liaison officer could also be attached to the LACC and TFPR secretariats. Another idea could be for MOP to create 'a small, high quality "coordination support unit", or an empowered "coordination advisor" to the Minister, intended to identify, catalyze and trail-blaze needed reforms' (Brynen 2003: 9–10).

The revitalisation of the SWGs and the evolution of the new intifada 'donor-only' forums such as the HEPG and the TFPR/RSGs to include Palestinian counterparts are also areas which will require serious attention and consideration. On the donor side, it is essential that coordination and harmonisation at project level are strengthened so as to avoid duplication. Donors should also harmonise their procedures (i.e. simplify them and pool resources) to avoid over-burdening the PNA unnecessarily.

Opening up the process so as to include actors from Palestinian civil society and the private sector in the development effort; ensuring greater transparency and public accountability[24]

Public participation should be encouraged. In particular, the relationship between the PNA and NGOs should be developed so as to take into consideration the views and roles of grass root organisations and other interested community groups. On the other hand, public hearings or public announcements by agencies implementing development work should be instituted and evaluation procedures formalised. Similarly, private sector initiatives need to be encouraged. The creation in 2003 of a National Task

Force on Economic Development comprising representatives from the public and private sectors and aimed at coordinating and leading the national input into a common strategy for Palestine's national development was a very positive initiative and one which can be built on. The establishment of a National Reform Committee regrouping PLC members, NGO leaders, academics and other civil society members to broaden the debate on the reform of the PNA was also a welcome measure, although many within civil society believe that this was still too hesitant an initiative and that public involvement in the reform process should be much more significant.[25]

Conclusion

It is beyond the scope of this chapter to tackle the issue of aid effectiveness and to assess the failures and successes of international assistance to the Palestinian people over the last decade. Clearly, aid did not succeed in its key priority, sustaining the peace process, but, as in most post-conflict peace-building situations, development and relief assistance can only help to buttress and enhance a political process: they cannot be a substitute for it. In the Palestinian case, the environment for the development effort has been all the more difficult as the international donor community has been operating in a unique situation of military occupation where the recipient of aid is not a sovereign independent state, and where, therefore, the recipient and host country have not been one and the same but two different interlocutors: on the one hand, the Palestinian National Authority, which up to 2000 had control over most of the Gaza Strip but only a series of disconnected enclaves containing most of the Palestinian population (areas A and B) in the West Bank; on the other, the government of Israel, which retained control over 60 per cent of the West Bank, including the roads linking these different Palestinian areas and all the points of entry/departure from the West Bank and the Gaza Strip. With the beginning of the intifada, the distinction between areas A, B and C became blurred, the economic crisis deepened and the closure regime imposed on the Palestinian territories became ever tighter, making it even more difficult for the donor community to operate and nearly impossible for it to continue to provide meaningful development assistance.

Given the situation prevailing at the time of writing (November 2003), and in particular the advanced process of economic and political fragmentation of the West Bank, the unabated growth of Israeli settlements and the construction of the Wall, one needs to be extremely cautious about making projections as to what would be the optimum aid strategy in the case of a sovereign, viable, independent Palestinian state. What has been suggested in this chapter are key elements of this strategy, based on general best donor practice, on the specific experience of international assistance to the WBGS over the last decade and on the critical need, in the future, to reconcile high aid dependency with political and economic independence. Ultimately, however, it will be up to the Palestinian government and its people, in close collaboration and partnership with the international donor community, to decide on the type of economic and institutional development that is most suitable for Palestine.

Notes

1 I would like to thank Stephen Lister and Nigel Roberts for their comments on first drafts of this chapter as well as Professor Neil MacFarlane, Dr Karma Nabulsi and Michael Keating.

2 Figures from World Bank (2002). Per capita assistance to the WBGS has been even higher since the beginning of the intifada with donors providing about US$315 per person per year, making the WBGS in recent years not one of the highest but *the* highest recipient of international financial funds. A comparison with other 'high profile' post-conflict cases makes this clear. According to the World Bank, per capita assistance for Bosnia over five years was US$215 per year and for East Timor over two years, US$235. See also World Bank (2003: xiv, 52).

3 According to the Development Assistance Committee of the OECD, foreign aid or official development assistance is defined as grants or loans to developing countries undertaken by the official sector with the promotion of economic development and welfare as the main objective and at concessional financial terms of at least 25 per cent. This embraces humanitarian assistance and emergency relief. See OECD website, www.oecd.org.

4 Co-Sponsors (1994). See also World Bank (1993, 1994), Paris Protocol (1994).

5 Closure refers to the restrictions placed by Israel on the free movement of Palestinian goods and people. It is three-fold:

   1 internal closure within the West Bank and Gaza through a dense network of military manned checkpoints and roadblocks, and reinforced by curfews;
   2 external closure of the border between Israel on the one hand and both the West Bank and Gaza Strip on the other, as well as between the West Bank and the Gaza Strip. This is being enforced by border checkpoints and a complicated travel permit system;
   3 external closure of international crossings between the West Bank and Jordan, and Gaza and Egypt, with passenger and commercial traffic through international crossings being severely limited.

   Israel's closure of the Palestinian territories began in the early 1990s and became systematic during the Oslo years (with its enforcement becoming stricter with the onset of the intifada and being accompanied by extensive siege, isolation measures and prolonged periods of curfews). For further details on the socio-economic and humanitarian impact of closures see World Bank (2002, 2003), Amnesty International (2003) and Special Rapporteur of the Commission on Human Rights (2003).

6 One should note, however, that the funds from the Arab League have been directed almost exclusively to budget support.

7 Figures do not include donor support to UNRWA's regular budget. Figures on combined EC/EU member states are indicative (World Bank 2003).

8 The working assumption of this article, following the overall line of this book, is the establishment of an independent, economically and politically viable and sovereign Palestinian state. This means, *inter alia*, a sovereign state:

1 with East Jerusalem at its capital;
2 whose territory is contiguous such that Palestinians can move freely within their state (i.e. within and between the West Bank, the Gaza Strip and their capital);
3 which has sovereign control over the movement of goods and people across its national borders;
4 which has independent control over its natural resources.

9 The poverty line used is US$2.1 per day. Figures from World Bank (2003).

10 In its May 2003 Assessment, the World Bank estimates that even if the internal closure were lifted for 2004 'real per capita incomes would still be 35 per cent lower [at the end of the year] than in 1999'. This gives an idea of the extent of the current economic crisis and the level and type of donor support that will continue to be required even if the political situation greatly improves.

11 The settler population nearly doubled during the Oslo years, from 247,000 in 1993 (including East Jerusalem) to about 420,000 in 2003. As of 2003, according to the Israeli NGO Peace Now, there were 145 settlements scattered in the West Bank and Gaza Strip (excluding East Jerusalem) as well as about 100 settlement outposts. In June 2002, the GoI began construction of a Separation Barrier ('the Wall') – a complex series of walls, barriers, trenches and fences physically separating the West Bank from East Jerusalem and Israel. The Wall is not constructed in Israel or along the 1967 Green line but in many places cuts eastwards many kilometres into the West Bank, separating Palestinian communities from each other, and isolating, fragmenting and impoverishing some hundreds of thousands in the process. The 2003 Report of the United Nations Special Rapporteur of the Commission on Human Rights states 'the evidence strongly suggests that Israel is determined to create facts on the ground amounting to de facto annexation'. See also B'Tselem (2002), HEPG (May 2003 and follow-up reports of July and September 2003).

12 The AHLC is restricted in its membership and composed of the United States, the European Union, Russia, Norway, Japan, Saudi Arabia and Canada. Associated members are the PLO/PA, Israel, Egypt, Jordan, Tunisia and the United Nations. It is chaired by Norway and, since 1999, co-chaired by each meeting's host. The World Bank acts as its secretariat. All decisions within the AHLC are taken by consensus.

13 Mirroring the AHLC, the JLC membership has been tightly restricted and composed of the United States, the European Union, Japan, Israel, with the PA acting as its chair, Norway as its secretariat and the United Nations and the World Bank as co-secretariat. It has met on average four times a year from June 1995 when it was first held until the beginning of the intifada, although its effectiveness was undermined as Israeli–Palestinian relations were soured after the May 1996 Israeli elections. Since late 2000, the forum has not been convened as a trilateral mechanism, though a few 'informal' donor-only JLC meetings took place up until June 2002.

14 LACC meetings are on average called on a monthly basis and chaired by Norway with, as co-chairs, the World Bank and the United Nations (also acting as co-secretariat).

15 The TFPR was established in July 2002. It reports to, and works under, the auspices of the Quartet (the highest political multilateral forum involved in the peace process since 2001 and comprising the US, EU, Russia and the UN). In addition to Quartet members, the TFPR is composed of Norway (also acting as convenor), Japan, Norway, Canada, the World Bank and the IMF.

16 In October 2003, the Civil Society RSG became dormant. A new Legislative RSG was created around the same time to follow up reform in this area.

17 The HEPG is chaired by the EC/EU, with the UN as deputy chair. Its other members are the US, Norway and the World Bank, with other countries or organisations such as specialised UN agencies, the ICRC and INGOs being invited on an ad hoc basis according to the topics under discussion.

18 This should be qualified, however: financial institutions such as the World Bank and IMF have played a crucial role in the international assistance process without having had much of a political role in the peace process.

19 In 1998, some 54 per cent of the PA budget was allocated to the wages and salaries of 89,130 public employees; in 2003, the salaries of 125,000 civil servants accounted for 78 per cent of the PA budget's cash expenditures. See World Bank (1999, 2003). As has been pointed out:

> The Palestinian Authority has a significantly inflated payroll. In the civil service there is overstaffing and job inflation in certain ministries and agencies and at certain levels of appointment. Others are understaffed, especially those requiring specialized or highly qualified personnel. The desire to ease unemployment, combined with political and personal factors, has partially converted public hiring into a means of rewarding loyalty and securing a mass constituency. This has left the Palestinian Authority with a much higher proportion of the labour force in public employment than is the case in other post-conflict situations.
>
> (Executive Summary, Independent Task Force 1999: 15)

20 See Independent Task Force (1999). We may note that, although there has been a widespread perception among both the Palestinian population and internationally, notably in the 1990s, that the PA has been corrupt and inefficient, there is to date actually very little dispassionate evidence to ascertain the degree to which funds have been misappropriated.

21 Best practice guidelines have been emphasising the importance that recipient countries 'own' their development process for some years now. The rhetoric of ownership is far from new (see for instance the 1969 Pearson Report, *Partners in Development*), but has gained renewed interest among international organisations, international financial institutions and bilateral development agencies since the mid 1990s, mainly as a way to enhance aid effectiveness in a context of spiralling conditionality, poor implementation rates, and limited donor success in fostering economic growth and reducing global poverty. See for instance OECD (1996) and World Bank (1998).

22 I am grateful to Tony Killick, discussant at the workshop in August 2003, for this point.

23 International best practice in aid management and recent literature on aid effectiveness stress the importance that foreign assistance should be 'programme-oriented', i.e. integrated within the recipient's overall budget, and programmed alongside internal resources rather than being earmarked for specific projects or uses (the fungibility of resources means that governments may simply divert their own funding elsewhere, leading to increasing scepticism in the effectiveness of the earmarking of donor funds). See for example, Foster and Fozzard (2000).

24 This has been advocated by many for a long time. See for instance the recommendations put forward in Jerusalem Media & Communication Centre (1999).

25 Some civil society initiatives already exist to promote reform and good governance. For instance, the Aman coalition for enhancing integrity, transparency and accountability in Palestinian society, which brings together

six Palestinian NGOs was created in 2000 to 'empower civil society to play an active role in combating corruption by mobilizing Palestinian efforts to develop and promote the initiative for the Palestinian National Programme against Corruption with focus areas being awareness raising, research, coalition building and capacity building'. See www.aman-palestine.org.

References

Amnesty International (2003) *Israel and the Occupied Territories. Surviving Under Siege: The Impact of Movement Restrictions on the Right to Work*, London: Amnesty International.

Brynen, R. (2003) *Aid Management and Coordination during the Intifada. Report to the LACC Co-Chairs. Peer Review and Commentary*, Jerusalem: LACC.

B'Tselem (2002) *Land Grab: Israel's Settlement Policy in the West Bank*, Jerusalem: B'Tselem.

Co-Sponsors (1994) 'Co-Sponsors' Summary, Conference to Support Middle East Peace, Washington, DC, 1 October 1993', in *Journal of Palestine Studies* 23: 128–129.

Foster, M. and Fozzard, A. (2000) *Aid and Public Expenditure: A Guide*, London: Overseas Development Institute.

Hooper, R. (1999) 'The international politics of donor assistance to the Palestinians in the West Bank and Gaza Strip, 1993–1997', *Research in Middle East Economics* 3: 59–95.

Humanitarian and Emergency Policy Group (HEPG) of the Local Aid Coordination Committee (LACC) (2003) *The Impact of Israel's Separation Barrier on Affected West Bank Communities*, May, Jerusalem: HEPG (see also July and September 2003 follow-ups).

Independent Task Force sponsored by the Council on Foreign Relations ('The Rocard Report') (1999) *Strengthening Palestinian Public Institutions*, New York: Council on Foreign Relations.

Jerusalem Media & Communication Centre (1999) *Foreign Aid and Development in Palestine*, Jerusalem: Jerusalem Media and Communication Centre.

Khan, M.H. (2003) Memorandum submitted to the House of Commons Select Committee on International Development, autumn 2003, available at http://www.publications.parliament.uk.

Lister, S. and Le More, A. (2003) *Aid Management and Coordination during the Intifada. Report to the LACC Co-Chairs*, Jerusalem: LACC.

Lister, S. and Venäläinen, R. (1999) *Improvement of Aid Coordination for West Bank and Gaza*, Jerusalem: LACC.

OECD (1996) *Shaping the 21st Century: The Contribution of Development Co-operation*, Paris: OECD.

Special Rapporteur of the Commission on Human Rights, (2003) *Report on the Situation of Human Rights in the Palestinian Territories Occupied by Israel since 1967, Submitted in Accordance with Commission Resolution 1993/2 A*, Geneva: UNHCHR.

United Nations Conference on Trade and Development (UNCTAD) (2003) *Report on UNCTAD's Assistance to the Palestinian People*, Geneva: UNCTAD.

World Bank (1993) *Developing the Occupied Territories: An Investment in Peace*, Washington, DC: World Bank.

World Bank (1994) *The West Bank and Gaza: the Next Two Years and Beyond*, Washington, DC: World Bank.
World Bank (1998) *Assessing Aid: What Works, What Doesn't and Why*, Oxford: Oxford University Press.
World Bank (1999 (unpublished)) *West Bank and Gaza: Public Expenditure Review*, Washington, DC: World Bank.
World Bank (2002) *Fifteen Months – Intifada, Closures and Palestinian Economic Crisis – An Assessment*, Washington, DC: World Bank.
World Bank (2003) *Twenty Seven Months – Intifada, Closures and Economic Crisis – An Assessment*, Washington, DC: World Bank.
World Bank and Japan (2000) *Aid Effectiveness in the West Bank and Gaza*, Washington, DC: World Bank.

Discussion

Tony Killick

Anne Le More has provided us with an admirably clear and authoritative description of the recent history of aid to Palestine and has drawn on this to point out ways in which the situation should be improved upon in future. I am certainly in no position to match her knowledge of the local scene and the purpose of this note is to build upon aspects of her chapter to address a crucial issue: what strategy might a future independent Palestinian state pursue for attracting and managing development assistance in ways that could reconcile its political independence with high levels of reliance on aid?

According to the World Bank, in 2001 (latest available) the West Bank and Gaza received $280 of aid per capita, which was greatly in excess of any other country recorded and compares, for example, with a regional average of $16 for the Middle East and North Africa as a whole.[1] It seems inevitable that an independent Palestine's reliance on such finance would remain high well into the future, so the question posed would be an important one.

Indeed, Le More shows that donor domination is already a major fact of life in the determination of relationships with the Palestine National Authority (PNA) and in efforts to coordinate the many sources of assistance. Unfortunately, as she also makes clear, neither they nor the PNA have taken a long-term strategic view of the development of a future Palestine and of how current assistance should be used to lay the foundations for that. An ineffective use of assistance is an almost inevitable consequence. So how might dependence and independence be reconciled, how might an aid strategy be prepared and what might be in it?

Dependence does not have to mean donor domination

A future government of Palestine (GoP) should recognise that it brings important assets to the negotiating table. First among these is its enormous geo-political importance in the Middle East and in the context of the 'war against terrorism'. Donor country self-interest will dictate that many of them will be anxious to maintain active and substantial programmes of assistance, a fact which gives a GoP substantial bargaining strength. The same interests are also likely to exert large pressures on agencies such as the IMF and World Bank to maintain large and active programmes.

Given that, a second factor will kick in: aid agencies will approve specific budget lines for utilisation in Palestine and the existence of such provisions will generate an 'imperative to spend'. This is a well-known phenomenon in the aid business: agencies defend their future budgets by making sure they spend their current ones. At least in the short-run, this makes it difficult for agencies to play hard-ball with intended recipients – which is one of the reasons why conditionality is so often flouted. Here, then, is another important leverage that a GoP could exert.

Lastly, norms of good donor behaviour are being developed which can offer recipient authorities a degree of protection against the worst tendencies of some of the donors. The most recent manifestation of attempts to move towards a rules-based aid regime is enshrined in the February 2003 *Rome Declaration on Harmonization.* According to this, donor agencies agree to reform their practices so as to ensure that assistance conforms better to recipient priorities and minimises transactions costs: 'The key element ... is a country-based approach that emphasizes country ownership and government leadership'. It would be easy to exaggerate the force of the commitments entered into in the *Declaration*, which remains entirely voluntary, but there are peer pressures at work and, at the very least, it provides a useful rhetorical stick which an assertive GoP could use in dealing with its donors.

Managing donors through inclusivity

The key words in present-day attempts to improve donor-recipient relations are 'partnership' and 'ownership'. In the context of an aid dependent state, 'partnership' implies a willingness by both sides to acknowledge the legitimate interests of the other. Specifically, it requires recipient governments to establish mechanisms and channels through which they can engage donors in policy and related discussions, as well as to monitor subsequent actions. If they work well, such channels can serve as at least a partial (and preferable) alternative to policy conditionality, increasing governments' room for manoeuvre.

But what of 'ownership'? This is an elusive notion but there would be general agreement that for recipient countries to fully 'own' a programme or process, it is not sufficient that it be sponsored by the central organs of state, e.g. by a Ministry of Finance and Development. For example, in connection with the HIPC debt initiative, donor countries have sought to ensure that the poverty-reduction strategies supported through debt relief are derived from widely-based participation and consultation processes, involving all relevant state agencies, non-government organisations, the churches, universities and think tanks, and other components of civil society. In this context, *donors are among those with a legitimate voice to be heard* – but are voices in a chorus.

It is intrinsically desirable that a strategy for Palestine's medium- and long-term development should be as consensual as possible and hence should be based on the principle of inclusivity. But besides being desirable for its own sake, such an approach should make it easier for a GoP to manage the donors, for their views will be among many others that need to be considered. An adept leadership ought to be able to utilise that to reduce donor influence.

What should be in an aid strategy?

An aid strategy designed to put a GoP in control should have at least four major building blocks.

First, a clear statement of the purposes for which aid is sought and of priorities among these purposes. Is it for agriculture and, if so, for what types of programme? Or is it for poverty reduction actions (donors would be happy with that)? Or infrastructure, law and order, private sector development…? The point about specifying such priorities is that it not only gives donors clear guidance but also provides a yardstick that can be used to turn down low-priority offers of 'assistance'. In fact, it would be a good idea to include a statement of areas in which assistance is *not* a priority, to make it harder for donors to come up with unwanted schemes.

What the last paragraph implies is that a GoP should be willing to say 'no' to donors promoting their own pet projects and schemes. This may be psychologically difficult in an aid-dependent regime but they should bear in mind the dubious value of low-priority aid. It is worth quoting from a recent report on donor–government relations in Tanzania on the low costs of declining unwanted 'aid':[2]

> the authorities might ask themselves what they are losing if they turn down offers of this kind. Typically, these will consist of specific projects, often to be operated outside the budget and to be implemented on the basis of special implementation units manned by expatriate 'technical assistance' personnel provided as a condition for undertaking the project, probably aided by Tanzanian officials receiving special incentive payments to give priority to the projects in question. All that we know about such aid suggests that it contributes little to the balance of payments (because of high project import content) and yields little or no net revenue to the budget and may well become a net drain upon the budget because of counterpart payments and consequential recurrent cost requirements. In addition, it contributes little to long-term development because it typically has low sustainability,

> i.e. it represents an investment with low, perhaps zero, returns; and, because of its enclave nature, it adds little to longer-term local human and institutional capacities. Instead, the parallel nature of such projects tends to undermine the already weak administrative machinery. The question arises, what is lost by refusing such assistance? Evidently not much. We believe that the fears that a lot of donor assistance would be foregone are not founded.

It goes without saying, however, that in order to be able to offer such a set of priorities to a GoP's aid partners it must first have developed a coherent and reasonably detailed development strategy for the country – a prerequisite which Le More shows to be far from being met in present conditions.

A second building block for the aid strategy should be a clear statement of the government's preferences as between alternative types of assistance. The main options here are between direct budget support (with debt relief as a category of that), humanitarian support (in which we might include food aid), sector-wide programmatic support, aid in the form of discrete development projects, and technical assistance.

The strong trend in thinking about cost-effective assistance is in favour of budget and other programmatic forms, with old-style project aid poorly regarded. Programme aid is favoured because it is more consistent with local ownership and conformity with local priorities, because it is conducive to more productive and coordinated relationships between donors and recipient authorities, and because the associated transactions costs are thought to be much lower than those resulting from project aid. A GoP would be well advised to state a clear preference for programmatic forms of assistance and to be firm in declining projects unless they clearly fit into national priorities.

Third, the strategy should make provision for a machinery for implementing and monitoring the priorities set out in the first two building blocks. Included here are provisions for adequate channels for dialogue between the Palestinian state and the donor agencies. An important aspect of the machinery established under this heading is that it becomes a means for coordinating the activities of the various donors and of integrating their work into the country's wider development efforts. An equally important aspect is that the government should be in charge of it. This is highly desirable, not only for the obvious 'ownership' reasons but also because the record has shown few examples of sustained successful donor coordination when this has been left to the donors themselves. The cliché here is that all donors are in favour of coordination but none wants to be coordinated.

Finally, if it is to reflect the principle of partnership – and if it is to be acceptable to the donors – the strategy must set out reciprocal commitments to be met by the GoP. These could include:

- An assurance that it would meet such basic criteria as the maintenance of human rights, respect for the rule of law, pursuit of prudent macroeconomic policies, and so on. An important aspect of such assurances relates to anti-corruption measures, the strengthening of accountability mechanisms and high standards of public financial management, so that donors may be assured that their money is going where it is supposed to go and is reaching those it is supposed to reach.
- A statement of the government's willingness to engage in dialogue with its donor partners on all matters which fall within their legitimate interest.
- The country's development programme itself: if the preference is in favour of programme aid then there must be a programme which donors regard as worthy of support.
- A statement of how the government envisages its reliance on aid could be reduced over time, so that donors can envisage at least an eventual exit from abnormally high levels of aid provision. Important here would be the development of policies to mobilise domestic resources and to attract private investment from outside.

Notes

1 World Bank (2003) *World Development Indicators*: Table 6.10.
2 Enhancing Aid Relationships in Tanzania: Report of the Independent Monitoring Group, Dar es Salaam: Economic and Social Research Foundation, November 2002: 29.

10 Absorbing returnees in a viable Palestinian state

A forward-looking macroeconomic perspective

Arie Arnon and Nu'man Kanafani

Introduction

The question of the Palestinian refugees is probably the thorniest aspect of the Israeli–Palestinian conflict. It involves a wide spectrum of issues ranging from the legal right of return, as a basic human right, to the technicalities of estimating the refugees' material losses and sufferings. And it inevitably triggers memories of the tragic experiences of exodus, relocation of families, disintegration of communities, and intolerable suffering over half-a-century of refugeehood. For many people, a solution which fails to undo the historic injustice and to point a finger at who was morally responsible is not worth consideration. For the Israelis, on the other hand, the 'return' is a concrete threat to their national existence and the material, let alone the moral, responsibility is the last thing they are ready to assume. Repatriation, return and restitution are extraordinarily charged terms, politically and psychologically, on both sides of the divide. And in addition to all of this the issue of refugees involves not only the two parties directly affected, the Palestinians and the Israelis, but also a number of other countries currently hosting the refugees.

Here, however, we shall not attempt to discuss the whole range of these issues. We take as our starting point the vision of the political settlement set out in the introduction to this book. In particular we shall assume that the major thrust of the Palestinian refugee problem will be resolved by granting the refugees the right to return to the sovereign Palestinian state in the WBGS and that a suitable package of compensation will be made available to facilitate the process of rehabilitation and absorption. In other words, we will avoid as far as is possible the highly sensitive legal and human complexities by assuming the existence of a political settlement. Our aim is to concentrate instead on the macroeconomic implications of different scenarios for implementing that vision of a peaceful settlement of the conflict.

We aim to integrate the two key challenges which will confront a future Palestinian state: securing a decent and sustainable standard of living for the current inhabitants of the WBGS, including the refugees, and accommodating and successfully absorbing those refugees and displaced persons who will return to settle in the state. In this sense, the elimination of the refugee problem and the process of nation-building become one and the same thing. The basic idea in the chapter is to establish a link between the macroeconomic cost of absorbing the refugees in a viable WBGS economy and the compensation package to the refugee. Rather than estimating compensation on the basis of the value of abandoned properties or some obscure arbitrary formula, we suggest the adoption of a forward-looking approach whereby compensation is determined in conjunction with the costs of resettling the refugees and securing the economic viability of the Palestinian state.

The next section deals with the issue of compensation. After a brief review of the developments in the early 1950s with respect to repatriation and compensation, we analyse three approaches for determining the pool of resources for compensating the Palestinian refugees. We discuss their pros and cons, with respect to both revenues and disbursements, stressing the significance of the forward-looking approach which links compensation to the cost of absorbing the returnees in a viable economy. The analysis recognises, nevertheless, the multi-dimensional nature of the refugee/compensation problem and leaves open the possibility of other forms of private/individual compensatory payments.

We then present a brief survey of the distribution of the Palestinian population and of refugees, and the factors which will affect the households' decision to relocate. We present, in non-technical terms, a macroeconomic framework which we use to estimate the cost of creating a viable West Bank economy and absorbing the returnees. We analyse various scenarios for the numbers and timing of returnees, with two different assumptions concerning the flow of Palestinian labour to Israel. We also incorporate the Gaza Strip into the analysis, by estimating the extra resources needed to secure its convergence on the standards of living in the more prosperous of the two different wings of the Palestine state. This analysis re-links the two regions economically and ensures that even under the assumption that all the returnees will be resettled in the West Bank, the economic effect will also be felt in Gaza. Next, we touch upon some aspects of absorption policy, using Israel's experiences in absorbing immigrants during the 1950s and 1990s to shed some light on the policy options which will confront the future Palestinian government in designing and implementing a successful absorption strategy.

Compensating the refugees

The aim of this section is to review various approaches for determining the pool of resources needed to compensate the Palestinian refugees. We will argue the need for a multiple-criteria approach, stressing the significance of taking the cost of rehabilitating and absorbing the returnees in a viable WBGS economy into account.

From repatriation to compensation

The first international resolution with reference to the Palestinian refugees affirmed their 'right of return' and envisaged compensation as an alternative that could be chosen by those refugees who freely opted not to exercise the right of repatriation. The UN General Assembly, in Resolution 194 of December 1948:

> Resolves that the refugees wishing to return to their homes and live at peace with their neighbours should be permitted to do so at the earliest practicable date, and that compensation should be paid for the property of those choosing not to return and for loss of or damage to property which, under principles of international law or in equity, should be made good by the Governments or authorities responsible.

To 'facilitate the repatriation, resettlement and economic and social rehabilitation of the refugees and the payment of compensation', the resolution established a Conciliation Commission (consisting of three countries, named in the following year to be the US, France and Turkey). The UN Conciliation Commission for Palestine (UNCCP) worked intensively during the first two years of its existence to secure the repatriation of the refugees, but was confronted by Israel's systematic refusal, and none of the various schemes for the repatriation of even a limited number were implemented.[1] Faced with this deadlock, the UNCCP started to shift its attention towards a new strategy under which compensation, rather than repatriation, would be considered as part of an overall settlement. The UNCCP thought that compensation could be a constructive step to ensure quick economic rehabilitation of the refugees in their new places of residence.

During its fifth session (December 1950), the UN General Assembly supported this shift in strategy and directed the UNCCP to survey the abandoned property of the refugees and 'take appropriate measures to settle the compensation issue' (Resolution 394 V). Soon thereafter the UNCCP produced what it called a 'global assessment' of the abandoned property of the Palestinian refugees. This assessment was at the heart of the UNCCP's proposals to the Paris Conference to settle the Palestine conflict (September 1951), which consisted of two components. First, Israel would agree to the repatriation of a 'specified number of Arab refugees who could be integrated into the Israeli economy'. Second, Israel would accept to pay 'as compensation for property abandoned by the refugees not repatriated, a global sum based upon evaluation arrived at by the Commission'. Furthermore, the payment of compensation should be planned in a manner that takes 'into consideration the Government of Israel's ability to pay' (Gabbay 1959: 331).

Thus there was a substantial shift in the attitude of the international community (or of the UNCCP, at least) to the repatriation of the Palestinian refugees. The 1948 UN resolution had considered compensation as payments to individuals who chose freely not to exercise their right to be repatriated (or to compensate them for damage), but the UNCCP proposal to the 1951 Paris Conference 'imposed' compensation on all of those refugees who could not be 'integrated in the Israeli economy' and who, therefore, were in practice denied the right of repatriation.

Compensation based on the value of abandoned property

The Paris Conference led nowhere, and the UNCCP declared its failure to the General Assembly at its sixth session in 1952. But the Conciliation Commission left a legacy behind it: the assessment of the value of abandoned Palestinian property in 1948. That assessment was a far from precise exercise. In fact, the team of experts which carried out the actual assessment asserted that 'no absolute evaluation could ever be obtained, and the whole estimation should be regarded with great caution'.[2]

The exercise was basically quite simple. Assets abandoned by the refugees were divided into immovable (land) and movable:[3]

Immovable assets: the experts estimated the size of the land area abandoned by the Palestinian refugees to be 16,324 sq. km (about 80 per cent of the total land area of the state of Israel). This was based on a highly imperfect statistical survey of rural Palestine, known as the *Village Statistics*, collected in 1945. 72 per cent of the total abandoned land was taken to be uncultivable (mainly in the Negev desert) and 28 per cent cultivable. The built-up area was estimated to cover 14 sq. km only. No value was placed on uncultivable land, while the values of the cultivable land and of the built-up area were fixed by the estimated productivity of crops and estimated rent. Both were derived from data on taxes paid on rural land and other real estate properties in the years preceding 1948. The experts put the total value of immovable property at £100.4 million (£69.5 million for rural land, £21.6 million for urban land and £9.5 million for land in Jerusalem).

Movable assets: the experts used three different approaches to estimate the value of movable assets:

1 assuming a fixed ratio between immovable and movable assets (the ratio was based on the actual proportions of assets for refugees in other parts of the world);
2 assuming the value of movable assets to be a fixed proportion of the national income (40 per cent);
3 directly estimating the value of various types of assets left behind by the refugees.

The experts concluded that the three methods gave somewhat similar results of about £18–20 million.

The UNCCP's global assessment, the sum of immovable and movable assets abandoned by the 1948 Palestinian refugees, was therefore put at £118–120 million.

The UNCCP's estimate confronted the Palestinians with a serious dilemma. On the one hand, they were reluctant to discuss the matter for fear of appearing ready to compromise on the right of return. On the other hand, the estimate was 'shamefully unrepresentative of the true market value' of the abandoned assets. This is especially the case when one recognises, as Gabbay (1959: 341) did, that:

> the Arab community in Palestine was regarded as one of the most prosperous Arab communities in the Middle East. Its holdings extended over hundred of thousands of dunums of fertile land ... business concerns, including factories and also houses, shops and movable property of great value.

Nevertheless, the Palestinian response came promptly, though with the assertion that discussing estimates of lost assets should be without prejudice to the refugees' right of return. The Arab Higher Committee (AHC, the body which represented the Palestinians up to 1948) and the League of Arab States produced counter-estimates to that of the UNCCP in the mid 1950s. These assessments included several additional non-real estate assets (such as jewellery, frozen and expropriated bank funds, livestock, or factories), along with the valuation of land on the basis of use (type of cultivated crops, location, detailed estimation of the prices of dwellings in cities, etc.). The two studies produced similar results, with a staggering value for total losses of £1,900 million in 1948 prices, i.e. 16 times the estimate of the UNCCP (Kubursi 1988).

Two other evaluations, much more disaggregated and better documented, have been made by Sayigh (1967) and Kubursi (1988) and (2001a). These included two new components in their assessment of the losses: first, various types of real estate whether privately or publicly owned, including public infrastructure and utilities; second, a wider range of movable assets, including households' durables, tools and implements, industrial and agricultural capital, financial assets, vehicles and stocks. The two studies arrived at a similar estimate, although their databases and valuation procedures were not identical. Sayigh's estimation of total losses, in mid 1940s prices, was £757 million, while Kubursi's was £743 million. Kubursi (1988: 186) concluded that 'The UN estimate of £120 million is a substantial undervaluation of Palestinian losses. The scale of underestimation is embarrassingly large: the UN estimate is 16.2% of ours'.[4]

Significantly, while the UNCCP study estimated the value of abandoned rural land to be £70 million, Sayigh and Kubursi estimated it to be five times higher, at £395 million. Also, against the UNCCP estimate of £30 million for urban real estate, Sayigh arrived at £254 million and

Kubursi at £130 million. In fact, the difference in valuing real estate assets explains more than 80 per cent of the difference between the UNCCP's and Sayigh's estimates of total Palestinian losses. Table 10.1 presents a summary of the various estimates in 1948 dollars and in 2000 dollars. Kubursi also applies an annual interest rate of 4 per cent on the 1948 losses to calculate the present real value of Palestinian losses, but this is not calculated in the table below.

Kubursi went further and attempted to calculate the human capital losses of the Palestinian refugees. Assuming that one-half of Palestine's national income in 1944 came from non-property income, and that 55 per cent of the Arab Palestinians became refugees, he put total human capital losses at £433 million. He pointed out that this was a maximum figure, since the refugees took with them at least part of their human resources, but he maintained that a good part of the human capital was lost because of the disappearance of jobs and complementary inputs.[5]

The above survey demonstrates how huge the gap is between the various estimates of Palestinians' assets in 1948.[6] And although it is often recognised that actual payments are only theoretically linked to the value of property lost, and that lump sum settlements, in practice, result in claimants receiving only a portion of their losses, it is difficult to see how a compromise can be arrived at on the basis of such divergent estimates (Workshop 1999). On the other hand, it is worth noting that the UNCCP approach of a lump sum payment on the basis of a global estimate has, according to Benvenisti (1999), much in common with current international practices in solving large-scale disputes.

Compensation based on economic and political feasibility

Instead of seeking to estimate the value of assets abandoned by the refugees, a number of studies have maintained that compensation will most probably be fixed through a process of political bargaining and will depend largely on Israel's (and the international community's) political willingness and economic ability to pay. These 'abilities' clearly differ from time to time and depend on the overall political environment. Similarly, Benvenisti (1999) has argued that compensation should be based on 'adequate' or 'just' principles, and that these criteria are more appropriate than restitution in kind, especially in cases of mass relocation and abandonment of property. Obviously, when based on political feasibility or 'fairness', estimates will differ widely, even more than when based on the value of lost assets.

Khalidi (1994) suggested that, if repatriation of the refugees was not attainable, then compensation might be fixed at about $20,000 per refugee, or a total of $40bn (assuming 2 million refugees). Gazit (1995), on the other hand, recognised that Israel should assume responsibility for providing the bulk of a compensation scheme to the refugees, which he put at

Table 10.1 Alternative estimates of Palestinian losses in 1948

	UNCCP (1951)	*LAS (1956)*	*Sayigh (1967)*	*Kubursi (2000)*	
				Material assets	*Human wealth*
In 1948 prices (£m)	120	1,933	757	743	433
In 1948 prices (US$m)*	484	7,790	3,050	2,996	1,745
In 2000 prices (US$m)**	3,636	58,503	22,921	22,500	13,200

Sources: Kubursi (1988), Kubursi (2001b) and Sayigh (1967).

Notes
*£1 = US$4.03.
**Adjusted for inflation, as measured by the US consumer price index (1948–2000).

$7–8bn. Al-Shikaki, in his joint work with Alpher (1998), cited a figure of $15–20bn as being a reasonable amount of compensation from a Palestinian point of view.

Brynen (1999) approached the matter in reverse, asking first how much resources can be expected to be made available in a fund for compensating the refugees. He analysed the question under two scenarios, pessimistic and optimistic, over a ten year period. His conclusion was that an amount between $6.7bn and $27.3bn was economically possible. Israel's contribution would range between 'a plausible lower margin' of $5bn, and 'an extreme upper boundary' of $25bn. Brynen pointed out, however, that although these amounts are economically feasible, this 'does not mean that they are politically feasible', and concluded that much would depend on how the compensation regime would be 'packaged and sold to the Israeli public'.

Arzt, in her comprehensive proposal for 'turning the refugees into citizens' (1997), pointed out that the amount of compensation needed is much beyond the capability of one country such as Israel. She did not cite a specific figure but argued that 'compensation must be paid out of a combined pool created as part of the final peace settlement'. She also gave some hints with respect to disbursement, advocating uniform payments to various categories of refugees, so that claimants would only be required to prove their membership in the particular class to be eligible. Arzt made two interesting suggestions in her book: that a ceiling on payment of compensation to individual refugees should be imposed so that greater sums could be directed to community projects to generate collective benefits to the refugees; and that the houses of the Jewish settlers 'who decided to leave the WBGS' could be included in Israel's compensation package to the Palestinian refugees. She estimated the number of those settlers to be around 10,000 persons (1997: 98).

Compensation based on the cost of absorption

A third approach for determining the pool of resources needed for compensation builds, though usually implicitly, on the cost of absorbing the refugees. Instead of referring merely to the past, basing compensation on the value of lost assets or on an arbitrary concept of feasibility, this approach assumes implicitly that the key to normalisation and reconciliation lies in addressing the current and future needs of the communities and individuals. The basic idea here was hinted at by BADIL (1999), a Palestinian NGO: 'Given the existence of favourable reintegration and peace-building efforts, refugees may find it acceptable to combine individual compensation ... or part of it, with cost of reconstruction of the physical and social infrastructure on their lands, hence a type of compensation in-kind'.

An important historical precedent for this type of compensation can be found in the reparation agreement between Israel and Germany in September 1952. The preamble to the agreement provided clarification of its background, saying:

> Whereas ... The State of Israel has assumed the heavy burden of resettling so great a number of uprooted and destitute Jewish refugees from Germany ... and has on this basis advanced a claim against the FRG for a global recompense for the cost of the integration of these refugees ... The parties agreed that Germany will pay to Israel the sum of 3,000 million DM.

In addition, Germany agreed to pay to Israel a total of DM450 million for the benefit of 23 Jewish NGOs (Sagi 1980: 212).

It is true that Germany's direct payment to the Israeli government represents a very small fraction of the DM85bn total of reparations, restitution, and indemnification made by Germany to the Jews since the end of the Second World War (Zweig 1987: 155). The vast bulk of this total was actually paid as indemnification to individuals (compensation for loss of property as well as loss of freedom, income, financial advancement, health and tranquillity, etc.). However, the significance of this small fraction, paid directly to the government of Israel, is what interests us here. In the deliberation which led to the agreement, Israel set out its *locus standi* for making claims against Germany in a series of Diplomatic Notes to the four Allied powers. The most important of these notes was presented on 12 March 1951. After arguing for and asserting Israel's right to make claims, as the only state which could speak on behalf of the Jewish people (and inherit from heirless Jews), the note advanced the claims on the basis of 'expenditure incurred and anticipated' for the resettlement of the Jewish immigrants. The number of immigrants was estimated to be 500,000 persons and the cost of transport, maintenance and resettlement to be $3,000 per person. Thus a total of $1.5bn (DM3bn) was demanded, and granted (Zweig 1978: 9). The German payments became one of Israel's most important sources for foreign exchange earnings by 1954.

The Harvard Project on Palestinian Refugees (HPPR 1998) made an attempt to estimate the cost of absorbing the Palestinian refugees and rehabilitating the refugee camps, though without making an explicit link between these and the issue of compensation. The study started by assuming that 250,000 to 750,000 people (50,000–250,000 households) would return to the WBGS within five years. Based on a direct cost of absorption of $7,000 per family, and additional cost of $25,000 for housing, infrastructure and education, the total cost of absorption was put at $1.6–4.8bn. As far as the rehabilitation of the refugee camps in the WBGS and Jordan is concerned, the study estimated the cost of improving the on-site physical infrastructure to be $94–188 million (depending on the extent of the improvement). When the cost of off-site infrastructure (schools and clinics, etc.) was added along with the costs of consolidation and land distribution, the total cost of rehabilitating the camps amounted to $5.4–8.2bn. The study concluded by suggesting that 'while this number is large in relation to the funding that UNRWA has received over the past thirty years, it is not large in relation to the sums that countries in the region now receive in economic and military assistance' (HPPR 1998: 25).

Tuma and Darin-Drabkin (1978) treated the issue of absorbing the returnees in a viable economy in an explicit and thorough manner. Their work was designed to answer one central question: how much extra resources are required to secure an economically viable state in the WBGS while allowing for the return of the refugees? To answer this question the authors started by giving a functional definition of economic viability. The term was taken to be consistent with three objectives: 'productive employment, an acceptable level of income per capita and the potential for saving and investment or a rate of growth that is comparable to the growth rates of other countries in the region' (1978: 73). The three objectives were fixed at 4 per cent structural unemployment, $800 annual per capita income (in 1975 prices), and a growth rate above 10 per cent per annum. They assumed that the returnees would be equivalent to the population of the WBGS in 1975, and that repatriation would be spread over a five-year transitional period, 1977–1982.

The solution of the exercise, which also covered the sectoral allocation of employment and the construction of new houses for both returnees and original inhabitants of the WBGS, corresponded with an investment schedule of $8.3bn over the five transition years. The authors went further and attempted to identify possible sources of funds. They suggested that 15 per cent of the total would come from domestic saving (assuming that the saving ratio in the WBGS would remain at its historic level of 15 per cent). The remaining 85 per cent was allocated somewhat arbitrarily: 50 per cent was assumed to come from Arab and international donors, and the remaining 35 per cent ($3bn) to come from Israel: 'it is our hunch', the authors wrote 'that the total sum of not less than $3bn will be expected' from Israel (1978: 94). Nevertheless, Tuma and Darin-Drabkin pointed out (in a footnote) that what Israel was expected to contribute was quite close to the UNCCP estimate of what the refugees had lost in 1948. Assuming a 6 per cent annual interest rate and an exchange rate of 4 between the pound and the dollar, the £120 million estimated by the UNCCP in 1948 would be equivalent to $2,600 million in 1976 (1978: 101).

Compensation, moral responsibility and disbursement

The above review has highlighted three different approaches to the issue of compensation to the Palestinian refugees: a backward-looking approach whereby the pool of resources is determined on the basis of the present value of the abandoned property; a more pragmatic method, in which a lump sum amount is determined on the basis of economic and political constraints; and a third approach in which compensation is linked to the cost of resettling the returnees and rehabilitating the refugee camps.

The issue of compensation, as an alternative to repatriation and to the exercise of the 'right of return', is more complex and more sensitive than the previous discussion suggests. One of the aspects not directly touched upon above is whether the resources designated for compensation (no matter how they are technically determined) are intended as an acknowledgement of Israel's moral responsibility for the tragedy and the suffering of the Palestinians in the past half century. Palestinian scholars (e.g. Khalidi 1994) accept compensation only on this basis, while Israeli scholars (e.g. Gazit 1995) stress that Israel's eventual contribution to a compensation scheme does not imply acceptance either of moral responsibility or of financial liability for the refugee problem. This explains the Palestinians' inclination to prefer an approach based on the valuation of abandoned property for determining compensation or, even better, an approach based on individual claims of lost assets and suffering. The claim-based approach emphasises the link between the money payment and the moral responsibility.

Another important aspect which has not been tackled explicitly here is the distinction between the criteria upon which the pool of resources for compensation would be determined and those upon which the disbursements to various beneficiaries would be based. A certain degree of harmony should probably exist between these two sets of criteria, in the sense that how the resources are estimated should have some bearing on what the resources will be used for. Such a linkage was made in the UNCCP proposal to the Paris Conference in 1951. After affirming that Israel should pay compensation based on the so-called 'global estimate' of Palestinian losses, the UNCCP established a committee of 'economic and financial experts' to decide how individual claims might be made and compensation be awarded.

Given compatibility between revenue and disbursement criteria, each of the three approaches to determining the pool of compensation would correspond with a pattern of allocation. When the pool is determined on the basis of the value of lost property, disbursement would be directed mainly toward compensating individuals for their losses (or on the basis of some other sort of measure of the suffering of individuals if human and psychological damages are taken into account). When the pool is fixed on the basis of what is politically and economically feasible, the lump sum payment would probably be disbursed in the form of unified per capita payments. Finally, when the pool is determined on the basis of the cost of resettling the refugees and rehabilitating the WBGS economy, the bulk of the compensation would be spent on public and community projects, budget support and the like.

Each of these patterns of disbursement has its advantages and drawbacks. A claim-based system whereby payments are made to compensate individual losses may satisfy the intuitive sense of justice. However, it would require detailed documentation of ownership, which may be practically impossible after more than half-a-century of exile and three generations born in the diaspora. Furthermore, even if sufficient documentation exists to warrant disbursement on the basis of private losses in 1948, the consequent reproduction of the income and social inequalities of the time may not be acceptable now.

Disbursement in the form of a lump sum cash payment for each refugee is probably the easiest and cheapest approach. But such a scheme carries with it serious concerns about sustainability and the possibility of payments being totally wasted or quickly consumed. The collective compensation approach has a number of advantages: it allows for the payments to be smoothed over time, reduces the negative socio-economic consequences of a sudden inflow of large funds in the form of individual compensation and allows for the inclusion of various forms of in-kind compensation in the scheme (such as Israel's settlements and other forms of infrastructure in the WBGS). Also, when compensation is linked to reconstruction and rehabilitation costs, other concessions from Israel, with regard to trade and labour flow for example, can conveniently be incorporated.

The main drawback of the approach which links compensation to the reconstruction of the WBGS is that the direct benefit would go to those Palestinians who live in (as well as to those who would return to) the WBGS. It may well be argued that the creation of a sovereign and prosperous Palestinian state would bring tangible benefits to all Palestinians, regardless of whether they choose to live in the WBGS or not. The existing relation between world Jewry and Israel, as well as different visionary ideas (such as the dual-citizenship proposed by Arzt 1997), exemplify the types of positive spillover effect to all Palestinians from the creation of a prosperous state. It is true that people may not find it easy to accept a collective, somewhat abstract and only probable gain in place of tangible personal compensation. The ability to see, let alone to agree, that personal justice and personal compensation can be integrated in collective benefits of national self-determination in a viable state requires a sophisticated political conscience and some altruism, neither of which may come easily to a population which has suffered so much in the past half century.

The above discussion highlights the complexity of the issues involved in any compensation scheme for the Palestinian refugees. A successful formula should strike a fine balance between justice and efficiency, between material and moral compensation, and between addressing the injuries of the past and tackling present suffering and future needs. Clearly, a single criterion for resource allocation cannot adequately encompass the multiple material, humanitarian and psychological dimensions of the refugee problem, nor secure an adequate and lasting closure of the most important file in the Palestinian–Israeli conflict. Adequate closure requires a multi-dimensional solution, with multiple criteria to determine both the pool of resources and their allocation. Our argument is that the macroeconomic cost of absorbing the Palestinian returnees in a viable and sovereign economy in the WBGS should be one of the core criteria. The main advantages of this approach have already been pointed out above: it puts the emphasis on the future rather than on the past, on securing the durability of the two-state solution, and on establishing a direct link between compensation for past grievances and the prerequisites for collective future prosperity.

The Palestinian refugees

The purpose of this section is to shed light on the number and distribution of the Palestinian refugees, and to put the number of those who would potentially return to the WBGS into perspective. It is useful to stress from the outset, however, that lack of comprehensive censuses and surveys makes the demographic data far from definitive. The geographical spread of the Palestinians and the successive and overlapping waves of exodus aggravate the data problems. Moreover, the number of refugees is a sensitive political issue, both to the parties directly involved and to the host countries. Therefore, all data presented here are merely tentative.

The refugees

A Palestinian refugee is a person who left, forcibly or voluntarily, the parts of Mandatory Palestine which became the State of Israel in 1948 and their descendants. The exact number of the 1948 refugees (and thus their number today), is one of the lasting disputes between the parties to the conflict. Estimates of the numbers of 1948 refugees range from as few as 520,000 to one million. The United Nations Conciliation Commission for Palestine (UNCCP) suggested a number of 726,000. This figure has been generally taken to be a reasonable estimate, not because it withstands serious scrutiny, but rather because it falls in the middle of other extreme estimates.[7]

The United Nations Relief and Works Agency for the Palestinian Refugees in the Near East (UNRWA) began its field work in 1950 and since then has kept records of the number and location of the refugees. However, the UNRWA definition of who was a refugee was different from that given above. The UNRWA definition is based on three criteria: need, displacement and original place of residence. Only a person whose 'normal place of residence was Palestine ... and who lost both home and means of livelihood as a result of the 1948 conflict' was registered as a refugee. Furthermore, only those who resided in UNRWA's fields of operations (WBGS, Jordan, Lebanon and Syria) were registered. Current UNRWA records register also the descendants of fathers who fulfilled the triple-criteria definition.[8]

UNRWA recognises the functional nature of its definition:

> It should be noted that UNRWA's definition of refugees is necessarily restricted ... Thus, for the purposes of repatriation or compensation, as envisaged in UN General Assembly resolution 194 (III) of December 1948, the term 'Palestine refugee' is used with a different, much less restrictive meaning as compared to UNRWA's need-based definition.
>
> (UNRWA 2003)

However, in the absence of a better alternative and because the UNRWA data are based on a clear, if restrictive, definition we shall use them to estimate the number of refugees. Table 10.2 is constructed on the basis of the UNRWA database for registered refugees and the PCBS's data for the number and distribution of the Palestinian people in 2001. The total number of registered refugees is 3.874 million, which seems reasonable. Starting from the UNCCP's estimate of 726,000 refugees in 1948, and assuming a plausible annual growth of 3.2 per cent, the number would have become 3.854 million refugees in 2001 which is almost identical with the figure cited in the table. However, if we take the commonly cited figure for the total number of Palestinians of 1.3 million in 1948, and assume the same annual growth (3.2 per cent), the total number of Palestinians worldwide would have amounted to around 7 million in 2001. This is about 20 per cent lower than the figure reported by the PCBS and cited in Table 10.2.[9]

In line with our focus on the potential returnees to the Palestinian state in the WBGS, we derive an index of 'diaspora Palestinians'. This refers to all the Palestinians who currently reside outside the territories of Mandatory Palestine, i.e. outside the WBGS and Israel. It is important to stress that diaspora Palestinians do not encompass all the refugees, since over one third of all the UNRWA registered refugees reside in the WBGS. The index is merely the absolute maximum of those who could return to the WBGS. The table indicates that about one-half of the total Palestinian people are currently in diaspora, and a little more than one-half of these are registered refugees. Furthermore, only a quarter of registered refugees in the diaspora lives in refugee camps in Jordan, Lebanon and Syria.

The decision to return

The likely number of returnees from the diaspora to the forthcoming state is a key question, because the size of the influx will determine the scale of economic adjustment required. It is obviously difficult to give a precise

Table 10.2 Total Palestinian population and UNRWA registered refugees, mid 2001

	Total Palestinians	*Registered refugees*	*No. of camps*	*Registered refugees in camps*	*Special hardship cases*
West Bank	2,102,360	607,770	19	163,139	30,702
Gaza	1,196,591	852,626	8	460,031	73,316
Jordan	2,637,076	1,639,718	10 (+3 unofficial)	287,951	42,364
Lebanon	391,240	382,973	12	214,728	42,448
Syria	411,119	391,651	10 (+3 unofficial)	109,466	28,513
Saudi Arabia	291,811				
Egypt	58,363				
Kuwait	37,140				
Other Gulf countries	117,099				
Other Arab countries	6,149				
USA	227,179				
Rest of world	289,289				
Israel	1,004,600				
Total	8,878,926	3,874,738	59 (+6 unofficial)	1,235,315	217,388
Total in diaspora*	4,575,375	2,414,342	32 (+6)	612,145	113,325

Sources: column 1 is from PCBS (2001), the rest of the table is from UNRWA (2001).

Note
*Total excluding WBGS and Israel.

answer since much will depend on the provisions of the future political settlement, on individual choices and on the future economic, social and political performance of the new state. Let us assume, for a start, that neither the provisions of the Israeli–Palestinian settlement nor the future Palestinian government nor the host countries would limit or force the movement of the diaspora Palestinians. In this case, the size of the immigration to the WBGS will depend totally on the free choices of the diaspora Palestinian individual/household.

Three sets of factors will probably have decisive effects on households' choices: potential improvement in standards of living and economic gain, family affiliation in the WBGS, and the value which diaspora Palestinians variously attach to the option of living in their own home country under their own sovereign authority.

There is abundant evidence that migration is very sensitive to economic conditions. Movement from one place to another proceeds in response to differences in earnings, actual and expected, as measured by the difference in wages weighted by the probability of obtaining gainful employment over a certain period of time. This suggests that the future influx of returnees to the Palestinian state would depend strongly on its economic performance: the better it performs relative to the neighbouring countries, especially with respect to creating jobs with high wages, the larger the migration would be. A dilemma seems to exist here, since the influx of the refugees would hamper economic performance, at least during the early stages. On the other hand, this suggests that the number of returnees to the WBGS would also depend on the efforts taken to improve and normalise the living conditions of the diaspora Palestinians in their current places of residence.

The discrepancy in per capita incomes and wage rates between the West Bank and neighbouring Arab countries is one indicator of the economic pull factors. In 1998, the average monthly wage of a full-time worker in the refugee camps in Jordan was JD146 compared with an average of JD190 in the West Bank, and about twice as much for Palestinians working in Israel (PCBS 1999b). This is an important pull factor and will probably continue in future as long as legal (or illegal) work opportunities in Israel remain relatively open for residents in the WBGS.

An allowance should be made, however, for the real purchasing power of the above figures. The WBGS's proximity and relative openness to Israel means that its PPP deflator must be substantially lower than that in other neighbouring countries. Table 10.3 shows that while nominal per capita GNP in Israel is more than ten times that in Jordan, the ratio is less than five times in PPP terms. If we assume that the price level in the WBGS lies in between those in Israel and Jordan, the average monthly wage in the WBGS would need to approach JD200 in order to secure the same purchasing power as JD146 in Jordan. In fact, only those Palestinians working in Israel and in the Israeli settlements were earning higher than

Table 10.3 GNP per capita in current and PPP dollars, 1999

	Per capita GNP, $	*Per capita GNP in PPP $*	*PPP deflator*
Egypt	1,400	3,303	2.359
Jordan	1,500	3,542	2.361
Lebanon	3,700	4,129	1.116
Syria	970	2,761	2.846
Israel (1998)	15,940	17,310	1.086
WBGS	1,610	NA	(1.723)*

Sources: World Development Report (1999/2000) and (2001/2002).

Note
*Assumed to be the average of the PPP deflators in Jordan and Israel.

that wage level. Unemployment is also relevant. For the refugee camps in Lebanon it was estimated at 40 per cent, which is higher than in the camps in the West Bank. Otherwise, unemployment in all diaspora refugee camps is lower than in the WBGS (HPPR 1998).

Another important factor that might weaken the economic pull from differential earnings is the cost of relocation which could exceed whatever capital assets the diaspora refugees might possess. The effects of differential earnings will probably be strongest for the poorer segments of the refugees, those living in the refugee camps in the diaspora, and particularly those which are defined by the UNRWA as 'special hardship cases' (see Table 10.2). However, as many as 74 per cent of the households in the camps in Lebanon have no savings of any kind. In fact, 50 per cent said that they would not be able to mobilise $130 if and when an emergency need for that amount arose (Ugland 2003: 177). On the other hand, the vast majority of the refugees in the diaspora camps have access to free housing, although this accommodation is often of very low standard. Eight out of every ten refugee households in Lebanon believe that they 'own' their houses. This is not strictly legally true, but it means that the refugees do not pay house rents (Ugland 2003: 190). Thus, unless the UNRWA or the PA were ready to provide comparable free accommodation for them in the WBGS, the decision of the refugees to return would involve substantial increases in their cost of living. On the other hand, in the wake of an overall settlement the refugees would probably receive compensation that would help them to relocate and permit the UNRWA to terminate its work.

The second set of factors which will affect the decision to move includes family affiliations in the WBGS and the degree of integration into the host societies. The unique surveys undertaken by FAFO in the refugee camps in Lebanon and Jordan provide enlightening information here. For while over 50 per cent of the inhabitants of the refugee camps in Jordan have first degree family relations in the WBGS, the ratio is negligible among the refugees in Lebanon (Khawaja and Tiltnes 2002: 40). In contrast, a high proportion of the refugees in Lebanon have close family relations in Europe or in Israel (Ugland 2003: 30). Yet, the surveys also reveal that the refugees in Jordan are much more integrated into the local society and environment than the refugees in Lebanon: 20 per cent of the households headed by a refugee in Jordan have a non-refugee member, mainly the spouse, and the majority of the refugees, while expressing dissatisfaction with their place of residence in the camps, expressed a strong desire to remain living within the camps' community (Khawaja and Tiltnes 2002: 18, 38). Actually, even in Lebanon, it is estimated that a quarter of third generation refugees have one Lebanese parent (Brynen 1997: 6). It is well known that large sections of the Palestinians in the diaspora, especially the middle class, are well established and well integrated into the communities within which they have lived for the past 50 years.

So far we have been dealing with the socio-economic factors on the basis of which a 'cool' calculation of costs and benefits may be made. However, no matter how important these factors are, it is doubtful that a refugee's decision on where to live in the future would be taken entirely on the basis of such a limited cost-benefit analysis. As pointed out by Arzt (1997: 62), after three generations of exile the image of a homeland becomes too abstract, too spiritual, to quantify in the manner of an economist or even a demographer. Undoubtedly, many Palestinians will attach a high value to living in their own home country under their own sovereign authority. However, moving from one place to another to live under one's own sovereign national authority rather than to return to one's original property and parent's place of residence requires a relatively high degree of political consciousness. When an average Palestinian, young or old, spontaneously affirms his or her readiness to return immediately, he or she is making a political statement regarding the fairness of the Palestinian cause rather than expressing a concrete plan to move from one place to another. The Palestinian identity has been sustained for more than 50 years as a form of deliberate resistance, and demanding that things be brought back to their original state prior to 1948 is a coherent component of the resistance mechanism. This phenomenon is not particular to the Palestinian refugees, for 'the majority of emigrants express desires for returning to their places of origin when asked, but a few do' (Khawaja and Tilnes 2002: 37, citing Portes and Bach 1988). Similarly, in the words of Brynen (1997), 'It is important to note that international experience suggests that the number of refugees who choose homeland repatriation is often much smaller than planners and activists initially anticipate. The proportion, moreover, usually declines over time'. This is not suggesting that refugees often lie, but rather that a distinction should be made between valuing an option and exercising it immediately. If a formula can be found whereby the refugees would be allowed to exercise the option of returning to the WBGS over a period of time, they would most probably then take their time and base their decisions more on their true needs and desires.

How many would return and from where?

The above discussion of the factors which affect the refugees' decision to move points at the complexity of the issue as well as the high uncertainty involved. As long as the provisions of the political settlement in the region are unknown and the future legal status of the Palestinians in the host countries is not clarified, only a tentative estimate of the number of returnees can be made.

Surprisingly, however, almost all the studies which have attempted to address this question have come up with figures which fall within a relatively narrow margin. Heller (1983) suggested, in his pioneering study, a figure of 800,000. Tuma and Darin-Drabkin (1978) argued that a little over one million would return to the WBGS during a transitional period of five years. Abed (1990: 37) worked with a figure of 750,000 (incorporating all the residents of the refugee camps in Jordan, Lebanon and Syria, an arbitrary 20 per cent of the other Palestinians in these countries, and 30,000–50,000 refugees from other countries). Abed suggested also that 50,000–100,000 refugees would return to Israel. The Harvard Project on Palestinian Refugees (1998) put the number of returnees somewhere between 250,000 and 750,000, with an average of 500,000, over a five-year period. The Palestinian Ministry of Planning and International Cooperation (MoPIC) came up with a figure of 700,000. Finally, the PCBS (1999a) assumed, in its population projection for 1997–2025, that net immigration to the WBGS would be 500,000 during 1997–2010, and zero thereafter.

Thus most of the studies seem to suggest between one half and one million returnees over a period of five years. Table 10.4 relates these numbers to the current population of the WBGS and the total number of refugees in the diaspora. It is interesting to note that any figure higher

Table 10.4 Number of returnees relative to basic population indices (%)

No. of returnees	*500,000*	*750,000*	*1,000,000*
Returnees relative to total WBGS current population	15	23	30
Returnees relative to total diaspora Palestinians	11	16	22
Returnees relative to registered refugees in diaspora	20	31	40
Returnees relative to registered refugees in diaspora camps	81	122	163

Source: Table 10.1.

than 650,000 allows in theory for the return of all the refugees who are registered in the diaspora refugee camps.

As to where the returnees would come from, Abed (1990) assumed explicitly that the inhabitants of *all* the refugee camps in the diaspora would constitute about 60 per cent of the returnees to the WBGS. As in other studies, this was justified on the grounds that the camps' residents are the most impoverished of the refugees and the least integrated into the host countries. It is also safe to presume that a future settlement in the region would require the elimination of the most striking symbol of the Palestinian tragedy, the refugee camps.

FAFO's recent surveys of the camps in Jordan and Lebanon document the poverty-enclave status of the camps. This is particularly true in Lebanon, where average household income in the camps was less than 30 per cent of the average income in Lebanon as a whole. Actually, nine out of every ten families in the camps in 1996 lived below the UNRWA poverty line (Ugland 2003: 157). The situation in the refugee camps in Jordan is less dramatic but the camp population is clearly worse off than the rest of the population in Jordan in terms of income, and this is especially true for the groups at the lower income indices (Khawaja and Tiltnes 2002: 55). The Jordan survey points out the 'presence of a rather vibrant "enclave" economy in the camps, with perhaps higher wages and a small affluent class of professionals, employers, and self-employed persons', but stresses that the 'camps suffer from a clustering of poverty, underemployment and other social dislocations' (2002: 68). The refugees in the camps in Lebanon are the least integrated and the most impoverished among all the Palestinian communities.

The suggestion that the economic 'pull' factor will be more powerful with respect to the most impoverished Palestinians is quite plausible. But for this to materialise some concrete form of support to cover the considerable relocation cost or to compensate for the free services which those refugees currently receive from UNRWA (especially free housing) will have to be in place. On the other hand, and along with the economic 'pull' factors, one also ought to consider the political 'push' factors. The situation of the Palestinian refugees in a number of places is particularly critical. For example, Brynen (1997) points out that in Lebanon there is very little support, at either the official or popular level, for the permanent settlement of a significant number of Palestinians. Abdullah (2002) has documented that since 1982 the Lebanese government 'has made every effort to make life uncomfortable, and Lebanon unwelcoming, for the Palestinian community'. In that sense most of the immigration out of the camps in Syria and Jordan would probably be 'pull' immigration, while that from Lebanon will be of the 'push' type.

FAFO's surveys reveal that the demographic structure of the Palestinians in the refugee camps in Jordan is quite similar to that among the refugees in the WBGS. The camps in Lebanon have substantially smaller families, with lower fertility and mortality rates and a larger number of female-headed households. However, the inhabitants of the refugee camps in Jordan as well as in Lebanon are remarkably poor in human capital: one-third of the camps' inhabitants in Lebanon are without basic education, while only 5 per cent have an education level higher than secondary (Ugland 2003: 107). The illiteracy rate is as high as 17.6 per cent (24 per cent for women and 10 per cent for men) among the camp population in Jordan (Khawaja and Tiltnes 2002: 74). The labour participation rate is also relatively low in both places, at about 40 per cent, and as low as 13 per cent for females in camps in Jordan. The sectoral allocation of employment exhibits a bias towards clerk and low-status manual occupations, with remarkably little occupational diversity.

However, as against this evidence of a relatively poor resource base among the current inhabitants of the diaspora camps, the potential returnees to the WBGS, the FAFO surveys hint at the high level of entrepreneurship, high social capital, optimism about a better future, and deep eagerness to improve their physical and socio-political environment among the refugees.

A framework for decision analysis

A solution to the refugee problem will have important consequences beyond the refugees themselves. Their decisions on whether to return or not, at what time and where to, will affect the WBGS economy as well as other economies in the region. The difficulty in assessing those consequences results from unavoidable uncertainties built into the process. The specifications of the peace agreements (between Israel and the Palestinians as well as between Israel and the countries currently hosting the refugees) are as yet unknown, while the reactions of the refugees to those agreements can only be guessed at. As pointed out above, their reactions will depend on both economic developments and the socio-political environment, in the new state as well as in the other countries in the region. None of these will be known to the refugees at the start of the process of implementing the agreements.

Figure 10.1 sketches the interlinkages between some of the factors that will affect, and be affected by, the refugees' reactions. We start from the peace agreement which will open the way for the return of the refugees and the payment of compensation. This, along with the initial domestic and international resources and the socio-political environment in the new state and the host countries, will determine the first round of the refugees' reactions. The number of returnees will have some bearing on the economic performance of the new entity, and this, along with the new extra resources and current socio-political conditions, will determine the second round of the refugees' reactions, and so on.

The reactions of the refugees will have immediate effects on several

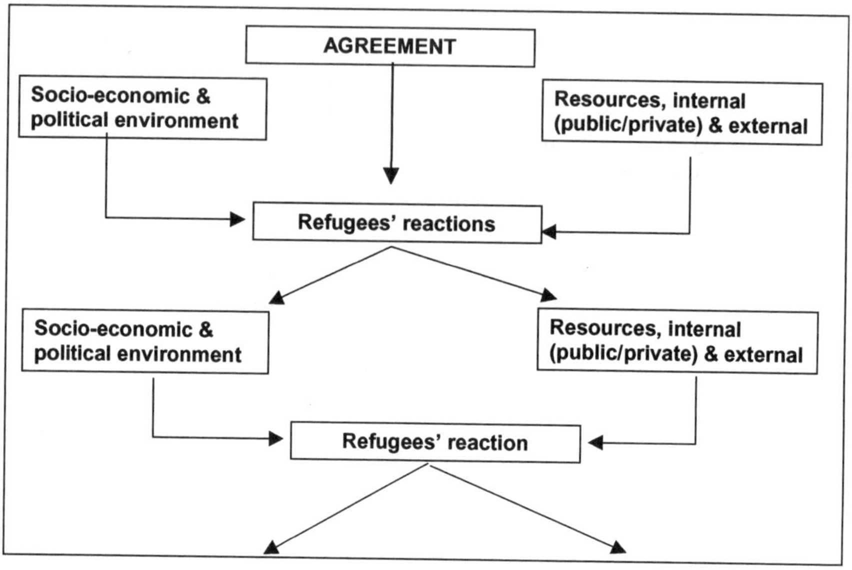

Figure 10.1 The decision to return.

economic factors such as the labour market, the housing market and disposable income. These effects will be incorporated in the model which we present in the following section. The graph makes clear that the reaction of the refugees will also depend on the resources which will be mobilised by the private and public sectors in the WBGS and by the international community. The private sector's reaction will be measured by the change in investment behaviour while the public sector's reaction will be reflected in its direct decisions with respect to public consumption and investment, taxes and the fiscal deficit, as well as the indirect effects of public policies. This latter influence will prove to be of the utmost importance since the policies will determine, to a large extent, how conducive the economic environment will be for growth and development. All those 'reactions' can be subsumed in macroeconomic scenarios described in terms of the standards of living, employment and balance of payments.

The exposition in Figure 10.1 subsumes two of the hypotheses which will be incorporated in the following section. First, the return of the refugees to the WBGS will be a process, i.e. it will be gradual and will extend over a number of years. Second, a certain amount of resources from external sources will be made available to facilitate the absorption of the returnees. Part of these resources will be associated with the comprehensive scheme of compensation to the Palestinian refugees. As we discuss below, there may also be in-kind compensation, in the form of housing units and other infrastructure which will be abandoned by Israel on the establishment of the Palestinian state.

A macroeconomic approach

In this section we use a macroeconomic framework to assess some of the implications of resettling the refugees in the Palestinian economy. We distinguish between the West Bank and the Gaza Strip because the economic structure in the two regions is substantially different, refugees face different conditions, and only a few returnees are likely to resettle in the Gaza region.[10] We focus first on the economics of resettlement in the West Bank and then analyse the cost of raising the living standards of the Gaza Strip to levels comparable to those in the West Bank. Our approach allows us to estimate the extra resources needed to improve the standard of living for *all* inhabitants in the WBGS, including the refugees currently residing there and the returnees, with emphasis on the creation of employment opportunities and housing. Our main concern here is to test feasibility and to determine the requirements for consistency rather than to provide a comprehensive model which captures behavioural and structural changes in the future. The analysis relies on a set of simplifying assumptions to deal with the enormous uncertainties involved in exercises of this sort, and it addresses only some of the aspects of the absorption and rehabilitation of refugees. However, its results clearly indicate that the economy of the WBGS could in principle absorb an inflow of refugees of the magnitude discussed earlier.

There are two important aspects to any attempt to quantify a resettlement and absorption of this kind: the creation of employment opportunities for the returnees and the provision of housing. In the quantitative evaluations we aim to measure the overall impact on the WBGS economy. Clearly the evaluation will depend crucially on assumptions concerning the reactions of the refugees. The current study will seek to present the complicated relationship between the number of returnees and the timing of the return, the expected changing patterns of aggregate demand schedules, and the additional resources necessary to secure compliance with certain constraints. In particular, we shall attempt to estimate the consequences of a number of scenarios on the labour market, capital accumulation, standards of living (including housing) and the balance of payments.

A macroeconomic framework

From a macroeconomic perspective, the most important parameters to consider are how many will return and how much new resources will be made available, and where do they come from? A related issue concerns the impact of the new setting, i.e. the establishment of a sovereign

Palestinian state, on private and public investment schedules: will entrepreneurs and government behave differently?

The answers to these questions will be captured by the various schedules where, for each year after the peace agreement, the appropriate changes will be specified. These schedules, which specify the number of returnees, the number of workers, the sums of additional resources and the parameters in the behavioural equations, will constitute the inputs in the detailed scenarios below.

The macroeconomic framework captures the essential elements of the newly established Palestinian state:

1 the peculiar structure of the labour market where, due to the differences in income levels and wages in the economies, an important segment of employment will be outside the domestic economy;
2 the impact of the substantial increase in population, and thus in labour supply, due to the 'return';
3 the effects of different assumptions concerning the availability of funds through either unilateral transfers or capital movements.

On the supply side, we assume a Cobb-Douglas production function relating output (GDP) to productive capital and domestic employment. Labour supply is determined by demographic trends, including natural growth and the ratio of working age population to total population, and the participation rate. Local labour demand is derived from the production function. Labour is also employed in the Israeli economy.[11]

On the demand side, the consumption function is linear and dependent on disposable income and the well known olive cycle, where in 'good' years consumers save more than in 'bad' years (see Arnon and Gottlieb 1996). We distinguish between investment in productive capital, which affects output via the production function, and investment in residential housing, which increases welfare but does not contribute directly to future production. For the former, a simple linear investment function is assumed which includes current output as its only variable. For investment in residential housing, it is assumed that behaviour during the first few years is similar to the historical trend, but the unusually high proportion of this type of investment will gradually decline in later years.

Government consumption is modelled as a proportion (22 per cent) of GNP. Exports must depend on foreign demand for the goods produced at home and on their relative price compared to that of the main competitors abroad. However, due to the lack of a good export function and the very stable ratio of exports to GDP in the past, we assume that, after recovery from the present difficulties, exports will continue to be 20 per cent of GDP. Imports depend on GNP. The balance of payments will be the result of exports, imports, unilateral transfers, factor income from abroad and capital movements. The latter are assumed to compensate for whatever imbalances are created by the other items: they are the residual in the model. Thus, the implied level of capital imports can be used to determine whether a particular scenario is feasible.

The scenarios

The model is solved first for a base scenario which assumes natural population increase only, i.e. no returnees, constructed on pre-intifada data on the economic structure adjusted for population increase. We then consider five different scenarios with respect to the number of returnees and the time span of the return, over a period of 20 years. This allows us to compare the economic changes which take place in each scenario with that of the no-returnees base scenario.

Concerning housing supply in the West Bank, one possible source that will be available immediately under the assumptions of an agreement on two states is that of the settlements. Since Palestine will be sovereign and its territory will have contiguity, the Israeli settlers now within this territory will leave unless the agreement will allow them to stay under Palestinian jurisdiction, which seems unlikely. The land will return to its owners, whether private or public, and the existing housing units where settlers live can then be used for absorption purposes. The exact number of housing units available for this purpose can be estimated at tens of thousands, reducing the cost of building as well as the time necessary for construction. We will not deal here specifically with the quantitative impact of this additional supply nor with the difficult issue of whether the value of these units will be part of the compensation package, nor will we address the issue of how they will be allocated. However, the value of these housing units will clearly affect the calculations of necessary capital imports provided below.

The base scenario

The base scenario assumes population and employment increase at an annual rate of 3.5 per cent in the West Bank, with a natural rate of unemployment of about 6 per cent; it is calculated with two different levels of labour integration with Israel: 'high labour market integration' where employment in Israel absorbs 28 per cent of the labour force, and 'low labour market integration' (18 per cent). The performance of the economy in this scenario is satisfactory. Per capita GNP increases over the 20 year period at an average annual rate of 3.1 per cent, and consumption per capita at 2.9 per cent. Productive capital per capita rises at an annual rate of 4.5 per cent, while government consumption and the housing stock grow at annual per capita rates of 3.1 and 3.6 per cent. These are typical rates for a reasonably growing economy. Under the high labour integration assumption, the capital imports needed to realise the base scenario amount to about $14bn in nominal value over the 20 years (or about $8bn in present value terms at year 1, with a 5 per cent discount rate). These capital imports represent about 9 per cent of the average annual GDP in the West Bank.

Five scenarios for the returnees

The five different refugee return scenarios are as follows:

1 500,000 returnees in two years (500, 2).
2 500,000 returnees in five years (500, 5).
3 1,000,000 returnees in two years (1000, 2).
4 1,000,000 returnees in five years (1000, 5).
5 1,000,000 returnees in ten years (1000, 10).

We assume two crucial mechanisms of adjustment. In the labour market the sudden increase in population from the influx of refugees causes unemployment to increase, the excess supply of labour pushes real wages down, and the economy adjusts towards a new equilibrium with one half of the excess supply of labour finding work in each period, until the involuntary unemployment has disappeared.[12]

Second, with respect to investment (both in productive capital and in housing) and consumption (both private and public), we assume in all the five scenarios that these variables increase with, but less than proportionally to, the increase in population relative to the base scenario, because the returnees' initial consumption and investment are smaller than those of the 'veterans'. The two sections of the population then converge gradually over the 20 years, so that by the end of the simulation the old base scenario functions hold again for the whole population.

The performance of the economy under the five scenarios makes clear that as the number of returnees increases and, especially, as the period of return gets shorter, absorption becomes more difficult and costly. Unemployment is highest (and real wages lowest) during the first five years of implementation under the third scenario (1 million returnees in two years), lower under the first and fourth scenarios (500,000 in two years and 1 million in five years) and much lower under the fifth and second scenarios (1 million in ten years and 500,000 in five years). There are corresponding declines in living standards, as measured by per capita GNP and consumption. Figures 10.2–10.4 exhibit the overall trends with respect to GNP per capita, unemployment and capital imports.

The results of the exercise imply a decline in the stock of housing per capita during the early stages due to the pressures caused by the increases in population. This is the case even in medium scenarios (like scenario 4) during the first five years. One possible way to ease this problem is the handing over of the existing Israeli settlements to the new Palestinian state as a part of a comprehensive peace deal in the region. A similar pattern is witnessed in productive capital per capita, although a compensating

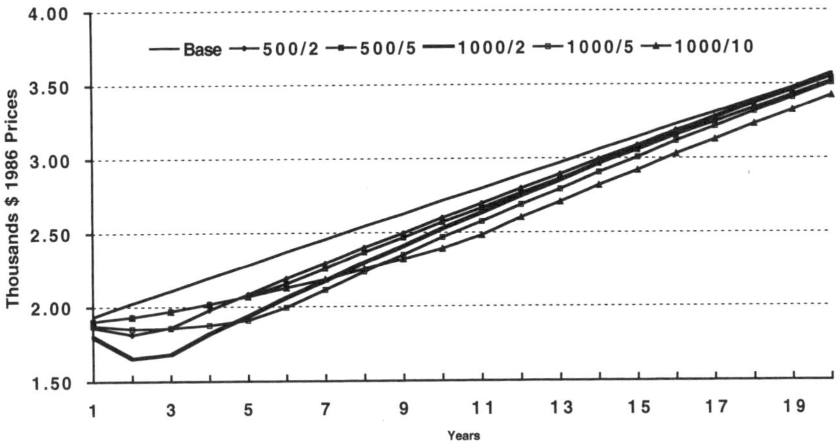

Figure 10.2 GNP per capita (2 year average) (US$1000 at constant 1986 prices).

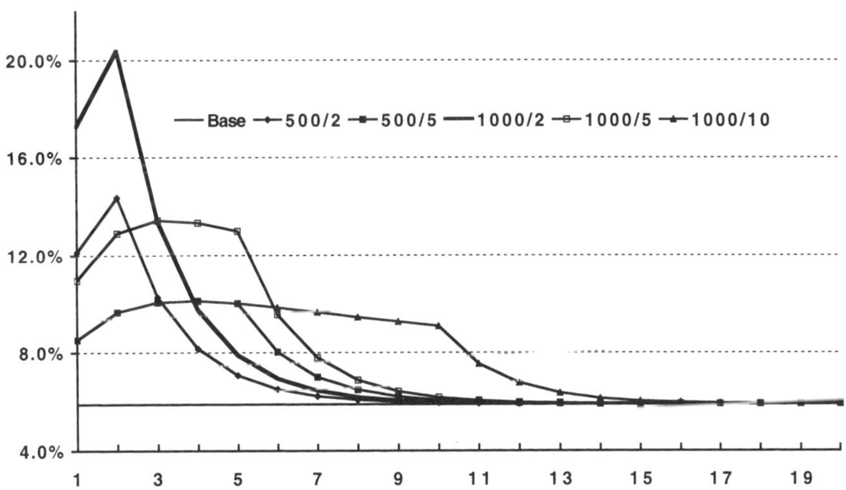

Figure 10.3 Unemployment rate (%).

mechanism is at work here. However, unlike residential housing, where the economy starts from a relatively high per capita stock, the initial levels of productive capital are very low in the Palestinian economy, and productive capital grows more quickly than the housing stock during the 20 years.

The short-term decline in living standards under the return scenarios can be seen in the low growth rates over the first five years for both per capita GNP and consumption. However, there is a marked 'recovery' in a

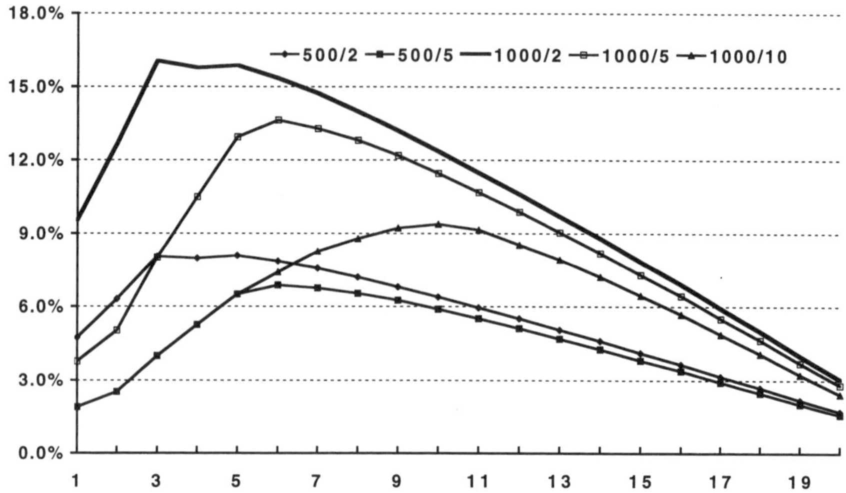

Figure 10.4 Capital imports beyond base scenario (as % of GDP, two-year average).

number of scenarios (with both low and high labour integration) after the first five years of implementation, notably in employment.

Table 10.5 presents the cumulative sums of additional capital imports necessary in each scenario, beyond what is required in the base scenario, calculated for the first ten years and for the whole 20 years of implementation. The table also presents the amount of capital imports needed to implement the base scenario (i.e. without returnees). Scenario 3 (1 million returnees in two years) is the most difficult to finance: $18.6bn in nominal terms or $11.5bn in the present value calculation. This is over and above the $14bn nominal dollars required in the base scenario. The second scenario (500,000 returnees in five years) is the 'cheapest', requiring $7.2bn in nominal terms and $4.4bn in present value (at a 5 per cent discount rate) beyond the base scenario.

The scenarios explicitly assume that the Israeli labour market will be relatively open to Palestinian workers. In fact changing this assumption could upset the outcomes of the scenarios, including the base scenario. In the first and second scenarios close to 290,000 Palestinian workers (and in the other three scenarios about 330,000) will be working in Israel at the end of the simulation period under the high labour integration assumption. Under the low labour flow hypothesis, the figures are about 185,000 and 215,000 respectively. These are lower figures than those experienced before the 'Oslo period', but much higher than those of recent years. Without this labour access the process of absorption would be much more difficult. The capital imports required depend partly on the links between the Palestinian and Israeli labour markets: the higher the flows of labour

Table 10.5 Capital imports with high and low labour flows (US$m)

Scenarios	*BASE*	*1*	*2*	*3*	*4*	*5*
		500, 2	500, 5	1000, 2	1000, 5	1000, 10
Years						
High labour flows (nominal sums)						
1–10	5,155	4,366	3,395	9,377	7,221	4,421
1–20	13,942	8,591	7,227	18,630	15,527	11,317
High labour flows (present value at year 1)						
1–10	3,895	3,271	2,475	7,004	5,251	3,148
1–20	8,017	5,337	4,350	11,536	9,321	6,523
Low labour flows (nominal sums)						
1–10	6,757	4,747	3,695	10,169	7,838	4,809
1–20	18,571	9,721	8,194	21,007	17,543	12,836
Low labour flows (present value at year 1)						
1–10	5,098	3,549	2,690	7,577	5,690	3,420
1–20	10,627	5,967	4,878	12,858	10,419	7,327

to Israel the easier the absorption process would be in terms of both the capital needed to finance it and economic performance in general. The cost of absorbing 1 million returnees in two years (scenario 3) is $18.6bn under high labour market integration but $21bn in the low labour flow case ($11.5 and $12.9bn in present values). However, the increase in the required capital imports between the low and high labour integration may appear to be small relative to what is suggested by other studies (see for example the World Bank 2002), at about 13 per cent in the various scenarios. This is probably because of the stringent adjustment process assumed here for the labour market.

The convergence of Gaza with the West Bank

The Gaza region, whose population is currently about one-third of the population of Palestine (see Table 10.1), deserves a closer consideration which would go beyond the scope of this chapter. However, it is clear that the impact of the above return scenarios on the Gazan economy will be different from that in the West Bank, since we have assumed that all the returnees will settle in the West Bank. We will nevertheless attempt here to incorporate Gaza into the analysis in a simple and straightforward fashion.

If Palestinian policy makers adopt the goal of securing convergence in the living standards of the two wings of the state, Gaza and the West Bank, then the Gazan population will be 'indirectly' affected even when all the returnees are assumed to settle in the West Bank. On the other hand, and since 70 per cent of Gaza's population is refugees, policies aiming at alleviating poverty and raising standards of living in Gaza to levels comparable with those in the West Bank will need to be specifically targeted towards the refugees. We will attempt here to estimate the additional external resources needed for these policies. Basically, we assume that the two regions will converge with each other so that gaps in standards of living, including in particular housing, will be eliminated over the absorption period of 20 years. We deploy a macroeconomic framework for Gaza similar in structure to the one used above for the West Bank. However, the driving force behind the calculations here is not the demographics of return, as in the West Bank, but rather the mechanism of convergence between the two regions.

The impact of the five scenarios on the Gaza Strip will depend, to a large extent, on the degree of economic integration of the West Bank and Gaza. The more integrated the economies will be in future the more similar will developments in the Gaza area be to those described above for the West Bank. In that sense, the five scenarios can be extended to Gaza so that the rehabilitation of the refugees currently resident in Gaza as well as the convergence process will take place at the same time. The analysis assumes that economic policies will be reflected in three variables: consumption, investment in productive capital and investment in housing. All three are based on their past behaviour in the economy of Gaza, supplemented by an adjustment mechanism which closes the gap over time between the levels of per capita consumption (and productive capital and housing stock) in the two regions. 40 per cent of the gap is closed in the first year, and lower proportions in subsequent years.

For each of our five scenarios we create a 'mirror' scenario for Gaza. These mirror scenarios capture the complex processes whereby refugees living in Gaza are rehabilitated and the two regions converge economically. The resulting rough estimates of the capital imports required in the five scenarios are presented in Table 10.6. They indicate that the macroeconomic costs of rehabilitation and convergence that will bring the Gazan economy close to that of the West Bank are between \$24bn and \$27bn in present value terms in the five scenarios.

The grand total for the cost of rehabilitating the economy of the WBGS and absorbing the refugees can be obtained by adding the estimated required capital imports in the base scenario, the additional amounts

Table 10.6 Additional capital imports necessary for the convergence of Gaza, US\$m (present value at year 1)

Scenarios	*1*	*2*	*3*	*4*	*5*
	500, 2	500, 5	1000, 2	1000, 5	1000, 10
Years 1–10	11,161	9,756	9,752	8,918	8,820
Years 1–20	27,222	25,694	25,390	25,059	24,381

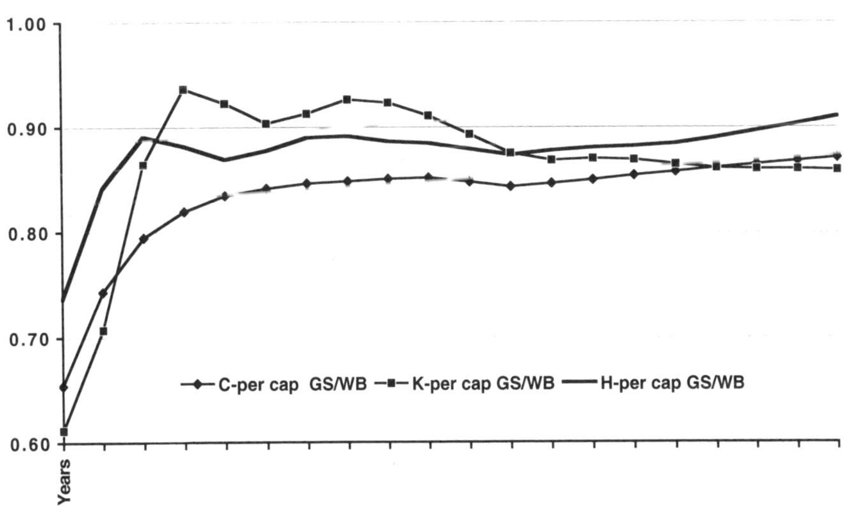

Figure 10.5 Convergence of Gaza's per capita consumption, capital and housing with the West Bank's (scenario 5: 1000/10).

needed under one of the five return scenarios, and the amount needed for the convergence of Gaza's economy. Under the high labour flow assumption, for example, the total cost of the fifth scenario amounts to about $40bn in present value terms.

It is clear that the capital imports necessary to make the scenarios 'work' are not negligible. However, the amounts are not outside the range of regional and international capacities, including the ability of Israel to contribute substantially to a fund which would create a sustainable Palestinian economy in conjunction with solving the problem of the refugees. Thus, our calculations indicate that although the additional capital imports are significant, they fall within what is 'feasible'.

The five scenarios show that, under the assumption that the external constraint can be lifted, the Palestinian economy could indeed absorb the returnees, rehabilitate the refugees and move towards sustainable growth. The absorption process, like other major shocks to an economy, is associated with many structural economic responses. The shocks were assumed in this exercise to be countered by 'positive' reactions from the various agents in the economy. In this sense, the right policies become crucial, since they have to 'convince' the various economic agents to behave 'positively' in order to allow the scenarios' results to materialise.

Absorption of returnees: policy options

When an economy faces the challenge of absorbing a significant number of returnees, the choice by policy makers of the right strategy is crucial, particularly for a new but impoverished state such as Palestine. Even if it can be assumed that additional resources (domestic or foreign) will be available, they must be used efficiently. The core challenge is to create employment opportunities and housing – which are long-term processes – and at the same time answer the immediate demands of the expanding population.

There are two major issues for absorption policy. First, should policy makers concentrate on housing and employment creation, or only on one of these goals? It can be argued, for example, that efforts should focus on job creation rather than upon housing or social benefits because 'If people have jobs they can provide for their own housing and social welfare'. Second, should absorption policy be implemented through a 'centralised' or a 'free market' model?

Israel's absorption experiences in the early 1950s and the 1990s shed light on these two central issues and provide some answers which could be useful for Palestine. Massive immigration in the early 1950s led to a doubling of the population (from 0.6 million) in four years (1948–1952). These immigrants were penniless and poorly skilled, with large families and low expectations. The waves of immigration in the 1990s increased the population by about one-fifth in five years. But unlike the early waves, these immigrants were highly skilled – a fifth of those of working age were engineers (Alterman 2002: 82) – and they were secular, with small families and with high expectations of Western standards of living: this was mainly 'pull' immigration.

In the 1950s the absorption strategy was designed to help achieve goals other than merely accommodating the immigrants. The public sector was seen as the only body which could provide comprehensive solutions to mass immigration, and it was involved directly, and in a very centralised fashion, in the planning and construction of new towns and houses, as well as in deciding who should live where. Immigrants were received in poor and primitive transit camps, and many of them remained there for a long time: about a fifth of Israel's population were living in temporary houses up to 1951 (Newman 2000). New Development Towns were built as permanent settlements for immigrants, 30 being established between 1948–1963. However, strategic considerations played a decisive role in selecting the locations of the new towns: the aim was to secure a strong Jewish presence in various parts of the country, especially the Negev and Galilee.

By the 1980s, however, new immigrants were more qualified and skilled, and coming mainly from developed countries. Moreover, the old absorption policy had been criticised for trapping the less dynamic immigrants in a vicious circle of poverty and dependency. Thus, the immigrants of the 1990s were met with a fundamentally different policy, which became known as 'Direct Immigrant Absorption'. Under the new strategy immigrants were given wide freedom to find work, and to choose where and how they wanted to live. They were provided with a generous package of support and subsidies, during the first year of their arrival, but then were left to make their own way. The package covered the costs of living (from the government's budget), house rent, language courses, and the fees for higher education (for three years). The subsidies were gradually phased out into the country's general social and national insurance systems (including unemployment benefits). Immigrants were also eligible for subsidised loans to buy their own houses.

The two strategies differ substantially in the role which they assign to the public sector. The latter was dominant in designing, executing and micro-managing the absorption of immigrants in the 1950s. Public agencies also carried out the construction works, first through the construction division in the Ministry of Public Works, then through the Ministry of Housing. 75 per cent of the housing units built during 1951–1961 were built by public agencies (Newman 2000). The Development Towns were established on public land and the government provided for all infrastructural work, planning, zoning, etc.[13]

The role of the public sector in the 1990s became a focus of heated political controversy in Israel. One camp, the '*housing first*' camp (led by Ariel Sharon, then Minister of Construction and Housing) argued that most, if not all, public investment should be diverted to secure an adequate supply of new houses. The '*economy first*' camp (led by Modaii, the Minister of Finance) maintained that immigrants needed jobs more than new houses, and public investments should be designed to create job opportunities: once incomes were generated, private developers would smoothly solve the housing problem. The 'housing first' camp won the day, and its strategy consisted of two programmes: one to be executed directly by the government, and another to be carried out by private real estate developers, supported by a wide range of incentives and subsidies. The government programme consisted of two components: temporary reception caravans (27,000 units) and the construction of 12,000 permanent, low-priced and small (45–60 sq. m) housing units).[14]

Israel's experiences with centralised and semi-free market approaches produced mixed results. The former were associated with severe housing shortages over a long period of time. Little attention was paid to the issue of quality, which proved to be expensive in the long-run. The new Development Towns were artificial creations and remained (until the new waves of immigrants in the 1990s) below the threshold needed to allow them to thrive economically, socially and culturally. They became (ethnically and socially) segregated ghettos with high unemployment and deteriorating environments. In contrast, the building programme carried out by private developers in the 1990s was relatively successful, unlike the public programme (caravans and emergency low-priced houses). It is thought that since potential buyers were not limited to new immigrants, high quality was maintained in order to attract buyers. However, the 'obsession' with housing first, at the expense of wider public investment to create jobs, was unfortunate. As Alterman (2002: 110) points out, the policy choice was politically motivated: it is far easier for politicians to build houses than to stimulate the economy and create new jobs.[15]

The right choice will depend on the conditions under which the economy operates. The 'free market' absorption strategy adopted by Israel in the 1990s would probably have been inapplicable in the 1950s. This is partly due to the substantial differences in the qualifications of the immigrants and in the resources which they brought with them, and partly due to the dramatic shifts in the Israeli economy and its ability to respond to market signals. However, even under the so-called free market model the public sector has played a significant role in the absorption process, either via the initial 'absorption package', or via a wide range of subsidies for housing and job creation (e.g. Eckstein and Weiss 2001).

It is probably fair to argue that, while current overall economic conditions in the WBGS are close to those which existed in Israel in the 1950s, construction skills, building techniques and financial resources are much superior. Thus the WBGS would be in a position to avoid the basic construction and quality flaws which accompanied Israel's massive housing programmes of the 1950s. Temporary, fast and 'cheap' solutions, including temporary 'returnee camps', should be avoided, not only because they are more expensive in the long-run but also because of the Palestinians' traumatic experience of 'temporary' camps, and because the first thing the returnees should get rid of is the mind set of refugeehood and temporariness.

The socio-economic and environmental implications of housing policy are just as important as the physical aspects. Although the returnees will probably have poor qualifications like the immigrants to Israel in the 1950s, they will be much younger, with a common language and with far less divergent cultural backgrounds. However, it will be just as important to avoid establishing 'ghettos' for returnees from specific places or for specific social groups. The new Palestinian state should also be in a position to avoid the creation of new artificial and non-viable urban centres, since its absorption policy will not be guided by strategic and ideological considerations as Israel's was.

The real challenge in designing and implementing a successful absorption policy will be in striking a balance between stimulating the returnees' (as well as the veterans') own initiatives to create foundations for their new lives on the one hand, and establishing efficient public institutions to trigger, aid, facilitate and sustain these initiatives. Absorption, especially in the case of the Palestinian refugees, should precisely mean breaking the vicious circle of dependency, temporariness and hand-outs. This implies, among other things, that the 'one absorption basket fits all' model should be avoided in favour of a 'multiple baskets' approach which takes into account the resources and the particular needs of each segment of returnees and veterans.

As pointed out earlier, the role of the public sector in absorption and reconstruction will need to be significant, especially under the current conditions of the Palestinian economy. However, it is important to emphasise that the government should not take upon itself direct involvement in spheres where the private sector can do better. An indirect approach, via financial arrangements to support private initiatives, would probably be more appropriate. We envisage, in particular, a set of financial arrangements which would answer the basic needs of the impoverished population, including the returnees, for a limited period of time. A comprehensive system of subsidised mortgage credit should be put in place, to be partly financed, perhaps, from the proceeds of selling the houses in the settlements. A parallel system of easy credit to support small and medium size enterprises and to provide liquidity for entrepreneurs and real estate developers will also be needed. Along with providing and improving the basic infrastructure in the existing camps and in the WBGS in general, the public sector should be ready to step in to ease any bottlenecks in the process, especially with regard to large-scale investment for upgrading human capital and vocational education and training.

Concluding remarks

We started the chapter with a survey of the literature on the issue of compensation, and concluded that the main body of compensation to the Palestinians may best be determined on the basis of a forward-looking approach which links it with the cost of absorbing the returnees in a viable and growing economy in the WBGS. We then surveyed the Palestinian population and the geographic distribution of the refugees, to arrive at an estimate of the number of potential returnees to the WBGS, and presented a framework for analysing the relocation decisions of individual households. We then presented a macroeconomic model through which the costs of establishing a thriving West Bank economy, absorbing various possible numbers of returnees there, and raising living standards in the Gaza Strip into line with those in the West Bank were estimated. Finally, the chapter discussed some policy options with regard to concrete strategies of absorption and economic reconstruction.

The exercise which we developed deals mainly with the limitations of the WBGS's absorptive capacity and tries to assess the restrictions on the ability of the Palestinian state to accommodate the returnees. The main conclusion, we argue, is that a solution to the problem of the Palestinian refugees along the lines discussed is feasible economically: under reasonable assumptions the return of the refugees can be economically as well as politically beneficial. The costs of absorption will be less painful the longer the period of implementation, and the lower the uncertainties related to the number and schedule of the returnees. The strategic decisions taken by the private and public sectors, as well those taken by the parties to the peace agreements and the international community will be crucial.

The forward-looking approach to refugee compensation is superior in many ways to the backward-looking approach based on evaluation of lost assets. However, there are real issues of historic justice and intolerable personal suffering which cannot be ignored and which should be addressed in order to heal the wounds and allow reconciliation. This would necessitate some form of personal compensation parallel with the collective fund. Israel's commitment to finance the individual compensation fund and the reconstruction and absorption fund (which is the main concern of this chapter) is a precondition for the healing process and for creating the foundation of a lasting settlement. Israel's payments, which would surely be augmented by international contributions, could incorporate certain concessions, whether with respect to labour or trade flows. They could also incorporate in-kind compensation, in the form of buildings and infrastructure currently in the Israeli settlements in the WBGS.

Finally, a word of caution. The exercise carried out in this chapter is limited and it does not cover all the aspects which should be taken into account in a comprehensive arrangement. We have not considered specifically the rehabilitation of refugees, whether within camps or outside, in the WBGS or elsewhere. More importantly, our macroeconomic framework is subject to a number of limitations: it is based heavily on the past and does not incorporate dynamic changes in behaviour of the kind that might be expected in the new situation, and it does not take into account all of the uncertainties involved. However, our main interest was to introduce an analytical framework for dealing with the issue of compensation, rather than to provide a precise estimation of the amount of compensation, and the model demonstrates the feasibility of the resettlement and absorption of the refugees.

Notes

1 The most important of these schemes was proposed in 1949 during the Lausanne conference where a figure of 200,000–300,000 refugees to be repatriated was discussed. Israel initially agreed to repatriate 100,000, but not to their original places of residence.

2 Gabbay (1959: 342). The team of experts which carried out the assessment was called the Refugee Office. The Refugee Office was appointed by the UNCCP in May 1951 to 'make such arrangements as it may consider necessary for the assessment and payment of compensation', in accordance with UN Resolution 394 V, December 1950.

3 The information about the evaluation is taken from Refugee Office: the 10th Progress Report of the UNCCP, A/1985, 1951, which is cited in Gabbay (1959, Chapter 7).

4 Kubursi (1988) utilised two different approaches to estimate material losses, an aggregate approach based on capitalisation of the national income in Palestine in the mid 1940s, and another approach based on detailed itemisation and valuation of different types of assets. The two approaches led to reasonably comparable results.

5 Kubursi (2001a) also estimated a third category of losses, following the approaches adopted in the German reparation schemes for world Jewry: compensation for psychological damage and pain. He put the figure for such losses at about £220 million (in mid 1940s prices). This brings total losses of physical assets and human capital and psychological damage of the 1948 Palestinian refugees to the staggering total of £1,395 million. Assuming an annual 4 per cent interest rate, and deflating with the US price index, Kubursi arrived at a total value of $327bn (in year 2000 prices).

6 The huge gap between various estimates is not totally due to alternative data sets. Kubursi (1988: 186) maintained that 'we used the UN data base, presumably the same that their assessors used to reach a different valuation. We were unable to find a vector of prices that is consistent with the UN estimate'. Also, 'What is surprising about this discrepancy is the fact that we have used exactly the same UN data that should have formed the basis for [the UNCCP's] valuation' (Kubursi 2001a: 246).

7 The jargon of the Palestine–Israel conflict distinguishes between two categories of Palestine refugees; *refugees* and *displaced*. The *displaced* refers to the indigenous inhabitants of the WBGS who left their residence following the Israeli occupation in 1967 (mainly to East Jordan, but also to Syria and Egypt). The number of the 1967 displaced persons is even less certain than that of the 1948 refugees, because the 1967 exodus also included people who were originally refugees (from the 1948 war) in the WBGS. Estimates of the

displaced (i.e. 'first-time' refugees in 1967) range between 180,000 and 240,000 persons. All the refugee data present in this chapter exclude the displaced persons.

8 Zureik (1996) pointed out that four main categories of Palestinian refugees are not registered by the UNRWA: those who moved to areas outside UNRWA's work fields, the Bedouins, the middle class Palestinians who are not in 'need' and the descendants of Palestinian women who married non-refugees. He estimated those to be 300,000 persons in the mid 1990s. Another reference argues that it is likely that as many as 12 per cent of what the UNRWA would define as 1948 refugees may never have registered with the agency (Schiff 1995: 24).

9 Arzt (1997: 60) estimated the total number of Palestinians to be 6.376 million in 1996. With annual growth of 3.2 per cent the figure would be about 8 million by 2001.

10 A number of different quantitative studies have made such a distinction between the West Bank and Gaza. See for example UNCTAD (1994).

11 The model draws heavily on Arnon and Gottlieb (1996) and Arnon *et al.* (1997).

12 Alternative assumptions, i.e. faster or slower adjustment, did not result in significant changes in the basic calculations.

13 Gabbay (1959: 362) points out that 'Of the 370 new Jewish settlements established between 1948–1953, 350 were set up on abandonees' property'.

14 Alterman (2002: 99). The government anticipated a repetition of the experience of the 1950s and was planning to import 60,000 'caravans' to be used as temporary arrangements. The actual number of immigrants turned out to be much smaller and only 27,000 caravans were made available. The incentive package to real estate developers consisted of five elements: free public land, subsidy for infrastructural works, bonuses for fast building, freedom to sell to all buyers, and finally (most importantly) a buy-up commitment – a guarantee to purchase 50 per cent of the units at a price of $80,000 per unit. Furthermore, to encourage the rental market, a 10 per cent tax reduction on income generated from house rents was adopted.

15 The government was obliged to buy up some 40,000 housing units from private developers. Alterman (2002: 110) argues that actually there was no over-supply of houses in the market: many immigrants were merely postponing the decision to buy a house until they had settled the issue of whether work could be found and where.

References

Abdullah, G. (2002) 'A review of the status of Palestinian refugees in Lebanon': http://www.hearpalestine.org/reports (accessed 22 November 2002).

Abed, G. (1990) *The Economic Viability of a Palestine State*, Washington: Institute for Palestine Studies.

Alpher, J. and Al-Shikaki, K. (1998) *The Palestinian Refugee Problem and the Right of Return*, Weatherhead Centre for International Affairs: Harvard University Press.

Alterman, R. (2002) *Planning in the Face of Crisis – Land Use, Housing and Mass Immigration in Israel*, London: Routledge.

Arnon, A. and Gottlieb, D. (1996) 'An analysis of the Palestinian Economy: the West Bank and the Gaza Strip, 1968–1991', *Bank of Israel Review* 69: 44–70.

Arnon, A., Spivak, A., Weinblatt, J. and Luski, I. (1997) *The Palestinian Economy:*

Between Imposed Integration and Voluntary Separation, Leiden: Brill Publications.

Arzt, D. (1997) *Refugees Into Citizens – Palestinians and the End of the Arab-Israeli Conflict*, Washington: Council on Foreign Relations.

BADIL (1999) 'The impact of return on compensation for Palestinian refugees', workshop on compensation as part of a comprehensive solution to the Palestinian refugee problem. Ottawa, July 14–15, http://www.arts.mcgill.ca/mepp/prrn/badil.html (accessed 12 February 2003).

Benvenisti, E. (1999) 'Principles and procedures for compensating refugees: International legal perspectives', workshop on compensation as part of a comprehensive solution to the Palestinian refugee problem. Ottawa, July 14–15, http://www.arts.mcgill.ca/mepp/prrn/benvenisti.html (accessed 12 February 2003).

Brynen, R. (1997) 'Imagining a solution: final status arrangements and Palestinian refugees in Lebanon', http://www.arts.mcgill.ca/mepp/prrn/papers/brynen2.html (accessed 12 February 2003).

Brynen, R. (1999) 'Financing Palestinian refugee compensation', workshop on compensation as part of a comprehensive solution to the Palestinian refugee problem. Ottawa, July 14–15, http://www.arts.mcgill.ca/mepp/prrn/brynen.html (accessed 12 February 2003).

Eckstein, Z. and Weiss, Y. (2001) 'Integrating immigrants from the former Soviet Union into the Israeli labour market', in A. Ben Bassat (ed.) *The Israeli Economy, 1985–1998: From Government Intervention to Market Economics*, Israel: Am Oved (in Hebrew). Also Cambridge, Massachusetts: MIT Press (in English).

Gabbay, R. (1959) *A Political Study of the Arab–Jewish Conflict*, thesis no. 117, Librairie Dooz, Geneva.

Gazit, S. (1995) *The Palestinian Refugee Problem*, Tel Aviv: Jaffee Centre for Strategic Studies.

Harvard Project on Palestinian Refugees (HPPR) (1998) Project on Palestinian refugees at Harvard University – summary report (eds G. Borjas and D. Rodrik). Mimeo, Harvard University.

Heller, M. (1983) *A Palestinian State: The Implications for Israel*, Cambridge: Harvard University Press.

Khalidi, R. (1994) 'Toward a solution', in *Palestinian Refugees: Their Problem and Future*, Washington: Centre for Policy Analysis on Palestine.

Khawaja, M. and Tiltnes, Å. (eds) (2002) *On the Margins: Migration and Living Conditions of Palestinian Camp Refugees in Jordan*', FAFO Report 357, Centraltrykkeriet, Norway.

Kubursi, A. (1988) 'An economic assessment of total Palestinian losses', in S. Hadawi (ed.) *Palestinian Rights and Losses in 1948*, London: Saqi Books.

Kubursi, A. (2001a) 'Valuing Palestinian losses in today's dollars', in *Palestinian Refugees – The Right of Return*' (ed. N. Aruri), London: Pluto Press.

Kubursi, A. (2001b) 'Palestinian losses in 1948: calculating refugees compensation', Centre for Policy Analysis on Palestine, information brief, no. 81. August, http://www.Palestinecenter.org (accessed 19 December 2002).

Newman, D. (2000) 'Palestinian refugee resettlement – learning from the Israeli development town and mass immigration experience of the 1950s and 1990s', Palestinian Refugee Research Net, http://www.arts.mcgill.ca/mepp/prrn/newman.html (accessed 25 June 2003).

PCBS (1999a) *Population Projections – Main Indicators*, http://www.pcbs.org/english/populati/proj_mai.htm (accessed 3 June 2003).

PCBS (1999b) *Labour Force & Employment Statistics*, http://www.pcbs.org/english/press_r/lab_pres.htm (accessed 3 June 2003).

PCBS (2001) *Estimates of Palestinian Population in Diaspora by Place of Residence*, http://www.pcbs.org/english/abs_pal/abs_pal3/tab01.htm (accessed 3 June 2003).

Sagi, N. (1980) *German Reparations – A History of the Negotiations*, Jerusalem: The Hebrew University, Magnes Press.

Sayigh, Y. (1967) *The Israeli Economy*, Beirut: PLO Research Centre (in Arabic).

Schiff, B.N. (1995) *Refugees Unto the Third Generation: UN Aid to Palestinians*, New York: Syracuse University Press.

Tuma, E. and Darin-Drabkin, H. (1978) *The Economic Case for Palestine*, London: Croom Helm.

Ugland, O. (ed.) (2003) *Difficult Past, Uncertain Future – Living Conditions Among Palestinian Refugees in Camps and Gatherings in Lebanon*, FAFO Report 409, Centraltrykkeriet, Norway.

UNCTAD (1994) *Prospects for Sustained Development of the Palestinian Economy in the West Bank and Gaza Strip, 1990–2010: A Quantitative Framework*, Geneva: UNCTAD.

UNRWA (2001) *UNRWA in Figures*, Gaza: Public Information Office, UNRWA Headquarters.

UNRWA (2003) *Frequently Asked Questions*, http://www.un.org/unrwa/overview/qa.html (accessed 25 June 2003).

Workshop (1999) Workshop report on compensation as part of a comprehensive solution to the Palestinian refugee problem. Ottawa, July 14–15, http://www.arts.mcgill.ca/mepp/prrn/prcomp3.html (accessed 12 February 2003).

World Bank (2002) *Long Term Policy Options for the Palestinian Economy*, World Bank: West Bank and Gaza Office.

World Bank (1999/2000 and 2001/2002). *World Development Report*, http://publications.worldbank.org (accessed 3 June 2003).

Zureik, E. (1996) *Palestinian Refugees and the Peace Process*, Washington: Institute for Palestine Studies.

Zweig, R. (1987) *German Reparations and Jewish World – A History of the Claim Conference*, Boulder: Westview.

Discussion

Osama Hamed

In their chapter, Arie Arnon and Nu'man Kanafani propose a macroeconomic approach that links compensation for Palestinian refugees to the cost of capital imports needed for building a viable Palestinian state and absorbing some of the refugees in this state. The chapter estimates the cost in three steps. In the first step, the chapter estimates the present value of capital imports needed to enable the West Bank GDP to grow at an average annual rate of 3.1 per cent over a 20 year period without taking into consideration the absorption of refugees. The estimates range between $8bn and $10.6bn. In the second step, the chapter estimates the present value of capital imports needed to absorb Palestinian refugees in the West Bank economy under different scenarios regarding the number of the absorbed refugees, the timing of their return, and the degree of integration between Palestinian and Israeli labour markets. These estimates range between $4.4bn (assuming half a million returnees over five years and a high degree of labour market integration) and $12.8bn (assuming one million returnees over two years and relatively low labour market integration). In the third step, the chapter estimates the present value of capital imports needed to improve the standards of living in the Gaza Strip to levels comparable with those in the West Bank, at between $24bn and $27bn.

The chapter is an important contribution to the debate about Palestinian refugee compensation. A genuine two-state solution to the Palestinian–Israeli conflict will very likely require substantial investment aimed at improving the standards of living of residents of WBGS refugee camps and the absorption of some of the diaspora refugees in the Palestinian state. The chapter provides us with an estimate of the cost of such investments and argues for using the estimate as a basis for providing financial compensation for Palestinian refugees. The macroeconomic approach developed in this chapter, however, provides compensation for only a fraction of Palestinian refugees. The chapter acknowledges this limitation and proposes using the macroeconomic approach in conjunction with other compensation schemes but does not suggest a specific mechanism for doing so. One way to extend the macroeconomic approach to cover the refugees not absorbed by the Palestinian state or resettled in Israel proper is to offer each of these refugees a financial compensation package equal in value to the absorption cost per capita estimated by the macroeconomic approach.

Financial compensation will no doubt be an important element of any settlement package for the Palestinian refugee question within the framework of a two-state solution. However, it is unrealistic to assume that it could constitute the whole package. To have a closure on the refugee question, the Palestinian refugees and the Palestinian public at large should be made to feel that the settlement package brings a certain degree of justice. To accomplish this, the refugee settlement package should include an official Israeli acceptance of historical responsibility for the displacement of Palestinian refugees. Such acceptance is essential to the healing process and to having a rational debate about pragmatic solutions to the Palestinian refugee question. The settlement package should also allow some Palestinian refugees to be resettled in Israel proper and should call for the handing over of Israeli settlements in the WBGS to the Palestinian state to be used for housing refugees. The most likely outcome of negotiations over the refugee question will probably allow only a limited number of Palestinian refugees to be resettled in Israel proper. The contribution of Israeli settlements in the WBGS can potentially be more substantial. The chapter acknowledges some role for Israeli settlements in resolving the refugee question when it refers to incorporating 'in-kind compensation, in the form of buildings and infrastructure currently in the Israeli settlements in the WBGS' as part of Israel's contribution to the refugee compensation fund. However, the chapter does not explore this potentially crucial element of the refugee settlement package in any detail.

Even without including the settlements annexed to Jerusalem, Israeli settlements in the WBGS could potentially house more than a quarter of a million refugees. Including the Jerusalem settlements would increase this figure substantially. The role of Israeli settlements in resolving the refugee question goes beyond their capacity to absorb a large number of refugees. Turning over tangible Israeli assets to Palestinian refugees in exchange for their tangible losses will bring an element of reciprocity to the compensation process that will help create a sense of justice.

Some may argue that handing over Israeli settlements in general, and Jerusalem settlements in particular, would be too traumatic for the Israeli public to accept. However, this is the kind of concession Israel needs to make to create an environment that allows the Palestinian public to overcome the trauma of accepting a permanent political settlement that effectively gives away the right of return.

Discussion

Athar Hussain

The chapter is ambitious in broaching the thorny issue of the resettlement of Palestinian refugees and is productive in proposing a solution that avoids the pitfalls of alternative proposals. The valuable contribution of this work is the quantitative framework it employs for estimating the compensation. In reaching the preferred option for compensation the authors observe the following guidelines:

- Mass return of refugees to the places of origin, now located in Israel, is impossible because it is impractical and will be rejected by Israel.
- Retrospective compensation based on the value of property left behind by refugees is infeasible because of the lack of generally agreed and verifiable estimates of the property left behind.
- The solution of the refugee problem should be linked to the establishment of a viable Palestinian state.
- The right of return should be interpreted as the right of Palestinian refugees outside the West Bank and Gaza Strip (WBGS) to settle there.

The authors' preferred option links the compensation to the costs of resettling the refugees in the Palestinian state comprising WBGS and securing the economic viability of the state. The implication is that for the most part the compensation will not paid to individuals and the bulk of it would be spent on public and community projects, budget support and also on housing. Israel provides a rich case for the study of problems in absorbing migrants and policy options.

Excluding the Introduction the chapter has four sections. The second part provides the background for the presentation of the authors' preferred approach to the compensation for the Palestinian refugees in the form of a review of three alternative schemes. Regardless of the particular scheme, compensation raises the questions of, first, who is a Palestinian refugee and, second, their total number. These questions are answered in the next section, which outlines the issues in defining a refugee and presents the distribution of the Palestinian population in Jordan, Syria and the Lebanon, the countries where the refugees are concentrated. The chapter then presents, in non-technical terms, the macroeconomic framework used to estimate the cost of creating a viable economy in the WBGS, including the resettlement of refugees. Estimates are presented with reference to five scenarios with different assumptions concerning the numbers and timing of returnees and the flow of Palestinian labour to Israel. It is assumed that all returnees will be resettled in the West Bank, which, as a result, will receive all the investment linked to the resettlement of returnees. To ensure the per capita income in the Gaza Strip, which is comparatively low, does not lag further behind that in the West Bank, the authors' cost estimate also includes expenditure aimed at reducing the income gap between the two parts.

The approach to the compensation proposed in the chapter makes a lot of economic sense and is not encumbered by the divisive baggage of history, which threatens to undermine any compensation package. The problem, however, is that history weighs heavily on the present and cannot be completely screened out. The refugee camps are reminders of the history and justice is the link between compensation and history as perceived by the Palestinian population, the refugees in particular. That perception cannot be erased, which raises the question of how can it be held back so as not to scuttle the compensation scheme proposed in the chapter. The likely answer is that the Palestinian state emerging out of a political solution has to hold sufficient promise for the Palestinian population so as to override the grievances of the past. The authors acknowledge that the issue of justice, although highly contentious, cannot be cast aside and may necessitate a supplementary gesture to provide compensation to individuals for the property they left behind. In order to be feasible such compensation will have to be a gesture of goodwill and reconciliation and not linked to the claims of lost property. A lump sum per person or household would seem to be appropriate.

Compensation raises a number of other issues. The first, which is already implicitly dealt with by the choice of the preferred compensation scheme, is who receives the compensation and benefits from it. The authors work in terms of the binary division of the recipients and beneficiaries being either individuals or a collective agency, such as the Palestinian government. Individuals are the recipients and beneficiaries when the compensation is linked to the loss of individual property. The authors assume that the recipient and, implicitly also, the beneficiary is the Palestinian state when the compensation takes the form proposed in the chapter. Although the government is always the recipient of funds, the beneficiaries may be individuals or households depending on how funds are used, for example for building homes. The difference between the two points to the need for a mechanism for the allocation of funds that is seen as equitable, and leads on to the issue of the refugees who would qualify for assisted settlement.

A crucial issue is who will finance the compensation. The authors assume that sources of funds would number two: first, the international community, meaning largely the US, the EU, richer Arab states and, second, Israel. The contribution from the former may be regarded as an enlightened investment in international peace. But Israel's contribution would have a special significance because it is seen by the Palestinians as the cause of their exile and suffering. The implication is that Israel's contribution has to carry a gesture of reconciliation. In its long-term interest Israel is advised by the authors to be generous in vacating Jewish settlements in WBGS and in allowing Palestinians to work in Israel. Further, Israel should be the principal source of funds for individual compensation, which the authors see as a general acknowledgement of the wrongs in the past. The question is whether the international community would provide enough assistance to solve the problem of Palestinian refugees entirely. A point not considered in the chapter is that the return of refugees and the eventual disappearance of the refugee camps is not only important for the Palestinians, and indirectly for Israel, but also for the Lebanon, Syria and Jordan. The chapter rightly assumes that the decision whether or not to return will rest with the refugees, which would be influenced by both the 'push' and 'pull' factors. A likely possibility that needs to be considered is when the push and pull factors do not lead to the return of all refugees. This raises the thorny issue of what happens to those refugees who choose not to return. This issue will be a major concern to the countries that house Palestinian refugee camps. The implication is that the solution of the refugee problem has to cover not only the return of refugees to WBGS but also the future status of refugees who do not return.

A final issue is who is a Palestinian refugee? The definition of a Palestinian refugee is clouded by the passage of time and successive waves of exodus. The difficulty is compounded by four factors. The Palestinian population is spread over many countries. Second, with the passage of time a significant number of Palestinians have married non-Palestinians. As a result, many Palestinian households are mixed, which raises the issue of how non-Palestinians are to be treated. Third, a significant percentage of the Palestinians in the neighbouring Arab countries are integrated with the local population and no longer live in refugee camps. Fourth, as yet there has been no comprehensive census or even a sample survey of the population; and the number of Palestinian refugees is a sensitive political issue for the Palestinian organisations, Israel and for the host countries. For the purposes of calculation, the authors use the restrictive UNRWA definition of refugee. That is, a person whose 'normal place of residence was Mandatory Palestine and who lost both home and means of livelihood as a result of the 1948 conflict and was registered as a refugee'. Only those who resided in UNRWA's fields of operations (WBGS, Jordan, Lebanon and Syria) were registered. Current UNRWA records also include the descendants of fathers who satisfy the conditions. The

UNRWA definition, as pointed out by the authors, is highly restrictive but it offers two advantages: first, it leads to a precise and easily verifiable estimate of the number of refugees and, second, it includes the most disadvantaged section of the Palestinian diaspora. The UNRWA definition may be suitable in determining the population in need of assisted resettlement; but it is too restrictive for specifying the people with the right of return to a would be Palestinian state.

A work such as this begs the question of relevance when the date of creation of a Palestinian state and its territorial boundaries are uncertain. The chapter does not address an immediate problem, but its value lies in providing a framework for thinking about an issue that will have to be resolved if and when a Palestinian state, acceptable to both the Palestinian population and Israel, is created.

11 Incomplete contracts, the port of Gaza and the case for economic sovereignty

Arie Arnon, Avia Spivak and Oren Sussman[1]

Introduction

The basic dilemma concerning economic relations between Israel and a (future) Palestinian state is the extent to which the two units should be economically integrated (or separated). On the one hand, it is argued that integration would generate more gains from trade, facilitate economic growth and maximise the peace dividend. On the other hand, it is argued that Israeli occupation has undermined economic development in the West Bank and the Gaza Strip, and that some separation is needed in order to turn things around. The former is sometimes considered as the economic approach, while the latter is sometimes described as an 'alternative' approach, which puts politics before economics. Indeed, as we shall see below, at least in some cases the international development agencies have used the 'economic argument' in order to advocate more economic integration.

At the heart of the debate lies the notion of *economic sovereignty*: the view that countries should have sovereign power over their vital interests, in particular strategic assets like ports, power stations, telecommunication systems and maybe some key industries. Indeed, most economists are hostile to the notion of economic sovereignty, believing that it serves a nationalistic, rather than an economic, purpose. Some might even argue that traditional economic theory cannot accommodate the notion of economic sovereignty: scarce resources should be allocated according to comparative advantage rather than some perceived strategic value.

The purpose of this short note is to point out that modern economic theory does not rule out a priori the notion of economic sovereignty (although it certainly does not argue that every asset is strategic and that countries should be autarchic with respect to every industry). Essentially, we argue that the notion of economic sovereignty is isomorphic to that of private property. It is well understood by now that firms may be forced to own and control certain assets rather than buy the services from external suppliers. This is because they cannot write down complete contracts that would protect them against opportunistic behaviour by these suppliers.[2]

Clearly, sovereign parties face even greater difficulties when they try to protect vital interests by way of a contract.

We use the port of Gaza as a leading example, although we believe that the argument is applicable more broadly. From the very beginning of the Oslo peace process,[3] the Palestinians considered a port in the city of Gaza to be an economic interest of vital importance. Most of the economists involved in the peace process considered such a port an extravagant symbol of national sovereignty which a poor Palestine could ill afford. It was argued that since ports are prone to significant scale economies, and since the nearby Israeli port of Ashdod still had excess capacity, buying services from Israel would prove more cost-effective.

In our view, this argument was based on narrow technological considerations and ignored the strategic issues that arise when contracts are incomplete. We construct a simple theoretical example where investment in strategic assets may actually facilitate, rather than impede, trade among nations. To understand why, suppose that the peace dividend is generated by a Palestinian development project that yields some exportable goods. Hence, the project is strongly complemented by a service generated by a specific asset, a port through which the goods are shipped to foreign markets. Now suppose that the Israeli port of Ashdod has excess capacity (even if it was operating at full capacity, due to significant scale economies in the technology of operating harbours it would be cheaper to expand capacity in Ashdod rather than construct a new port in Gaza). Hence, in a first-best world the parties may benefit from trading port services.

Note, however, that such a trade presupposes the ability to contract upon, and enforce, the 'access fee' to the port. Suppose, to the contrary, that contracts are incomplete or un-enforceable. In that case, the access price will be determined according to the *ex post* bargaining power of the parties. Possibly, that price will fail to compensate the home country for the sunk cost of its investment in the development project. If that is foreseen in advance, the whole deal will fall apart and the potential peace dividend will never materialise. In such a world, the only remedy may be to locate another port within the sovereign territory of Palestine. Obviously, such a solution will decrease the peace dividend; however, a decreased peace dividend may be better than no peace dividend. One practical implication from our analysis is that accounting-based rates of return on the port will fail to capture its social welfare. We highlight this result by the following argument: a port in Gaza may stand idle as Palestinian exporters use cheap port services in Israel; a Gaza port is nevertheless essential in preventing Israel from behaving opportunistically and charging fees that drive the *ex post* rate of return on the development project down to zero.

Our analysis is an application of the property-rights incomplete-contracts literature. It is interesting to note, however, that while Hart (1995) emphasises the 'under-investment' result, ours is an over-investment result: second-best investment is higher than first-best investment.

In that respect, our result is closer to the 'strategic excess capacity' result, derived in the context of international trade; see Tirole (1988). It is also interesting to note the relation of our analysis to the sovereign-debt literature; see Eaton and Fernandez (1995). Note, however, that the latter literature emphasises that sovereignty is an obstacle to trade, because it weakens enforcement. While we agree with this observation, we point out that, given that the parties are sovereign and enforcement is already weak, strengthening the sovereign position of the weaker party may balance the relationship and thus ease, rather than disrupt, trade among nations.

This chapter is organised as follows: more details on the Oslo Declaration of Principles (DOP) and on the Gaza port decision can be found in the next section. We then provide a very simple example indicating that a Gaza port might have made sense. A brief conclusion follows.

Some history of the Gaza port

The Gaza port is already mentioned in the DoP signed first in Oslo and then in Washington on 13 September 1993. The economic section of the declaration states that there will be 'co-operation in the field of transport and communications, including a Program, which will define guidelines for the establishment of a Gaza Sea Port Area'.[4] The issue of a port in Gaza receives more detailed attention in the Interim Agreement of 28 September 1995. It is stated that 'plans for the establishment of a port in the Gaza Strip in accordance with the DOP ... will be discussed and agreed upon between Israel and the Council'.[5] To resolve the security issues, it was agreed that ships would have to harbour first in an Israeli port.

However, the Gaza port was never built, partly because of the recommendations of the international development agencies. It is well known that ports are prone to significant economies of scale, which imply, according to standard analysis, that one is better than two. Thus, for example, a report by the Armand Hammer fund calculates that the 'use of [the] Ashdod Port would cost [neighbouring Arab] countries (Jordan and Iraq) at least $7 per ton [i.e. 50 per cent] less than the use of a yet un-built Gaza port' (net of investment required to expand capacity at Ashdod). Indeed, the report states explicitly that the construction of a port in Gaza can be justified only on the grounds of 'non-economic considerations'.[6] More significantly, the World Bank has argued that other infrastructure projects such as roads, water treatment facilities and housing were more urgently needed. This is because:

> the region is presently served by modern facilities in the existing Israeli ports on the Mediterranean coast and the Port of Eilat and the Jordanian Port of Aqaba in the Gulf of Aqaba. Therefore, the economic viability of a new port at Gaza will need to be assessed within the regional context. However, [the report still mentions that] the Palestinians consider the port an essential element.[7]

Unfortunately, this optimistic spirit of cooperation has never materialised. The year 1994 saw some of the worse acts of violence so far in the history of the Israeli–Palestinian conflict, committed by extremists from both sides, a violence that has been escalating ever since. In response, the Israeli government has implemented a policy of closures, preventing Palestinian access to Israeli territory in general, and particularly to the port of Ashdod. The Israeli government has usually argued that the measures are necessary for security reasons, but the Palestinians have always argued that the closures are ineffective security-wise, and are rather a means to penalise the Palestinian civil population, or even worse to pressure it towards renegotiating the Oslo Agreement. As we shall see below, an important aspect of our theoretical argument is that no third party can verify such claims. It is telling, however, that some outsiders found them to be credible.[8] For example, the head of the World Bank delegation to the West Bank and Gaza argued that:

> the Paris Protocol created a de facto customs union. But a union that works presupposes mutual interests, good will and an environment of trust and respect. This environment had eroded over the past two years. Increasingly adversarial relationships between the Palestinian Authority and the Israeli Government put a customs union implementation at risk... Private Israeli–Palestinian trade relations are close and in many cases parties are satisfied. However, when the interests are not identical, the Palestinians have little control. Israeli commercial interests can be advanced either by various traditional obstacles (port delays, claims of failures to meet standards, etc.) or by means of other barriers and costs, which may be intertwined with security or safety procedures. Israel defends its fiscal interests by enforcing limits on Palestinian direct imports, by its control of external market access and its control of all import tax remittances, essential to Palestinian fiscal health.[9]

The model

We now present a simple example that uses incomplete-contract theory to argue that a port in Gaza would make economic sense in a second-best world where inter-state enforcement mechanisms are weak.

The setting

There are two periods: *ex ante* and *ex post*. The real interest rate is assumed to be zero. There are two players: i and p, which we dub 'Israel' and 'Palestine', respectively. *Ex ante*, player p can implement a development project, which costs c *ex ante*, and would yield an output $d>c$ *ex post*. We may think of the development project as either public (e.g. infrastructure, training and education programmes) or private (new business implemented in a decentralised manner with aggregate yield and cost of d and c). We also assume that the output of the project is an export commodity so that realising the income is contingent upon accessing foreign markets. We interpret $(d-c)$ as a 'peace dividend'.

To reach the international markets, player p must access a harbour from where the goods can be shipped abroad. Now suppose that player i has a harbour which is in excess capacity. For simplicity, the existing capacity of i's harbour is sufficient to accommodate all of p's exports at a shadow-price of zero. More specifically, we assume that player p can access i's port at a zero marginal cost, without any additional investment in infrastructure. In contrast, it is costly for player p to construct its own harbour: we assume that the fixed cost of a new harbour is k; the marginal cost of exporting goods via the new harbour is assumed to be zero. Obviously, in a first-best world, investing in a new harbour is wasteful. However, we assume that the surplus generated by the project is large enough to cover the cost of constructing a harbour, namely:

$$d-c-k>0. \tag{1}$$

We also assume that there is a production lag in the construction of the harbour: it has to be built *ex ante* so as to be operational *ex post* when the project comes on stream.

Clearly, p's access to i's port needs to be guaranteed by way of a contract at the time that the investment decision is made. However, contracts are valid only to the extent that they can be enforced. Obviously, international transactions are notorious for the weakness of their enforcement mechanisms, and we assume that no contractual obligation is enforceable internationally. However, we assume that the international community can punish any action of one player against the territory of the other. We discuss this assumption further later in the chapter.

Our last assumption is that player i has all the bargaining power both *ex ante* and *ex post*. This assumption is made for simplicity: the result will not change qualitatively if we allocate the bargaining power more evenly. As it happens, the assumption is not at odds with the Israeli–Palestinian reality.

First-best

It has already been noted that there is no first-best rationale for player p to construct a harbour in its own territory. Therefore, the only purpose of the present sub-section is to explain what contracts and enforcement mechanisms are required to support the first-best outcome. Hence, assume for the time being that everything is contractible and enforceable. We shall argue that this assumption is not very realistic, for it assumes a powerful and well-informed enforcement agency, a counterfactual.

The first-best contract contains an access price t^*, at which player p may export its goods via player i's harbour. Under the assumption that i has all the bargaining power, t^* is trivial to compute:

$$t^* = Min(d - c, k) = k. \quad (2)$$

That is, player i uses his bargaining power to extract all the surplus from the transaction, subject to the constraint that player p cannot be charged more than the cost of constructing its own harbour. Using equation (1) we get that the second constraint is binding.

Obviously, the contract should require that while player p crosses i's territory it obeys i's traffic laws, its pollution standards and safety requirements, as well as abstaining from any criminal activity. If not, player i may use its sovereign power to stop player p from accessing the harbour. These conditions may seem technical, but they are not. *Ex post*, player i will try to behave opportunistically, and renegotiate the access price t upwards. Since c is already a sunk-cost, and since the option of building a harbour is no longer available, there is nothing that prevents player i from renegotiating the access price up to d.[10] The practical way to do this is by using the 'law abiding' clauses in the contract as an excuse for stopping player p from crossing i's territory to access the harbour. Note that even if there exists an international agency that is responsible for enforcing the contract, it is unlikely to be able to establish whether denying access is strategic or justifiable under the law-abiding clauses. In the language of the incomplete-contracts literature, player p's conduct within player i's territory is 'observable but not verifiable'.

Second-best

It is quite obvious that once player p foresees that player i would behave opportunistically and will expropriate the peace dividend, it will not invest in the development project. But it is quite obvious that had player p been allowed to construct its own harbour, it would collect a surplus of:

$$d - c - k > 0.$$

Hence, building its own port, though first-best wasteful, is second-best welfare enhancing, supporting international trade between player p and the rest of the world.

Three points are worthy of some elaboration. First, note that it is likely that the port will lose money. The reason is the following: suppose that player p supplies port-services to its own citizens at some fee $t_p > 0$. Whatever this fee is, player i would have an incentive to undercut it. This is because its own harbour is in excess capacity; at a zero marginal cost, it is profitable to expand traffic at any positive price. The exact equilibrium price depends on how we model the oligopolistic competition among the two players. Let us note that under the plausible assumption of Bertrand competition, the equilibrium fee t_p* would be zero. Thus, from an accounting point of view the harbour is a pure waste of money. Hence, standard net-present-value rules for evaluating investment projects may not be valid for strategic assets in a second-best world. In our setting, the value of the harbour is not captured by the cash-flow that it (does not) generate, but rather by the fact that it prevents player *i* from behaving opportunistically. Without such a guarantee, player *p* cannot implement its development project.

Second, comparing the first- and the second-best, it is easy to see that player *p*'s profits are the same. Hence, the whole dead-weight loss, *k*, resulting from the contractual imperfection falls on player *i*. If player *i* could pre-commit itself not to behave opportunistically towards player *p*, it could collect the amount that player *p* spends (in the second-best world) on constructing the harbour. Also, comparing the 'no project' state with the second-best, it is easy to see that player *i* has no share in the peace dividend, and is thus indifferent to whether the development project is implemented or not. It is easy, however, to amend the example giving player *i* some bonus in case the development project is implemented. (It can be interpreted as profits of *i*'s suppliers to *p*'s producers while operating the project.) Once that is done, it is actually in *i*'s best interest to allow the construction of a port so as to pre-commit itself not to behave opportunistically and to enable the generation of the peace dividend both for its own and its neighbour's sake.

Third, it is worth noting that the second-best arrangement (trade supported by a strategic asset) works under the crucial assumption that player *i* will not use its military power to block player *p*'s harbour because the international community is able to stop such an action. Why would the international community stop an action of player *i* against the territory of player *p*, but not enforce a contract that allows player *p* access to player *i*'s harbour? The reason is that when player *i* denies access to the harbour, the international community cannot verify whether this action is opportunistic, or whether it is a 'justifiable' response to player *p* breaching the 'law-abiding' condition in the contract. We believe that this is, essentially, what happened in the Israeli–Palestinian case. Israel denied the Palestinians access to Israeli harbours on grounds of defence against terrorism. While terrorism was a fact, it was impossible to establish whether the Israeli steps were genuine, or whether these were opportunistic steps intended to renegotiate the contract.

Conclusions

We have started this chapter by identifying two seemingly conflicting views regarding the desired economic relations between Israel and an independent Palestine: on the one hand, the economic approach that recommends integration so as to maximise the peace dividend; on the other hand, the 'alternative' approach that argues that integration would lead to Israel's continued control of Palestine, which would undermine the latter's economic development (as it has done in the past).

The main purpose of this chapter is to provide a synthesis of the two approaches. We have shown that modern economic theory does not support a priori the view that the optimal level of integration is full integration. In a sense, the analysis implies that one cannot clearly distinguish between the economic and the political aspects of Israeli–Palestinian relations. We have constructed a simple example where allowing Palestine to hold a strategic asset separately from Israel is a necessary condition for the generation of the peace dividend. Investment in the strategic asset is justified even though the actuarial rate of return on the asset is likely to be negative. Hence, a certain amount of separation is actually a necessary condition not just for the political stability of an Israeli–Palestinian peace treaty, but also in order to support international trade between Palestine and the rest of the world.

It is important to emphasise that the analysis is not limited to the port of Gaza alone. Rather, we use the port of Gaza as a leading example that helps to explain what we mean by 'strategic assets'. It is obvious that the port is not unique. The argument would apply immediately to other border points, such as airfields or land exits. Indeed, any asset or policy that may be used by Israel in order to disrupt the normal operation of the Palestinian economy should count as well. For example, internal routes within the Palestinian territory that are used for the delivery of labour, raw materials and finished goods may also be considered strategic. Indeed, we have observed in recent years many cases where such roads were blocked in order to impose internal closures, with enormous damage to the Palestinian economy.

At the same time, it is important to emphasise that our argument is not in favour of autarchy, but rather in favour of trade and cooperation supported by the establishment of sovereign power over strategic assets. It is worth repeating some of the key assumptions. First, strategic assets have some crucial technological properties; most importantly they strongly complement a broad range of economic activity, and they are specific in the sense of not having any close substitute. Second, we deal with parties emerging out of a long and bloody conflict, having no mutual trust, goodwill or reputation on which cooperation could be maintained. Third, the parties are highly asymmetric. It follows from our technological assumptions that while Israel may hold up Palestine, the converse is unlikely. It is only the interaction of the technological and the political factors that makes certain assets strategic in nature.

Lastly, we would like to raise the following question: why should the above analysis be applied to Israel and Palestine, but not to peaceful neighbouring countries in, say, Western Europe? The answer is that our game-theoretic model is well suited to capture the state of conflict within which Israel and Palestine operate. Probably, a more peaceful situation is characterised by some additional factors that would allow the parties to establish a cooperative solution. Some 'social capital' of good will or reputation may be one of these factors. Another may be a web of interwoven interests between individuals within those countries so that a majority of people in both countries lose from breaking down the relations. Analytically, modelling the cooperative solution is probably a more demanding task than modelling the conflict. Unfortunately for Israel and Palestine, we have not yet reached the point where dealing with such an analytical challenge is a matter of practical urgency.

Notes

1 The authors are solely responsible for the views expressed in this chapter, regardless of any institutional affiliation. We would like to thank seminar participants in the St Andrews workshop (29–30 August 2002), particularly David Cobham, Nu'man Kanafani and Jonathan Thomas, for their helpful comments.
2 See Klein *et al.* (1978) and Hart (1995).
3 For more background see Arnon *et al.* (1997).
4 Article 5, Annex III-Protocol.
5 Annex 1, Article XIV, paragraph 4.
6 See Ben-Shahar *et al.* (1989: 141).
7 See World Bank (1993).
8 Arguably, the government sought concessions payable in political rights rather than money, but this bears little effect on the analysis.
9 Dr Joe Saba, the Resident Mission Director of the World Bank in the West Bank and Gaza Strip, in a speech delivered in Nablus on 29 September 1998. Quoted in the *Palestine Economic Pulse* 3: 5, September–October 1998: 4–5.
10 Payment may be extracted in kind, an interpretation that fits better the description in the historical section: according to the Palestinian side, Israel's closure policy was intended to renegotiate the Oslo Agreement and extract more concessions, territorial and other.

References

Arnon, A. Luski, I., Spivak, A. and Weinblatt, J. (1997) *The Palestinian Economy: Between Imposed Integration and Voluntary Separation*, Leiden: Brill.

Ben Shahar, H., Fishelson, G. and Hirsch, Z. (1989) 'Regional cooperation in the development of transportation infrastructure in the Middle East', in M. Merhav (ed.) *Economic Cooperation and Middle East Peace*, London: Weidenfeld and Nicolson.

Eaton, J. and Fernandez, R. (1995) 'Sovereign debt', in G.M. Grossman and K. Rogoff (eds) *Handbook of International Economics*, Oxford: North-Holland, volume 3: 2031–2077.

Hart, O. (1995) *Firms, Contracts, and Financial Structure* (Clarendon Lectures in Economics), Oxford: Oxford University Press.

Klein, B., Crawford, R. and Alchian, A. (1978) 'Vertical integration, appropriable rents, and the competitive contracting process', *Journal of Law and Economics* 21: 297–326.

Tirole, J. (1988) *The Theory of Industrial Organization,* Cambridge and London: MIT Press.

World Bank (1993) *Developing the Occupied Territories: An Investment in Peace* (six volumes), Washington, DC: The World Bank.

Discussion

Jonathan Thomas

The model is certainly parsimonious, and it makes a very interesting point. It demonstrates nicely how a judicious use of economic theory can get to the heart of an issue. Rather than speculating on possible ways of complicating the model, which one could imagine doing, but would be rather against the spirit of the analysis, I shall concentrate on a discussion of the key assumptions.

Let me give a brief summary of the model. Palestine (p) has a project which costs c and yields a return $d > c$. In order to realise d, it has either to use a port located in Israel (i), or to construct its own port at a cost k (see the timeline in Figure 11.1). In the absence of a complete contract, i will behave opportunistically and expropriate to the maximum extent possible – demanding the highest price that p will accept (i.e. so that p is just indifferent about accepting or rejecting). Thus the model assumes that i has all the bargaining power, and can extract the entire surplus (d) leading to a loss for p – so anticipating this p will not incur the cost of c if it had not earlier decided to build the Gaza port. The conclusion is then that p will build the port, and is not dependent on i's port later. So it realises d but at

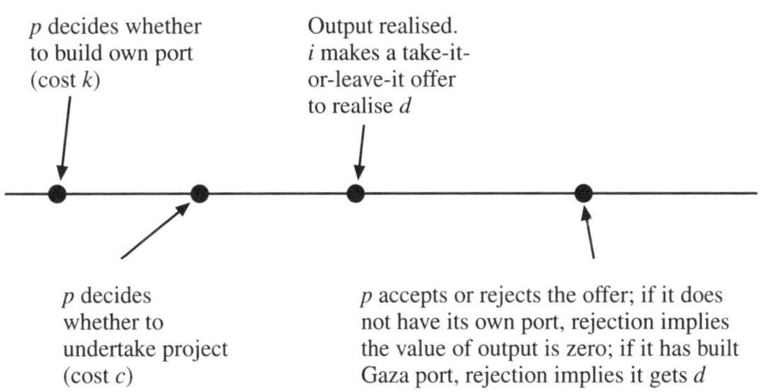

Figure 11.1 Timeline for model.

a cost k in addition to the project cost c. (The project proceeds under the assumption that $d-c-k>0$.)

The conclusion is that building the Gaza port enhances welfare *even though* it may be inefficient, and hence integration can adversely affect profitable economic activity.

An absolutely crucial assumption is that Israel cannot commit *not* to expropriate the value of the project. Two reasons for this are highlighted in the chapter:

1 It is not possible to enforce contractual obligations if entered into by sovereign states; they can renege because there is no mechanism for enforcement.
2 Contracts must include unverifiable elements – notably security performance. So i can always claim that security is being breached, and on this basis deny access to the port.

While it is true that sovereigns do have legal power to renege on such agreements, it is nonetheless difficult to do so. An explicit breach of a treaty would be damaging politically. Indeed this point is made in the chapter in relation to the possibility of i blockading p's harbour – such an overt act for economic ends would presumably be unacceptable to the international community. The second reason given is, in my view, likely to provide a better underpinning of these incomplete contracts. Even here, however, i would have to avoid behaving in an overt way to carry through expropriation of surplus. For example, i could hardly get away with an explicit statement of the form, 'Unless you are prepared to renegotiate the price of using our port up towards d, we will claim that there is a potential security problem and bar you from using the port'. A more subtle approach would be to lever up the price *ex post* claiming it as the 'costs of increased security'. Since security information is generally not observed or verifiable by outside parties, it is difficult to imagine that such an action by i could be prevented, even by international pressure.

A question I would like to raise at a more general level relates to the fact that these issues do not seem peculiar to potential interactions between Israel and a future Palestine. Certainly if we take the first view of why contractual incompleteness obtains – due to the ability of sovereigns to act in a way that is unconstrained by prior commitments – then similar considerations should arise in many other areas of international relations.

A possible answer is that the analysis here is peculiar to hostile states. A standard – and more efficient than constructing a new port – resolution of a hold-up problem in the sort of context we are looking at is to suppose that interaction between the two parties occurs over more than just one period. Then as in a standard repeated game analysis, reneging on a current agreement will have adverse long-term consequences. Thus if i attempts to expropriate, even though it succeeds in the short-run, future investment by p will be zero (or p will build her own port) and hence i will not be able to expropriate in future. Instead she should content herself with a low but positive price each period. Thus expropriation leads to a breakdown of 'trust' in that in the future the worst is expected of the other party. (In game theory parlance, there is reversion to the static Nash equilibrium.) Provided parties are sufficiently patient, an equilibrium without expropriation and in which p invests but does not build her own port, can be implemented by the credible threat of breakdown occurring in response to contract breach. This is efficient. See Halonen (2002) for analysis of this kind of resolution to a hold-up. A reason why this sort of repeated game analysis may not be applicable in the Palestinian context is that we are already effectively in breakdown for other reasons. There is already no trust. Hence long-term contracts as a response to contractual incompleteness are not viable. While I do not think there is a formal way of showing why a breakdown of trust would spillover from other issues to this one, it is certainly plausible. (Somehow, to get a handle on this, I suspect that one might need to appeal to psychology, something that we usually try to abstract from in our simple economic models.)

A final issue I would like to raise concerns whether this is really about political states or just opportunism by economic agents. The argument actually only requires the Israeli port to behave opportunistically, something that is in its interest to do. If the contractual incompleteness is due to factors that are under the control of the port, then it does not need support by the state. The same analysis should go through. On the other hand the implications of this opportunism would probably need to be countered by the *state* of Palestine. As shown in the chapter, any new port is likely to be loss-making – once it is built it will have to compete with the existing port which in practice will price competitively and take its share of trade. Nevertheless, the argument of the chapter is that it would pay the state to subsidise a loss-making Palestinian port *because* that will keep charges down. On the other hand, of course, there would surely be other strategic dimensions to take into account. Restrictions on access to Ashdod for strategic reasons would no longer be a threat that could be used, so the value of a port to Palestine would probably be understated by the arguments presented here.

Reference

Halonen, M. (2002) 'Reputation and the allocation of ownership', *Economic Journal* 112: 539–558.

Index